Introduction to Criminal Justice

Cliff Roberson LL.M., Ph.D.

COPPERHOUSE PUBLISHING COMPANY
901-5 Tahoe Blvd.
Incline Village, Nevada 89451
(702) 833-3131 • Fax (702) 833-3133
http://www.copperhouse.com/copperhouse

Your Partner in Education
with
"QUALITY BOOKS AT FAIR PRICES"

INTRODUCTION
TO
CRIMINAL JUSTICE
2ND EDITION

Library of Congress Catalog Number 93-73918
ISBN 0-942728-71-8 Paper Text Edition

3 4 5 6 7 8 9 10

Printed in the United States of America.

DEDICATION

This book is dedicated to the men and women serving and those that have served in America's criminal justice system. We are truly fortunate to have such fine devoted professionals ever tending that fine blue line. For your anonymous help in our times of need and to perhaps make up just a little for the thanks never given or thought of too late. *Thank you!*

— Cliff Roberson

ACKNOWLEDGEMENTS

In writing this book, the number of debts accumulated to colleagues is surprisingly large. Thank you to Lance Parr, Warren Nichols, Glenda Hunt and Michael Kane for their review of the completed manuscript and for their comments that helped produce a better text. Finally, I wish to express my appreciation to a wide range of persons who remain anonymous, yet without whom this book could not have been written.

Special thanks goes out to all the agencies and photographers who made many of the photographs contained in the book possible. They are:

Tom Myers
Greg Clark
Costa Mesa Police Department
Los Angeles Police Department
St. Paul Police Department
Tucson Police Department
Denver Police Department
Houston Police Department
Sacramento Police Officer's Association
Folsom Prison
Mule Creek Prison
El Dorado County Sheriff's Department
Sacramento County Sheriff's Department
Broward County Sheriff's Department

PHOTOGRAPHY CREDITS

PREFACE

The primary goal of this text is to present a clear and balanced overview of the entire criminal justice system. The system is examined from its historical foundation through its contemporary form with the material presented in an easy-to-comprehend manner, thus freeing the instructor from text review during class time. Therefore, the instructor may pursue more meaningful discussions and group exercises involving the criminal justice concepts.

The text is organized in five parts. Part I provides a basic foundation for our criminal justice system. Part II discusses law enforcement issues and concepts. Part III deals with our court system. Part IV introduces the students to correctional concepts and juvenile justice. Part V addresses criminal victimology and victims' rights along with the impact of drugs on the system. The final chapter summarizes the present and calculates the future of criminal justice in America. Case studies and discussion questions are presented in each chapter to provide the framework for classroom discussion on complex criminal justice problems or issues.

Introduction to Criminal Justice will conform well to a single semester survey course in Administration of Justice or Introduction to Criminal Justice. If the instructor wishes to delete material to shorten the course, Part V may be deleted. If further material is needed, the Instructor's Manual contains additional material.

TABLE OF CONTENTS

PART I
GENERAL CONCEPTS

CHAPTER 1

PART II
LAW ENFORCEMENT IN AMERICA

CHAPTER 5

THE DEVELOPMENT OF THE CRIMINAL JUSTICE SYSTEM .. 139

CHAPTER 6

ORGANIZATION AND OPERATION
OF LAW ENFORCEMENT SYSTEMS 167

CHAPTER 7

CRITICAL ISSUES FOR LAW ENFORCEMENT PERSONNEL 201

CHAPTER 8

POLICE OPERATIONS 227

PART III
THE COURT SYSTEM

CHAPTER 9

CHAPTER 10

CHAPTER 11

PRETRIAL AND TRIAL PROCESS 309

CHAPTER 12

SENTENCING 335

PART IV
CORRECTIONS

CHAPTER 13

STRUCTURE AND PURPOSE
OF THE CORRECTIONAL SYSTEM 367

CHAPTER 16

CHAPTER 17

CHAPTER 18

PART I

GENERAL CONCEPTS

THE ECONOMICS
OF CRIME

SHATTERED LIVES
$170,000,000,000

CRIMINAL JUSTICE SYSTEM
$90,000,000,000

PRIVATE PROTECTION
$65,000,000,000

URBAN DECAY
$50,000,000,000

PROPERTY LOSS
$45,000,000,000

MEDICAL CARE
$5,000,000,000

Rampant crime is costing America
$425 billion a year.

* BusinessWeek December 1993

OVERVIEW OF THE SYSTEM

There is one universal law. That law is justice. Justice forms the cornerstone of each nation's law.

—Alexis De Toqueville

PHILOSOPHY OF THE CONTEMPORARY SYSTEM

W e refer to criminal justice as a "system," as if it were truly a system. It would be more accurate to refer to it as a non-system. The term "system" refers to the interrelationship among all those agencies concerned with the prevention of crime in society. It implies that a closely knit, coordinated structure of organization exists among the various components of the system.

The system, however, is not a close-knit, coordinated structure of organizations. The criminal justice system is actually three separate elements: police, courts, and corrections. Each operates almost independently of the other. In many cases the goal orientation of the various elements within a local jurisdiction are in conflict with each other as to the main functions of the criminal justice system. Thus, the system can best be described as "fragmented" or "divided." Accordingly, the criminal justice system is a group of agencies organized around various functions that each is assigned. While there is no single criminal justice system in this country, we have many systems that are similar but individually unique. For convenience and out of habit, however, we will use the phrase "criminal justice system" to collectively refer to all three components.

We apprehend, bring to trial, and punish criminals by means of this loose confederation of agencies at all levels of the government. As will be discussed later in this text, our system of justice has evolved from the English common law into a complex series of procedures and decisions. Unlike many other nations, private citizens are actively involved in our justice system.

Under our form of government, each state and the federal government has its own criminal justice system. While state constitutions and statutes define each state's criminal justice system, all the systems must respect the rights of individuals as set forth in the U.S. Constitution and interpreted by our courts. Later in this chapter, we

Chart 1.
A General View of The Criminal Justice System

This chart seeks to present a simple yet comprehensive view of the movement of cases through the criminal justice system. Procedures in individual jurisdictions may vary from the pattern shown here. The differing weights of line indicate the relative volumes of cases disposed of at various points in the system, but this is only suggestive since no nationwide data of this sort exists.

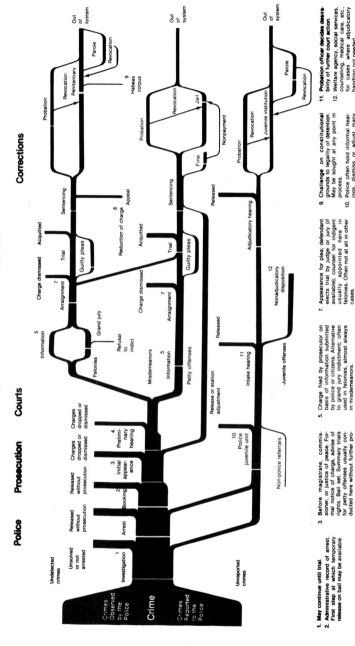

1. **May continue until trial.**

2. **Administrative record of arrest. First step at which temporary release on bail may be available.**

3. Before magistrate, commissioner, or justice of peace. Formal notice of charge, advise of rights. Bail set. Summary trials for petty offenses usually conducted here without further processing.

4. Preliminary testing of evidence against defendant. Charge may be reduced. No separate preliminary hearing for misdemeanors in same systems.

5. Charge filed by prosecutor on basis of information submitted by police or citizens. Alternative to grand jury indictment; often used in felonies, almost always in misdemeanors.

6. Reviews whether Government evidence sufficient to justify trial. Some States have no grand jury system, others seldom use it.

7. Appearance for plea; defendant elects trial by judge or jury (if available), counsel for indigent usually appointed here in felonies. Often not at all in other cases.

8. Charge may be reduced at any time prior to trial in return for plea of guilty or for other reasons.

9. Challenge on constitutional grounds to legality of detention. May be sought at any point in process.

10. Police often hold informal hearings, dismiss or adjust many cases without further processing.

11. **Probation officer decides desirability of further court action.**

12. Welfare agency, social services, counseling, medical care, etc., for cases where adjudicatory handling not needed.

will examine the rights of the individuals and the issue of individual rights versus law and order.

As we begin our study of the justice system, several important concepts should be considered:

—The response to crime is mainly a state and local function.

— Police protection is primarily a function of cities and towns.

— Corrections is primarily a function of the state governments.

— More than 60 percent of all persons employed in the justice system are employed at the local (city and county) level.

Citizen Involvement in the Justice System

As the *Report to the Nation on Crime and Justice* indicates, our response to crime is a complex process that involves both citizens and agencies at all levels.[1] Often the private sector initiates the response to crime. This first response may come from any part of the private sector—individuals, families, neighborhoods, associations, business, industry, the news media, or other private service organizations.

Citizens' response to crime involves crime prevention as well as participation in the criminal justice process once a crime has been committed. Private crime prevention is more than participating in neighborhood watch or providing private security. It also includes a commitment to stop criminal behavior by not engaging in it nor condoning it when it is committed by others.

Citizen involvement in the criminal justice process includes:

1) reporting crimes to the police,

2) being a reliable participant as a witness or juror in a criminal proceeding, and

3) accepting the disposition of the system as just or reasonable.

As voters and concerned citizens, individuals also participate in criminal justice through the policy-making process that affects how the criminal justice process operates, the resources available to it, and its goals and objectives. At every stage in the process, from the original formulation of objectives to the decision about where to locate jails and prisons and to the reintegration of inmates into society, the private sector has a role to play. Without such involvement, the criminal justice process cannot serve the citizens it protects.

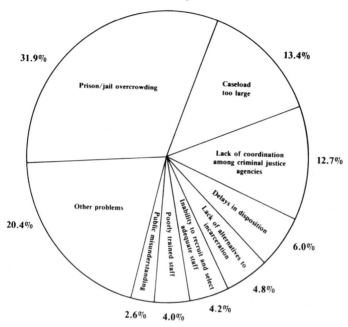

National survey results identifying important issues facing the criminal justice system. Percentages indicate relative seriousness of the problem by respondents.

EXHIBIT 1-1

The Challenge of Crime in a Free Society

(President's Commission on Law Enforcement and Administration of Justice, Washington, D.C., 1967, pp. 3-5.)

Many Americans think of crime as a very narrow range of behavior. It is not. An enormous variety of acts make up the "crime problem." Crime is not just a tough teenager snatching a lady's purse. It is a professional thief stealing cars "on order." It is a well-heeled loan shark taking over a previously legitimate business for organized crime. It is a polite young man who suddenly and inexplicably murders his family. It is a corporation executive conspiring with competitors to keep prices high. No single theory, no single generalization can explain the vast range of behavior called crime.

...The most understandable mood into which many Americans have been plunged by crime is one of frustration and bewilderment. For "crime" is not a single simple phenomenon that can be examined, analyzed and described in one piece. It occurs in every part of the country and in every stratum of society. Its practitioners and its victims are people of all ages, incomes and backgrounds. Its trends are difficult to ascertain. Its causes are legion. Its cures are speculative and controversial. An examination of any single kind of crime, let alone of "crime in America," raises a myriad of issues of the utmost complexity.

Components of the Justice System

As noted earlier, our justice system is composed of three basic components: law enforcement, courts, and corrections. The common goals of the justice system include:

1) deterring crime,

2) maintaining peace and order,

3) investigating crime, and

4) apprehending and punishing criminals.

"Law enforcement" is a generic term used for agencies whose tasks normally include: enforcing criminal law, exercising the power to arrest, maintaining public order and peace, providing emergency services to the public, and generally serving the public at large. "Courts" are the agencies which have the authority to decide on cases and controversies in law brought before them. "Corrections" is used to include those agencies involved in probation, incarceration, and parole.

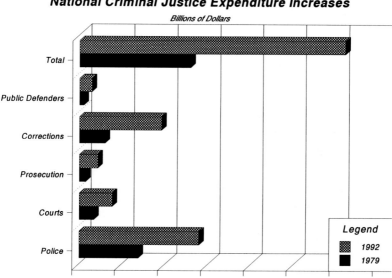

National Criminal Justice Expenditure Increases

Billions of Dollars

Source: U.S. Dept. of Justice

Adversarial System

Early English criminal justice was based on two fundamental premises. First, the responsibility for accusing an individual of a crime rested with the victim or the victim's family. If no private accuser came forward, there was no prosecution. The second premise was the adversarial nature of criminal procedure. Our system of justice today is still based on the adversarial concept. The role of the judge was that of an impartial referee between two contending parties. In criminal cases, the adversaries were the accused and the private accuser. The private accuser was later replaced by the police or public prosecutor and, in the U.S., a district attorney.

CRIMINAL JUSTICE ADMINISTRATION

In this section, a brief overview of criminal justice administration is presented. Individual chapters of this book focus on each major component of the system.

The primary state agency involved in criminal law administration in most states is the State Department of Justice or Office of Attorney General (Criminal Division). This department is usually composed of the State Attorney General and the Division of Law Enforcement. The typical goals of the department are:

1) to seek to control and eliminate organized crime in the State,

2) publish and distribute a compilation of the state laws relating to crimes and criminal law enforcement that are of general interest to peace officers,

3) operate the state's teletype and law enforcement telecommunications systems, and

4) promote training and professionalism of peace officers.

State & Local Justice System Expenditures
1992 Per Capita National Average in Dollars

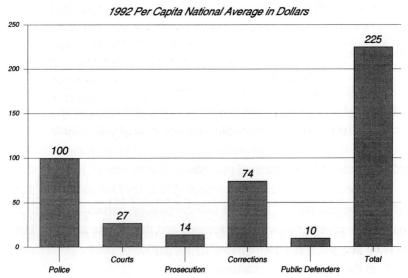

Source: U.S. Dept. of Justice

State Attorney General

The chief law officer of a state is the attorney general. It is the state attorney general's duty to see that all laws of the state are uniformly and adequately enforced. The attorney general usually has limited supervisory authority over district attorneys, sheriffs, and other law enforcement officers in matters pertaining to the duties of their respective offices. The attorney general may require any of these officers to make reports concerning the investigation, detection, prosecution, and punishment of crime within their jurisdiction.

The attorney general in most states may prosecute any violations of law of which a superior or district court has jurisdiction when he or she is of the opinion that the law is not being adequately enforced in any county. Also, when directed by the governor, the attorney general shall assist any district attorney in the discharge of his or her duties. If a district attorney is disqualified to conduct a criminal prosecution, the attorney general may appoint a special prosecutor.[2]

Regarding the broad authority given the attorney general by the state constitution, one court opinion noted that the authority has been tempered by "judicial construction." The court stated:

"These officials are public officers, as distinguished from mere employees, with public duties delegated and entrusted to them, as agents, the performance of which is an exercise of a part of the governmental functions of the particular political unit for which they, as agents, are active.... It is at once evident that 'supervision' does not contemplate control, and that sheriffs and district attorneys cannot avoid or evade the duties and responsibilities of the respective offices by permitting a substitution of judgment."[3]

District Attorneys

District attorneys in most states are elected county or judicial district officers. They are also officers of the state.[4] The district attorney is, in most cases, the public prosecutor. Duties of a district attorney in criminal matters normally include:

1) institution of proceedings before magistrates (judges) for the arrest of persons charged with or reasonably suspected of public offenses,

2) presenting cases to the grand jury in those states that use grand juries for indictments, and

3) conducting all prosecution for public offenses.

In a few states (i.e., Illinois, Florida and Rhode Island for example), there are "state attorneys" who are appointed rather than elected and perform those duties normally performed by the district attorney. In some states, they are called "county attorneys."

The Police

As we will discuss in Chapter 5, we have no national police force. There are federal law enforcement agencies, such as the FBI, but all of them have limited subject matter jurisdiction. Policing is mainly a function of local cities and counties. Accordingly, we have thousands of independent police agencies in the United States. In spite of this independence, the organization of most police departments is very similar.

As a general rule, within city limits the police have primary jurisdiction for keeping peace and enforcing the laws; whereas the sheriff has the similar responsibilities in areas outside the cities. It is not unusual, however, for some of the smaller communities to contract with the sheriff for law enforcement services within their communities.

The Courts

We operate in the United States under two separate court systems, the federal and state. Ninety-five percent of all criminal trials in the United States are conducted in state courts and involve violations of state law. Federal courts are involved only in matters involving federal issues.

The primary federal trial courts are the U.S. District Courts. There is at least one federal district court in each state. In states with more than one district court, the districts are divided geographically. For example, the U.S. District Court, Southern District of California is the federal district court for San Diego and the southern-most part of California. [*Note:* Within a district there may be more than one district court judge each acting as the district court. For example, the U.S. District Court, Southern District of New York (including New York City) has over 100 judges, each acting as the district court.]

The appellate courts in the federal system are the U.S. Court of Appeals and the U.S. Supreme Court. The United States is divided into circuits and each has a court of appeals. For example, the U.S. Court of Appeals, Ninth Circuit includes the western part of the United States.

In the state system, the trial courts are usually the lower courts (municipal or justice) and the courts of general jurisdiction (superior or district) courts. Most states also have courts of appeal and a supreme court.

Corrections

Corrections consists of probation departments usually operated by the superior court judges, jails which are locally controlled, parole departments which are generally state operated, and state operated correctional institutions. In addition, there are numerous community correctional programs that may be state, county or locally operated.

INDIVIDUAL RIGHTS V. LAW AND ORDER

The history of criminal justice in the United States represents a pendulum-like swing between the public's fear of crime and the concept of individual rights. Criminal justice professionals generally are oriented toward one of two opposing directions— "law and order" or "individual rights." The "law and order" orientation stresses the need to solve the crime problem. The "individual rights" orientation stresses the need to protect an individual's rights and often considers this need greater than the need to punish offenders. Too great an emphasis on individual rights will restrict law enforcement and allow offenders to escape punishment. Arbitrary police practices that may occur under the "law and order" orientation may infringe on human and constitutional rights. As Chief Justice Earl Warren stated in *Miranda v. Arizona*[5]:

The quality of a nation's civilization can be largely
measured by the methods it uses in the enforcement of the
criminal law....All of these policies point to one overriding
thought: the constitutional foundation underlying the
privilege is the respect a government—state or federal—must
accord the dignity and integrity of its citizens. To maintain
a fair state–individual balance, the government must shoulder
the entire load.

THE DUE PROCESS CONCEPT

Associated with the individual rights v. law and order issue is the
concept of "due process." This concept restricts the power of the state
and more particularly the police, courts and corrections. The Bill of
Rights, the first eight amendments to the U.S. Constitution, contains
23 separate individual rights, 12 of them concern procedural rights for
persons accused of criminal conduct. In 1798, the U.S. Supreme Court
ruled that the prohibitions against government action contained in those
amendments were restrictions only on the federal government and not
on state governments. The case, *Calder v. Bull*, involved a statute
passed by the legislature of Connecticut which set aside a probate court
judgment and directed the probate judge to refuse the recording of a
will (an ex posto law).[6] The justices noted that the Bill of Rights was
designed to prevent the federal abuse of power, not state abuse.

AMENDMENT XIV

Section 1. All persons born or naturalized in the
United States, and subject to the jurisdiction thereof, are
citizens of the United States and of the State wherein they
reside. No State shall make or enforce any law which shall
abridge the privileges or immunities of citizens of the
United States; not shall any State deprive any person of life,
liberty, or property, without due process; nor deny to any
person within its jurisdiction the equal protection of the
laws.

The Fourteenth Amendment, one of the anti-slavery amendments enacted in 1865, however, has been used by the courts to place "due process" requirements on the states and the state's criminal justice system in criminal matters.

The clause "without due process" of the Fourteenth Amendment has been interpreted by the U.S. Supreme Court as "incorporating" most of the provisions of the Bill of Rights. Accordingly, those rights which are incorporated under that clause apply to state as well as federal criminal proceedings. In 1897, the Court using the "due process" clause of the Fourteenth Amendment applied the Fifth Amendment's requirement of payment of "just compensation" for the taking of private property for public use to the states. Later in 1925, in *Gitlow v. New York,* the Court held that the First Amendment's protection on free speech restricted the states right to control free speech. The Sixth Amendment's right to counsel was imposed on the states by *Powell v. Alabama* (1932) and the requirement of a trial by "an impartial jury" in jury cases was imposed by *Norris v. Alabama* (1935).

The Incorporation Controversy

For many years, there was a controversy over whether all of the rights contained in the Bill of Rights were incorporated into the due process clause of the Fourteenth Amendment, and thus applied to the states, or only to those that are considered "fundamental" to due process. Justice Hugo Black, in his many years on the court, contended that not only should there be total incorporation of the Bill of Rights, but also some other "fundamental" rights not included in the Bill of Rights. While the Court never adopted Black's "total incorporation" concept, it has adopted his concept that the due process clause includes other "fundamental" rights not contained in the Bill of Rights.

The Modern Approach

Presently the Court is using the "selective incorporation" approach. The Court has accepted the concept that not all rights enumerated in the Bill of Rights are necessarily fundamental, and that other rights may be fundamental even though not contained in the Bill of Rights. To determine if a right is "fundamental," the Court looks at whether the procedural safeguard is "fundamental to the American scheme of justice" or "necessary" in the context of the criminal process maintained by the various states.

The following Bill of Rights guarantees have been "selectively incorporated" and thus held enforceable against the states to the same standards that the rights protect against federal encroachment.

First Amendment
— free speech (*Gitlow v. New York*)

— freedom of press (*Near v. Minnesota*)

— freedom of assembly (*Dejonge v. Oregon*)

Fourth Amendment
— general right to privacy (*Griswold v. Connecticut*)

— protection against unreasonable searches and seizures (*Wolf v. Colorado*)

— exclusionary rule (*Mapp v. Ohio*)

— requirement of probable cause to arrest (*Terry v. Ohio*)

Fifth Amendment
— protection against self-incrimination (*Malloy v. Hogan*)

— protection against double jeopardy (*Benton v. Maryland*)

Sixth Amendment
— right to trial by jury in serious cases (*Duncan v. Louisiana*)

— right to speedy trial (*Klopfer v. North Carolina*)

— right to be informed of nature of charges (*Connally v. General Construction Co.*)

— right to confront and cross-examine adverse witnesses (*Pointer v. Texas*)

— right to subpoena witnesses in a criminal case (*Washington v. Texas*)

Eighth Amendment
— protection against "cruel and unusual" punishment (*Louisiana ex rel. Francis v. Resweber*)

The following rights, although required in federal criminal proceedings, have not been imposed on the states:

Fifth Amendment

— right to grand jury indictment (*Hurtado v. California*)

Sixth Amendment

—right to jury trial in minor criminal cases (*Duncan v. Louisiana*)

Eighth Amendment

— prohibition against excessive bail (The Court has never decided this issue, but indicated in *Schilb v. Kuebel* 404 U.S. 357 (1971) that it would apply to the states.)

==

EXHIBIT 1-2

Mapp v. Ohio

==

Dollree Mapp was convicted of knowingly having in her possession and under her control some lewd and lascivious pictures. The pictures, which were used as evidence in her conviction, were seized by police officers during the execution of an illegal search.

Ms. Mapp lived alone, with her 15 year old daughter, in a second floor apartment in Cleveland, Ohio. On May 23, 1957, three police officers arrived at the home, rang her doorbell, and were asked the purpose of their visit. The police stated that they desired to talk to her. Ms. Mapp informed them that she would admit them only if they had a search warrant. The officers did not enter at that time but kept the home under observation for the next three hours. Other police officers arrived. The police then broke a glass to the rear door and entered the apartment. An officer waved a piece of paper, purporting to be a search warrant, at her. Ms. Mapp grabbed the paper and placed in down her dress. [There was no warrant.] The officer, after a brief struggle, was able to retrieve it. Ms. Mapp was then handcuffed and forced to sit on her own bed.

The officers searched her upstairs bedroom. In her dresser, a photo album and other personal papers were taken. A trunk was also searched and found to contain obscene materials. At Ms. Mapp's trial in a state court, her attorney objected to the introduction of the pictures and other obscene materials that were taken from her apartment in violation of her rights under the Fourth and Fourteenth Amendments of the U. S. Constitution. She was convicted and the conviction was upheld (approved) by the Ohio Supreme Court. Ms. Mapp appealed to the U.S. Supreme Court alleging that the conviction was in violation of her U.S. Constitutional rights as a U.S. citizen. The high court agreed with her and reversed her conviction. [*Note*: During the decision in this case, the Supreme Court instituted the "exclusionary" rule.]

THE LEGAL FOUNDATIONS OF CRIME

What is Crime?

Important words often go beyond the assigned boundaries of their dictionary meanings. Crime is one such important word, a word that signifies different meanings to many different people and is always straining at the boundaries of its conventional meaning.[7]

Crime is one of the oldest problems faced by civilizations. The act of defining "crime" is however a difficult task. At first glance, it seems simple why we call certain acts "crimes" and certain people "criminals"; crimes are acts that pose threats to our society and criminals are people who commit those acts. This simple approach fails to consider the relativity of criminal definitions.

The relativity of criminal definitions indicates that every definition of an act as a crime must be viewed as tentative and subject to redefinition. For example, if in 1932 John and Jill Smith had walked down a street in New York City and John had a pint of whiskey in his pocket and Jill had a gold coin in her pocket, John would be committing a criminal act because of the prohibition statutes. Two years later under the same circumstances, John's conduct would be lawful since the prohibition statutes had been repealed, but Jill's would be illegal because of the new currency statutes which made the possession of gold coins for currency illegal.

The question, "What is crime?" focuses on four issues. First, the relationship between crime and law. Which gives rise to which? Second, the problem of measurement. How much crime is there in society today and what do the crime rates tell us? Third, the problem of causation. What causes crime? And fourth, who is a criminal? Each of these issues will be discussed in the first four chapters of this text.

Prostitution and Sex Crimes

Drugs

Bribes to Public Officials

Gambling

Obscene Material

Shylocking

Illegal Liquor

Vice Offenses

We generally assume that the law criminalizes particular behaviors that most people disapprove of. From this point of view, designating some acts as crimes is a simple way of sanctioning certain conduct while condemning other conduct. The law under this perspective is a protective reaction against behaviors and people considered by society as unacceptable.

In measuring crime, we have a tendency to accept official crime statistics at face value. Crime is what is reflected in and measured by official crime statistics. A common criticism of official crime statistics, however, is that they measure only one kind of crime — the street crimes of the poor and the working-class. Another criticism is that statistics measure only that crime which is reported.

Gwynn Nettler once remarked that, "Crime is a word, not a deed."[8] In this context, crime constitutes a category of events that contains numerous subcategories. And at the same time, the category of crime is itself a subcategory of a larger set of events (e.g., socially harmful acts).

Terming an act a crime involves a series of judgments. First, the judgment is made that the act is harmful. Next is the decision that the act should be regulated by law. Finally, the decision that the law regulating the act should be a criminal statute rather than a civil one.

Webster's New Universal Unabridged Dictionary provides us with four definitions of **crime**.

1) An act committed in violation of a law prohibiting it, or omitted in violation of a law ordering it; crimes are variously punishable by death, imprisonment or the imposition of certain fines or restrictions.

2) An extreme violation of the law; wrongdoing of a criminal nature, as felony or treason, which affects the whole public and not just the rights of an individual; distinguishable from a misdemeanor.

3) An offense against morality; sin.

4) The acts of a criminal; habitual violation of the law.

The above definitions present two basic positions; first, crime is a defiance of a positive law and second, crime is a breach of moral law. Henry Campbell Black in *Black's Law Dictionary* defines crime as "a positive or negative act in violation of penal law; an offense against the State.*" Black then proceeds to discuss crimes which are *malum in se* (evil in themselves) and crimes which are *malum in prohibitum* (which are crimes simply because statutes have made them crimes). It appears that both dictionaries suggest that crime has a positive definition (i.e., that which the State condemns) and a moral dimension (i.e., an offense against morality).[9]

The above analysis of the definitions of crime fails to explain why a given act is a crime and another similar act is not. Johnson states that crime, as a concept, does not emerge full grown in any society. It develops out of experience and is conditioned by social and cultural attitudes.[10] Accordingly to understand why some acts are considered crimes and similar acts are not, not only do we need to look at the current values of our society, but also the historical background of the prohibited or sanctioned conduct.

Since religious beliefs are one of the most formative influences upon us, there is still a moral dimension to the definition of crime. At the time that our country was founded, most of our crimes were also considered moral sins. In Colonial America, those who committed crimes were also considered to be "offenders against the divine." Over the passage of time, the diversity in our society on matters of religion tended to separate crime from moral wrongs. Our movement to secularize the criminal statutes has resulted in the definition of crime as an offense against the laws of state without reference to the divine. When legislatures or judges participate in the law-making processes, however, they are strongly influenced by their religious or lack of religious beliefs.

A working definition of crime that has been adopted by most criminologists is the one proposed by Edwin Sutherland:

> The essential characteristic of crime is that it is behavior which is prohibited by the State as an injury to the State and against which the State may react, at least at the last resort, by punishment.[11]

The above definition limits crimes only to those acts which violate a criminal statute. It does not address the morality aspects of human behavior. For purposes of our discussions in this text, we will use Sutherland's definition.

Types of Law

Law can be divided into several different classifications. The most common ones include:

— crimes and torts, and

— common law and statutory law.

A **crime** is a wrong involving the violation of the peace and dignity of the State. In theory, it is committed against the interest of all of the people of the State.[12] Accordingly, crimes are prosecuted by the prosecutor in the name of the "State," "People," or "Commonwealth."

A **tort** is a wrong that is a violation of a private interest and thus gives rise to civil liability. The same conduct, however, may be both a crime and a tort. For example, a woman is forcibly raped by a neighbor. The criminal aspect of the conduct is a violation of the peace and dignity of the State and therefore a crime against all the people in the State. It is also a violation of the private interest of the victim, and she may file a civil suit and obtain civil damages against the offender. [*Note:* The offender may be acquitted at the criminal trial where proof of his or her guilt is required to be established beyond a reasonable doubt and yet held accountable at the civil trial where the degree of proof required to hold the offender accountable is much less.]

Common law developed during the Middle Ages in English society as a body of unwritten judicial opinions which were based on customary practices of Anglo-Saxon society. The decisions that British justices made in new situations became the precedents for such future situations. Common law, in large part, forms the basis of our modern statutory and case law.

Statutory law is law that originates with specifically designated lawmaking bodies. It is enacted by legislative bodies of government. The primary statutory laws dealing with crimes and criminal procedure are the state penal codes.

The Nature of Criminal Law

Criminal law is the ultimate form of legal control by the State. By use of the provisions for punishment and sanctions, the State can use criminal law to repress any conduct that threatens the State. The concept of criminal acts as injuries to the State developed when the custom of private or community redress was replaced by the principle that the State is wronged when it or one of its subjects are harmed.

A rule of conduct is a criminal law only if it is created by the State (or federal government), contains provisions for punishment to be administered upon the conviction of its violation and the punishment is administered by the State in the name of society. The basic conceptual difference between civil law and criminal law is that criminal law defines conduct that is considered against the interest of the society, whereas civil law refers to conduct that is against the interest of the individual. Crime is therefore a social wrong and a tort is a private wrong.[13]

Substantive and Procedural Criminal Law

There are two basic types of criminal laws: substantive and procedural. Substantive criminal law defines crimes. It lists the elements that constitute each act or omission that is classified as a crime. Substantive criminal law also attaches penalties for violations of the crimes.

Procedural law controls the manner in which substantive criminal law is involved. It provides the rules by which we investigate, bring to trial and punish criminals. To be legally convicted of a crime, a person must be tried according to procedural criminal law and convicted of committing an act or a failure to act in violation of the substantive criminal law.

SOURCES AND CLASSIFICATIONS OF CRIME

This section contains a discussion of the sources of our law, our crime classification systems, general rules regarding criminal punishment, and the repeal of criminal statutes.

General and Specific Sources of Law

The criminal laws in most states come from three primary sources:

1) Federal and state constitutions,

2) Statutory law, and

3) Case law.

Generally, constitutions provide rights and protections for individuals and restrict the power of the government to prosecute or punish. Statutes contain the substantive acts and procedural requirements for prosecution. Case law contains interpretations of constitutional and statutory provisions.

Constitutional Law

Both the U.S. Constitution and the state constitutions are sources of criminal law for the courts. Constitutions provide the framework for criminal law by:

1) Limiting the power of the government;

2) Establishing individual rights; and

3) Providing for the establishment of a judicial system.

As noted earlier, constitutions generally leave the creation and definition of crimes to statutory enactments. The U.S. Constitution, for example, defines criminal acts in only two sections, Article III, Section 3 on treason and Amendment 13 which forbids involuntary servitude except as punishment for crime. The state constitution defines criminal acts in a few more areas, but for the most part, the state constitution, like the federal, focuses on individual rights and limitations of governmental power.

Statutory Law

Generally, there are two types of statutory law, (1) statutes which are passed by the legislators and (2) initiatives which are passed by the voters. Under most circumstances, the power to designate state criminal offenses and provide for the punishment of prohibited acts is reserved for the state legislature and cannot be delegated.[13] In establishing the elements of a crime, the legislature may depart from the norm or common law concepts as long as the elements do not conflict with federal or state constitutions or federal law.[14]

Many of the state crimes are set forth in the Penal, Health and Safety and Vehicle Codes. Other state codes that contain numerous crimes are the Welfare and Institutions Code, Business and Professions Code, Fish and Game Code, and Government Code.

In some states, like California, the voters have the power via the initiative petition process to propose and approve statutes and amendments to the state constitution. An initiative measure is started by presenting a petition to the Secretary of State that has been signed by the number of voters that is equal to at least 5 percent of the number that voted in the last gubernatorial election for all the candidates for governor. The Secretary of State is then required to submit the measure at the next general election held at least 31 days after the petition is certified or a special election may be called.[15] A simple majority of votes is sufficient to pass the measure and it takes effect the day after the election unless the measure provides otherwise. Initiative measures should be interpreted liberally to give full effect to its objective and the needs of the people.[16]

All laws of a general nature have uniform operation within the state. A local or special statute is invalid in any case if a general statute can be made applicable. A statute or initiative must embrace only one subject, which shall be expressed in its title. If a statute or initiative embraces more than one subject or the subject is not embraced in its title, the provision is void. The one subject limitation must, however, be interpreted liberally to uphold legislation whose various parts are reasonably germane to the subject contained in its title.[17]

Substantive and Procedural Laws

Laws relating to criminal conduct may be divided into two general areas— substantive and procedural. Substantive law defines crimes and establishes punishments. Procedural law sets forth the rules and requirements that must be followed during the investigation, apprehension and trial of individual defendants. That portion of the penal code that prohibits theft of another's property (larceny) is substantive in nature, whereas, the Evidence Code is a procedural code.

Felony or Misdemeanor

The most popular classification of crimes is by the categories of treason, felonies, misdemeanors, and infractions. Treason is defined in the U.S. Constitution as levying war against the United States, or in adhering to our enemies by giving them aid and comfort. Treason, since it threatens the very existence of our nation, is considered the most serious. Because of its rarity of occurrence, will not be further discussed in this text. The majority of our crimes are classified as either felonies or misdemeanors. The key to distinguishing between a felony and a misdemeanor is not the punishment actually given in court, but the punishment that could have been imposed. For example, a person who commits the crime of burglary could receive 10 years in prison. The judge only sentences him to six months in local jail, the sentence typically given for a misdemeanor crime. That person has been convicted of a felony, even though he only received a jail sentence.

At common law a felony was considered as any crime for which the offender would be compelled to forfeit property to the King. Most common law felonies were punishable by the death penalty. The common law felonies include murder, rape, assault and battery, larceny, robbery, arson and burglary. Presently, only aggravated murder subjects the offender to the death penalty.

Most states distinguish between misdemeanors and felonies on the basis of place of incarceration. If the offender can only be incarcerated in a local jail, then the offense is a misdemeanor. Felony offenders can be incarcerated in prisons or correctional institutions. Other states use a combination of place of incarceration and character of offense to make the distinction between felonies and misdemeanors.

The Model Penal Code provides that a crime is a felony if it is so designated, without regard to the possible penalty. In addition, any crime for which the permissible punishment includes imprisonment in excess of one year is also considered a felony under the Code. All other crimes are misdemeanors.

Several states, like California, have crimes that are referred to as "wobblers" based on the fact that they can be considered by the court as either a felony or a misdemeanor.

Infractions are considered the lowest level of criminal activity. An infraction is an act that is usually not punishable by confinement, (i.e. a traffic ticket). In several states, the term "petty misdemeanors" is used in lieu of infractions.

Similar to infractions are violations of municipal ordinances. In some states, ordinance violations are not considered crimes based on the theory that a crime is a public wrong created by the state and thus prosecuted in the name of the state. An ordinance is a rule created by a public corporation (the municipality) and prosecuted in the name of the municipality.

The classification of a crime as a felony or misdemeanor is important for several reasons. First, a felony conviction on a person's record can prevent the individual from entering many professions and obtaining certain jobs. A felony conviction has been used to deny a person the right to enter the armed forces, to obtain employment with a law enforcement agency, and may even affect the ability of a person to obtain credit or adopt a child. In one state, a felon (person who has been convicted of a felony) may not obtain a license to sell chickens wholesale. In addition, the conviction of a felony can be grounds to impeach a public official. At one time, many states did not allow a person who had been convicted of a felony to vote, hold office or serve on a jury. Today, in all but eight states, many of the sanctions commonly associated with a felony conviction have been abolished.

EXHIBIT 1-3

Felony or Misdemeanor

California Penal Code 17 —
Felony and Misdemeanor Defined

(a) A felony is a crime which is punishable with death or by imprisonment in the state prison. Every other crime or public offense is a misdemeanor except those offenses that are classified as infractions.

(b) When a crime is punishable, in the discretion of the court, by imprisonment in the state prison or by fine or imprisonment in the county jail, it is a misdemeanor for all purposes under the following circumstances:

(1) After a judgment imposing a punishment other than imprisonment in the state prison.

(2) When the court, upon committing the defendant to the Youth Authority, designates the offense to be a misdemeanor.

(3) When the court grants probation to a defendant without imposition of sentence and at the time of granting probation, or on application of the defendant or probation officer thereafter, the court declares the offense to be a misdemeanor.

(4) When the prosecuting attorney files in a court having jurisdiction over misdemeanor offenses a complaint specifying that the offense is a misdemeanor, unless the defendant at the time of his arraignment or plea objects to the offense being made a misdemeanor, in which event the complaint shall be amended to charge a felony complaint.

(5) When, at or before the preliminary examination or prior to filing an order pursuant to Section 872 [that section pertains to holding the accused over to answer for a felony], the magistrate determines that the offense is a misdemeanor, in which event the case shall proceed as if the defendant had been arraigned on a misdemeanor complaint.

(c) When a defendant is committed to the Youth Authority for a crime punishable, in the discretion of the court, by imprisonment in the state prison or by fine or imprisonment in county jail, the offense shall, upon the discharge of the defendant from the Youth Authority, thereafter be deemed a misdemeanor for all purposes. [Subparagraph (d) omitted.]

California Penal Code 177 —
Public Offenses Not Otherwise Defined Are Misdemeanors

When an act or omission is declared by a statute to be a public offense, and no penalty for the offense is prescribed in any statute, the act or omission is punishable as a misdemeanor.

California Penal Code 19d —
Application of Misdemeanor Law to Infractions

Except as otherwise provided by law, all provisions of law relating to misdemeanors shall apply to infractions, including but not limited to powers of peace officers, jurisdiction of courts, periods for commencing action and for bringing a case to trial and burden of proof.

The Nature and Classifications of Crimes

Crimes are classified as "mala in se" or "mala prohibitum" crimes. Other classifications include "crimes involving moral turpitude," "infamous crimes" and "high crimes."

Mala in Se and Mala Prohibitum Crime

An act is said to be malum in se when it is inherently and essentially evil, that is, immoral in its nature and injurious in its consequences, without regard to the fact that it is a violation of the law.[18]

Malum Prohibitum

A wrong prohibited; a thing which is wrong because prohibited; an act which is not inherently immoral, but becomes so because its commission is expressly forbidden by positive law (Black's Law Dictionary).

At common law, crimes were classified as either "mala in se" or "mala prohibita". Mala in se crimes involve conduct that is inherently and essentially wrong and injurious. Crimes such as murder, rape, incest, arson, etc. are considered as mala in se crimes. Mala prohibita crimes are wrong only because they violate legislative acts and not because they are inherently and essentially wrong in themselves. Most mala prohibita crimes involve traffic, social and economic behavior. Criminal violation of a rent control statute is an example of a mala prohibita crime.

Moral Turpitude

Moral turpitude is a classification used to describe acts that are contrary to justice, honesty, modesty, or good morals.[19] It has also been defined as an act of baseless, vileness, or depravity in the private and social duties which one person owes to others, or to society in general.[20] Crimes that suggest a lack of honesty, or that imply immoral conduct are considered as crimes involving moral turpitude. For example, perjury, theft, and rape are considered crimes involving moral turpitude. [*Note:* Crimes involving moral turpitude may also be considered as mala in se crimes.]

Conviction of a crime involving moral turpitude may disqualify a person from holding a professional qualification such as an "attorney at law."[21] The conviction of an attempt to commit a crime involving moral turpitude has the same disqualifications attached as a conviction of the actual offense.[21]

Infamous Crimes

While various crimes are referred to as infamous crimes in the state constitutions and statutes, there is no statutory definition. An infamous crime is one that entails infamy upon the one who committed the crime.[23] At common law, the term infamous was applied to those crimes upon the conviction of which, the person became incompetent to testify as a witness on the theory that they were so depraved as to be unworthy of credit (*Black's Law Dictionary*). It was not the character of the crime that determined whether or not it was an infamous crime, but the punishment that may be imposed for conviction of it.[24]

Crimen Falsi

"Crimen falsi" is a phrase used to describe those crimes that involve the element of falsehood and includes everything which has a tendency to injuriously affect the administration of justice by the introduction of falsehood and fraud (*Black's Law Dictionary*). The phrase is, also, used as a general designation of a class of offenses involving fraud and deceit. Crimen falsi crimes include forgery, perjury, using false weights or measurements, and counterfeiting.

High Crimes

"High crimes" is a phrase used to describe those crimes that, if convicted of, will disqualify the offender from holding public office or making the person incompetent to act as a juror.[25] High crimes include bribery, perjury, forgery, and malfeasance in office by a public official.

Wobblers

In most cases, it is not the punishment awarded by a court that determines whether or not a crime is a felony, misdemeanor or infraction; but the punishment that could have been imposed. There are some offenses, however, that are considered as "wobblers." Wobblers are offenses that are either felonies or misdemeanors depending on the sentences awarded at court or action by the court after conviction. Wobblers are treated as felonies until sentencing time unless the crimes are formally charged as misdemeanors.

For example, California Penal Code 524 provides that an attempted extortion may be punished by imprisonment in the county jail or in a state prison. Accordingly, it is a "wobbler." If the accused on conviction receives a jail term, then it is a misdemeanor conviction.

If he or she receives a prison term, then it is a felony conviction. [*Note:* The district attorney can charge it as a felony or misdemeanor. If the DA charges the offense as a felony offense, at the preliminary hearing the judge may reduce it to a misdemeanor offense.]

Punishments

When an act or omission is declared by a statute to be a crime and punishment is provided for, but no specific penalty is prescribed in the statute, then the general punishment statutes prevail. For example in most states, even in jury trials, the judge has the duty to impose sentences.

In capital cases with a jury, however, the jury must make a finding as to whether special circumstances exist and if so, do they outweigh the mitigating circumstances before the death penalty can be imposed. For example, if the accused with no prior criminal record intentionally kills his girlfriend by administering poison, the jury must decide that the special circumstances (death by poisoning) outweigh the mitigating circumstances (no prior criminal record) before the death penalty may be imposed.

Concurrently or Consecutively

When the accused is convicted of two or more crimes, the judge is required to make a determination as to whether or not the sentences will be served concurrently or consecutively. Sentences that are served concurrently are served at the same time. Consecutive sentences are served one at a time; one following the other. For example, the defendant is convicted of two crimes, arson and robbery. If he received two years for each offense and the sentences are served concurrently, he will serve a maximum of two years. If the sentences run consecutively, he will first serve one sentence and when that sentence is completed, he will serve the other (two years plus two years for a maximum of four years). [*Note:* If the accused has pending confinement from a previous court, the court should also indicate whether the present sentence will be served concurrently or consecutively with the sentence given in the prior court.]

White Collar Crimes

"The best way to rob a bank is to own it."

(A joke that recently circulated in Washington, D.C.)

White collar crimes are nonviolent crimes committed for financial gain by means of deception by persons having professional status or specialized skills. The most common white collar crimes include: counterfeiting, embezzlement, forgery, fraud, and regulatory offenses. Generally, prosecuting white collar crimes is more complicated than street crimes. There is often one single victim or no one to report the commission of the offense. The crime is often based on trust between the victim and the offender. Normally the building of trust expands the time frame of the crime, permitting repeated victimizations of an unsuspecting victim.

The extent of white collar crime has been estimated at over 50 billion dollars a year. Despite its potential for extensive damage, citizens do not regard it with the same fear as they do "street" crime. Except in exceptional cases, such as the savings and loan frauds, the consequences of corporate or white collar crime are generally ignored. It is estimated that the savings and loan debacle of the 1980s was at least a decade in the making and will cost every person in this country at least $1,200 to repair its damage. In addition, the FBI contends that banks and credit unions lose over $1.3 billion each year to fraud and embezzlement by tellers and loan officers.

Computer-assisted crime is presently a major part of white collar crime. Like corporate crime, the majority of it goes undetected or unreported. There is no central data bank for computer crime statistics. The National Institute of Justice has defined computer-assisted crime under three classifications:

1) Computer abuse— An intentional illegal act involving knowledge of computer use or technology. For example, wrongly obtaining bank withdrawal codes by the use of computer equipment.

2) Computer fraud— The use of a computer either directly or as a vehicle for deliberate misrepresentation or deception usually to hide embezzlement or thefts.

3) Computer crime— The violation of a computer crime statute.

Crimes Without Victims

Crimes without victims or "victimless crimes" are those crimes that have no adverse impact on persons other than the actor. They can also be considered as "consensual crimes." Gambling, prostitution and drug abuse have traditionally been considered by some as victimless crimes. One problem with the enforcement of victimless crimes is that the police will often not have an aggrieved victim to testify against the offender. Criminologists have traditionally debated as to whether or not acts between consensual adults should be considered as criminal. The justification for imposing criminal sanctions for the violation of those statutes on victimless crimes is that there are at least "moral victims" to those crimes, and that society, in general, is a victim in those situations.

Repeal/Amendment

Criminal statutes are repealed or amended by other legislation either directly or by implication.[26] A statute is repealed directly by legislation expressly repealing the statute in question.

Repeal by Implication

Repeal by implication is not favored by the courts.[27] A statute is repealed or amended by implication when a later statute is enacted that is inconsistent with it. Normally, a general statute will not be considered as repealed by a special statute or statute of limited applicability unless the intent of the legislature is clear.[28] It is assumed that the legislature did not intend to repeal a former statute by a later statute if, by a fair and reasonable construction, effect can be given to both statutes.[29] [*Note:* If two general statutes are clearly in conflict with each other, the presumption is that the latest enacted statute prevails.]

Effect of Repeal

The repeal of a statute under which a person has been convicted does not affect the conviction if the conviction is final. All states have a "general saving clause" for repealed criminal statutes. It modifies common law by allowing for the prosecution of acts which were criminal at the time of commission even though the statute which made them criminal has since been repealed. Its purpose is to authorize prosecution under a former statute in order to avoid a situation where the defendant could not be prosecuted under any law, simply because the legislature has modified the statute in question between the time that the act was committed and the time of trial.[30] The California Supreme Court decided in 1893, that a person should be punished under the state law as it existed at the time of the commission of the offense rather than subsequent amendment to such law. This principle has since been upheld by the U.S. Supreme Court.[31]

The above rules apply even where the act is no longer a criminal offense. For example, if a state were to repeal its traffic laws as of January 1, 19XX; an accused could be convicted and punished on January 3, 19XX on a traffic violation that occurred prior to January 1.

LEGAL RESEARCH AND METHODOLOGY

Administration of Justice is normally one of the first courses taken by criminal justice majors. Accordingly, this section is included to introduce the students to the basic concepts of legal research and methodology. Researching legal issues and cases is different from standard literature research. Once the student has mastered the concepts and methodology, however, legal issues, case law, and statutes can be located quickly and efficiently.

In conducting legal research, the researcher should:

1) Research the subject systematically, going sequentially from one source (e.g., statutes, court decisions, or law reviews) to the next.

2) Check to insure that the latest available information has been consulted. For example, use only the latest copy of the penal code. Using only the latest references is essential because legal information and points of authority change frequently as the result of statutory modifications and new court decisions.

3) In researching legal questions, be patient and thorough. To many questions, the law frequently does not yield easy "yes or no"

answers. At times, the answers will be considered ambiguous and conflicting.

Legal Citations

Legal citations are a form of shorthand used to assist in locating legal sources. Appellate court decisions are published in case law books, more popularly known as "reporters." The basic rules of legal citation are as follows:

1) In most citation formats, the volume or title number is presented first.

2) Following is the standardized abbreviation for the legal reference source.

3) Finally, in the case of court cases, is the page number of the first page of the decision. In the case of statutory references, it is the section number of the statute.

For example, the citation, 107 U.S. 468, refers to the case starting on page 468 of volume 107 of United States Reports. A citation of 18 U.S.C. 347, refers to title 18 U.S. Code, section 347.

National Reporter System

West Publishing Company's *National Reporter System* is the standard for researching court reports. The system includes, in bound volumes and advance sheets, decisions of all state and federal appellate courts and selected trial court opinions. Included in the bound volumes are the table of cases, table of cited statutes, criminal and appellate procedure tables, words and phrases, and a key number digest.

The Reporter System was started in 1876 by two brothers doing business under the name of "John B. West and Company." The brothers reported the decisions of courts in Minnesota in a series of pamphlets known as "The Syllabi." In 1879, the name of the series was changed to "North Western Reporter." By 1887, the venture had expanded to a total of seven regional reporters covering all the states. The seven regional reporters are still being published with only slight modifications in state coverage. The present day coverage is as follows:

1) *Atlantic Reporter*: Me., N. H., Conn., Vt., Pa., Del., Md., and N.J.

2) *North Eastern Reporter*: Mass., N.Y., Ohio, Ind., and Ill.

3) *North Western Reporter*: N.Dak., S.Dak., Nebr., Minn., Iowa, Wis., and Mich.

4) *Pacific Reporter*: Kan., Ok., N.M., Col., Wyo., Mont., Id., Utah, Ariz., Nev., Or., Wash., Ca., Alaska, and Ha.

5) *South Eastern Reporter*: Ga., S.Car., N.Car., Va., and W. Va.

6) *South Western Reporter*: Tex., Ark., Tenn., Ky., and Mo.

7) *Southern Reporter*: La., Miss., Ala., and Fla.

In addition to the regional reporters, West publishes the *Supreme Court Reporter* which reports only decisions of the U.S. Supreme Court; The *Federal Reporter* which reports decisions of the U.S. Courts of Appeal, and the *Federal Supplement* which reports selected U.S. District Court decisions, decisions of federal judicial panels, and other special federal courts. The *New York Supplement*, which also reports New York state appellate cases, was started in 1887, and the *California Reporter*, which reports current decisions of the California Supreme Court, District Courts of Appeal and Superior Court (Appellate Department) decisions, was started in 1960.

Official Reporters

As noted above, West's *National Reporter System* is the standard case reporter; however, in most cases they are not considered the "official reporter." Each high court designates a publisher as the "official reporter." For example, the official reporter of the U.S. Supreme Court is the U.S. Reports (U.S.), whereas the reporter is the Supreme Court Reporter (S. Ct.). Contained in each case reported in the West reporter is the official reporter citation.

Legal Digests

Legal digests are not legal authorities. They are used as research tools. Legal digests identify and consolidate similar issues by topical arrangement. Most legal digests, using West's standard format, divide the body of law into seven main divisions, thirty-two subheadings and approximately four hundred topics. West also publishes a digest for each series of case reporters. Each topic is assigned a digest "key" number. For example, Crim Law 625 is the key number for the legal issue of "exclusion from criminal trial."

The key number is the same for each digest published. Legal points from court decisions are published with a brief statement of the legal point involved and the case citation for the court decision being digested. If, for example, a point being researched is located in a digest under Crim Law 625, then reference to other digests using the same key number (Crim Law 625) will help locate other court decisions on the same or similar issues.

Shepard's Citations

Shepard's Citations, started in 1873 by Frank Shepard, are widely used to ascertain the current status of a statute or court decision. *Shepard's Citations*, more popularly known as citators, analyze each appellate court decision as to the history of the case, other decisions where that decision has been cited, and whether or not the rule of the case has been modified, overruled, or approved by other cases. A similar analysis is used for statutes. For a detailed explanation of how to use *Shepard's Citations*, read the first pages of any citator volume.

Legal Dictionaries and Encyclopedias

Like *Shepard's Citations* and legal digests, legal dictionaries and encyclopedias are not legal authorities, but research tools. The most popular legal dictionary is *Black's Law Dictionary*.

Legal encyclopedias provide discussions on various legal points in encyclopedic form based on court decisions and statutes. They are arranged by broad legal topics and subdivided by individual areas. Most state legal encyclopedias provide detailed discussions on state legal issues. For example, the citation "17 Cal Jur 3d (Rev) 125" refers to volume 17 of California Jurisprudence, Third Edition (Revised), section 125. The cited section provides a detailed discussion on robbery.

Law Reviews

The major law schools publish law reviews. In general, the law reviews contain scholarly articles on various aspects of California law. They are not legal authority but are often cited as persuasive authorities.

Law reviews are cited similar to court cases. For example, an article in volume 50 of the Standard Law Review which begins on page 192 would be cited as: 50 Stan. L. Rev. 192.

Standard Jury Instructions—Criminal

Standard Jury Instructions—Criminal are collections of standard jury instructions that a judge may use to instruct the jury regarding elements of crimes, defenses, and other matters relating to the trial. They are also used by non-judges as references, since the instructions contain explanations of crimes and criminal procedural matters.

Consolidated Indexes

A convenient research tool is the consolidated index of your state. For example, LARMAC is a consolidated index to the constitution and laws of California. It is an index of the state constitution, all twenty-eight codes, and the general laws of California under one alphabetical listing. It is the most complete index available on California law. Similar indexes exist for most states.

Attorney General Opinions

Generally, the State Attorney General has charge, as attorney, of most legal matters in which the State is interested.

The Attorney General is normally required to provide legal opinions in writing to the Legislature or either house thereof, and to the Governor, the Secretary of State, Controller, Treasurer, State Lands Commission, Superintendent of Public Instruction, any state agency prohibited by law from employing legal counsel other than the Attorney General, and any district attorney when required, upon any question of law relating to their respective offices.

The opinions are generally of two types: formal and informal. Formal opinions concern legal questions that are of general statewide concern. Formal attorney general opinions are usually published in volumes similar to case reports. Informal opinions normally concern problems that are of local interest only. Informal opinions are not usually published, but many are available to the public from the Attorney General's Office. Informal opinions are generally issued in letter format.

Attorney General opinions are considered as "quasi-judicial" in character. While they do not have the force and effect of statutes or court decisions, they are entitled to great weight and are persuasive to the courts.[32]

DISCUSSION QUESTIONS

1. Timmer states that "A definition of crime represents the legal conditions under which the State, as an instrument of an economically dominant class, exercises its power to punish."[33] Do you agree or disagree with this statement? Explain your opinion.

2. What are the requirements for qualifying conduct as a crime?

3. Define the differences between a tort and a crime.

4. Distinguish between procedural and substantive criminal law.

5. Is a state statute that defines the crime of criminal homicide a procedural or substantive law?

6. Explain the various classifications of crime.

7. What constitutes white collar crime?

ENDNOTES

[1] U.S. Department of Justice, *Report to the Nation on Crime and Justice*, 2nd ed., (Washington D.C. 1988): pp. 56-60.

[2] *Sloane v. Hammond*, 81 CA 590; 254 P 648 (1927).

[3] *People v. Brophy*, 49 CA2d 15, 28; 120 P2d 946 (1942).

[4] 80 ALR2d 1067.

[5] 384 U.S. 436 (1966).

[6] 3 U.S. 386 (1798).

[7] Richard Quinney and John Wildeman, *The Problem of Crime*, 3rd ed., (Mountain View, Ca.: Mayfield, 1991), p. 1.

[8] James F. Gilsinan, *Criminology and Public Policy*, (Englewood Cliffs, NJ: Prentice-Hall, 1990), p. 17.

[9] Herbert A. Johnson, *History of Criminal Justice*, (Cincinnati: Anderson, 1988).

[10] Ibid. p. 7.

[11] Edwin Sutherland, *White Collar Crime*, (New York: Holt, Rinehart and Winston, 1949).

[12] *People v. Morrison*, 54 CA 469, 202 P 348 (1921).

[13] *People v. Knowles*, 35 C 2d 175.

[14] *People v. Perini*, 94 C 573.

[15] Cal. Const. Art II, sec. 8.

[16] *Mills v. Trinity County*, 108 CA 3d 656.

[17] *Fair Political Practices Comm. v. Superior Court*, 25 C 3d 33.

[18] *State v. Shedoudy*, 45 N.M. 516.

[19] *Marsh v. State Bar of California*, 210 C 303.

[20] *Traders & General Ins. Co. v. Russell*, S.W. 2d 1079.

[21] *Re Application of Westenberg*, 167 C 309.

[22] *Re O'Connell*, 184 C 584.

[23] *Butler v. Wentworth*, 24 A. 456.

[24] *Brede v. Powers*, 263 U.S. 4.

[25] California Code of Civ. Pro. 199 (b).

[26] *People v. Dobbins*, 73 C. 257.

[27] *People v. Armstrong*, 100 CA 2d Supp 821.

[28] *People v. Deibert*, 117 CA 2d 410..

[29] *People v. Armstong*, 100 CA 2d Supp 852.

[30] *Re Estrada*, 63 CA 2d 740.

[31] *McNulty v. California*, 149 US 645.

[32] *D'Amico v. Medical Examiners*, 6 CA 3d 716, and People v. Berry, 147 CA 2d 33.

[33] *Crime in the Streets and Crime in the Suites*, (Needham Heights, Ma.: Allyn & Bacon, 1989), p. 27.

Upper part of the pillar upon which the legendary Code of Hammurabi was inscribed.

EVOLUTION OF THE
PRESENT SYSTEM OF
JUSTICE

*When is conduct a crime? When somebody up
there — a king, dictator, legislator, or Pope so
decrees!*

—Jessica Mitford

FOUNDATIONS OF OUR JUSTICE SYSTEM

In this section, we will explore the ancient foundations of our justice system. In studying them, it is difficult to separate the early law from the early searches for crime causation and the system for enforcing the law. The concepts are interwoven until at least the 17th century. Accordingly, the ancient foundations of our law, the early searches for crime causation and the foundations of our justice system are presented together in a rough chronological order.

In looking at the evolution of our criminal justice system, we note that it is English in origin. To understand its development, however, we need to look at the roots of western civilization beginning with the first known written criminal codes along with three ancient systems of law; Biblical Israel, Classical Athens, and the Roman Empire. Each of these systems contributed to the system that we have today. Israel's system developed during the period 1200-650 B.C. when Israel was transformed from a nomadic existence based on herding sheep and goats to a farming society. Athens' system developed during the period 596-410 B.C. when Athens thrived on the Mediterranean commercial activity. The Roman system was developed during the period 520-25 B.C.

Code of Hammurabi

Our present criminal codes grew out of custom, tradition, and actual written codes. The first known criminal code was the Code of Hammurabi about 2100 B.C. The Code of Hammurabi was named after the King of Babylon. The code was engraved on a pillar of stone and contained specific laws governing the conduct of people. It was comprised of some 4,000 lines of writing which were preceded by a poetic prologue of one long sentence that ended with the phrase: "Law and justice I establish in the land and promote the welfare of the people."

The code was a comprehensive series of laws covering not only crime, but property rights, family law and other civil matters. The Code of Hammurabi also contained rules protecting victims of crimes. The concept of "an eye for an eye and a tooth for a tooth" was first introduced by King Hammurabi with his "lex talionis." [*Note:* The above concept was based on the premise that the punishment should fit the crime.]

The code had a certain systematic order. It began with a discussion of murder and sorcery and then covered all grades of social behavior. The three essential features of the code were that it was based on individual responsibility under the law, a belief in the sanctity of the oath to God, and the necessity of written evidence in all legal matters.

Biblical Israel

Biblical Israel's criminal justice centered around the concept that the descendants of Abraham were the chosen people of God. Rules of behavior as well as the structure of criminal law and punishments reflected this influence. Wrongful conduct was offensive because; first, it tended to destroy the bonds of society and caused dissension among the people and second, it could easily bring divine wrath down on the entire nation.

The most common trial court was the "court at the gate." This court originated with the authority of the clan elders to determine controversies within the clan. With the establishment of towns and cities and the mixing of clans, the elders established the court at the gate to assist in resolving controversies. The court was usually convened in the mornings at the gate to the town. The elders on the way to the farms would stop and do justice. Both civil and criminal cases were tried by the court. By holding the court at the gate, the maximum number of people could witness the proceedings. From this practice developed the concept of a public trial.

In criminal cases, the accusing party stood to the right of the accused. The elder who was acting as a judge was seated in the center. An accused person could be assisted by a defense witness who later became known as a "defender." The accusing party acted also as the prosecutor. If the death penalty was imposed, the accusing party was responsible for throwing the first stone. A person giving false testimony was subject to the same punishment as that of the accused.

The court instructed the witnesses not to give testimony that was second hand or supposition. Similar restrictions on witness testimony exists today in our evidence codes. In most cases, it took at least two witnesses to convict an accused. If there was insufficient evidence to convict, the accused was asked to take an exculpatory oath denying his guilt. The accused was then required to call upon God to curse him if he swore falsely, and the case was dismissed.

To them, the law was an expression of God's command and violation of it was a transgression against God. God was all knowing and jealous. Deviant behavior, at that time, was believed to destroy the bonds of society. It was also believed that antisocial acts caused dissension among the people of Israel. In addition, it was thought that deviant/criminal behavior on the part of any member of God's chosen people could incur God's wrath on everyone. Hebraic laws, therefore, were developed to appease God's displeasure. For example, consider the following quotation that explains how the ancient Hebrews dealt with homicide:

> ... Israelite law demanded that one who killed should be put to death, a relatively harsh punishment principle that developed from the theological connection between the blood of the victim and the spirit of God.
>
> Yahweh (God) was believed to possess the blood of a man which, in turn contained the spirit given to the individual by the Creator. In shedding human blood, a murderer took what rightfully belonged to Yahweh (God), only his death and the shedding of his blood was adequate compensation. If a murdered man should be found in a field, the nearby village was expected to sacrifice an animal if the culprit could not be found....[1]

The idea was that the blood of the animal and the animal's spirit would be returned to God and, thus, "balance" would be restored. Until balance was restored, God would not be satisfied.

Athens

The early Greeks initiated a series of reforms in both the law and its enforcement. Around 593 B.C., Solon, the chief magistrate of

Athens drafted a code of behavior which prohibited slavery for indebtedness, divided the population into classes based on property, and granted citizenship to even the lowest classes. At that time, the administration of justice was the responsibility of the Heliaea which were juries chosen by lot from among 6,000 representatives of the Athenian tribes. The parties involved in a grievance took their claims to the Heliasts, who decided the question of conviction or acquittal by secret ballot. The law specified that a trial must be finished in one day or less.

Athenians, because of their experience with harsh rulers, were convinced that the rule of the people was essential to their happiness. As the state became more prosperous, so did their insistence upon protections that would discourage any citizens from attempting to establish a tyranny.

The Athenians relied on self-help in arresting persons accused of criminal behavior. This was probably the first use of "citizen's arrest." In addition, the accusing party could ask that a magistrate be present to help make an arrest. In most cases, the prosecution began by filing a complaint with the magistrate with the delivery of a copy on the accused. With all parties present, including witnesses, the magistrate would hold a preliminary hearing regarding the charges. He then could either dismiss the complaint or hold it over for the next session of the court.

Murder cases were assigned to a special court consisting of all serving and previously commissioned magistrates. The court would meet in the marketplace. Originally, the decision of the court could be appealed to the entire people of Athens for review. Later, a panel of 50 citizens were selected to decide appeals. The appeals were decided by secret written ballot.

Like the Israel courts, oaths played a significant role in the criminal procedure of Athens. Both the accused and the accusing party were required to take an oath to the accuracy of their pleading. In early Athenian criminal procedure, the accused and his family could take an exculpatory oath and if the "oath-helpers" outnumbered the persons who supported the accuser's oath, the charges were dismissed. In this latter case, the accused was required to invoke a curse on himself and his family if his oath of "not guilty" was false.

Later, the reliance on oaths declined and was replaced by an emphasis on the reliability and accuracy of the evidence. After the submission of evidence the parties could present speeches in favor of their position. If the accusing party lost the case and received less than 20 percent of the jury's votes, he could be fined 1,000 drachmas. The fine was to discourage citizens from bringing unsubstantiated criminal offenses.

Capital punishment was carried out by either throwing the criminal in an open pit or allowing the criminal to drink hemlock. Non-capital punishment included banishment and public degradation. Flogging was used only for slaves. In some cases, the convict was sold into slavery.

The Greek philosophers considered crime as an offense against the society or the state. They were also concerned about ameliorating a higher power, but they were convinced that the rule of the people was critical to the prevention of tyrannies. The Greeks believed that anyone who committed homicide was infected with corruption and evil. Merely being accused of homicide made a person corrupt, and his movements were sharply circumscribed to keep him away from places of assembly and from sites of religious significance. Later, however, the Greeks developed a naturalistic explanation of criminal behavior. Plato and Aristotle, for example, appeared to believe that the cause of criminal behavior was based on physical factors.

Plato (428-348 BC) taught that man had a dual character. He believed that a person was rational and sought perfection, but was limited by his or her own weaknesses and imperfections. Plato also contended that crime would always exist because of man's greedy nature. An examination of his *Republic* leads to the conclusion that he believed that we have the freedom to choose between right and wrong. He also contended that punishment was man's right to cleanse himself of evil.

Aristotle (384-322 BC) divided law into two classes— natural and man-made. Natural law concerns those values that are universally accepted as correct. Man-made laws were those that were created by man to promote equality and fairness. According to Aristotle, our ability to reason separates us from animals, and crime is caused by our irrational acts. Unfortunately, he was not clear on the cause of the irrational acts. It does appear, however, that he believed the irrational acts (crimes) were the result of the individual's deliberate choices.[2]

[*Note*: Did Aristotle mean that if we "reason", we will not commit crimes?]

The Romans

While the Romans shared the Greeks antipathy with tyranny, their system was founded on the concept of the citizen-soldier to ensure Roman dominance of the world. The Roman system of criminal justice was designed to protect the citizens of Rome from unjust prosecution and to provide the citizens with a clear understanding of their rights and responsibilities to the state.

The Roman system provides a series of checks and balances over the exercise of judicial power. For example, the two principle magistrates were the consuls. Each consul's term of office was only one year, and each needed the consent of his colleague to govern. All magistrates had the authority to veto a colleague's action. In addition, criminal judgments against citizens could be appealed to the body of the people. After, 25 B.C., however, appeals were decided by the emperor. A magistrate could avoid an appeal by bringing the matter before a council of advisors which was composed of the other magistrates.

Since the magistrates were selected from the senatorial class, the common people established their own tribunals similar to the magistrates. The tribunals could conduct a criminal proceeding before either their own assembly of other tribunes or before an assembly of the people as a whole.

Later as the process became too cumbersome, beginning in about 190 B.C., lesser magistrates were authorized to assemble juries composed of an equal number of patricians, knights, and plebs. The juries decided on the guilt of the accused. If the magistrate agreed with the jury and entered a conviction, no appeal was allowed. The court utilized one presiding officer and a jury varying in size from 32 to 75 individuals. Since these courts were presided over by the lessor magistrates, they were not guided by legally trained individuals.

The mode of trial was adversarial in nature. Both the accused and the accuser were arraigned against each other, and the issues were submitted to the jurors who were considered as impartial. Later these courts tended to shift toward police courts which acted as investigatory agencies and became inquisitorial in nature.

Procedures before the Roman courts tended to provide maximum flexibility and hearsay evidence was permitted. Often testimony was presented by the use of affidavits. In most cases, the reputation of the accused was the main point of issue, and character evidence was freely admitted into evidence. It appears that the Romans, during this later period of time, achieved efficiency at the expense of individual rights.[3]

The Romans in their search for the causes of crime, integrated the spiritualism of the Hebrews with the naturalism of the Greek scholars to develop laws that were based on the "nature of things." The chief contribution of the Romans was their focus on "justice" and codes of law, not a search for crime causation.[4]

About 500 B.C., in response to public pressures, a committee of ten distinguished leaders compiled a legal code based on Roman customs. The code was set up on ten bronze or wooden tablets in the Forum. Later two more tablets were added. These twelve tablets formed the basis of Roman civil law. During the height of the Roman Empire, the most important enactments were leges (legislation), which were rules of conduct announced by the emperor or by the assembly. It was also customary for magistrates and governors to issue edicts which gave their interpretation of the law and the actions that the officials would take or permit under various circumstances.

The edicts and the leges were exhibited in the Forum. As new magistrates and governors adopted many of their predecessors' edicts, the emperor in 130 A.D. instructed the jurists to codify the edicts and leges into a permanent code, Edictum Perpetuum. In 27 B.C., the Roman emperor created the Vigiles of Rome, the first nonmilitary force. The Vigiles were a group of approximately 1,000 men whose job it was to keep peace in the city and to fight fires.[5]

The Early Western Europeans

The early European churches equated crime with sin. Criminals were possessed by the devil. For example, St. Augustine (354-430 AD) contended that God gave Adam a choice between good and evil and that Adam chose evil. To St. Augustine, evil (crime) resulted from influences of the devil. Criminals, therefore, had to have the devil driven from them. The church rite of "exorcism" was used for this. If exorcism failed to drive the devil out of the "sinners," then they were turned over to civil authorities where capital punishment or other brutal punishments were used to eradicate the devil.[6]

St. Thomas Aquinas (1225-1274) contended that the "soul" is implanted in the unborn child by God and that the "soul" is the source of our reasoning power. The conscience is that part of our soul that guides us toward rational and just behavior. It is our human appetite (influenced by the devil) that causes us to seek worldly pleasures. When the human appetite overrules our conscience, evil (crime) occurs.[7]

Another popular explanation of criminal behavior during the 15th and 16th centuries included astral influences (moon and stars). A Swiss physician, Hohenheim (also known as Paracelsus, 1490-1541) was a proponent of the idea that criminal behavior was caused by influences of the stars and the moon. According to this explanation, astral influences controlled human behavior and caused people to act in strange and irrational ways.[8] [*Note:* The word "lunatic" comes from the Latin word "luna", meaning moon.]

The English

When the Anglo-Saxon tribes from central Europe invaded England in 500 A.D., they brought with them a tribal police system. This system was vastly different from the Roman influence that had prevailed upon England for over four hundred years. Whereas the Roman law was based on government legislation, the Germanic (Anglo-Saxon) law was comprised of customs and was generally unwritten.

The first known English code was written in the Seventh century by King Aethelbert. The proclamations of the code were called "dooms." The dooms were social class orientated. For example, theft was punishable by fines which ranged widely in magnitude according to the status of the victim. Stealing from the King was punishable by a fine equal to nine times the value of the property stolen. Theft from a person of the holy order was punishable by a fine three times the value of the property taken. Crimes committed in the presence of the King were considered a violation of the "king's peace" and increased the punishment for the crime. In the Ninth and 11th centuries, the code was rewritten, but little new substance was added.

Most historians trace the common law of England to William the Conqueror who invaded England in 1066. At the time of the invasion, each county was controlled by a Sheriff (shire-reeve), who also controlled the courts in that county. Accordingly, there was no uniform English system. William took over the courts and made them royal court—under the control of the King. He sent representatives to the many courts in England to record the decisions of the judges. William distributed selected decisions of the judges to all the judges. Judges then utilized the selected decisions in making their own decisions. As the routine of these courts became firmly established, it was possible to forecast decisions based upon previous decisions of similar cases. From this developed the doctrine of *stare decisis* which means "to stand on the decision" (i.e., legal precedent).

William also compiled a list of crimes that were found to be common in most areas of the kingdom. These crimes became the "Common Law Crimes" of England. Later new statutory crimes were added by the King and Parliament. [*Note:* The concept of common law crimes was so ingrained in England that the traditional crimes of burglary, larceny, murder, etc., were not defined by statute in England until the 1960s.]

An artist's conception of a public execution in early London, England.

Justice In Early America

Our system of criminal justice is based on English common law. The colonists brought English traditions and concepts with them when they settled our country. Included was the English concept of justice, which is the foundation of our system. To this foundation, a bit of Spanish and French influence was added as the system was developed and changed to meet the requirements of a growing nation.[9]

There was a clear tendency in early America, to equate crime with sin, pauperism, and immorality. The first explanations of crime in American colonies were linked to the devil. For example, there were three "crime waves" during the first 60 years of the Massachusetts Bay Puritan Colony. All were blamed on the "devil." The most serious of the crime waves occurred in 1792 and was thought to be caused by witches.[10]

Beccaria's *Essay on Crimes and Punishments* in 1766 marked the apex of the "Age of Enlightenment." At this time the colonies in North America were being settled. The Age of Enlightenment and its reliance on the role of reason in understanding human behavior was very popular in the new world. The "Age of Enlightenment" made its influence felt throughout the western world and led to the American Revolution and the adoption of a government marked by constitutionalism and limited political power. After the American Revolution our system of criminal justice expanded and developed its own unique identity. The idea of clear and precise criminal laws (one of the hallmarks of the "classical school" discussed in Chapter 3) evolved at this time.

American Criminology came into its own in the 19th century. It developed from the fields of sociology and psychology and was directly influenced by the positivist school and the "Age of Realism." Accordingly, American criminal law scholars embraced the "classical" school and American correctional scholars embraced the "positivist" school which will be further discussed in chapter three. The result was a clear division between the legal and corrective aspects of our criminal justice system. The law tended to be based on the concept of "free will" (the offender can freely choose to perform a criminal act) and corrections were based on the "treatment" (the offender's behavior was the result of factors beyond his control) concept. This division was apparent until the late 1950s. Beginning in the late 1950s and the early 1960s, the "positivist" influence on the penal aspects of our criminal justice system lost much of its influence.[11]

This decline of the "positivist" influence was likely caused by the social and political unrest and the increase in crime rates that occurred in the late 1950s and the 1960s. In addition, in the 1960s our society began moving in a decidedly conservative direction. One implication of the conservative movement was the way that criminals were viewed. The classical view, which considered criminals to be rational beings who chose to commit crimes, appeared and the sympathetic treatment of criminals disappeared. The classical view continues still to dominate the American criminal justice system.

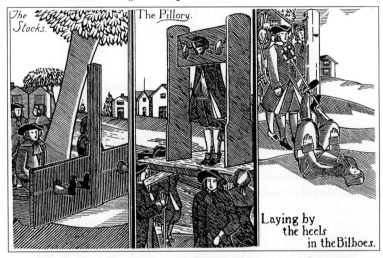

The end result of criminal justice in Colonial America often meant punishment by simple yet effective devices. (Courtesy of Patterson Smith Publishing Corp.)

EXHIBIT 2-1

The Capital Laws of Massachusetts in the Years 1641-1643

—partial list—

1. If any man after legal conviction, shall have or worship any other God, but the Lord God, he shall be put to death.

2. If any man or woman be a Witch, that is, hath or consulteth with a familiar spirit, they shall be put to death.

3. If any person shall blaspheme the Name of God the Father, Son, or Holy Ghost, with direct, express, presumptuous, or high-handed blasphemy, or shall curse God in like manner, he shall be put to death.

4. If any person shall commit any willful murder, which is manslaughter, committed upon premeditate malice, hatred, or cruelty, not in a man's necessary and just defense, nor by near casualty, against his will; he shall be put to death.

5. If any person slayeth another through guile, either by poisoning, or other such devilish practice; he shall be put to death.

6. If any person shall slayeth another suddenly in his anger, or cruelty of passion, he shall be put to death.

7. If a man or woman shall lie with any animal, by carnal copulation, they shall surely be put to death and the animal shall be slain and buried.

8. If any person committeth adultery with a married, or espoused wife, the Adulterer and the Adulteress, shall surely be put to death.

9. If any man shall unlawfully have carnal copulation with any woman-child under ten years old, either with or without her consent, he shall be put to death.

10. If any man steals, he shall be put to death.

11. If any man rise up by false witness, he shall be put to death.

DEVELOPMENT OF THE TRIAL SYSTEM

Prior to the invasion by William the Conqueror and the Normans, England first used blood feuds and later a system called "compurgation" to keep law and order. Under compurgation, when an individual was accused of a crime or the wrongful withholding of property, he could take an oath that he was innocent of any wrongdoing. He then called other witnesses (oath-helpers) to swear, not to the facts of the case, but that they believed the accused told the truth. If the accused gained the support of a sufficient number of "oath-helpers," he was acquitted. The system was based on the widespread fear of divine retribution for false swearing. It was from this practice that the present-day requirement for the witnesses to present their testimony under oath originated.

If the accused was unable to obtain sufficient oath-helpers, the judges had the alternative of leaving the case undecided or referring the case to a trial by ordeal. There were several forms of trial by ordeal. One test required the accused to put his hand in a kettle of boiling water. When the hand was withdrawn, it was bound with cloth for three days. At the end of three days when the cloth was removed, if the hand was unscathed, the accused was acquitted. Another ordeal required the accused to carry in his bare hands a red-hot bar of iron. If the accused was unable to carry the iron for a given distance without dropping it, he was considered guilty. Another ordeal consisted of walking barefooted across a number of heated plowshares placed side by side.

Still another popular method of trial by ordeal was to lower the accused with his hands tied behind his back into a body of cold water. If he floated, it meant that he was possessed by the devil and thus was guilty. This was based on the concept that when Satan invaded a person's body, his specific gravity was less than that of the water. If he sank, he was considered innocent. One problem with this ordeal was that often the "innocent" person drowned before he could be rescued. In most cases, the ordeals by hot irons were used for the nobility and ordeals by water for the commoners.

As the Normans gained power, they re-introduced the old feudal concept of "trial by duel." Under this system, in the case of a dispute, a duel would be fought, and the winner of the duel became the winner of the case. Later, "champions" could be hired by those involved to fight a duel.

Trial by jury emerged in the 12th century to replace trial by ordeal and trial by duel. The county sheriff selected members of the jury. It was a common practice to select members who were favorable to the Crown. The sheriff also had the power to withhold food from the jury until they reached a decision. If the jurors made a "wrong decision" they could also be punished. The power to punish jury members was considered necessary to prevent the jury from siding with the accused against the Crown. The determination that a jury had made a wrong decision was based upon a retrial of the case before a jury of Knights.

In 1166, the King ordered that twelve family heads from each one hundred families be placed under oath and report to the King all individuals accused or known to be robbers, murderers, or thieves. This order was known as the Assize of Clarendon. "Assize" referred to an order of the King. Henry II provided that certain questions regarding conduct of an accused were resolved by a jury of twelve men selected from those who lived nearby. The procedure used to comply with the assize was similar to the process now used by grand juries. [*Note:* A grand jury is presently used as an investigative body that investigates and indicts persons suspected of committing criminal behavior. This also appears to be the origination for the size of a trial jury being twelve in number.]

By 1240, the use of trial juries was common. Persons accused of a crime by a grand jury were given the option of banishment or trial by a jury. To discourage some persons accused of serious crimes from choosing the option of banishment, many were tortured until they accepted the trial by jury alternative. The most common form of torture used was "pressing to death." The accused was first placed in solitary confinement, then stripped naked, and starved. His body was subjected to increasing weights of iron until he pleaded to the indictment and accepted a jury trial or died. Pressing to death lasted until the 1800s and was finally replaced with the automatic entry of a "not guilty" plea when the accused refused to plea.

CORNERSTONES OF OUR PRESENT TRIAL SYSTEM

No study of the development of our trial system is complete without examining the Magna Carta and the "common law." In addition, to understand our present system it is essential that the student have a basic knowledge of each. Our present system today is based on principles that can be traced directly to the Magna Carta. Our present trial system is a common law system. Accordingly, these two concepts will be examined in the next two sections. For a discussion of our present court system, please refer to Chapter 8.

Magna Carta

One of the greatest documents in English legal history was the Magna Carta, also known as the Great Charter. It was signed in 1215 at Runnymede by King John. The King was forced to sign the charter by the barons. The Charter greatly influenced the later drafting of our federal constitution. Under the charter, certain rights and privileges were guaranteed to "freemen." [*Note:* The term "freemen" did not include ordinary English citizens. King John and later kings, however, had a habit of ignoring the guarantees.]

The Magna Carta introduced the concept that people governed by a government should have a voice in establishing the government. Included is the concept that people who live under a system of law should have a voice in deciding the principles of law.

EXHIBIT 2-2

Selected Provisions of the Magna Carta

Article 38: No bailiff shall henceforth put any one to his law by merely suit without trustworthy witnesses presented for this purpose. [From this article evolved the right of the accused to confront the witnesses against him.]

Article 39: No freeman shall be captured or imprisoned or disseised (dispossessed of property) or outlawed or exiled or in any way destroyed, nor will we go against him or send against him, except by the lawful judgment of his peers or by the law of the land. [From this article evolved the right to a trial by jury of one's peers.]

Article 40: To no one will we sell, to no one will we deny or delay right or justice. [The right to a speedy and just trial evolved from this article.]

Common Law

Common law originated during the period of time that William the Conqueror was the King of England. At the time of the Conquest (1066), there was no uniform criminal law in England. Individual courts were dominated by sheriffs who enforced village rules as they saw fit. In order to reduce the arbitrary aspects of the law, William decreed that all prosecutions would be conducted in the name of the King. [*Note:* A similar practice exists today where all cases are prosecuted in the name of the People, the State, or the Commonwealth.]

To understand common law, we must first understand the English customs and traditions that evolved into what is now known as "common law." Medieval England was divided into tribal areas known as "shires." The King's justice was administered by "shire-reeves", who presided over the shire courts. A sheriff is the modern counterpart of the "shire-reeve." The law was based on ancient custom and varied with each tribal area.

Common law crimes have not existed in most states since the adoptions of state penal codes.[12] Also, there are no federal common law crimes.[13] Accordingly, for conduct to be criminal under either state or federal law, there must be a statute, ordinance, or regulation denouncing it.[14] Even though common law crimes have been abolished, common law principles with regard to criminal procedure and construction of corresponding statutory crimes still apply.[15] As stated in *People v. Giles*, with respect to criminal procedure, the common law has the force of law in absence of statutory provisions at variance with it.[16]

Civil Code 22.2 Common Law—When Rule of Decision

The common law of England, so far as it is not repugnant to or inconsistent with the Constitution of the United States or the Constitution or laws of this State, is the rule of decision in all courts of this State.

California Penal Code 6

No act or omission, commenced after twelve o'clock noon of the day on which this code takes effect as a law, is criminal or punishable, except as prescribed or authorized by this code, or by some statutes... or by some ordinance, municipal, county, or township regulation.... [*Note:* Since Penal Code 6 applies only to acts or omissions, it appears that the civil code provision also applies to criminal proceedings.][17]

EXHIBIT 2-3

TAYLOR v. KENTUCKY

U. S. Supreme Court, 436 U.S. 478 (1978)

Justice Powell delivered the opinion of the Court. Only two Terms ago, this Court observed that the "presumption of innocence," although not articulated in the Constitution, is a basic component of a fair trial under our system of criminal justice.... In this felony case, the trial court instructed the jury as to the prosecution's burden of proof beyond a reasonable doubt, but refused petitioner's (accused) timely request for instructions on the presumption of innocence and the indictment's lack of evidentiary value.

We are asked to decide whether the Due Process Clause of the Fourteenth Amendment requires either or both instructions.

The petitioner was tried for robbery in 1976, allegedly having forced his way into the home of James Maddox and stolen a house key and a billfold containing $10 to $15....The Commonwealth's only witness was Maddox. He testified that he had known the petitioner for several years and had entertained petitioner at his home on several occasions. According to Maddox, petitioner and a friend knocked on his door on the evening of February 16, 1976, asking to be admitted. Maddox refused, saying he had to go to bed. The two left, but returned 15 minutes later. They forced their way in, hit Maddox over the head, and fled with his billfold and house key, which were never recovered.

Petitioner then took the stand as the only witness for the defense. He admitted having been at Maddox's home on other occasions but denied going there on February 16 or participating in the robbery.... Defense counsel requested that the Court instruct the jury that "the law presumes a defendant to be innocent of the crime." The Court declined to give the instruction and instructed the jury that the Commonwealth had the burden of proving the accused's guilt beyond a reasonable doubt. The petitioner was found guilty and sentenced to five years in prison....

This Court has declared that one accused of a crime is entitled to have his guilt or innocence determined solely on the basis of evidence introduced at trial.... And it long has been recognized that an instruction on the presumption is one way of impressing upon the jury the importance of that right....

We hold that on the facts of this case the trial judge's refusal to give the requested instruction resulted in a violation of his right to a fair trial as guaranteed by the Due Process Clause of the Fourteenth Amendment. The judgment of conviction is reversed, and the case is remanded for further proceedings not inconsistent with this opinion. [Justice Brennen wrote a concurring opinion and Justices Stevens and Rehnquist wrote dissenting opinions.]

Discussion: Since the majority of people are aware that the accused is presumed innocent of the charge until his or her guilt is established beyond a reasonable doubt, should it make any difference in the case if the jury was aware of this requirement without being so instructed by the judge?

EXHIBIT 2-4

Robinson v. California

Supreme Court of the United States, 1962 (370 U.S. 660)

Mr. Justice Stewart delivered the opinion of the court:

A California statute makes it a criminal offense for a person to "be addicted to the use of narcotics." This appeal draws into question the constitutionality of [the statute]...

The broad power of a State to regulate the narcotic drug traffic within its borders is not here in issue... There can be no question of the authority of the State in the exercise of its police power to regulate the administration, sale, prescription and use of dangerous and habit-forming drugs.... The right to exercise this power is so manifestly in the interest of the public health and welfare, that it is unnecessary to enter upon a discussion of it beyond saying that it is too firmly established to be successfully called in question.

This statute... is not one which punishes a person for the use of narcotics, for their purchase, sale or possession, or for antisocial or disorderly behavior resulting from their administration. It is not a law which even purports to provide or require medical treatment. Rather, we deal with a statute which makes the "statute" of narcotic addiction a criminal offense, for which the offender may be prosecuted "at any time before he reforms." California has said that a person can be continuously guilty of this offense, whether or not he has ever used or possessed any narcotics within the State, and whether or not he has been guilty of any antisocial behavior there.

It is unlikely that any State at this moment in history would attempt to make it a criminal offense for a person to be mentally ill, or a leper, or to be afflicted with a venereal disease. A State might determine that the general health and welfare require that victims of these and other human afflictions be dealt with by compulsory treatment, involving quarantine, confinement, or sequestration. But, in the light of contemporary human knowledge, a law which made a criminal offense of such a disease would doubtless be universally thought to be an infliction of cruel and unusual punishment in violation of the Eighth and Fourteenth Amendments.... We hold that a state law which imprisons a person thus afflicted as criminal... is cruel and unusual.

Questions: Do you agree with the Supreme Court that it is cruel and unusual to label a person a criminal because the person is afflicted with a disease? Does the case imply that the Supreme Court is of the opinion that narcotic addiction is a disease?

[*Note:* In *Powell v. Texas*, (1968) 392 U.S. 514 the U.S. Supreme Court held that a Texas statute punishing a person for being drunk in a public place was constitutional.]

EXHIBIT 2-5

The Queen v. Dudley and Stephens (Queen's Bench, 1884)

Decision by Lord Coleridge, Chief Justice:

Two prisoners, Thomas Dudley and Edwin Stephens were indicted for the murder of Richard Parker on the high seas on the 25th of July in the present year. The special verdict of the jury was as follows:

That on July 5, 1884, the prisoners, with one Brooks, all able-bodied English seamen, and the deceased also an English boy between seventeen and eighteen years of age, the crew on an English yacht, were cast away in a storm on the high seas 1600 miles from the Cape of Good Hope, and were compelled to put to sea in an open boat. In this boat, they had no water supply and no food. For three days, they had nothing to eat or drink. On the fourth day, they caught a small turtle, upon which they subsisted for a few days. They had no fresh water, except such rain as they from time to time caught in their oilskin capes. That on the eighteenth day, when they had been seven days without food and five without water, the prisoner Dudley proposed to the others that lots should be cast who should be put to death to save the rest. They could not agree on this. Next it was agreed that since all but the youth had family in need of support that the boy should be killed. On the next day, Dudley with the consent of Stephens, went to the boy, and telling him that his time was come, put a knife into his throat and killed him then and there; the three men fed upon the body for three days and were rescued on the fourth day. The boy because of his weakened condition would not have lived for two more days and had the others not fed upon the body of the boy... would have within four days died of starvation.

The real question in this case is whether the killing under the circumstances set forth in the verdict be or be not murder... if a person, being under necessity for want of food or clothes... steal another man's goods, it is a felony and punishable by death.... If, therefore, that extreme necessity of hunger does not justify larceny, ... necessity would not justify murder.

It must not be supposed that in refusing to admit temptation to be an excuse for crime it is forgotten how terrible the temptation was; how awful the suffering; how hard in such trials to keep the judgment straight and the conduct pure. We are often compelled to set up standards we cannot reach ourselves, and to lay down rules which we could not ourselves satisfy. But a man has no right to declare temptation to be an excuse, though he might himself have yielded to it, nor allow compassion for the criminal to change or weaken in any manner the legal definition of the crime... in our unanimous opinion the prisoners are upon this special verdict guilty of murder. [The court then proceeded to pass sentence of death upon the prisoners. The sentence was later commuted by the crown to six month's imprisonment.]

Discussion: This case raises some interesting questions. First, the contention that the killing of the boy was essential for self-preservation and that no evil motive was evolved; that the act was based on a decision to preserve life of three other persons. Second, what law should apply since the crime occurred on the high seas in a make-shift raft. The court held that English criminal law should apply because the men were shipwrecked from an English vessel.

DISCUSSION QUESTIONS

1. Explain the development of our present trial system.

2. What is the significance of the Magna Carta?

3. Explain the role of common law in modern criminal trials?

4. Explain the difference between common law and statutory law.

ENDNOTES

[1] Edward Westermarck, *The Origin and Development of the Moral Ideas*, vol. 1, 2nd ed. (London: 1912); Herbert Johnson, *A History of Criminal Justice*, (Cincinnati: Anderson, 1988); Sir Henry Maine, *Ancient Law*, 10th ed., (London: John Murray, 1905); Richard R. Korn and Lloyd W. McCorkle, *Criminolgy and Penology*, New York: Holt, Rinehart and Winston, 1966).

[2] Sir Henry Maine, *Ancient Law, Its Connection With the Early History of Society and Its Relation to Modern Ideas*, (London: John Murray, 1861); Lon Fuller, *The Morality of Law*, (New Haven: 1964); George Calhoun, *The Growth of Criminal Law in Ancient*

Greece, (Berkeley: Univ. of California Press, 1927); F.M. Conford (translator), *The Republic of Plato*, (New York: Oxford Univ. Press, 1941).

[3] Herbert A. Johnson, *History of Criminal Justice*, (Cincinnati: Anderson, 1988).

[4] Rene A. Wormer, *The Story of Law*, (New York: Simon and Schuster, 1962) and M.F. Morris, *The History of the Development of Law*, (Washington D.C.: John Byrne, 1909).

[5] John Liversidge, *Britain in the Roman Empire*, (New York: Praeger, 1968).

[6] Carl Joachin Friedrich, *The Philosophy of Law in Historical Perspective*, (Chicago: 1963); Paul C. Higgins and Richard R. Butler, *Understanding Deviance*, (New York: McGraw-Hill, 1982); St. Augustine's "On Christian Doctrine," translated for *Library of Liberal Arts Series*, (New York: Bobbs-Merrill, 1961).

[7] Carl Joachin Friedrich, *The Philosophy of Law in Historical Perspective*, (Chicago: Univ. of Chicago Press, 1963).

[8] Arnold Lieber and Carolyn R. Sherin, "Homicides and the Lunar Cycles: Toward a Theory of Lunar Influence on Human Emotional Disturbance," *American Journal of Psychiatry*, vol. 129, July 1972, pp.101-116.

[9] Herbert A. Johnson, *History of Criminal Justice*, (Cincinnati: Anderson, 1988).

[10] Richard Quinney, *The Problem of Crime*, (New York: Dodd, Mead & Co.. 1971).

[11] C. Ray Jeffrey, "The Structure of American Criminological Thinking," *Journal of Criminal Law, Criminology and Police Science*, vol. 46, (Jan.-Feb. 1956): pp. 663-674.

[12] Cal. Jur. 3rd. (Rev.) Part 1, page 27.

[13] *United States v. Eaton*, 144 U.S. 677 (1892).

[14] *People v. Talbott*, 65 CA2d 654; 151 P2d 317 (1944).

[15] *Lorenson v. Superior Court of Los Angeles County*, 35 C2d 49, 216 P2d 859 (1950).

[16] 70 CA2d Supp 872, 161 P2d 623 (1945).

[17] See 17 Cal. Jur. 3rd (Rev) Part 1, page 57.

EXPLANATION OF
CONTEMPORARY CRIME

*The inescapable conclusion is that society se-
cretly wants crime, needs crime, and gains
definite satisfactions from the present mishan-
dling of it.*

—Karl Menninger, The Crime of Punishment

CONCEPTS OF CRIME CAUSATION

The two oldest and most basic theories of crime causation are the classical and the positivist schools. All other theories of crime causation are based in part on the key principles of one of those schools. The classical school was founded on the concept of "free will" and that the decision to commit criminal behavior is a voluntary act. The positivist school, on the other hand, stresses the lack of free choice and the concept of determinism.

Classical School

The classical school was one of the first attempts in the modern Western world to explain crime causation. The label "classical" is used to refer to the fact that it was the first group to develop an organized perspective on crime causation. "Classical" is used as a descriptive term like classical language or classical music. The classical school dominated European thinking for three-quarters of the 18th century.

The classical school theorists see human beings as being governed by the doctrine of "free will" and rational behavior. Accordingly, humans, including criminals, can freely choose either criminal paths or noncriminal paths, depending on which path they believe will benefit them the most. The general principles of the classical school include:

1) People, including criminals, will avoid behaviors that bring pain and will engage in behaviors that will bring pleasure;

2) Prior to deciding whether or not to commit criminal acts, a person will weigh the expected benefits against the expected pains (i.e., incarceration, fines, and the expectation of "getting caught"). The decision to commit or not commit criminal acts depends on which course of action is more beneficial to the person;

3) Criminals are responsible for their own behavior. They have the ability to interpret, analyze, and dissect the situations in which they find themselves;

4) Criminals are not victims of their environment. They act over and against their environment;

5) Individuals, including criminals, are totally responsible for their behaviors;

6) Criminal acts are deliberate and are committed by rational individuals; and

7) Since criminals are responsible for their criminal acts, they should be held accountable.

EXHIBIT 3-1

Cesare Beccaria 1738-1794

Cesare Beccaria is considered the founder of the classical school of criminology. He has been described as lazy and easily discouraged. His 17 page essay on penal reform, however, is a classic in its field. It was his only work of distinction.

He was born in Milan, Italy in 1738. His parents were members of the aristocracy and both had distinguished professional careers. Beccaria attended college at Jesuit College in Parma, Italy and later studied law at the University of Pavia. His mother was concerned about his ability to function in the business climate. It appeared that she wanted her son to have a prominent place in the community, yet a position that would not be demanding upon him and one that did not require much effort. Accordingly, she secured his appointment as a college professor by making a large donation to the university.

At the age of 26, he published his famous essay, *On Crimes and Punishment*. Since the essay attacked the justice system in Italy, it was originally published anonymously. At the time, the existing criminal justice system in Italy was repressive and barbaric. His essay was considered a blueprint for reform. It advocated changes that were quickly supported by the public.

In the essay, Beccaria applied the "social contract" theory to penology. According to the social contract theory, a person is bound to society only by his consent, and therefore, this makes society responsible to him as well as he being responsible to society. He concluded his essay with the recommendation that all social actions should be based on the concept of the greatest happiness for the greatest number. His influence can be found today in modern English law.

The classical school advocated that punishment should be swift, certain, and should fit the crime. The only purpose of punishment was to protect society. The certainty of punishment was a necessity to prevent crime. Beccaria also advocated that the punishment be prompt. According to Beccaria, if an individual knew for certain that he would be promptly punished, he would be less likely to commit the crime. [*Note*: Our punishment today is neither certain nor prompt.]

The Positivist School

Positivist thinking represented a major shift from the classical school. According to the positivists, behavior is governed by physical, mental, environmental and or social factors that are not controlled by the offender. Accordingly, the offender lacks "free will" and his behavior is determined by factors beyond his control.

Cesare Lombroso was one of the early founders of the positivist school. He is also considered the father of modern criminology. Lombroso was influenced by Charles Darwin's *Descent of Man*, and Darwin's theory of evolution. According to Lombroso, the criminal was a throwback who never fully evolved and was "subhuman." He spent much of his life considering these "biological throwbacks" and trying to identify their physical characteristics. He was also the first criminologist who "got his hands dirty." He spent numerous hours measuring criminally insane persons' skulls. Lombroso is credited

Issue	Medical Model 1930-1974	Justice Model 1974-Present
Cause of Crime	Disease of society or of the individual.	Form of rational adaptation to societal conditions
Image of Offender	Sick, product of socio-economic or psychological forces beyond control.	Capable of exercising free will; of surviving without resorting to crime.
Object of Correction	To cure the offender and society; to return both to health; rehabilitation.	Humanely control offender under terms of sentence; offer voluntary treatment.
Agency/Institution Responsibility	Change offender, reintegrate back into society.	Legally & humanely control offender; adequate care & custody; voluntary treatment; protect society.
Role of Treatment & Punishment	Voluntary or involuntary treatment as means to change offender; treatment is mandatory, punishment used to coerce treatment, punishment & treatment is viewed as same thing.	Voluntary treatment, only; punishment & treatment not the same thing. Punishment is for society's good, treatment is for offender's good.
Object of legal Sanctions (Sentence)	Determine conditions which are most conducive to rehabilitation of offender.	Determine conditions which are just re: wrong done, best protect society and deter offender from future crime.
Type of Sentence	Indeterminant, flexible; adjust to offender changes.	Fixed sentence (less good time).
Who determines release time?	"Experts," (parole board for adults, institutional staff for juveniles).	Conditions of sentence as interpreted by Presumptive Release Date (PRD) formula.

with being one of the first persons to use statistical techniques to understand patterns of crime.

In determining the type and amount of punishment that should be handed down in a case, the positivists emphasized not the crime (as had the classical thinkers) but the criminal as an individual. They conferred on what treatment was necessary to correct the individual. The central theme was not "free will" but determinism — the criminal had no choice. A person is propelled by social, biological, emotional, and or spiritual forces beyond his or her control. Accordingly, the amount of treatment necessary depended not on the criminal act, but the criminal's needs. Punishment (treatment) should be individually tailored to meet the needs of the individual offender.

The Sociological Theories

The sociological theories have always been popular in the United States. The theories include as a major assumption the idea that crime is caused by factors such as poor education, poverty, inadequate housing, inadequate socialization, broken families, delinquent peer relations, poor parenting, family difficulties, and criminogenic social conditions. The more popular social theories include: strain, control, conflict, radical, cultural deviance, labeling and differential association.

Strain Theories

The strain theories assume that excessive pressures or strain on individuals often results in criminal behavior. The basic assumptions of the strain theories include:

1) If the criminal fails to conform to social norms (rules) and laws, it is because there is excessive pressure or strain placed on him by society that causes him to commit criminal behavior;

2) People are basically moral and desire to conform to society's rules; and

3) The nature of the strains or pressures cause an offender to commit criminal conduct.

EXHIBIT 3-2

Emile Durkheim 1858-1917

Emile Durkheim, a French sociologist, contributed to both the strain and control theories. He is credited with introducing the term "anomie" into the literature. He defined "anomie" (a Greek term defined as "lawlessness") as a state or a condition that exists within people when a society evolves or changes from a primitive to a modern entity. Anomie is the condition of normlessness (norms of conduct have lost their meaning and become inoperative for large numbers of people). An individual has the feeling of being a number, social isolation, or social loneliness. He believed that anomie was the product of societal transition from a primitive to a modern complex society.

Durkheim's theory of anomie was also used to explain the phenomenon of suicide. According to him, there are four types of suicide: "altruistic," where the individual feels it is necessary to sacrifice his or her life for a higher goal; "egoistic," where the individual is inadequately integrated into society and sees himself as an outcast; "fatalistic," where the individual feels that he or she is backed into a corner and that there is no way out; and "anomie," where the person is totally alienated from society.

Durkheim is also credited with the concept that crime serves a useful purpose in society. According to him, crime has the following functions:

— Crime provides us with a method to measure good and bad in society. We are considered as good because we do not commit crime;

— Crime is a major industry. [Over 600,000 people are employed in the criminal justice system in the United States. There would be a depression if crime is eradicated and all 600,000 persons have their jobs eliminated.];

— Crime serves to unite segments of the population. It causes people to unite against the "bad guys";

— Crime serves as a warning that something is wrong with society. [For example, riots may alert the society that there are significant societal problems that need to be corrected.]

Control Theories

The social control theorists contend that criminal behavior occurs when a person's bonds to society are weakened or severed. They believe that people are by nature amoral and will commit deviant acts if provided the opportunity. Societal controls are necessary to prevent criminal behavior. When the controls are weak, people commit crime.

One social control theorist, Walter Reckless contended that we have a number of social controls, containments and protective barriers to help us resist the pressures that propel us toward criminal behavior. He contended that there are two types of containment that prevent us from committing criminal behavior: inter containment and outer containment.

Inter containment consists mainly of self components, such as self-control, good self-concept, ego strength and goal orientation.

Outer containment consists of those social buffers such as family identification, discipline, opportunity for acceptance, identity, and belongingness. If our containments are strong, we will be prevented (controlled) from committing criminal behavior.

A similar control theory is Travis Hirschi's social bond theory. Hirschi believes that if a person has strong bonds to mainstream society, the bonds will prevent criminal conduct. According to Hirschi, there are four basic bonds: attachment, commitment, involvement, and belief. Attachment refers to the person's ability to be sensitive to others. Commitment refers to the investment the individual has in conformity. For example, a person who has spent a great deal of time and energy going to college is more likely to refrain from endangering his or her standing in the community by committing criminal acts. Involvement refers to the degree that a person is involved in conventional society. Belief refers to the person's belief in the values of that society.

Conflict and Radical Theories

The conflict theories focus on the political nature of crime. They contend that our criminal laws are designed to protect and serve the elite of the community. The central theme of both the radical and the conflict theories is that criminal behavior can be explained in terms of economic conditions and is an expression of class conflict. The radical theorists contend that the capitalist economic system encourages people to be greedy and selfish and to pursue their own benefits without regard to the needs and wishes of others. They also contend that the criminal justice system criminalizes the greed of the poor but allows the rich to pursue their selfish desires. To eradicate crime, according to the conflict theorists, we need to reform society. According to the radical criminogolists, we need a rebellion to change the political structure of the state to eradicate the crime problem.

Cultural Deviance Theories

Cultural deviance theories assume that people are not capable of committing deviant acts; acts are deviant only by mainstream standards, not by the offenders' standards. For example, if a person is raised by parents belonging to the Nazi party, the person would most likely accept or hold beliefs supported by that party. A person becomes deviant by being socialized with non-mainstream values. Another central theme of the cultural deviance theories is that people are social animals and human behavior is a direct product of our social environment.

Thorsten Sellin, a leading spokesperson for the cultural deviance theories, summarized the cultural deviance theories as follows:

— For every person, there is a right or wrong way to act in each situation. The right or wrong is determined by the conduct norms of the group to which we are a member.

— Conduct norms (rules of conduct) of one group may allow a person to act in one way, whereas conduct norms of another group would prohibit such conduct.

— The problem occurs when a person acts in a manner permitted by his or her group, but not permitted by the conduct norms of the groups in control of the political organizations of the state. That person's actions, since in violation of the norms of the controlling group in society (which are reflected in our criminal laws), may be considered as criminal.[1]

There are two types of cultural conflicts: primary and secondary. A primary cultural conflict occurs when one's native cultural conduct norms conflict with the laws of the new culture. Secondary conflict occurs in complex societies that have a variety of subcultures, and there is a conflict between the behavioral norms of the subculture and the norms (as enacted into law) of the dominant culture.

Marvin Wolfgang, a prominent spokesperson on subcultures, contends that there is a subculture of violence. His theory is summarized as follows:

— Members of a subculture hold values different from those of the dominant parent culture.

— Certain subcultures have norms or values that are favorable to the use of violence and its members learn a willingness to resort to violence.[2]

Differential Association

The differential association theory of crime causation has been the most popular theory for the past sixty years. It was developed by Edwin Sutherland. According to his theory, criminal behavior is learned behavior. We learn to commit crimes the same way that we learn to play sand lot baseball. Sutherland contended that we learn criminal behavior from our associations with others. His theory looks at the ratio between associations with persons whose attitudes are favorable or unfavorable to the violation of criminal behavior. If there is an excess of associations favorable to the violation of criminal behavior, then the individual will likely commit crime. The associations that influence us are differential in that the influence of a close personal friend or close relative will have far more impact on our behavior than will the influences of a distant but socially prominent figure (e.g., hard-rock singer).

Labeling

The process of making a person a criminal according to the labeling theory is a process of labeling. After one is defined as a criminal (i.e., labeled a criminal), the individual becomes what he is labeled. There are two types of deviance: primary and secondary. Primary deviance is the first involvement that a person has with the criminal justice system. Secondary deviance is that deviance that is committed after an individual has been labeled a criminal.

The labeling theory is based on the following hypotheses:

— No act is intrinsically criminal.

— The act of "getting caught" starts the labeling process.

— After a person is labeled a criminal, the individual becomes what he is labeled.

Biological Theories

While the sociological theories have enjoyed popularity in the United States, the biological theories have had similar support in Europe. The common theme of the biological theories is that crime is caused by biological processes.

Inferiority Body-Type Theories

The inferiority body-type theories contend that crime is the direct result of the criminal's inferior body. The theories assume that the offender's constitution, physique or inferior mental state is responsible for his or her behavior. For example, one physical anthropologist (Hooten) after extensive study concluded that criminals tend to have low foreheads, compressed faces, and narrow jaws.[3] W.H. Sheldon studied 200 delinquent boys and concluded that body type was innately related to personality.[4] Sheldon concluded that delinquents tended to be big-boned and muscular.

Biochemical Imbalances

The concept of biochemical imbalances as a factor in crime causation was first developed by Fredrick Wohler, a German chemist in 1928. According to this theory, the chemical imbalances cause emotional disturbances which result in deviant behavior. The imbalances may be caused by a number of factors including nutrition. The leading biochemical imbalance theories are the XYY chromosome abnormality and PMS/PMT.

In the normal person, there are twenty-three pairs of chromosomes in each cell, including a pair of sex chromosomes. Most women have two X chromosomes. Most males have an X and a Y chromosome. A small percentage of males have a XYY chromosomal abnormality. According to the XYY theory, the extra Y chromosome causes more aggressive behavior. This is based on the theory that men are innately more aggressive than women and that the absence of a Y chromosome in women explains why women are less aggressive than men. This theory was very popular in the 1940s and 1950s. Over 200 research studies on the XYY condition, however, fail to support the conclusion that XYY men are more aggressive and violent than XY men.[5]

EXHIBIT 3-3

People v. Tanner

California Court of Appeals, Second District

Tanner was charged with kidnapping, forcible rape and assault with intent to commit murder. He pled guilty to the charge of assault with intent to commit murder and was remanded to the Atascadero State Hospital in California for further study as a "possible" mentally disordered sex offender. While at Atascadero, Tanner was discovered to possess cells with an extra male or Y chromosome. He petitioned for a withdrawal of his guilty plea, so that he could enter a plea of not guilty by reason of insanity based on his XYY condition.

Judge Cobey in his opinion stated:

Appellant's (Tanner) sole contention on appeal is that this evidence (of the extra male chromosome) was sufficient to support a change of plea by him from "guilty" to "not guilty by reason of insanity."

The studies of the "XYY individuals"... are rudimentary in scope, and their results are at best inconclusive.... The behavioral effects of this abnormal condition, the testimony of appellant's expert witnesses suggests only that aggressive behavior may be one manifestation of the XYY Syndrome. The evidence collected by these experts does not suggest that all XYY individuals are by nature involuntary aggressive. Many identified XYY individuals have not exhibited such behavior.... The experts could not determine whether appellant's aggressive behavior, namely, the commission of an assault with the intent to commit murder, resulted from his chromosomal abnormality. The deficiencies in the geneticists' testimony renders that testimony unconvincing that his chromosomal abnormality made him legally insane at the time he committed the assault.

The judgment of conviction of assault with the intent to commit murder is affirmed (approved).[6]

Premenstrual syndrome (PMS)/premenstrual tension (PMT) may affect 40 percent of women between the ages of 20 and 40. The symptoms usually begin about ten days prior to the onset of the menstrual period and become progressively worse until the onset of menstruation. In some women it continues for several days after the onset. Katherine Dalton, an English physician, states that there is a greater likelihood of accidents, alcohol abuse, suicide attempts, and crime committed by women suffering from PMS/PMT. According to her, many women during this time are "mean" and "irritable."[7] The chances of a woman suffering from severe PMS/PMT are increased if the woman is between 30 and 40 years of age, is under emotional stress, has poor nutritional habits, has side effects from birth control pills and fails to exercise. It appears that the popularity of the PMS/PMT theory exceeds the empirical evidence supporting it. It was successful, however, in two English cases in reducing murder to manslaughter.

EXHIBIT 3-4

Sandie Smith

Sandie Smith, an English barmaid, was convicted of carrying a knife and threatening a police officer. At the time of her offense, she was on probation for stabbing another barmaid to death. Her background includes nearly thirty convictions for assault and battery and at least eighteen suicide attempts.

At court, her attorney introduced evidence that her outbursts of erratic behavior always occurred several days prior to her menstrual period and that except for those periods she was a mild mannered person. The court accepted the evidence as a mitigating factor. Since the trial, Smith receives a daily injection of progesterone. It appears that she has not been involved in any violent criminal behavior while under medication.

Nutrition and Criminal Behavior

In recent years, considerable attention has been focused on the relationship between sugar, preservatives, diet, and involvement in criminal behavior. The concept of nutrition as a factor in causing criminal behavior can be traced to the development of the chemical imbalance theories. Many researchers claim that malnutrition is a causative factor in violent criminal behavior based on the fact that individuals involved in such behavior normally have poor nutritional habits. Other researchers are of the opinion that food allergies can trigger violent behavior.

Carlton Fredericks, a researcher who has conducted numerous studies on the effects of nutrition on behavior, has asserted that during World War II in Greece, when the Nazi occupation made bread, a staple in the Greek diet, scarce, there was a marked improvement in Greek schizophrenics and paranoids.[8] The case of Dan White, discussed below, has some interesting information regarding nutrition and criminal behavior.

EXHIBIT 3-5

Dan White and the "Twinkie" Defense

When considering nutrition and criminal behavior; consider, also, the fact that Americans buy 700 million "Twinkies" a year. Eighty percent of them on impulse. Over 50 billion Twinkies have been sold in the past 60 years.

On May 22, 1979, Dan White, a former San Francisco, California, County Supervisor was convicted of voluntary manslaughter for the November, 1978 killing of San Francisco Mayor George Moscone and Supervisor Harvey Milk. White was originally charged with first degree murder (a capital offense). The prosecutor argued to the jury that White was guilty of cold-blooded murder. It was established that White had gone to city hall to talk to the mayor. He had entered through a window to avoid the metal detector at the main entrance. At the time, he was carrying a snub-nosed revolver. He shot Mayor Moscone and Harvey Milk nine times with the weapon, killing both of them. Note: White readily admitted killing the mayor and Supervisor Milk, who was his most vocal opponent on the San Francisco Board of Supervisors.

White's defense attorney, Douglas Schmidt presented evidence to establish that White had suffered from "diminished capacity" caused by a "biochemical change" in his brain. According to the defense's theory of the case, White was incapable of premeditation, deliberation and malice required to obtain a murder conviction. Evidence at trial indicated that White was a manic-depressive with a high degree of stress caused by financial and other personal problems. A defense medical expert testified that White suffered from a "genetically caused melancholia" and, at the time, he was "discombobulated." Defense witnesses, which included family members, friends, and experts testified about White's moods and his diet. One defense psychiatrist testified that White's compulsive diet of candy bars, Twinkies, and cokes was evidence of a deep depression and resulted in excessive sugar which either caused or aggravated a chemical imbalance in his brain.

The Superior Court jury in finding White guilty of only manslaughter and not first degree murder, apparently accepted the "Twinkie" defense.

Associated with nutrition is the effects of alcohol as a causative factor in criminal behavior. For many people, alcohol appears to relax normal inhibitions and behavioral restraints. When this occurs, a person is more likely to engage in criminal conduct. Alcohol may also be used to provide an offender with courage to commit an act.

It appears that alcohol may affect criminal behavior in three ways:[9]

1) Direct criminal activities that result from the fact that alcohol is a regulated and taxed substance, e.g., illegal selling of alcohol;

2) Indirect behavioral effects of alcohol acting as an anesthetic, with the potential to frustrate social goals; and

3) Acts resulting from alcohol addiction and physical dependence on alcohol.

Some facts regarding the relationship between alcohol consumption and criminal behavior include:

— One-third of all arrests by the police are for alcohol-related crimes;

— A significant number of violent crimes involve alcohol abuse;

— In criminal homicides, research indicates that 80 percent involve a drinking offender and/or victim;

— In approximately 75 percent of the robbery cases that are solved by the police, the offender had been drinking immediately prior to the robbery and in 67 percent the victim had been; and

— Approximately 60 percent of the people arrested for criminal conduct admit to having a drinking problem.

Psychological Theories

The psychological theories all assume that there is something wrong with the criminal's mind that causes him or her to commit criminal behavior. Each theory emphasizes factors or defects within the individual that cause crime. Like biological theories, they overlook the impact of economic, social and political factors on human behavior. Psychological theories developed from the fields of psychiatry and psychology in the early 20th century and are based primarily on the works of Sigmund Freud (1856-1939).[10] Psychological theories were also a major catalyst in the growth of corrections and penology in the United States.

Sigmund Freud believed that aggression and violence are rooted in instinct. He saw violence as a response to thwarting the pleasure principle. Freud contended that each of us possessed a "death wish" and that this wish was a constant source of aggressive impulses.

Freudian theorists view criminal and delinquent behavior as largely caused by guilt, unconscious conflicts, repression, inadequate personality development, traumatic developmental stages, and weak superego development. Many criminologists, however, contend that there is a lack of evidence that psychological factors such as mental and emotional difficulties are important in criminal behavior.[11] The Freudian views have been criticized for their overemphasis on the sexual aspects of behavior and motivation and for not dealing with the social factors that affect human behavior.

EXHIBIT 3-6

Past Molestation as a Defense

Recently, there have been instances where offenders have used the fact of past molestation as a defense for criminal behavior. In the typical case, a defendant attempts to justify his or her violent conduct on the fact that he or she was molested as a child and that the molestation psychologically affected his or her thinking processes. A variation of that theme occurred in 1993 in the Ellie Nesler case.

Ellie Nesler was being led to the witness stand to testify in a case where the defendant, Daniel Driver, was charged with molesting her son at a church camp. Mrs. Nesler pulled out a small handgun and shot Driver several times in the back of the head. Mrs. Nesler was charged with the murder of Driver. After the shooting, Mrs. Nesler received overwhelming support. Lawyers, including famed attorney Melvin Belli, offered their services to Nesler. Two trust funds were established to help in her defense and many cars in the area had signs reading "L.E. Law" for Ellie.

At her trial, she was found guilty of manslaughter rather than murder. Manslaughter is a lesser charge to murder and is loosely defined as a killing done in the "heat of passion." Her defense included the fact that psychologically, because of the trauma she suffered as a molested child, she was unable to control her actions and, therefore, claimed "temporary insanity."

EXHIBIT 3-7

Commonwealth v. Marshall

(Supreme Court of Pennsylvania, 1974; 318 A. 2d. 724)

Justice Manderino:
The appellant, Eugene Marshall, allegedly shot his estranged wife in full view of several eyewitnesses.... He was given a psychiatric examination... The psychiatric report diagnosed the appellant as a "Schizophrenic Reaction, Paranoid Type, Acute," and recommended his incarceration in the Institute for Criminally Insane... The diagnostic formulation in the report of that examination said "this man is seen at this time as continuing in a Schizophrenic Reaction of the Paranoid Type with inappropriate affect, delusional ideation and apparently hallucinatory phenomenon of a religious nature." The report also said the appellant "displayed poor judgment... and it was obvious that he was in reality unable to understand or fully appreciate his situation because of the degree of his present illness."

The mental competence of an accused must be regarded as an absolute and basic condition of a fair trial. The conviction of an accused person while he is incompetent violates due process... and ... state procedures must be adequate to protect this right.

Emotional Problem and Mental Disorder Theories

The emotional problem theories, unlike the psychological theories, view the offender as having the same psychological makeup as non-offenders, but he is unable to cope with his or her environment. The emotional problem theories assume that the criminal is unable to cope with life's problems and, thus, turns to crime. According to these theories, the way a criminal perceives how he or she looks can create emotional problems that are factors in the causation process. The offender being unable to cope with every day problems acts out criminally.

The mental disorder theories emphasize neuroses, psychoses, and personality disorders as factors in crime causation. The mental disorders can be organic or functional. The two main psychoses that have been linked to criminal behavior are schizophrenia and paranoia. The organic disorders have an identifiable physiological cause such as head injuries that affect the functioning of the mind. In the functional disorders, there is no apparent brain pathology that can be identified by existing techniques. An example of a functional disorder would be a person with no apparent brain pathology who hears voices that others do not hear or sees things that others do not see. In both types of disorders, the person's cognitive, perceptual, and memory functions do not operate normally.

Thinking Pattern Theories

Thinking pattern theories are psychological theories that deal with the criminal's cognitive processes, logic, rationality and language usage. According to these theories, how an offender processes things, objects, events, and situations in his or her mind will determine the offenders behavioral choices. Some of the thinking pattern theories contend that the criminal has a distinct criminal mind. Others contend that the criminal's mind is no different from noncriminal minds. All of them agree that the thinking patterns of a criminal are different than those of a non-criminal.

Techniques of Neutralization

Sykes and Matza researched the question, "Why do people violate laws in which they believe?" They concluded that criminals use "techniques of neutralization" to justify the commission of criminal acts. The techniques include:

— Denial of responsibility. The offender denies having responsibility for his or her behavior.

— Denial of injury. The offender denies that the victim is injured.

— Denial of the victim. The victim deserved it concept.

— Appeal to higher loyalties. The gang, peer group, etc. are more important than the victim.

Multifactor Approach

For many years, researchers have debated the causes of criminal behavior as if there was only one single cause. Attributing a single cause to all types of criminal conduct is similar to assigning a single cause to all types of medical illnesses. The causation factors that result in an individual robbing a convenience store are completely different from those that result in tax evasion. Most researchers now take the multifactor approach. This approach assumes that many different variables contribute to criminality. It is now generally accepted that psychological, biological, and sociological factors contribute to criminal behavior alone or in combinations and that different crimes will be the result of different combinations of factors.

EVOLUTION OF SOCIAL CONTROL

In looking at the evolution of social control, we need first to look at our process of labeling a person a "criminal" and the relationship between sin and crime.

Who is a Criminal?

After pleading "no contest" to charges of taking kickbacks on government contracts, a former governor of Maryland and U.S. vice-president stated: "Honesty is different things to different people."

In defining one a "criminal" we have the same difficulty that we discussed above in determining what a crime is. It would appear that one who commits a crime is subject to being labeled a "criminal." The article in Exhibit 3-9, however, indicates that we all commit crimes. Is it necessary to be convicted in a criminal trial before being considered a criminal? Using this approach would mean that a father who regularly sexually abuses his daughter is not a criminal until the daughter reports it and he is convicted. If the daughter never reports it, is he any less a criminal?

The Relationship Between Sin and Crime

Before the American Revolution, the colonies were subject to the law handed down by the English judges. Accordingly, the common law of England with its Anglo-Saxon concepts became the basic criminal law of the colonies. After the revolution, the common law was later modified and changed by state legislatures. During the modifications, the colonies' religious beliefs became a part of our criminal code, and criminal law was used to regulate morality. To some extent, we still use criminal law to regulate morality. According to Norval Morris and Gordon Hawkins, our present criminal codes in the United States are some of the most moralistic criminal laws in history.[15]

EXHIBIT 3-8

Common Criminals

We are a nation of law breakers. We exaggerate tax-deductible expenses, lie to customs officials, bet on card games and sports events, disregard jury notices, drive while intoxicated and hire illegal child care workers....Nearly all people violate some laws, and many people run afoul of dozens without ever being considered, or considering themselves, criminals. The authors of this article admit, between them, to having committed 16 of the 25 offenses listed on the chart (below) carrying maximum jail time of 15 years and fines of as much as $30,000. Most of the dozens of people interviewed for this article have violated eight or more of these offenses. An article in a Canadian prison newspaper stated: "There is only one difference between the men in this prison and a great number of your readers. We were caught."[14]

Psychoanalytic Approach

Why do we break the law? Is it, as some psychologists suggest, because the law is our symbolic parent, whom we both adore and abhor and whom we enjoy disobeying? Or is it, more prosaically, that many laws seem too foolish, unfair, burdensome, or intrusive for even the most law-abiding to obey slavishly? Or is it simply that we know we can get away with it?

Some people who deal with serious crime scoff at these questions, arguing that routine, nonviolent infractions are too trivial to worry about in a nation threatened by murder, rape, armed robbery, gang warfare and drug trafficking. But other social scientists take seriously the phenomenon of lawbreaking among the ostensibly law-abiding. They say our willingness to break laws undermines respect for ourselves, for one another and for the rule of law.

As a practical matter, laws that are often broken with impunity make it difficult for people to predict the consequences of their acts. In the 1970s, Douglas Ginsburg smoked marijuana, as did many of his contemporaries; in 1987 he lost the chance to be a Supreme Court justice as a result. Perhaps a young lawyer who now tosses soda cans into the garbage will be next: In the year 2001, failing to recycle could disqualify someone for the cabinet.

Longtime Practice

Lawbreaking among the mostly law-abiding isn't new, of course. Tax evasion dates back to biblical times. Avoiding jury duty has been common sport at least since the 17th century. Millions drank liquor during Prohibition. People have been driving while intoxicated since the invention of the automobile. Criminologists say they believe that there are more such crimes than there used to be, but there are no figures to back up that claim.

Academic studies do show how widespread lawbreaking is today. University of Colorado sociologist, Delbert Elliott has tracked a group of young adults since 1976, when they were junior-high and high-school age. The tally thus far: 90 percent of the group has broken the law at some time. Other studies yield similar results.

One reason for so much lawbreaking, criminologists say, is that there are so many laws, with new ones being added every year. A state's statutes including the regulations of businesses, can fill 40 volumes or more. State criminal codes average about 1,000 pages each. And on top of the state tomes sit the U.S. laws; Federal criminal provisions fill some 800 pages. Town and city ordinances add to the list.

Pleading Ignorance

"There are so many things legally one can get in trouble for breaking, it would be difficult not to be a lawbreaker in our society," says Paul Fromberg, an Episcopal priest at Christ Church Cathedral in Houston, who admits to having broken 12 laws on the chart. "If you don't know what the rule is, how do you follow it?" wonders Jack Greene, a criminal law professor at Temple University.

Also, in a nation that is increasingly multicultural, many laws don't represent shared values. Laws restricting gambling, drinking, fortunetelling, extramarital sex, sexual behavior and the use of fireworks, for example, are more acceptable in some communities than in others. In many states, adds James Fyfe, a criminal justice professor at Temple University, the legislature is still dominated by rural law-makers whose laws "reflect the values of the farms but not of the urban areas."

Under the circumstances, people who seek to maintain high moral standards often make sharp distinctions between the laws they will break and those they won't. Some people who steal, for example, do so only when they believe they have a moral right to what they are taking. "Just because something is against the law doesn't mean its wrong," says San Francisco author Timothy Ferris. "I've stolen legal pads from every office I've ever been in. But I use those legal pads to write books. That's a good use of the legal pad."

Crimes that are seen as victimless, or as invasions of privacy, are often broken without much soul-searching. "There is a huge number of people who violate drug laws because they believe it is their own private business," says Arnold Trebach of the Drug Policy Foundation in Washington, which advocates decriminalization of some illegal drugs. "To a large number of drug users, the law is an ass."

Faceless Victims

But people differ as to which crimes are victimless and which victims merit concern. Who is the victim when one cheats on one's taxes or lies to the insurance company or makes illegal home repairs? Whoever the victim is, it is nameless, faceless and too distant to concern many people. This may be why people so readily cheat the Internal Revenue Service, even though the economy may suffer as a result. "We would have no national debt if people would pay the taxes they owe," says Todd Clear, a criminal justice professor at Rutgers University.

Clearly, the more distant or abstract the victim, the less incentive there seems to be to respect or protect that victim. Kenneth Lenihan, a professor at John Jay College of Criminal Justice in New York, says he witnessed this phenomenon a few years ago when he employed several ex-prisoners. After one apparently stole the professor's checkbook and forged some checks, two of the others indicated that they would cooperate with the bank's investigation. But when they learned the loss would be the bank's and not Mr. Lenihan's, they changed their minds, he says.

Thrilling Experience

Another obstacle to good citizenship is that lawbreakers are often admired, both for taking the risk and for profiting from doing so. Says Prof. Greene of Temple: "There's an under-the-table ideology in this country. People want a good deal."

This attitude seems to be particularly prevalent in the workplace, where competition dictates straddling a fine line between shrewd and shady. "What a lot of people do is, they hang their ethical hat at the door," says Michael Daigneault whose Falls Church, Va. firm, Ethics Inc., teaches ethics to businesspeople.

But some law-and-psychology specialists say something far deeper is at work in lawbreaking. "Our emotional stance toward the law isn't one of unequivocal respect, but one of ambivalence," says Martha Grace Duncan, a professor at Emory University's law school.

"From a psychoanalytic perspective, it makes sense that this should be so," she adds, "for the law represents the parent [and] thus serves as a repository of powerful feelings from early childhood — complex feelings of affection and disdain, attraction and repudiation."

If so, the national parent may need a lesson from Dr. Spock in the virtues of consistent discipline. Civil libertarians warn that when too many rules exist, and only some are enforced, the law becomes capricious and unsettling. The legal system starts to resemble a lottery.

One solution is to repeal or amend laws that don't make sense to a lot of people. Indeed, the Zoe Baird flap seems likely to result in more sensible rules for paying Social Security taxes for domestic employees. But most of the often-disobeyed laws are likely to stay on the books, either because they are sound public policy or because it is easier to pass a new law than to repeal an old one. Particularly when morals are thought to be an issue, many legislators don't want to appear to be on the side of sin. Even some people who admit to occasional lawbreaking say they are happy the laws are there "just so people don't get really out of hand," as Los Angeles teacher Janie Teller puts it.

Inevitably, then, some long-dormant law will awaken periodically and, like a B-movie monster, wreak havoc for a time. But fear of the consequences probably won't increase adherence to the law. Just ask Los Angeles architect Steven Wallock, who says he has violated 22 of the 25 laws on the chart. Some of the prohibited acts "are just too much fun" to resist, he explains. And, like most of us, he doesn't expect to get caught. "Why would someone doubt me?" he asks, "I'm a good guy, and I look honest."

[reprinted with permission from the Wall Street Journal,
March 12, 1993]

COMMON OFFENSES
How Many Have You Committed?

Taking office supplies or using office services for personal use
Up to 1 year in jail and/or up to $1,000 fine.
Evading income taxes (failing to report tips, exaggerated deductions)
Up to five years in jail and/or up to $250,000 fine.
Gambling illegally (betting on a card game or sporting event)
Up to six months in jail and/or up to $10,000 fine
Committing computer crimes (copying software illegally, gaining illegal access)
Up to three years in jail and/or up to $10,000 fine
Serving alcohol to minors
Up to one year in jail and/or up to $5,000 fine
Possession of a small amount of illegal drugs (marijuana or cocaine)
Up to four years in jail and/or up to $10,000 fine
Committing adultery in states where it is illegal
Up to one year in jail and/or up to $1,000 fine
Shoplifting
Up to one year in jail and/or up to $1,000 fine
Stealing TV signals (cable or satellite hookups)
Up to one year in jail and/or up to $1,000 fine
Speeding or other moving violations
Up to one year in jail and $1,000 fine
Parking illegally
Up to $500 fine and your vehicle towed and impounded
Lying to a customs agent to avoid duties
Fine not to exceed the value of the merchandise
Importing prohibited products (Cuban cigars, tortoise shell jewelry, plants, etc.)
Up to one year in jail and/or up to $100,000 fine
Buying stolen goods (watches, books, jewelry, stereos, newspapers, etc.)
Up to one year in jail and/or up to $1,000 fine
Unauthorized sale of tickets to events for above the listed price
Up to six months in jail and/or up to $1,000 fine
Patronizing a prostitute
Up to one year in jail and/or up to $5,000 fine
Lying on a government job application
Up to one year in jail and/or up to $1,000 fine
Disregarding a jury summons
Up to six months in jail and/or a $750 fine
Drinking in public (e.g., a park or beach where prohibited)
Up to 30 days in jail and/or up to $100 fine

NOTE: laws and penalties vary among states

THE CYCLE OF VIOLENCE

Does childhood abuse lead to adult criminal behavior? How likely is it that today's abused and neglected children will become tomorrow's violent offenders?

In one of the most detailed studies of the issue to date, research sponsored by the National Institute of Justice (NIJ) found that childhood abuse increased the odds of future delinquency and adult criminality by 40 percent overall. The study followed 1,575 cases from childhood through young adulthood, comparing the arrest records of two groups:

— A study group of 908 substantiated cases of childhood abuse or neglect processed by the courts between 1967 and 1971 and tracked through official records over the ensuing 15 to 20 years.

— A comparison group of 667 children, not officially recorded as abused or neglected, matched to the study group according to sex, age, race, and approximate family socioeconomic status.

While most members of both groups had no juvenile or adult criminal record, being abused or neglected as a child increased the likelihood of arrest as a juvenile by 53 percent, as an adult by 38 percent, and for a violent crime by 38 percent.

Male vs. Female

Experiencing childhood abuse or neglect even had a substantial impact on individuals with little likelihood of engaging in officially recorded adult criminal behavior. Thus, although males generally have higher rates of criminal behavior than females, being abused or neglected in childhood increased the likelihood of arrest for females by 77 percent over comparison group females. As adults, abused and neglected females were more likely to be arrested for property, drug, and misdemeanor offenses such as disorderly conduct, curfew violations, or loitering but not for violent offenses. Females, in general, were less likely to be arrested for street violence and more likely to appear in statistics on violence in the home.

Race

Both black and white abused and neglected children were more likely to be arrested than comparison children. However, the difference between whites was not as great as that between blacks. In fact, white abused and neglected children do not show increased likelihood of arrest for violent crimes over comparison children. This contrasts dramatically with findings for black children in this sample who show significantly increased rates of violent arrests, compared with black children who were not abused or neglected. This is a surprising finding and one that may reflect differences in an array of environmental factors. Investigation of a number of explanations for these results, including differences in poverty levels, family factors, characteristics of the abuse or neglect incident, access to counseling or support services, and treatment by juvenile authorities is in process.

Juvenile Record

Abused or neglected juveniles were at higher risk of beginning a life of crime at a younger age with more significant and repeated criminal involvement. Notably, however, among those arrested as juveniles, abused or neglected persons were not more likely to continue a life of crime than other children.

In short, childhood abuse and neglect has no apparent effect on the movement of juvenile offenders toward adult criminal activity. Distinguishing the factors that promote the onset of criminal behavior from those that affect persistence in a criminal career is clearly an important topic for future research.

Does Only Violence Beget Violence?

The "cycle of violence" hypothesis suggests that a childhood history of physical abuse predisposes the survivor to violence in later years. This reveals that victims of neglect are also more likely to develop later criminal violent behavior as well. This finding gives powerful support to the need for expanding common conceptions of physical abuse. If it is not only violence, but also neglect, far more attention needs to be devoted to the families of children whose "beatings" are forms of abandonment and severe malnutrition.

The physically abused (as opposed to the neglected or sexually abused) were the most likely to be arrested later for a violent crime. Notably, however, the physically abused group was followed closely by the neglected group.

Perpetrators of Abuse

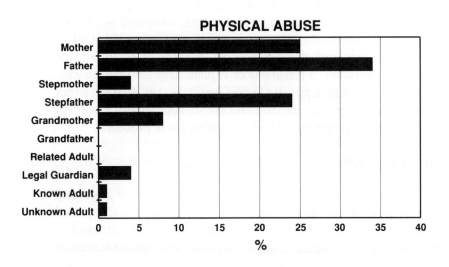

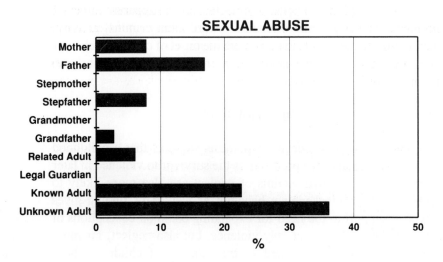

Source: U.S. Dept. of Justice

Because different types of abuse and neglect are not distributed evenly by age, race, and sex, these frequencies present an oversimplified picture. Even after controlling for age, race, and sex, however, a relationship between childhood neglect and subsequent violence remained evident.

These findings offer persuasive evidence for the need to take concerted preventive action. Nationwide, in 1986 the incidence of neglect was almost three times that of physical abuse (15.9 per 1,000 children, compared to 5.7 per 1,000 for physical abuse, and 2.5 per 1,000 for sexual abuse). Neglect also is potentially more damaging to the development of a child than abuse (providing the abuse involves no neurological impairment). In one study of the influence of early malnutrition on subsequent behavior, malnourished children had attention deficits, reduced social skills, and poorer emotional stability than a comparison group. Other researchers have found an array of developmental differences associated with childhood neglect. This study now suggests that those differences include a greater risk of later criminal violence.

Conclusion and Implications

Childhood victimization represents a widespread, serious social problem that increases the likelihood of delinquency, adult criminality, and violent criminal behavior. Poor educational performance, health problems, and generally low levels of achievement also characterize the victims of early childhood abuse and neglect.

This study offers at least three messages to juvenile authorities and child welfare professionals. They suggest that the following must occur:

1) Early intervention.

2) Development of policies that recognize the high risks of neglect as well as abuse to the future criminality of the individual.

3) Re-examination our out-of-home placement policies. Studies suggest that separation may intensify, rather than relieve, a child's problems.

DISCUSSION QUESTIONS

1. If PMS/PMT explains female crime, why are most violent crimes committed by males?

2. What are the critical differences between the classical and positivists theories of crime causation?

3. Explain and contrast the differential association and control theories.

4. Which theory of crime causation appeals to you? Why?

5. What criteria should be used before identifying someone as a criminal?

6. Explain the concept of the "cycle of violence."

7. List the three conclusive steps that should be taken to control a cycle of violence and briefly explain the purpose of each.

ENDNOTES

[1] Thorsten Sellin, *Cultural Conflict and Crime*, (New York: Social Science Research, 1938).

[2] Marvin Wolfgang, *Crime and Culture: Essays in Honor of Thorsten Sellin*, (New York: Wiley, 1968).

[3] E.A. Horton, *The American Criminal*, (Cambridge, Mass.: Harvard Univ. Press, 1939).

[4] W. H. Sheldon, *Varieties of Delinquent Youth*, (New York: Harper, 1949).

[5] William Chamblis, *Exploring Criminology*, (New York: Macmillan, 1988), p. 186.

[6] 91 Cal. Rpt. 656 (1970).

[7] Katherine Dalton, "Menstruation and Crime," *British Medical Journal*, vol 3. 1961, pp. 1752-1753.

[8] Carlton Frederick, *Psycho-Nutrition*, (New York: Grossett and Dunlap, 1976), p. 26.

[9] Russell Smith, "Alcoholism and Criminal Behavior," in Leonard Hippchen, ed. *Ecologic-Biochemical Approaches to Criminal Behavior*, (New York Van Nostrand, 1978), p. 21-30.

[10] Donald Gibbons, *The Criminological Enterprise*, (Englewood Cliffs, NJ: Prentice-Hall, 1979).

[11] Ibid. p. 214.

[12] Norval Morris and Gordon P. Hawkins, *The Honest Politician's Guide to Crime Control*, (Chicago: Univ. of Chicago Press, 1969).

SCOPE OF THE CRIME PROBLEM

*You can't measure what a patrolman standing on
a corner has prevented. There is no product at
the end of a policeman's day.*

—*Charles E. McCarthy, 1968*

I n this chapter, we will examine the nature and scope of the "crime problem." The crime data indicates that crime is increasing in the United States. Experts, however, continue to debate whether the increase in crime, as reflected by the crime data, is an actual increase or a reflection of the more accurate methods of obtaining and maintaining data on crime.

SOURCES OF CRIME DATA

The first major crime statistics were used to measure the society's "moral health." Later they were used to measure the effectiveness of criminal justice agencies. They are still used today to measure the effectiveness of our police departments, courts, and corrections. There is considerable debate as to their ability to measure the effectiveness of the agencies. While the public holds the agencies responsible for the crime problem, seldom do those same agencies receive any credit when crime rates drop.

The U.S. Department of Justice uses the Uniform Crime Reporting Program (UCR) and the National Crime Victimization Survey (NCVS) to measure the magnitude, nature and impact of crime in the United States. The two measures differ in the methodology used to collect the data and their coverage of crime. Accordingly, there are inconsistencies between their results. Looking at both together, however, enhances our understanding of the crime problem. While these reports contribute to our knowledge of crime, crime victims, and offenders; none portrays completely and accurately the kinds and amounts of crime that goes unreported and unrecorded. The phrase "dark figure of crime" is commonly used to refer to crimes that are committed but not discovered, reported, or recorded by law enforcement agencies.

Uniform Crime Reports

The collection of crime statistics on a national basis began in 1927. At the annual meeting of the International Chiefs of Police, a committee was appointed to respond to the demand for a national crime data. Based on the recommendations of the committee, Congress, in 1930, authorized the FBI to collect and compile nationwide data on crime. At first, the Uniform Crime Reports were issued on a monthly basis, then later on a quarterly basis until 1941. From 1949 to 1957 they were issued semiannually. Since 1958, they have been issued on a yearly basis. As early as 1932, FBI director J. Edgar Hoover boasted of the value and usefulness of the UCRs in testimony to Congress.

The UCRs have help establish the FBI's reputation as the nation's leading authority on crime trends. The UCRs are also relied on by administrators, politicians, and policy makers. Many researchers contend, however, that the UCRs are incomplete and structurally biased which results in the creation and persistence of many myths about crime in the United States.

The UCRs collect information on crimes reported to law enforcement authorities. The UCRs classify reported crime as either index (Part I) or non-index crimes (Part II). The index crimes are homicide, forcible rape, robbery, aggravated assault, burglary, larceny-theft, motor vehicle theft, and arson. Other crimes are recorded as non-index crimes. Only arrest data are reported for Part II offenses. Only the index crimes are used to measure crime rates, etc.

Part I Offenses — Index Crimes

As noted earlier, Part I offenses include all events either reported to or observed by law enforcement agencies of those categories of crimes known as index crimes. The eight Part I crimes are defined below.

Criminal homicide— The murder and non-negligent manslaughter of one human being by another. Deaths caused by negligence, suicides, accidental deaths and justifiable homicides are excluded. Traffic fatalities are also excluded.

Forcible rape— The carnal knowledge of a female forcibly and against her will. Included are rapes by force and attempts or assaults to rape. Statutory rapes (where no force is used) are excluded. Homosexual rapes and date rapes are also excluded.

Robbery— The taking or attempting to take anything of value from the care, custody, or control of a person or persons by force or threat of force or violence and or by putting the victim in fear.

Aggravated assault— An unlawful attack by one person upon another for the purpose of inflicting severe or aggravated bodily injury. This type of assault usually is accompanied by the use of a weapon or by means likely to produce death or great bodily harm. Simple assaults are excluded.

Burglary (breaking or entering)— The unlawful entry of a structure to commit a felony or a theft. Attempted forcible entry is included.

Larceny-theft (except motor vehicle theft)— The unlawful taking, carrying, leading, or riding away of property from the possession or constructive possession of another. Examples are thefts of bicycles or automobile accessories, shoplifting, pocket-picking, or the stealing of any property or article which is not taken by force and violence or by fraud. While attempted larcenies are included, embezzlement, "con" games, forgery, worthless checks, etc. are excluded.

Motor vehicle theft— The theft or attempted theft of a motor vehicle. A motor vehicle is self-propelled and runs on the surface and not on rails. Excluded are motorboats, construction equipment, airplanes and farming equipment.

Arson— Any willful or malicious burning or attempt to burn, with or without intent to defraud, a dwelling, house, public building, motor vehicle or aircraft, personal property of another, etc.

The local law enforcement agencies make direct monthly reports to the FBI or to a centralized state agency who then reports to the FBI. Each report received by the FBI is examined for reasonableness, accuracy, and deviations that may indicate errors. Any unusual variations are verified with the reporting agency for possible error. For each calendar year, the UCRs are published in a detailed annual report, *Crime in the United States*. The report includes information on crime counts and trends. This data is classified as to crimes cleared, persons arrested by sex, race, and age, characteristics of homicides, victim-offender relationships, weapons used, and circumstances surrounding homicides. In addition to the annual report, special reports are frequently issued. The UCR program provides crime data for the Nation as well as for regions, states, counties, cities, and towns.

Major problems with the UCR include: (1) only index offenses are used to determine crime rates; (2) many offenses are never reported to the police and therefore are not entered into the system; and (3) not all index offenses known to law enforcement are recorded. Regarding the latter problem, if a victim reports that her home was broken into and she was physically assaulted and raped, only the most serious offense (i.e., the rape) will be recorded. The other two index offenses will not be recorded.

The phrase "cleared by arrest" is misleading. Under the UCR reporting system, a crime is also reported as cleared by arrest under any of the following circumstances:

1) the victim indicates a refusal to prosecute and the suspect is not arrested;

2) the suspect is located in another state and the other state refuses to extradite the suspect;

3) police release the suspect;

4) there is insufficient evidence to charge the arrested person; or

5) the defendant is acquitted without being arrested.

The Future

Presently, the UCRs are being redesigned by a five year program with the goal of converting the reports to more comprehensive and detailed reports called the National Incident-Based Reporting System (NIBRS). Whereas most of the information contained in the UCRs is based on the eight index crimes, the NIBRS will provide detailed information regarding 22 broad categories of offenses, involving 46 specific offenses.

The advent of NIBRS marks the transition to an automated system of retrieving crime data directly from law enforcement records. With NIBRS, law enforcement agencies can transfer crime information directly from the local computer systems to national and state levels through automated processes. As a result, crime statistics should become more comprehensive and flexible than under the UCR system that uses standardized reporting forms.

NIBRS is an incident based reporting system. This means that as law enforcement agencies collect data on each single occupance (crime), the data is transmitted to the NIBRS computers. The goal of NIBRS is to collect most of the data on each incident currently being maintained in law enforcement records. For example, when NIBRS is operating fully, it will collect up to 53 different facts about each incident, thus allowing more correlation among offenders, property, victims, offenders, and arrestees. NIBRS will retain many of the general concepts currently being used by the UCRs, including the basic measurements of crime rates and guidelines for reporting offenses.

The implementation pace of NIBRS will depend upon the resources, abilities, and limitations of the contributing law enforcement agencies. As with the UCRs, the adoption by local law enforcement agencies will be voluntary. [*Note:* To qualify for certain types of federal assistance, the local agencies must currently participate in the UCRs. It would appear that the same "voluntary" methods will be used to encourage local agencies to participate in NIBRS.] From a practical point of view, it appears that only when local agencies modify or update their records system, will they implement NIBRS. Until then, the FBI will continue to accept and publish the traditional UCR data. The FBI will also produce interim NIBRS reports from available input to that system. The interim reports will serve as a supplement to the UCRs. [*Note:* NIBRS documents and interim reports may be obtained by writing the Uniform Crime Reporting Program, Federal Bureau of Investigation, Washington, D.C. 20535.]

The Crime Clock

The annual report of the UCRs begins with the "crime clock." A look at the clock suggests that we have one murder every twenty-eight minutes. The reader is cautioned that the crime clock display should not be interpreted to imply a degree of regularity in the commission of crimes; that it merely represents the annual ratio of crimes to fixed time intervals. Unfortunately, many people ignore the caution and refer to the clock using its literal measuring of the time interval of crime.

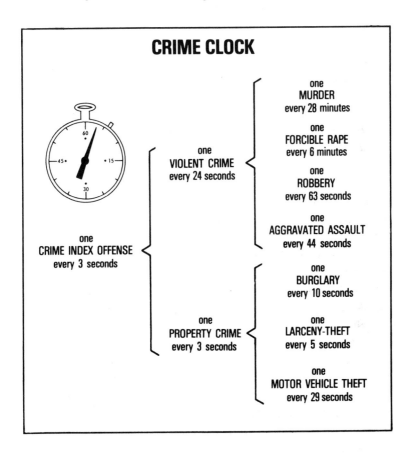

National Crime Victimization Survey

In an effort to determine the parameters of crime that were not in the official crime statistics, The President's Commission on Law Enforcement and Administration of Justice conducted the first national survey of crime victimization in 1965. During that year, 10,000 households were surveyed to determine if any member of the household had been the victim of a crime during the preceding year and if so, whether the crime had been reported to law enforcement. In those cases where no report was made to law enforcement, they were asked the reasons for not reporting.

The households were selected in an attempt to ensure a representative sample of the nation as a whole. The victimization surveys indicated that the actual amount of crime in the United States was much higher than reflected in the UCRs. For example, forcible rapes were almost four times the number reported in the UCRs. Burglaries and robberies were twice as high as the numbers reported in the UCRs.

The success of the early victimization studies stimulated the Law Enforcement Assistance Administration to finance a survey by the U.S. Bureau of Census in 1972. The Bureau of Justice Statistics (BJS) NCVS began in 1973. The NCVS collects detailed information on the frequency and nature of the crimes of rape, personal robbery, aggravated and simple assault, household burglary, personal and household theft, and motor vehicle theft. It does not include data on homicide or crimes against commercial entities such as store robberies.

The surveys target not only victimizations but also public conceptions of the fear of crimes, characteristics of the victim and offender, conceptions of police effectiveness, as well as other data. The major problem with the surveys is their accuracy. Victims tend to incorrectly remember exactly when a crime occurred. They tend to forget the value of the property stolen. In addition, since the same respondents are used from year to year, they may be subject to "panel bias," (less willing to cooperate in the long and complex interviewing process). Another major problem with the surveys is the costs involved.

The U.S. Census Bureau personnel annually interview approximately 49,000 households (about 101,000 personnel). Households selected for interview are kept in the sample for three years and are interviewed at six month intervals. New households are rotated in as old ones are rotated out.

The NCVS collects data on crimes suffered by individuals and households, whether or not those crimes are reported to law enforcement. From the sample households, estimations are made regarding the amount and type of personal crime in the U.S. during a given period of time. Data is collected on the victims by age, sex, race, ethnicity, marital status, income, and educational level. Similar information, as available, is collected regarding the offenders. Other information provided by the surveys include the time and place of occurrence of crimes, weapons used, nature of injuries, and economic consequences. Questions on the survey also cover the experiences of victims with the justice system, details on self-protective measures used, and possibility of substance abuse by offenders. In addition, supplemental questions are added to the survey when special topics are being researched. Recently, the NCVS expanded its questions to include questions concerning victimizations that occurred at work, while shopping, on public transportation, and during leisure outings. They also added vandalism to the list of crimes covered.

The findings from the NCVS are published for each calendar year, normally in April of the following year. A more detailed report is released in June. Periodically special and technical reports of specific crime topics are also published.

Comparison of UCR and NCVS

The NCVS includes crimes both reported and not reported to law enforcement, whereas the UCR contains only those crimes reported to law enforcement. The NCVS excludes homicide, arson, crimes against commercial entities, and crimes against children under age 12. All of these are included in the UCR. In determining crime rates, the NCVS includes simple assaults whereas under the UCR, simple assaults are reported as Part II crimes and not included in computing crime rates. In addition, it is noted that there are differences in crime definitions between the two data collections.

Another major difference is that the UCR rates crimes per 100,000 persons per year and the NCVS rates crimes per 1000 households per year. Since the number of households may not grow at the same rate each year as the total population, trend data for rates of household crimes measured by the two data collections may not be comparable.

The UCRs are based on actual counts of offenses reported to law enforcement agencies. The NCVS is based on an extensive scientifically selected sample which is then used to make an estimate of the actual crime rates for the population. Accordingly, the NCVS is subject to sampling variations.

While the results of the two data collections are not strictly comparable, a comparison of crime data from the two provides us with greater understanding into the crime problem. While both the UCRs and the NCVS use extensive accuracy checks in their data collection processes to minimize errors, there are many possible sources of error.

Measuring Occupation-Related Crimes

As noted earlier, the UCR measures only the eight index crimes. The NCVS, also, does not include those crimes like embezzlement or tax evasion. At the present time, there are no significant data bases that measure the extent of "white collar" crime that exists in the United States. [*Note:* "White collar" crime refers to those crimes usually committed by persons who traditionally wore white shirts and ties.]

Other Crime Statistics

Another data collection used in trying to determine the nature and extent of crime is the "self-reported crime." The first major study of crime was in 1947. In that study, approximately 1,700 persons who had been convicted of criminal behavior completed questionnaires regarding their involvement in criminal behavior. It appeared from the answers received that criminal activity was considerably more than the official crime data suggested. Similar self-reported surveys were conducted in Miami, Florida between 1988 and 1991. These studies also suggested that there was considerably more criminal activity than indicated by the UCRs.

The impact of drug use has resulted in more than 20 data collections involving drug usage patterns, trends, and correlates. The most significant of the data collections are the National Household Survey of Drug Abuse, the High School Senior Survey and the Drug Use Forecasting. Since the Drug Use Forecasting (DUF) is a high profile data base, it is discussed in a separate section.

The National Household Survey of Drug Abuse is sponsored by the National Institute on Drug Abuse and is conducted on a regular basis. This survey is used to estimate the patterns of drug abuse by persons in the general household populations of the United States. The estimates are incomplete in that they do not include people living in jails, prisons, military bases and the homeless.

The High School Senior Survey is also sponsored by the National Institute on Drug Abuse. It is conducted annually by using a representative sample of high school seniors. The survey examines drug use patterns, alcohol use, and life-style of American youths. Since it only surveys high school seniors, it misses most high school dropouts who are likely drug abusers.

Hate crime statistics are being collected on a five year data collection program that was mandated by the Hate Crime Statistics Act passed by the federal government in 1990. The first statistics collected under this program were published in 1992.

Drug Use Forecasting Program

The Drug Use Forecasting Program (DUF) has since 1987 collected data on drug use from booking facilities throughout the United States. The purpose of DUF is to provide cities with the necessary information for the early detection of drug epidemics, planning and allocation of law enforcement resources, and determining local drug abuse treatment and prevention needs. The data is collected for approximately 14 consecutive evenings each quarter through voluntary and anonymous interviews and urine specimens from selected arrestees. According to the reports received in this program, cocaine is the most frequently used drug.

During the first few years under the DUF, the data indicates that between 54 and 82 percent of men arrested for serious offenses in 14 major cities tested positive for illicit drugs. Cocaine use was the most used illegal drug by arrestees.

VOLUME AND RATES OF CRIMINAL ACTIVITY

In this section, we will examine individual crimes and assess criminal activity in general. Unless otherwise indicated, the data used in this section is from the UCRs and the National Crime Surveys.[1]

Murder suspect being taken into custody.

Individual Crimes

Murder

Murders occur less often than any other index crime. Murder is defined as the unlawful killing of a human being. Deaths caused by negligence, suicides, accidental deaths, and justifiable homicides are excluded. Traffic fatalities are also excluded. The total number of murders in 1991 was 24,703. This was an all time high. More murders occurred during August than any other month of the year with the fewest occurring in February. The Southern states had 43 percent of the total number, Western states had 21 percent, the Midwestern states had 19 percent, and the Northeastern states had 17 percent. Only the Northeastern states had a decline in murders from the previous year. Approximately 70 percent of murders are cleared by the police (those cases in which the police have made an arrest or have otherwise identified the offender).

More than three out of four murder victims are male. The overall murder rate is approximately 10 per 100,000 per year. On a regional basis, the South's murder rate was 12, the West's was 10, and the Midwest's and Northeast's were eight. Approximately 58 percent of the known murderers were relatives or acquaintances of the victim. About 20 percent occurred as the result of some felonious activity such as robbery. Twenty-eight percent of the female murder victims were killed by their husbands or boyfriends. Out of every 100 murder victims, approximately 47 are white, 50 are black, and three are of other races. Considering the total population in the United States, the murder victimization rate for blacks is about six times as that for whites. Approximately 49 percent of the victims are between the ages of 20 and 34. In the majority of cases, the offender and the victim are of the same race. About 87 percent of the male victims were killed by males. Only 10 percent of the female victims, however, are killed by females. About 12 percent of the murders were committed by relatives and about 34 percent by other acquaintances.

Arguments were listed as the causation factor in about 32 percent of the cases and felonies (robbery, arson, etc.) in about 21 percent of the cases. Firearms were used to commit about 62 percent of the murders.

Criminal homicide has the highest clearance rate of all the index crimes. The police generally clear about 67 percent of the cases. The average sentence received by defendants convicted of murder is 19 years and 11 months.

Forcible Rape

Forcible rape, the carnal knowledge of a female forcibly and against her will, mostly involves a lone victim and a lone offender. It is the least reported of all violent crimes. It is to be noted that statutory rape differs from forcible rape in that it involves sexual intercourse with a female who is under the legal age of consent, regardless of whether or not she is a willing partner.

Approximately one-third of rapes occur in the victim's home. Approximately 20 percent of the rapes occur in the home of a friend and about 20 percent on the street. About 75 percent occur between sunset and sunrise. Approximately 58 percent of the victims are under the age of 25. Rapes occur more frequently during July and August and less frequently during December, January and February. The highest rates (91 per 100,000 females) occur in the Western part of the United States. The Northeastern states have the lowest rate (57 per 100,000).

Approximately 83 out of every 100,000 women are raped each year. Black women are more likely to be raped than white women. Women who are divorced, separated, or who have never been married are nine times more likely to be raped than women who are married or widowed. Unemployed females are three times more likely to be raped than employed females. Female students are one and one-half times more likely to be raped than an employed female.

It appears that approximately 80 percent of the rapes are acquaintance rapes (the victim knows the offender). The police clear about 50 percent of reported rapes. Of the persons arrested for rape, 55 percent are white and about 43 percent are black. Thirty percent are under the age of 25 years.

Robbery

Robbery is the violent crime that most often involves more than one offender. It is defined as the taking or attempted taking of anything of value from the care, custody, or control of a person or persons by force or threat of force or violence or by putting the victim in fear.

Armed robbery refers to the use of a weapon. Approximately one half of all robberies involve the use of a firearm. The average loss in robberies is about $820 dollars. The average loss for bank robberies is about $3,200. Only about 24 percent of the robberies are cleared. In metropolitan areas, the robbery rate is about 341 per 100,000 inhabitants. In the rural areas it is about 70 per 100,000. The Northeast has the highest robbery rates (about 352 per 100,000) and the Midwest the lowest (223 per 100,000).

Sixty-one percent of those arrested for robbery are black and about 38 percent white. Males account for over 90 percent of those arrested for robbery. Most (62 percent) are under 25 years of age.

Assault

Assault is the unlawful attack by one person upon another for the purpose of inflicting severe or aggravated bodily injury. There are two types of assaults — aggravated and simple. Aggravated assaults usually involve the use of a weapon or means likely to result in death or great bodily harm.

Simple assaults occur more frequently than aggravated assaults. Simple assaults may be described as "second degree" assaults which may involve fistfights and scuffles. Most assaults involve one victim and one offender. About one-third of the aggravated assaults are committed with blunt objects or other dangerous weapons. Approximately 55 percent of assaults are cleared by the police.

Americans are victims of aggravated assault at a rate of about 433 per 100,000 per year. In Metropolitan areas, the rate is about 487 per 100,000 and only about 170 in rural areas. The South accounts for about 39 percent of the cases and the Northeast only about 17 percent of the cases. The months of July and August have the highest rates for aggravated assault and February the lowest.

Males constitute about 86 percent of those arrested for aggravated assault. Approximately 60 percent of those arrested were white and about 38 percent were black.

Burglary

Burglary is the unlawful entry of a structure to commit a felony or a theft. Attempted forcible entry is included under the burglary definition. Burglary may include violence or personal encounters; however, it is most often a property crime. Residential property is targeted in two out of every three reported burglaries. About 42 percent of residential burglaries occurred without forced entry. About 37 percent of the non-forced burglaries are known to have occurred during hours of daylight. Burglaries occur more frequently in the summer months of August and July and least frequently in the winter months of January and February. The average loss per burglary is about $1,250 dollars. The police clear only about 13 percent of burglaries.

The burglary rate is the highest in the South (about 1,500 per 100,000 population per year) and the lowest in the Midwest. The Northeast has only about 1,000 per 100,000. Of the individuals arrested for burglary 19 percent are under the age of 18. Approximately 91 percent of those arrested are male. Whites accounted for 69 percent of those arrested and blacks accounted for 29 percent.

Larceny-Theft

Larceny is the most common of the eight major offenses. It is defined as the unlawful taking, carrying, leading or riding away of property from the possession or constructive possession of another. Larceny, in some states, may be divided into two forms — simple larceny and grand larceny. Grand larceny involves the taking of valuables worth over a set amount. Typically this amount is set at $200.00.

Less than 5 percent of all personal larcenies involve contact between the victim and offender. Pocket picking and purse snatching most frequently occur inside nonresidential buildings or on street locations. About 37 percent of the reported larceny-theft incidents involved the theft of automobile accessories and auto parts. The average loss per crime is about $478.00. Theft crimes have the lowest clearance rate of all index crimes. Burglaries have the second lowest.

Larceny-theft rates are the highest for the Western states (about 3,500 per 100,000) and the lowest for the Northeastern states (about 2,600). Larceny-thefts occur more frequently in July and August and less frequently in February. Females account for about 32 percent of those arrested for larceny-theft. Forty-four percent of the arrestees are under the age of 21. Whites account for about 67 percent of the total arrestees and blacks account for about 31 percent.

Motor Vehicle Theft

Motor vehicle theft is relatively well reported to the police, probably because of insurance requirements. It is defined as the unlawful taking or attempted taking of a self-propelled road vehicle owned by another, with the intent to deprive him or her of it permanently or temporarily. It should be noted that the stealing of trains, planes, snowmobiles, boats and farm machinery is classified as larceny under the UCR reporting program.

A stolen motor vehicle is more likely to be recovered than any other type of stolen article. Each year, about one car in every 100 is stolen. The most likely victims of this crime are black and Hispanic households headed by people under age 25 living in center-city multiple or low-income housing (those who can least afford it and who are most likely not to have insurance).

This is the only crime that is more common in the Northeast (795 per 100,000 per year) than other sections of the U.S. The lowest area is the Midwest at 507 per 100,000. The average value per stolen vehicle is about $5,000. The Volkswagen and Cadillac models were the automobiles stolen most often during the years 1988 to 1992. Eighty percent of the motor vehicles stolen are cars. Fifteen percent are trucks and buses. Ninety percent of the people arrested for this crime are male and 62 percent are under the age of 21.

Arson

Arson was the latest crime added to the Index. Arson involves the unlawful, willful, or malicious burning or attempted burning of property with or without intent to defraud. Single family residences are the most frequent targets of arson. About 16 percent of the structures where arson occurred were vacant. Only about 18 percent of the arson cases are cleared by the police. About 40 percent of those that were cleared involved offenders under the age of 18 years, a higher percentage of juvenile involvement than for any other index crime. Arson has the highest rate of involvement by whites than any other index crime. Seventy-seven percent of the people arrested for arson are white. About 87 percent are male. The South has the highest rate of involvement, 67 per 100,000 and the Midwest the lowest at 44 per 100,000.

Illegal Drugs and Alcohol Offenses

Individuals between the ages of 25 and 34 are most frequently arrested for drug and alcohol offenses. Since 1982, there has been a large increase in drug abuse arrests, especially for women. The impact of drugs has been felt throughout the whole spectrum of the criminal justice system — from street crimes to crack babies, from violent gang turf wars to the increasing offender population crippling our correctional system. See Chapter 17 for an in-depth discussion on drugs.

Administration of Breathalyzer test to a drunk driving suspect.

EXHIBIT 4-1

Theories Of Corruption

(Excerpt from Law Enforcement Assistance Administration, *Report of the Task Force on Organized Crime*, GPO: Washington, D.C., 1976)

Why do public officials violate the laws they have been selected to implement or enforce and often become the instruments of organized crime? This question has been debated for many years, and a variety of explanations — some conflicting, some complementary — have been offered. Some of these explanations focus on the individuals involved and their backgrounds and personalities; others focus on the situations in which corruption arises and their relationship to broader social and political environments. This report will not provide a complete statement of these theories, or even select one that seems superior; all the explanations have a degree of validity and are useful in explaining some facets of the problem. As in any complex human behavior, the reasons for and reactions to the situation are multifaceted and, therefore, not subject to simple labeling or explanations....

Examinations of corruption have differed in their conclusions in part because they have analyzed different factors. Some authors have focused on the acts of corruption, seeking to ascertain whether they are isolated events or parts of systemic patterns of illegality. A second set of studies looked at the characteristics of the participants in the corruption. In some cases they are merely the few "rotten apples" that one might, on a statistical basis, expect to find in any group; in other cases they seem to be average persons representative of their society. Finally, a third body of research attempted to measure the significance of the settings in which corruption occurs, asking whether it arises from the ways in which governments conduct their business....

Corrupt Acts: Premeditated Greed or Crimes of Opportunity? For over a century, criminologists and psychologists have sought explanations of criminality in family relationships, personalities, medical histories, job and educational skills, friendships, and other characteristics of offenders. During the past decade, scholarly attention also has been directed at the nature of the crimes committed, distinguishing between premeditated crimes and the so-called "crimes of opportunity." For example, one homicide may be a carefully planned gangland execution, while another the unfortunate consequence of an overheated barroom brawl.

In terms of corruption, some acts involve systematic looting of the public till — often by organized crime — using the skills of many conspirators and developing complicated procedures to conceal the frauds. By comparison, the decision of a traffic officer to accept $10 in lieu of writing a ticket might be made on the spur of the moment. The latter type of corruption presumably could be reduced by removing the opportunities. However, the reduction of planned corruption, including that perpetrated by organized crime, will require more complicated steps to alter the costs and benefits perceived by potential offenders....

What determines whether a particular governmental activity might be seen as an opportunity for a potential corrupter or corruptee? Among the factors that first come to mind are legal constraints, surveillance and supervision practices, and market demand for the activity.

Whether some public employees succumb to the temptation to abuse their offices may depend on the degree to which they are bound by legal constraints and citizen attitudes. Are government purchases left to the discretion of purchasing agents or do they require advertisements, competitive bidding, and independent auditing? Do the laws and regulations governing the officials' conduct —those the police officer enforces or the bureaucrat implements — allow substantial or even excessive discretion, or are they specific?

One of the major facilitators of official corruption is secrecy, and those governmental activities that go unnoticed are most susceptible to abuse by organized crime and other corrupting influences.... Few people are likely to notice the approval of a minor zoning variance, a technical amendment to the tax code, or a police officer's on-the-street evaluation of a drug purchase.... This situation suggests that, to maximize both the possibility and the probability of detection, a comprehensive program to reduce corruption must include accountability and supervision.

The level of demand for the goods and services controlled by public officials — the funds, jobs, contracts, programs, privileges, and restrictions that can be allocated as prescribed by law or the highest bidder — also can determine the frequency of corruption.... If an office supply contract with city hall offers no greater reward than that available from other business opportunities, a stationery supply house would have no incentive to offer a bribe to get the contract.

The Participants. Whenever corruption is uncovered, the first impulse is to question the character of the people involved.... One must avoid simplistic theories that offer easy explanation of why people are or may become corrupt. Many grafters act simply on the basis of greed, while others seek prestige or power. Some may be coerced into cooperating — because of threats by organized crime figures, for example — and then subjected to threats of blackmail. Others may rationalize their behavior by thinking that they will be subject to "enforcement" by organized crime. And still others may be involved in corruption or organized crime activities to advance the interests of relatives or friends.

Settings for Corruption. A final set of theories addresses the environment of corruption, the broader political and structural settings that may determine whether specific reforms will succeed. The first theory argues that corruption will thrive in a setting in which the public does not support the laws or is divided about their values. The second is that a weak government, one that is poorly organized to carry out its duties, is less able to mount an effective fight against the major source of corruption — organized crime.

Victimization by Race, Gender, and Age

Race

Generally, blacks have the highest victimization rate for crimes of violence. Hispanics have the next highest rate for victimization; whites the lowest. In rural areas, however, whites tend to have higher rates of victimization for crimes of violence than non-whites. For crimes of theft, whites have a greater victimization rate than blacks.

Households Experiencing Crime

by race of household head, 1991

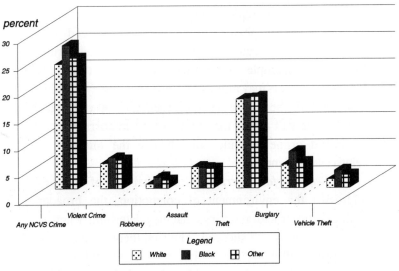

Source: U.S. Dept. of Justice

Women

Women are generally less likely than men to be crime victims. Their rate of victimization is about 60 percent of that of men. In two classes of victimization, however, female victims predominate. The two classes include rape and violence between intimates. Violence between intimates refers to crimes committed by one spouse on the other, by ex-spouses and by live-in partners. Women are victims in crimes involving intimates at a rate of three times that of males. Among crime victims, 25 percent of the women and only 4 percent of the men were victimized by persons whom they knew intimately. About 85 percent of the crimes against a female by an intimate involved assaults and/or batteries, and 11 percent involved robberies. It appears that women report only about 57 percent of the violent crime by intimates to law enforcement agencies.

Black women experienced violent crime at a higher rate than that of women of all other races. A Hispanic woman was more likely to be a victim than a non-black/non-Hispanic woman. Separated or divorced women are six times more likely to be the victim of a violent crime than married or widowed females.

Age

In general, the higher the age category, the lower the probability of both violent and theft victimization. Individuals ages 12 to 24 have the highest rate of victimization while those age 65 and older have the lowest rate. Females under the age of 35 have a higher rate of victimization than men or women above the age of 35. Men between the ages of 12 and 34 have the highest victimization rates.

Seventeen is the most frequent age to be arrested for an offense of any kind and to be arrested for a violent offense. The most frequent age to be arrested for property offenses is 18. Nineteen is the most frequent age to be first imprisoned as an adult.[2]

Family Income

The higher the income level, the less likely a person is subject to violent crime victimization. Employed and retired persons are less likely to be victimized than the unemployed, members of the Armed Services, or students. Renters, also, experience a higher rate of victimization than homeowners.

Victimization is studiied more thoroughly in Chapter 16.

Prisoners

In this section, we will look at the statistics involving persons confined in jails and other correctional institutions.[3]

While we often use the terms "jail" and "prisons" interchangeably, jails are generally locally operated institutions used to confine people awaiting trial or convicted of misdemeanors. Prisons are generally operated by the state and are used to confine persons convicted of felonies.

The United States confines a larger share of its population than any other nation. The U.S. incarceration rate is about 455 per 100,000 persons. The second highest nation is South Africa with a rate of 311. Sweden and Japan incarcerate only about 42 per 100,000—less than 10 percent of our rate. In 1991, the Soviet Union imprisoned 268 persons per 100,000. It is estimated that on any given day, there are over 400,000 persons in the United States being held in jails or about one in every 460 adult residents.

The use of fines in lieu of jail/prison time has not been very popular in the United States. A fine is one of the oldest forms of punishment and is widely used in Western Europe as the sole sanction for the major portion of cases coming before the criminal courts. Sweden, England, and West Germany use fines as the sole punishment in about 65 percent of criminal cases. In the U.S. fines are widely used, but in connection with other sanctions. In addition, recent studies indicate that the amounts of fines levied in the U.S. are relatively small compared to other countries. Critics of the use of fines contend that given the poverty of most offenders, fines cannot be collected; they are difficult to enforce; and their use adds to the courts' administrative burdens.

There are approximately 1,200 prisons in the United States. Forty-seven of these are federal institutions. The rest are state prisons. Of those, 11 percent are maximum security, 11 percent are high/closed, 28 percent are medium, 25 percent are minimum and 25 percent are community facilities. Approximately 96 percent of the prisoners are serving sentences in excess of one year.

Cohort Studies of Juveniles

In the 1960s, Marvin Wolfgang studied some 10,000 males born in Philadelphia in 1945. He concluded that by the time of their 18th birthdays, some 627 youths had been arrested five or more times. He also concluded that less than seven percent of the youth were responsible for nearly 70 percent of the crimes attributed to the 10,000. He repeated his study later for youths born in 1958 with similar findings. Similar studies were conducted for other cities in the U.S. The generalized findings of those studies are as follows:

— Juvenile violent offenders were a very small fraction of the total number of youth.

— As a rule, juveniles do not typically progress from less serious to more serious crimes.

— It is difficult to predict which juveniles will progress to more serious crimes.

— A relatively small number of juveniles are responsible for most of the arrests involving juveniles.

— Violent juveniles do not generally specialize in the types of crimes they commit.

— Most violent juvenile crimes do not involve the use of weapons.

EXHIBIT 4-2

National Survey on Law and Order

A 1993 national survey on law and order resulted in the below listed conclusions:

1) Eighty-two percent of the public has a positive attitude toward the police.

2) Only 23 percent of the public believes that juries convict the guilty and free the innocent.

3) Approximately 87 percent of the public feels that the criminal justice system does not treat all people equally.

4) Thirty percent feel that juries are right only about half of the time.

5) Sixty-two percent do not approve of plea-bargaining.

6) About 90 percent feel that repeat offenders who commit serious crimes should not be eligible for parole.

7) Seventy-one percent feel that juveniles between the ages of 13 and 17 who commit violent crimes should be tried as adults.

8) About 70 percent feel that police treat date rape less seriously than other crimes.

The above conclusions were based on an exclusive survey of 2,512 men and women, aged 18 to 75 and representative of the population as a whole.[5] From the above conclusions, it appears that the public, as a whole, has a higher opinion of the police than they do the court system or corrections.

THE ROLE OF DISCRETION IN CRIMINAL PROCESSES

Our laws do not apply automatically. They must be enforced by *the system*. The criminal justice system, however, is not designed for total enforcement of our laws. The system is a discretionary one. Discretion must be used in determining which crimes will be prosecuted and which offenders will be punished. The justice system consists of a series of discretionary points, places where the decision to arrest, prosecute, or punish must be made. The key discretion points in the handling of a criminal conduct include:

— the citizen reports the crime to the police;

— the police investigate the report;

— the police apprehend and arrest;

— the prosecutor charges the suspect;

— the suspect plea bargains;

— the judge sentences;

— convicted appeals; and

— correctional decisions.

Officer discretion comes into play most often during the enforcement of traffic infractions. Shown above is a sobriety checkpoint where officer discretion is used to determine if further testing, for driving under the influence of drugs or alcohol, is needed.

At each of the above points, the decision maker may decline to take official action. If this occurs, normally the criminal is not punished for his or her crime. The person with the most discretion is the police officer on the street. If the officer resolves the issue on-site or chooses to not take any action, an official case is never opened on the crime and the crime goes unreported.

Since the police officer has considerable personal discretion, the use of discretion by officers has been the subject of many research projects. According to the results of those projects, the major variables that affect an individual officer's discretional decision during a typical encounter between an officer and an offender include the below factors:

— **The seriousness of the crime.** The most important variable is the seriousness of the crime. Major felonies (e.g., murder, rape, serious batteries) will in all likelihood be handled as crimes and will be treated as law enforcement functions.

— **Demeanor of the offender.** In less serious crimes, often the demeanor of the offender is a significant factor in the officer's decision to handle the matter officially. Think about the last time that you were stopped for a traffic violation. When the officer first approached your automobile, why did you treat the officer with respect? Were you hoping that your pleasant demeanor would influence the officer not to write you a ticket?

— **Offender's previous involvement in the criminal justice system as a client.** If the officer is aware that the individual has a prior record, the officer is more likely to handle the matter as a law enforcement function (i.e., an arrest or citation).

— **Presence of a victim who requested official action.** Studies indicate that officers are more likely to cite or arrest offenders if there is a victim present who demands formal police action. [*Note*: One of the effects of the recent victims' rights movement is the limitation of police discretion when dealing with certain categories of crime.]

EMERGING CRIME TRENDS

Time has a way of changing all things. Crime is no exception to this rule. What we know about yesterday's crimes will become even more clear as we review and analyze them with future technologies. With today's technology, we have the ability to correlate a vast array of information from individual crimes, reports of crime, and historical crime review. With such information we can more accurately determine our current situation and better forecast emerging trends.

Reports indicate that we are now beginning to see what hopes to be a reduction in violent street crimes. With a reduction of street crimes comes the trend for safer cities as crime moves into rural areas. As the population relocates to rural areas, crime moves with it. White collar crime is on the rise along with crimes against the elderly. More females are now involved with crime and this trend should continue to accelerate. The most rapidly increasing type of crime is generally accepted as high-technology crime.

The Fear of Crime

It is important to note that along with the above trends comes the more pervasive aspect of crime — the fear of crime. Reports show that those most fearful of crime are often the least apt to experience what they fear. Unfortunately, this insidious fear of crime touches virtually everyone. The irony of this all is that those that fear crime least, young males, tend to experience crime the most often. Along with this is the fear of strangers which is not proved out by the findings that most violent crimes are committed by someone known to the victim.

Men vs. Women

The number of women committing crimes seems to be rapidly growing. Current trends over the last 10 years show that crimes committed by men have grown by approximately 15 percent while crimes committed by women have grown by approximately 35 percent. Violent crimes committed by men and women have grown 43 percent and 62 percent, respectively. Property crimes committed by men and women have grown 8 percent and 32 percent, respectively.

Does this mean that women are approaching the point where they rival men for criminal activity? No! What current reports suggest is that more women are being arrested on drugs, alcohol, larceny, fraud and white collar related crimes. In only two reported areas do women outnumber men in committing crime — runaways and prostitution.

The general conclusion is that although women are becoming more criminally active, there is little evidence towards the emergence of a new female criminal.

School Crime

An overwhelming majority of students experience fear of crime at school. Although rates of victimization are low, the fear of crime is still pervasive at school much like that found out on the streets. An estimated nine percent of students, ages 12 to 19, were crime victims in or around their schools this year. Violent crimes were experienced by over two percent of students with seven percent experiencing property crimes. The violent crimes were composed mainly of simple assaults (attacks without weapons) and usually resulting in minor injuries.

It was significant to note that firearms were not found to be an issue except in very isolated instances. Students feared less the possibility of someone being armed as opposed to being in the wrong place at the wrong time. Hallways, restrooms, and certain routes to and from school were the most feared by students.

Fifteen percent of students said their school had gangs, and 16 percent claimed that a student had attacked or threatened a teacher at their school.

Students of different races experienced about the same amount of violence and property victimization in and around their schools. Hispanics were shown to have experienced a higher rate of property crime. Victimization seems to directly correlate to age. The older the student the less likely the student was to be victimized. Victimization by violent crime also showed no consistent relation to the income level of the victims' families.

As the students age, drugs appear to become more available or known to the student. Students over the age of 15 were more likely to say that drugs were available at school. Public school students were more likely to say that drugs were available at school than those who attend private schools.

The emerging patterns for schools tend toward more security measures employed by the school and by the student. Locker checks, metal detectors, hall patrols, and, in some instances, bullet-proof vests are being encountered. By-in-large the majority of crimes committed at school are the same today as they were a decade or two ago. Fist fights, petty thefts, vandalism, alcohol and drug use are the main reports of criminality in our schools.

Hate Crimes

Unfortunately, trends indicate that hate crimes will again be on the increase much like what was seen in the 1970s. Bombing, shootouts, kidnappings, and the like will be brought forward by groups ranging from underground survivalists to foreign terrorist agents.

Many of those groups now thought of as hate mongers (i.e., KKK, the Order, neo-Nazis, white supremacists, etc.) are the ones most feared. These groups tend to be well entrenched into our society. They are well-financed, highly organized, and armed with modern arsenals.

Drugs

Drugs will continue to play a major role in crime. They are often linked to crime through their use by the criminal and by their manufacturing and trafficking. Trends indicate that little will change in this area. Our "War on Drugs" has been ineffective in limiting drug use and has mostly resulted in simply more creative trafficking. The proposed use of our military for border patrol and drug importation eradication is good theory, but successful practical application has yet to be seen. Chapter 17 will discuss, in more detail, the effects of drugs on the criminal justice system.

High-Tech Crimes

Most agree that this area will be the most rapidly increasing segment of criminality. Some say this area of crime will not just grow but rather explode into the 21st century. With the increased sophistication of this type of crime will come the inability of law enforcement to effectively deal with it. As we march to cope with current high-tech crime, criminals will be sprinting ahead with state-of-the-art procedures, software and hardware. Our only hope seems to be in the allocation of funds to modernize and anticipate high-tech's future in crime. Law enforcement must be prepared to battle a point/counter-point war against these high-tech criminals.

DISCUSSION QUESTIONS

1. Compare and contrast the Uniform Crime Reports with the victim surveys.

2. What are the problems with our present crime reporting data bases?

3. What steps should be taken to improve our knowledge regarding the amount of crime that exists in our society?

4. Why is it important to determine crime trends?

5. What types of action do you employ due to the fear of crime?

6. How might high-tech crimes be discovered and discouraged? How might these types of crime effect your life?

ENDNOTES

[1] Most of the information presented in this section is presented in the present tense. The information used to estimate those percentages is, however, based on past data which may be only approximations.

[2] U.S. Department of Justice, *The Young Criminal Years*, (1992).

[3] Bureau of Justice Statistics, *Probation and Parole*, (1991): and Bureau of Justice Statistics, *Jail Inmates*, (1991).

[4] *Wall Street Journal*, (April 19, 1993), p. B-2.

[5] *Parade Magazine*, (April 18, 1993), pp. 4-7.

PART II

LAW ENFORCEMENT IN AMERICA

August Vollmer, Chief of Police, Berkeley, California from 1905 to 1932.

5

THE DEVELOPMENT OF
THE CRIMINAL JUSTICE
SYSTEM

*The policeman is the little boy who grew up to be
what he said he was going to be.*

—Raymond Burr, 1968

The largest and most visible segment of the justice system is the police. American taxpayers spend approximately $30 billion a year on police protection compared to $15 billion on courts and $20 billion on corrections. Accordingly, for every dollar spent on criminal justice, about 45 cents goes to law enforcement agencies.

The police are charged with the prevention and detection of crime and the apprehension of offenders. Other responsibilities of the police include the protection of society and the preservation of civil order. Our police are considered by many as the "thin blue line" between order and disorder. Others have a less flattering description of the police. In this chapter, we will examine both the historical development and the present state of our police departments.

One of our first problems in examining the development of modern day policing is to define "policing." What does it mean? There are many books on police, but only a few attempt to define the concept of policing.[1] *Webster's Ninth New Collegiate Dictionary* has the following definition of police:

> **police** n. The department of government concerned primarily with maintenance of public order, safety, health and enforcement of laws and possessing executive, judicial, and legislative powers.

There are at least two problems with the above definition. First, historically most policing has been done by organizations that were not "departments of government." Second, police are not always primarily concerned with the maintenance of public order, safety, health and enforcement of laws. Webster's definition attempts to define police by its ends rather than its means. Egon Bittner defines police as "a mechanism for the distribution of a non-negotiably coercive force employed in accordance with the dictates of an intuitive grasp of situational exigencies."[2] As you can see this definition is not one that is considered a model for clarity. It does, however, point out the problem with defining the concept of policing. The most important difference between police and other organizations is the ability of the police to use **coercive force**. Therefore, we can define **police** as:

"Those nonmilitary organizations who are given the general right by the government to use coercive force to enforce the law and whose primary purpose is to respond to problems of individual or group conflict that involve illegal behavior."[3]

Our policing is a product of its English heritage. When the British colonists brought their criminal justice system to the colonies, they included the English common law, the high value placed on individual rights, the court system, and law enforcement institutions. This English heritage contributed three enduring features to American policing. First, a tradition of limited police authority; second, the tradition of local control; and third, a highly decentralized and fragmented system of law enforcement.[4]

We demand a lot from our police. They are the only around-the-clock, 365 days a year public service agency with the authority to use coercive force to settle disputes. We expect our police to settle our problems immediately. Demands for police services fall into one of four categories: (1) crime fighting, (2) maintaining order, (3) providing informational services, and (4) providing emergency services.

FROM THE ENGLISH MODEL
AND OTHER INTERNATIONAL HERITAGE

The modern police department can be traced to the Ninth century when Alfred the Great of England structured his kingdom's defenses to prepare for the Danish invasion. To establish internal security, he instituted the system of **mutual pledge**. This system organized the country at the lowest level into groups of ten families. These groups were called **tithings**. Next, ten tithings were grouped together into a hundred families called **constables**. Next, the constables within each geographic area were combined to form the administrative units called shires (later called counties). Each shire was governed by a shire-reeve (later called sheriff).

In the 13th century the **night watch** was established to protect the streets in urban areas of England during the hours of darkness. The night watch was the first rudimentary form of metropolitan policing. From the 13th to the 17th centuries there was little development in the area of policing. During that period of time in theory each citizen in England was a policeman since all citizens were charged with the enforcement of the laws of England. In actual practice, however, law enforcement was almost non-existent.

By the 17th century, the chief law enforcement officials were the magistrates and the parish constables. The magistrates presided over courts, ordered arrests, called witnesses to investigate criminal behavior and examined prisoners. The parish constables were holdovers from the days of Alfred the Great. They had only limited authority to arrest and the authority was confined to small districts. In addition, in some urban areas there were constable's assistants called **beadles.** The beadles were used primarily to clear the streets of vagrants. Many of the constables, magistrates and beadles were corrupt.

Highway robbery was flourishing in England during the 16th and 17th centuries. To combat this problem, Parliament, in 1693, passed an act providing a reward of 40 pounds be paid for the capture and conviction of any highwayman or road agent. From this act emerged the **thief-takers.** The thief-takers were private detectives who were paid by the Crown on a piecework basis. They had no official status and only the authority of private citizens. Anyone could be one. They received rewards in return for the apprehension of criminals. The reward was payable upon the conviction of the thief. In addition to the reward, the thief-takers also received any property that belonged to the thief unless someone could prove that the property was stolen. During serious crimes waves, the Parliament increased the bounty to 100 British pounds for certain crimes. Later the system was expanded to include burglars, housebreakers, and street robbers. In addition, in some villages the landowners banded together and offered supplemental rewards. Many people trace the origin of the bounty hunter of the American West to thief-takers.

As the system of thief-takers grew, a class of professional thief-takers developed. While many criminals were apprehended by the thief-takers, probably more crime was created by the system than it suppressed. Many of thief-takers were criminals themselves, since often pardons were used as rewards. In addition, many of them became thief-makers. They would entice people to commit crime and then arrest the unsuspecting people for the rewards. There were also cases where innocent people were framed by the planting of stolen property on them in order to collect rewards.[5]

The period 1750 to 1850 witnessed a marked growth in the development of modern policing. By 1829, there were over 3,000 uniformed constables in the London Metropolitan police force. Henry Fielding, an eighteenth-century novelist who wrote *Tom Jones*, is credited with laying the foundation for the first modern police agency. Fielding was appointed as a magistrate in Westminster near London in 1748. At the time, he lived on Bow Street. It was in his home where he first opened his office and there formed the first modern police department. Fielding's goal was to reduce the burglaries, street and highway robberies, and thefts which were flourishing at the time.

Fielding established a relationship with the local pawnbrokers and requested that they notify him when someone tried to pawn stolen property. He ran advertising in the London and Westminster newspapers inviting anyone who was the victim of a crime by robbers or burglars to immediately send or bring to his Bow street office a description of the property stolen and a description of the criminal. Prior to his actions, there were no formal provisions for the reporting of crimes to authorities. Next, with the help of Saunders Welch who was the Constable of Holborn he formed a small unofficial investigative group of assistants. This group is considered as the first organized police force used in England and were nicknamed the "Bow Street Runners." The Bow Street Runners were not salaried. They earned their money under the standard thief-takers' reward system.

Later, the government supplemented Fielding's efforts by periodically providing financial support for the Bow Street Runners. In 1752, however, Fielding because of his poor health was confined to a wheelchair. He persuaded the government to appoint his brother, John Fielding as his chief assistant. John took over control of the operations of the runners. Since John was blind, he was referred to as the "Blind Beak." [Beak is an English slang word for judge.]

Henry Fielding died in 1754. In 1763, his brother John was provided with government funds to establish a civilian horse patrol of eight men to patrol the streets of London. After less than a year, however, the horse patrol was disbanded. Later a permanent foot patrol was established and in 1804 a new horse patrol was started.

The new horse patrol was outfitted in red vests and blue jackets and trousers. They became England's first uniformed police. One of the promises made to Parliament in establishing the new police was that they would wear uniforms to ensure that they were not used as spies and that people who gave information to a constable would know that it was a constable.

In 1789, a Glasgow businessman, Patrick Colquhoun was appointed a London magistrate. He attempted to get authorization to establish a large, organized police force for greater London. His efforts were unsuccessful because of the English people's love of freedom, their faith in private enterprise, and their distrust of government. He did establish a special river police patterned after the Bow Street model. The majority of his efforts, however, were unsuccessful because of the traditional mistrust of authorities by the English.

As a result of the riots between the Irish immigrants and local English citizens in 1780, the Parliament began debating on how to provide better public safety. Parliament debated this question for almost fifty years until 1829. In that year, Sir Robert Peel, England's Home Secretary influenced Parliament to pass the "Act for Improving the Police In and Near the Metropolis." This act established the first permanent police force in London. It was composed of over 1,000 men. The force was structured along military lines. The police were required to wear distinctive uniforms and were under the leadership of two police commissioners (one a lawyer and one a military officer). At that time, they were known as "the new police." Later they became known as "bobbies" in reference to Sir Robert Peel's nickname.[6]

The Act was referred to by the citizens of England as the "Peelian Reform." The basic tenets of the act are as follows:

1) The police must be stable, efficient, and organized along military lines.

2) The police must be under government control.

3) The best evidence of the efficiency of the police will be an absence of crime.

4) The distribution of crime news is essential.

5) The policeman should have a perfect command of his temper and a quiet and determined manner.

6) Good appearance commands respect.

7) The selection of proper persons and then properly training them is the root of efficiency.

8) Police headquarters should be centrally located and easily accessible to the police.

9) Policemen should be hired on a probationary basis.

10) Police records are essential to the necessary distribution of police strength.[7]

Colonel Charles Rowan, the commissioner who was a military officer, wanted to instill mutual respect between the police and the citizenry. Accordingly, he attempted to recruit young men who would inspire the highest personal ideals for the departments. Unfortunately, they were not immediately well received. Often open battles ensued between the bobbies and the citizenry.

The London Metropolitan Police introduced four new concepts to policing that exist today:

1) new mission,

2) new strategy,

3) new organizational structure, and

4) continual presence of the police.

The new mission was one of crime prevention. Until then, the chief role of law enforcement was catching criminals. The strategy was the concept of preventive patrols. The bobbies maintained a visible presence in the city by the use of fixed "beats." The organizational structure was the development of a quasi-military style. In addition, the police were professional in that they were full-time paid employees.

EMERGING LAW ENFORCEMENT SYSTEM IN THE U.S.

The first law enforcement agencies in America were created as soon as communities were organized. Whereas the English were reluctant to establish police forces, the colonies did not hesitate in the establishment of local law enforcement agencies. The Puritans who dominated the intellectual life of colonial America included in their ideology the belief that government was necessary because man was by nature sinful. Accordingly, it was essential that the government force people to conform to the requirements of the law.

Colonial America

Samuel Walker observes that the colonials borrowed their law enforcement practices from the English, the Dutch, and the French.[8] Walker states that the colonials had stronger biblical influences than were found in the English laws at that time and that the death penalty was used less frequently than in England.

The law enforcement officers in the colonies were the sheriff, the constable, the watch, and the slave patrol. The sheriff who was appointed by the colonial governors was the chief law enforcement officer. His responsibilities included the collection of taxes, conducting elections, maintaining bridges and roads, and criminal law enforcement. The sheriff did not patrol his area, but was a reactive agent of social control. The sheriffs received no salaries and were paid through a system of fees. Corruption was common.

The constable was initially an elected official in the colonial towns and cities. His duties included criminal law enforcement. Later in some of the larger cities, including Boston, the position became a semiprofessional appointed position. As a general rule in the larger cities, the constable provided law enforcement during the day and the night-watch during hours of darkness.

The watch is the closest to our modern-day police force. Members of the watch patrolled the cities to guard against fires, crimes and disorders. At first, the watch was only a night-time activity. Later in the larger towns and cities it evolved into a 24 hour activity and became a paid professional force. At first, following the English tradition all adult males were required to serve as a part of the watch. As more males attempted to evade their service in the watch and many hired others to take their place, the volunteers were replaced by paid persons.

In 1801, Boston became the first city to be required by law to maintain a permanent night watch. The people hired were paid fifty cents a night. The same year, Detroit appointed its first civilian full-time police officer.

The slave patrol was a distinctly American form of law enforcement. It started in the Southern states to guard against slave revolts and to capture runaway slaves. In 1837, the Charleston, South Carolina slave patrol with about 100 officers was the country's largest police force.

In 1789, the U.S. Congress created the first federal law enforcement agency when they created the office of federal marshall. In 1829, the Congress in passing the Postal Act conferred police powers to the postal department (later re-designated as the U.S. Postal Service). Later postal inspectors were appointed to enforce postal laws.

Frontier Justice

While the cities on the Eastern seaboard were concerned with law and order, there was little law and order on the colonial frontier. Accordingly, two distinct patterns of law enforcement developed— the quest for law and order in the cities on the Eastern seaboard and the lawlessness of the frontier. As a general rule, the only law enforcement officials available on the frontier were the elected county sheriffs and the appointed town marshals. Often crime fighting was a secondary duty to the sheriff. His primary concerns were collecting taxes and judicial assistance duties.

When extra help was needed by a sheriff or marshall for crime sprees or the apprehension of particularly dangerous criminals, they would call upon the male citizens of the local area to form a posse. The posse is slang for "posse comitatus," a common law descendant of King Alfred's "hue and cry." By common law, no man could refuse to serve as a member of a legally constituted posse.

Officials in a few frontier states also created their own law enforcement organizations. One of the more famous was the Texas Rangers which was formed in 1823 by Stephen Austin who hired a dozen bodyguards to protect fellow Texans from the Indians and bandits. Similar organizations included the Arizona Rangers formed in 1901 and the New Mexico Mounted Patrol (1905).

The present popular opinion of what a policeman is is based to a great extent on the image created by the Eastern press regarding the

western law man. The image created of the ideal policeman was one
who:

— was large in stature,

— harsh in attitude,

— had a low tolerance,

— extreme courage, and

— had ample firepower.

The "Law West of the Pecos." circa 1876.

Vigilantism

The lack of law enforcement caused the citizens on the frontier
to take justice into their own hands. This lead to the rise of vigilantism
on the frontier. The word **vigilante** is of Spanish origin and means
"watchman."

The vigilance groups were groups of organized citizen volunteers
that patrolled the local communities to guard against criminals. The
first vigilante movement in America occurred in Piedmont, S.C. in
1767.[9] However, the Atlantic seaboard states had very few vigilante
movements. There were vigilante groups in all the Western and

Southern states. It appears that there were at least 326 movements identified in the South and West.

Vigilantism arose as a typical response to the absence of effective law and order. The main thrust of most of the movements was to re-establish the conservative values of life, property, and law and order. Vigilante action was intended to be a clear warning to disorderly inhabitants that the newness of settlement would not provide an opportunity for ignoring the values of civilization. Most movements lasted only a few weeks or months. The vigilante movements are distinguished from the lynch mobs in that the vigilantes had a regular organization (though illegal) and existed for a definite period of time (though possibly a short one). Richard Maxwell Brown states that there were two models of vigilantism; the socially constructive model that dealt with a problem of disorder straightforwardly and then disbanded, and the socially destructive model that encountered such strong opposition that the result was civil conflict such as feuds and range wars.[10] Brown also contends that the movements appeared in two types of situations: (1) where the regular criminal justice system was absent or ineffective, and (2) where the regular system was operating satisfactorily. In the first situation, a void was filled by the movement. In the latter situation, the vigilantism functioned as an extralegal structure that paralleled the regular system. Brown also contends that the most important result of vigilantism has not been its social-stabilizing effect but the subtle ways in which it persistently under-mined our respect for law by its repeated insistence that there are times when we may choose to obey the law or not.[11]

It appears that at one time or another vigilantism was supported by many prominent Americans. For example, President Andrew Jackson is reported to have advised Iowa settlers to punish a murderer by vigilante action. Theodore Roosevelt sought unsuccessfully to join a vigilante movement. Leland Stanford, Sr. a California Governor and founder of Stanford University was a member of a San Francisco vigilante movement in 1863.

Presently, any organized group effort by citizens designed to combat crime that is not sanctioned by official law enforcement agencies is considered a form of vigilantism. There are still vigilante movements in the United States today. They tend, however, to be less violent that in the past. The most famous movement today is probably the "Guardian Angels." To many people, the concept of vigilantism is associated with mob violence and the punishment of innocent victims.

Policing in the 19th Century

As occurred in England, the old system of law enforcement could not handle the problems caused by urbanization, industrialization, and immigration.[12] Boston had major riots in 1834, 1835, and 1837. Racial violence grew in the years before the civil war. Angry depositors stormed and destroyed banks. Despite the problems, the cities were slow in creating new police forces. New York City did not create a new police force until 1845 and Philadelphia finally created a consolidated city wide police force in 1854. Two commonly accepted reasons for the delay in establishing new police forces are: 1) to the Americans, police officers dispersed throughout the community brought to mind the hated British army, and 2) others were afraid that rival politicians would gain control of the police departments and use them for their own partisan advantages.

Detroit's "Flying Squad" sped to the scene of crimes on its trusty two-horsepower vehicle.

Four theories are commonly used to explain the development of police agencies during the 19th century after the delayed start.

1. **Disorder-control theory**— explains the development in the need to control mob violence that existed in the United States during that time period.

2. **Crime-control theory**— suggests that the increases in criminal activity and the failure of the old systems of law enforcement created a perceived need for a new type of police.

3. **Class-control theory**— blames the creation of police departments on class-based economic exploitation. Advocates of this theory note that the development of new police agencies coincided with the development of urbanization and industrialization. According to those who support this theory, the police are merely tools used by those in power to suppress the lower classes.

4. **Urban dispersion theory**— holds that many of the urban police departments were created just because other cities had them.[13]

Policing in the Early 20th Century

At the turn of the century, politics influenced every aspect of the American police agencies. For example, to obtain an appointment to the New York City Police Department, all one needed to do was to pay $300 to the Tammany Hall political machine. Officers were selected entirely on the basis of their political connections. In most cases, the composition of the local police department reflected the ethnic and religious makeup of the cities. Police officers had no job security and could be fired at will. It was not unusual for an entire police force to be fired after a new mayor was elected.

Few departments had any formal training requirements. New officers were handed a badge, a baton, and a copy of department rules (if any). The first police academy was formed in Cincinnati in 1888, but it lasted only a few years. In 1895, New York City started a special training course for new officers, but the course covered only the use of a pistol. It wasn't until 1909 that New York City offered training other than weapons training for new officers. As late as 1913, the New

York Police Academy gave no tests and all students were automatically passed.

For the most part, officers patrolled on foot. The foot patrols were, however, inefficient. The officers were thinly spread. For example, the foot patrols in Chicago were often longer than four miles. The lack of a communications system made it difficult for officers to respond to crime and disorder. Supervision was weak, and officers could easily avoid patrolling by spending their time in the local bars and restaurants.

The world's first police car was a Detroit Police Model T Ford with homemade antenna. (Courtesy of the Detroit Police Department).

Reform Movement

As police agencies slowly evolved in the latter part of the 19th century, the control of the departments by the local politicians impeded effective law enforcement and created an atmosphere of corruption. In the 1850s to curb police corruption, community leaders in many of the cities created police administrative boards with the power to oversee police agencies. For the most part, the boards failed to curb police corruption since the private citizens appointed lacked the necessary expertise in the intricacies of police work.

In some cities, including New York City, the police departments were taken over by state legislatures. These takeovers resulted in police departments that were funded by local budgets but under the control of state legislators. Since most state legislatures at that time were controlled by rural politicians, the control of the police in those cities was also under the control of the rural politicians.

The International Association of Chiefs of Police (IACP) was formed in 1902. One of its first actions was to advocate a national clearing house for criminal identification. The IACP became the leading voice for police reform. They called for the creation of a civil-service police force, the removal of political influence and control, and the centralized organizational structure to curb the power of precinct captains.

The first police labor union was the Fraternal Order of Police (FOP) which was formed in 1915. The FOP prohibited striking and accepted police of all ranks. Also in 1915, the International Association of Policewomen was formed in Baltimore, Maryland.

On September 9, 1919, the Boston police went on strike. The strike was caused by the police officers' dissatisfaction with the status that they held in society and their low salaries. Earlier, the police had formed the Boston Social Club. They then voted to change the club to a union and to affiliate with the American Federation of Labor (AFL). As a result of the strike, rioting and looting broke out. Then Governor Calvin Coolidge mobilized the state militia to take over the city. Public support was strongly against the police and the strike was broken. All the striking officers were fired and replaced by recruits.

The unsuccessful strike is credited with ending police unionism and taking police departments out of the hands of autocratic police administrators. In addition, crime commissions on the local, state, and national level began to investigate the ability of the criminal justice system to deal with crime. The most famous of those commissions was the Wickersham Commission. The Wickersham Commission and other reformers expressed a common concern: "get the police out of politics and get politics out of the police."[14]

The early police reformers appeared to share the following common goals:

— the establishment of a civil service type system to replace the political patronage system;

— increased job security for police supervisors;

— centralized policing within each city or urban area; and

— the implementation of standards for hiring, training, and promotion of officers.

Artist's conception of the brutal police riots which erupted during the late 1850s. The above depicts the riot in the city of New York between the state appointed force named the Metropolitan Police and the City Police.

Wickersham Commission

The Wickersham Commission was appointed in 1931 by President Herbert Hoover. It was officially known as the National Commission of Law Observance and Enforcement. While the commission did a detailed analysis of the justice system and helped establish the philosophy of treatment and rehabilitation of prisoners, it is best remembered for its exposition of police brutality and corruption. Another finding of the commission was that the Volstead Act (prohibition) was not enforced because it was basically unenforceable.

The commission issued a multi-volume report. Two volumes dealt directly with the police: "Lawlessness in Law Enforcement" and "The Police." August Vollmer was the principle author of the volume "The Police." Vollmer's contributions to law enforcement are discussed later in this chapter.

The commission concluded that the average police supervisor's term of office was too short and that his or her responsibility to political officials made the position insecure. The commission found a lack of effective, efficient, and honest police officers and that there was no intensive effort to educate or train officers. Other faults found in police departments included the lack of communications and necessary equipment. The commission also concluded that too many varied duties were placed on individual police officers. Unfortunately, at the time the commission report was issued, America was in the depths of the depression and criminal justice reform became less important. Accordingly, only few changes were made in police departments as a result of the report of the commission.

EXHIBIT 5-1

August Vollmer

August Vollmer was first a town marshall and then chief of police in Berkeley, California from 1905 to 1932. He was the leading spokesperson for the professionalization of police departments. He is considered the "Dean of Modern Police Administration." His contributions to policing include the early use of motorized patrols, the advocating of a centralized fingerprint system that was later established by the FBI, utilization of psychological screening for police applicants, creation of the first juvenile unit, and emphasizing the importance of college training for police officers. Vollmer wrote several books on police administration. In 1923, he was interim Chief of Police for Los Angeles. He suggested many reforms for the then corrupt police department.

Vollmer was instrumental in the establishment of a criminology program at the University of California and assisted in the development of the first degree-granting law enforcement program at San Jose State College (now California State University, San Jose).

The Kefauver Committee

After World War II, the traditional problems of corruption, graft, and bribery were still common to police agencies. In response to these problems, in 1950, the U.S. Senate established the Senate Crime Committee. Senator Estes Kefauver was the first chair of the committee which became known as the Kefauver Committee. For the first time, a senate investigation was televised to the American public. The public was treated to revelations that included the fact that many police departments were lead by corrupt top-level administrators. There was an immediate public outcry for action. Accordingly, a new series of police reform efforts were made.

As a result of that committee and other public pressures, the concept of the "new police professional" developed. The lessons of the first half of the century were applied during the latter half of the century. While the reforms were a welcomed change, unfortunately, the image of the "new professional" resulted in a depersonalization of policing in the 1950s. We attempted to demand uniformity and downgraded individualism in our march to professionalism.

EXHIBIT 5-2

O. W. Wilson

Orlando Winfield Wilson, better known as O. W. Wilson, worked for August Vollmer in Berkeley. Wilson, after obtaining his degree from the University of California, became Chief of Police in Fullerton, California. However, he lasted only a short time because his ideas about modern law enforcement were not acceptable to the local citizens in Fullerton. In 1928, he became Chief of Police in Wichita, Kansas. He turned a corrupt police department into the "West Point of law enforcement." Wilson left Wichita in 1937 because his strict enforcement of vice laws alienated the city's politicians.

Orlando W. Wilson — One of the most respected names in the history of American law enforcement.

From 1939 to 1960, Wilson was a professor of Criminology at UC Berkeley. In 1950, his book *Municipal Police Administration* was published. Many consider this book the most influential book written on police administration.

Policing and the Great Society

During the period from 1960 to 1980, policing underwent a great deal of turmoil and crisis. Some of the reasons for the turmoil and crisis include: Supreme Court decisions emphasizing the concept of "individual rights" over "law and order"; the "hippie" movement; the unpopular war in Southeast Asia; the civil rights movement; and the rising crime rates.

The U.S. Supreme Court decision of *Ohio v. Mapp* in 1961 marked a decade wherein the Court began to scrutinize police activities. The period from 1961 to 1972 has been referred to as the "criminal justice revolution" or "the due process revolution." During this period, the Court restricted what the police could do. The Mapp case imposed the exclusionary rule on the states. Police were also told what they could and could not do in the areas of search and seizure, interrogations, and apprehensions of persons suspected of criminal behavior. Many new restrictions were placed on the police. These restrictions are discussed in Chapter 7.

The police objected loudly to the *Mapp* case, the *Miranda* case (which dealt with in-custody interrogation) and other criminal cases decided in favor of the defendants. Police advocates contended that the Court had handcuffed the officers and had favored the rights of criminals at the expense of the rights of victims and law-abiding citizens.

The 1960s was an active time period for the civil rights movement. Riots occurred in cities in New York and New Jersey and in Philadelphia, Los Angeles, Chicago, San Diego, Omaha, Cleveland, and Detroit. The riots were caused by the institutionalized racism that existed in most of our cities during that period of time. The specific acts, however, that precipitated the riots were often police actions such as routine traffic stops or other law enforcement confrontations. In addition, the police were used in an attempt to restore peace. Accordingly, the police became the convenient targets of angry minority groups. To add to the problem, most police officers were not properly trained nor equipped to respond appropriately.

The police responded to the unrest by establishing police-community relations programs and adding neighborhood storefront offices to facilitate communications with citizens. Many researchers, however, felt that the police-community relations programs had little impact on day-to-day operations. Civil rights leaders demanded that civilian review boards be established to review complaints about police misconduct. Such boards were established in many cities including Philadelphia and New York City. However, by 1966 most of the boards had been abolished.

In 1965, President Johnson called for an escalation of the Vietnam war. Our involvement in the war was never solidly supported by the public. By 1965, it was evident that the governments we supported in South Vietnam were corrupt, an increasing number of our youth (especially minorities) were being killed, and money needed to fight the "War on Poverty" and other social ills at home was being used in South Vietnam. The antiwar movement grew in strength. To a large extent, the antiwar movement was a young white-middle-class movement. The police who, unfortunately, had been involved in the middle of the civil rights movement as the "guardians of public order" were again brought into the middle of the antiwar demonstrations. The most famous conflict was the one between the police and the antiwar activists at the Democratic National Convention in Chicago in 1968. From this confrontation came charges of police brutality and other misconduct.

The 1960s was also a period of rising crime rates. The police departments grew in the 1960s and early 1970s, mainly because of the public fear of crime. The number of sworn officers in the United States increased from 333,000 in 1960 to about 555,000 in 1980.[15] However, in 1986, a survey concluded that almost half of the police budgets had not kept pace with inflation and that almost a third of the departments had experienced budget cuts since 1980.

In response to the increasing public concern regarding crime, President Johnson appointed the President's Commission on Law Enforcement and Administration of Justice in 1965, more popularly known as the President's Crime Commission. The commission published a report in 1967 entitled "The Challenge of Crime in a Free

Society." The report offered many recommendations for reform. It endorsed the need to professionalize our police by higher police personnel standards, more training, and better management and supervision. The report subconsciously implied that we could solve the crime problem by spending more money on crime prevention.

The Law Enforcement Assistance Administration (LEAA) was formed within the U.S. Department of Justice by the Omnibus Crime Control and Safe Streets Act of 1968. LEAA spent approximately 8 billion dollars between 1969 and 1980. The LEAA was responsible during its existence for assisting thousands of police officers with a college education. In 1960, only 20 percent of the police officers had any college education; by 1988 the percentages had increased to over 65 percent. The LEAA also funded numerous applied research projects and assisted police departments in upgrading their departments. The LEAA went out of existence in 1982 when Congress failed to appropriate any lead funding for it.

The 1980s was a period of fiscal austerity for police departments. Most of the federal grants were no longer available. As noted earlier, many of the police departments' budgets did not keep up with the rate of inflation. The 1980s was also a period when the task-force approach was used to combat crime problems. The task-forces included: CRASH, in Los Angeles, to deal with the gang related criminal homicides; and DART, in Houston, to attempt to reduce street-level drug sales. This was also a period of technological revolution. The use of in-car computers and cellular phones made the communications network between the officer on the street and headquarters more reliable and secure. Computers also permitted better inter-agency communications and basic record keeping.

The late 1980s was also the period of President Bush's War on Drugs. This war was based on two premises: first, drugs are a major source of police corruption; and second, the drug dealers and suppliers had almost unlimited resources. Accordingly, federal assistance was needed. The major efforts used to combat this war placed heavy demands on the limited resources and training available to most local policing agencies. Unfortunately, it appears that the results have been less than desired.

During the period 1960 to 1990, the profile of the police officer changed significantly. The number of sworn police officers who were female or of a racial minority group increased during that period. The number of black officers increased from 3.6 percent in 1960 to about 11 percent in 1992.

PUBLIC-PRIVATE CONTEMPORARY LAW ENFORCEMENT SYSTEMS

In this section, we will examine the contemporary law enforcement systems in the United States. Presently there are over 15,000 state and local police departments in the United States. Approximately 80 percent of the agencies are local police departments. About 20 percent are sheriff's departments. There are only 49 state police or highway patrol agencies. Federal law enforcement agencies are a very small fraction of the total law enforcement industry. As noted earlier, American policing is highly fragmented. Accordingly, any generalizations about police departments are usually made toward a "typical" department.

Citizen as a Police Officer

As noted in Chapter 1, citizens have traditionally been involved in the criminal justice process. Their involvement includes: the reporting of crime; crime prevention programs, like neighborhood watch and marking our property; and supporting local police departments. Historically, citizens have been more directly involved than they are now. For example, most states have laws that require citizens to assist police officers when requested and to join when requested the posse comitatus. These laws are seldom used now. A third and more controversial involvement is membership in those groups known as vigilantes.

Public Police Officer

The public police refers to those police employed, trained and paid by a governmental agency and whose purpose is to serve the general interest of all citizens through the enforcement of our criminal laws.

Private Police Officer

Allan Pinkerton is often credited with being the first modern day private security officer. He worked mainly for the railroads and factory owners. He provided security during the union strikes. Presently, private security is one of the fastest growing segments of law enforcement.

Private police refers to those police-type organizations whose members are employed and paid to serve specific purposes, within the law, by individuals or organizations. A city cop is a public police officer. The guard at the local bank is a private police officer. [*Note*: In many situations, an individual may be both a public and a private officer.] Many municipal police officers work part-time for private employers. In these cases, the officers, when on their part-time jobs, are both public and private. One research report estimates that by the year 2000, there will be 750,000 private contract guards and 410,000 proprietary security forces in the United States.[16]

Public Safety Officer

In some communities, there is an integration of police, firefighters, and other services like emergency medical services into the concept of a public safety officer. In some cases, this integration is limited to administrative purposes. In other cases, the officer is expected to perform joint duties involving public safety. In addition, often the term "public safety officer" is used to include police officers, firefighters, etc.

Police Services

In a typical police department, the law enforcement agency performs the following services to the citizens of the community:

— prevents crime;
— investigates crimes and apprehends criminals;
— maintains order; and
— provides other miscellaneous services.[17]

EXHIBIT 5-3

COPS

As noted earlier, the slang term for British police officers is "bobby." The American slang term is "cops." However, the origin of the term "cops" is not as clear as the origin of the term "bobby." One dictionary suggests that the word is short for "copper" which means to capture. Another dictionary suggests that the word emerged as a slang for police because the early city police officers wore uniforms that had large copper stars on them.

DISCUSSION QUESTIONS

1. Explain the present day concepts of policing that we obtained from the English?

2. Why were the cities slow in establishing city police departments?

3. What are Sir Robert Peel's contributions to policing?

4. What was the reason that the English first started requiring their police officers to wear distinct uniforms?

ENDNOTES

1 Carl B. Klockars and Stephen D. Mastrofski, *Thinking About Police*, (New York: McGraw-Hill, 1991).

2 Egon Bittner, *The Functions of Police in Modern Society*, (Washington D.C.: Government Printing Office, 1971).

3 Roy R. Roberg and Jack Kuykendall, *Police & Society*, (Belmont, Ca.: Wadsworth, 1992).

4 Samuel Walker, *The Police in America*, (New York: McGraw-Hill, 1992).

5 Patrick Pringle, *The Thief-Takers*, (London: Museum Press, 1958).

6 Charles Reith, *A Short History of the British Police*, (London: Oxford University Press, 1948).

7 T. A. Critchley, *A History of Police in England and Whales*, 2nd ed., (Montclair, NJ: Patterson Smith, 1972).

8 Samuel Walker, *Popular Justice: History of American Criminal Justice*, (New York: Oxford University Press, 1980).

9 Richard Maxwell Brown, "Vigilante Policing," in *Klockars and Mastrofski* (1991), pp. 58-64.

10 Ibid. p. 60.

11 Ibid. p. 72.

12 Samuel Walker, *The Police in America*, 2nd ed., (New York: McGraw-Hill, 1992).

13 Roy R. Roberg and Jack Kuykendall, (1993), p. 58.

14 Samuel Walker, *Popular Justice: History of American Criminal Justice*, (New York: Oxford University Press, 1980), p. 134.

15 Samuel Walker, *The Police In America*, 2nd ed., (New York: McGraw-Hill, 1992), p. 27.

16 Melissa Davis, Richard Lundman, and Ramiro Martinez, Jr., "Private Corporate Justice: Store Police, Shoplifters, and Civil Recovery," *Social Problems*, vol. 38, (1991): pp. 395-408.

17 Samuel Walker, (1992), p. 37.

ORGANIZATION AND OPERATION OF LAW ENFORCEMENT SYSTEMS

The act of organizing is indispensable to proper management, and without some form of organizational structure, most police operations could not be carried out.

—*O.W.Wilson*

I n this chapter, we will focus on the organization and operation of law enforcement agencies. Before we study them, we will take a brief look at the basic goals of a law enforcement agency. Henry Tosi states that all organizations have three goals which may be either intermeshed or independent. The goals are (1) growth, (2) stability, and (3) interaction. The interaction goal refers to organizations which exist primarily to provide a medium for association of their members with others. While Tosi was referring to business organizations, these goals apply equally to police departments.[1]

The primary goal of a police department should be to serve and help protect the public. It would also appear that police departments have the secondary goals of growth, stability, and interaction in order to help in accomplishing the primary goal of serving and protecting the public. All policy decisions made by the top management should be made only after considering how the decision will help the department accomplish its goals with the maximum utilization of resources.

LOCAL LAW ENFORCEMENT

Metropolitan Police

As noted earlier, city police constitute the majority of the sworn police officers in the United States. Police departments range in size from the 33,000 in New York City to one officer departments in smaller cities. More than half of all police departments have 10 or less sworn officers. Nearly 1,000 departments have only one officer. The FBI estimates that approximately 390,000 officers and civilians work in city police departments in the U.S.

Almost all police departments, from the largest to the smallest, have the same standard goals as noted above. Most maintain jurisdiction over law enforcement matters within their city boundaries. There are a number of auxiliary police agencies that assist them. The most common auxiliary agencies are park police, airport police, transit police, and university police. The auxiliary police are created to handle special problems or special jurisdictional areas like the airports and parks. The relationships between the city police and the auxiliary agencies differ in almost every city. In general, the auxiliary agencies have carved out a small portion of the city police's jurisdiction (normally geographic) over law enforcement. In most cases, in those limited geographic areas like our airports, both the city police and the auxiliary police have concurrent jurisdiction. Police departments are headed by a police chief who is appointed by the mayor or city council.

Law Enforcement Workforce
percentage distribution by employer

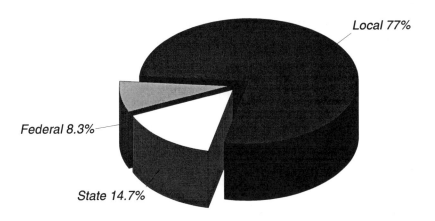

Local 77%

Federal 8.3%

State 14.7%

Source: U.S. Dept. of Justice

Rural Law Enforcement

While city police have jurisdiction over law enforcement within their respective city, outside of city boundaries the jurisdiction is normally with the sheriff's office. In all states, except Rhode Island and Hawaii, the sheriff is an elected official. The county sheriff's office has evolved from that of the early sheriff in England. There are approximately 3,400 rural law enforcement agencies in the United States.

The duties of a sheriff vary according to size and population of the county. The sheriff's role is more complex than the role of the urban police. The county sheriff may serve in three major capacities: (1) law enforcement, (2) service to the courts, and (3) corrections. In many rural counties, the sheriff is also the coroner. In most counties, the sheriff is the process server for court processes such as summons and writs of execution. In general, the sheriff's law enforcement duties are restricted to the unincorporated areas of the county. In counties where the entire county is within an incorporated area (like San Francisco), the sheriff generally has no law enforcement duties. In addition, most sheriffs are charged with the responsibilities of operating the county jails.

Lee Brown classifies the sheriff departments into four models. First, is the **"full service" model**. This is the department that performs in all three major capacities— law enforcement, courts, and corrections. The second model is the **"law enforcement" model** where the department has only law enforcement duties. A third model is the **"civil-judicial" model** where the sheriff's duties are limited to court service with no law enforcement or corrections responsibilities. The fourth model is the **"correctional-judicial" model** where the sheriff has no law enforcement duties but operates the jails and provides service to the courts. The San Francisco Sheriff's Department could be considered a correctional-judicial model, since the San Francisco police department has the law enforcement responsibilities. [*Note*: The entire county is within the city limits of San Francisco.][2]

Sheriff's departments have traditionally been considered the weak link in the law enforcement chain. One reason for this status has been the partisan nature of the sheriff's departments. Sheriffs are elected in all but a few counties. The sheriff must be political in order to be elected. The fact that one is a good campaigner is no guarantee that one will be a good law enforcement administrator. After the sheriff is elected, unlike the chief of police, the sheriff is accountable to no one until the next election. In recent years, great strives have been made to improve the quality of sheriff's departments.

The improvements have been motivated, to some extent, by the work of professional organizations such as the National Sheriffs' Association. The improvements include upgrading the entrance requirements for deputies, increasing in-service training, better pay and better working conditions, and the establishment of civil service protection for deputies.

STATE POLICE

Unlike city police, state police are generally created by the legislatures to deal with specific problems. Presently, Hawaii is the only state without a state police. Historically, the state police do not have general law enforcement jurisdiction. The trend, however, is to vest the state police with such authority. For example, there are presently 23 state police agencies in the United States with general law enforcement duties. The largest and best known state police agency is the California Highway Patrol (CHP). The CHP specializes in the protection of motorists and directs most of their attention to the enforcement of laws involving traffic safety. The CHP has approximately 6,200 officers and 2,500 civilian employees. The smallest state police unit is probably Wyoming with about 160 officers and 55 civilian employees.

NATIONAL LAW ENFORCEMENT AGENCIES

There is no federal law enforcement agency with unlimited jurisdiction. Unlike Italy or France, there is no national police force. Each federal law enforcement agency has been created to enforce specific laws and cope with particular problems or issues. The more important agencies are discussed below.

U.S. Department of Justice

The legal arm of the federal government is the U.S. Department of Justice which is headed by the attorney general. The attorney general is appointed by the president and confirmed by the senate. The attorney general, like other cabinet members, serves at the pleasure of the president. The general duties of the Department of Justice are to: (1) enforce federal laws, (2) provide representation in court when the U.S. is a party to a court action, and (3) conduct investigations of possible violations of federal law through one of its agencies.

The chief divisions within the department include:

— the Civil Rights Division which protects citizens from illegal discrimination;

— the Tax Division which prosecutes tax violators; and

— the Criminal Division which prosecutes non-tax violations of federal criminal law.

The Federal Bureau of Investigation (FBI) is an investigative agency, not a police agency. Its jurisdiction is limited to investigating violations of federal law. The FBI is the most glamorous of the federal law enforcement agencies. It was started in 1870 when the attorney general hired investigators to investigate violations of the Mann Act (forbidding transportation of women across state lines for immoral purposes). The investigators were formalized into the Bureau of Investigation in 1908. In 1930, the Bureau was re-organized into the FBI under the direction of J. Edgar Hoover. He directed the FBI until 1972.

The FBI currently employs about 21,500 people. In addition, the FBI provides a number of services to local law enforcement agencies including its sophisticated crime laboratory, Uniform Crime Reports, the National Crime Information Center, and a vast fingerprint file. The Director of the FBI is under the direction of the attorney general.

The Drug Enforcement Administration (DEA) was organized in 1973 when a group of drug enforcement units including the Bureau of Narcotics and Dangerous Drugs were combined. Agents of the DEA assist local and state agencies in their investigation of illegal drug use and trafficking. The DEA also conducts international investigations of drug operations that impact the U.S. The DEA is also under the administrative supervision of the attorney general. The DEA currently employs approximately 5,000 persons.

Other agencies under the Department of Justice include the U.S. Marshals and the Immigration and Naturalization Services (INS). The

U.S. Marshals Office is the oldest federal enforcement agency. In the frontier days, they were the primary law enforcement in many western areas. Presently, the U.S. marshals are court officers who help implement federal court orders, transport prisoners to federal court, and track down federal fugitives. The INS is responsible for the administration of immigration laws, the exclusion and deportation of illegal aliens, and the naturalization of aliens.

In 1924 an unknown young attorney, John Edgar Hoover, was appointed Director of the FBI .

Treasury Department

There are also several law enforcement agencies under the Treasury Department. They include the Secret Service; Bureau of Alcohol, Tobacco, and Firearms; the Customs Service; and in times of peace, the Coast Guard.

The Secret Service was established in 1865 to investigate counterfeiting and forgery of government currency and checks. It is best known today for its role in protecting the president and other government officials. Presently there are about 1,500 agents in the service.

The agents of the Bureau of Alcohol, Tobacco and Firearms (ATF) are treasury agents with the responsibility to enforce federal tax laws and regulations relating to alcohol, tobacco and firearms. In 1993, the ATF became highly visible for their involvement in the Branch Davidian Cult standoff in Waco, Texas.

The Customs Service inspectors are responsible for enforcing U.S. laws and regulations regarding the importation of foreign goods into this country. They are also responsible for collecting import duties and fees.

The U.S. Coast Guard performs both military and domestic law enforcement duties. In time of war, the Guard is under the direction of the Department of Defense. In times of peace, the Guard in under the control of the Secretary of the Treasury. During peacetime, the Guard enforces boating laws and helps prevent violations of customs and immigration laws and regulations.

National Guard

The National Guard serves both a military and a domestic role. As a military unit, it is under federal control. As a domestic law enforcement agency, it is under the control of the governor. The Guard may be activated by the governor when there is a natural disaster or to help enforce the law in times of civil unrest.

STYLES OF POLICING

A Harvard University symposium divided American policing into three historical eras. The administrative approach to each era provides us with three different styles of policing. The first period, from 1840 to 1930, was characterized by the interrelationships between the police and politics. The second era was the reform era which lasted from about 1930 to the 1970s. The reform area was characterized by the growth of police professionalism. The present era, from the 1970s to present, is the era of community problem solving. The present era is characterized by a concept of a partnership between the police and the community and the stressing of the service role of police.[3]

James Q. Wilson contends that each era contributed to three styles of policing. His three styles are:

1) the watchman style (from the first period),

2) the legalistic style (from the growth of police professionalism era), and

3) the service style (from the present era).[4]

The watchman style of policing has an overriding concern for order maintenance. The police are employed to keep the peace. The average officer sees his or her goal as one of controlling criminal activity and disruptive behavior. Often informal police intervention is used to keep the peace, such as persuasion and threats. In some cases, "roughing up" tactics by the police are used on disruptive persons. Many researchers have condemned this style of policing as being focused on the lower to lower-middle class neighborhoods within a city, especially those neighborhoods where a fair amount of violence or physical abuse is traditionally present.

The legalistic style focuses on enforcing the law "to the letter." The legalistic style has also been called the "laissez faire" style because of its "hands-off" approach to behaviors which are not criminal in nature. Often under this style of policing, police do not get involved in community disputes that do not break the law. Uniform, impartial arrests or citations for all violators of the law characterize the legalistic style. An example of this style of policing would be to issue speeding tickets to motorists who are caught driving 56 mph in a 55 mph zone. This style of policing tends to increase the number of criminal complaints filed.

The service style of policing is marked by a concern to provide service to the community and to assist the community in solving problems with less emphasis on the enforcement of the law. The police see themselves as helpers rather than enforcers of the law. Often persons who commit criminal acts are not prosecuted if the individuals agree to seek voluntary treatment from behavior modification courses. Instead of arresting, the officers counsel, issue written warnings, or issue oral instructions to offenders in many cases. The service style of policing tends to blend into the characteristics of the community. [*Note*: The service style of policing tends to reduce the number of criminal complaints filed especially in misdemeanor cases.]

STRUCTURE AND OPERATION

Police departments in the United States are not substantially different from the original British style of policing.[5] There are certain organizational features common to almost all urban departments. The three most important features are bureaucracy, semi-military model, and organizational environment.

The International City Manager's Association *Municipal Police Administration* offers six general principles of organization for law enforcement agencies:

1) The work should be apportioned among the various individuals and units, according to some logical plan. (Homogeneity)

2) Lines of authority and responsibility should be made as definite and direct as possible. (Delineation of responsibility)

3) There is a limit to the number of subordinates who can be supervised effectively by one officer, and this limit seldom should be exceeded. (Span of Control)

4) There should be "unity of command" throughout the organization. (Subordinates under the direct control of only one supervisor)

5) Responsibility cannot be placed without the delegation of commensurate authority, and authority should not be delegated to a person without holding him/her accountable for its use. (Delegation of responsibility)

6) The efforts of the organizational units and of their component members must be coordinated so that all will be directed harmoniously toward the accomplishment of the police purpose. The components thus coordinated will enable the organization to function as a well-integrated unit.[6]

Bureaucracy

Bureaucracy is a form of organizational structure that was developed by Max Weber, a German social scientist. Bureaucracy is defined as (1) government by bureaus, administrators, and petty officials, (2) the body of officials and administrators of a government or government departments, or (3) the concentration of power in administrators. Presently, bureaucracy is a term generally cast in an unfavorable light. We blame a lot of our problems and inactions on the "bureaucracy."

Max Weber (1864-1920) is famous for his study on bureaucracy.[7] Weber was convinced that the organizational forms that were appropriate for a rural society were no longer useful in an industrialized world, and as those forms declined, a new organizational type, the bureaucracy, would be created. According to him, a bureaucracy is an organization that has numerous formalized rules and regulations and therefore can be administered by bureaus.

Weber thought that a bureaucracy was the most rational system of organization available. He felt that managers who want to obtain efficiency and optimal organizational performance were forced to use a bureaucratic form of organization. One constant criticism of bureaucracy is that it dehumanizes the employees in its use of standardized procedures for completing task assignments. Rather than defending the dehumanizing aspects of a bureaucratic form, Weber stated that bureaucracy was an irresistible organizational wave.

As noted earlier, bureaucracy is the basic organizational structure of police departments.[8] Applying Weber's theory to a police agency, for it to be rational (i.e., a bureaucracy) the agency must contain the following elements:

1) A continuous organization of official functions bound by formal rules — According to Weber, bureaucracies have well-articulated policies which are impersonally and uniformly applied through-

out the organization. Police departments uniformly have well-articulated polices which are impersonally and uniformly applied throughout the departments.

2) A specific division of labor — Bureaucratic organizations have divided labor to an intensive degree of refinement. Tasks are broken down into the most minute particles of specialization so that even the newest unskilled employee can master a task with a minimum of skill and training. Most police departments have divided their tasks and assigned officers to specialized tasks such as patrol, communications, traffic, etc.

3) Hierarchy of authority — This involves the progressive concentration of control over subordinate units in successively higher levels of authority in an organization's vertical command structure. Police departments are generally organized in successively higher levels of authority in a vertical command structure with the police chief at the apex.

4) Expertise — Employees are selected by comparing objective standards established for the organization for adequate performance of a job with the qualifications of the applicant. The chief criteria is how well the potential employee is suited by way of education, training, knowledge, and skill to perform the assigned function in the organization. This element is present in the average police department.

5) Written records — Bureaucratic organizations keep elaborate records for the purpose of achieving uniformity of action. Police departments are noted for keeping elaborate records and the establishment of standard or standing operating procedures (SOPs) to achieve uniformity of action.

Semi-Military Model

Police departments not only tend to be bureaucratic, but are also modeled loosely after the military style of organization. The characteristics in law enforcement agencies taken from the military style include:

— centralized command structure with a rigid chain of command;

— clearly marked lines of communications;

— strong discipline;

— differentiation between ranks or positions;

— authoritarian leadership; and

— status quo emphasis.

The operational units within a police department are also similarly classified to the military units of line, staff, and auxiliary units.

Performing an officer inspection at the beginning of a shift.

Police Organizational Environment

Police departments are "open" systems as opposed to "closed" systems. A **closed system** is a system that is independent of external influences. An **open system** is one which is not independent of external influences. The police are influenced by the political, economical, and social pressures of the community in which the department is located. The external (environmental) influences on a police department require the department to be flexible to adapt to those pressures.

Organizational Clarification

To prevent internal conflict, members of an organization need to understand their duties and the duties and assignments of others. Two devices commonly used to demonstrate the structure of an organization and inform members of the organization of their duties and assignments are organizational charts and position descriptions.

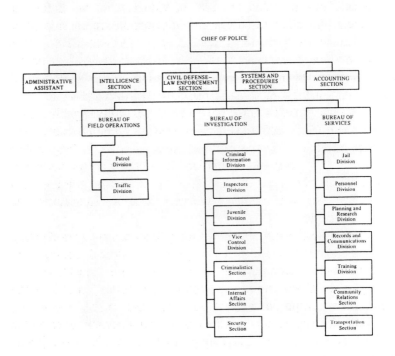

A typical organization chart of a police department serving a city of 500,000.

Organizational charts are pictorial representations of the agency and they map lines of authority for the entire organization. One major limitation of organizational charts is that they fail to delineate the informal structure that exists in every organization. Each position within a police department normally has a position description. Each position description should include basic job functions and their relationship to others.

Management

Police management is normally divided into three broad categories: top management, middle management, and first-line supervision. Top management is the chief and his or her immediate subordinates (deputy chiefs or assistant chiefs). Middle management are generally the captains and the lieutenants. First-line supervision includes those leaders who operate at the performance level, usually the sergeant.

A police department has two major inputs—human and nonhuman resources. Human inputs are the individuals who work for the department. All other resources and information are considered as nonhuman inputs. A manager has the duty to coordinate the activities of the human inputs and the expenditures of nonhuman inputs. Whether the department is small or large, management must work toward making sure that the department's missions are accomplished.

Top managers determine policy, set organizational goals, direct program execution, coordinate the processes of administration, and are responsible for the department attaining its goals. In large police departments, environmental conditions require that the top managers be generalists who can view their department and its programs as a whole. The essence of top management is the ability to influence the actions of people.

Middle-level management's primary functions include activating departmental policies, maintaining operational control, setting standards, reviewing accomplishments, and utilizing personnel to accomplish goals. While top management sets policy, middle-level management's responsibility is to translate those policies into action.

First-line supervisors are the persons who actually oversee the work of the line officers. Their duties include devising work plans, making assignments, training, and evaluating the persons they supervise. Other duties include maintaining records, developing team spirit, presenting departmental policy to subordinates, and cooperating with managers above them and other first-line supervisors.

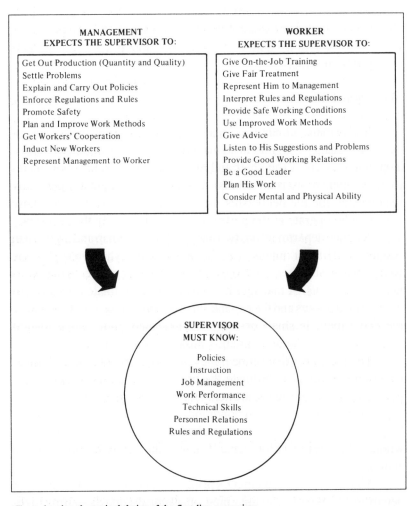

MANAGEMENT EXPECTS THE SUPERVISOR TO:	WORKER EXPECTS THE SUPERVISOR TO:
Get Out Production (Quantity and Quality)	Give On-the-Job Training
Settle Problems	Give Fair Treatment
Explain and Carry Out Policies	Represent Him to Management
Enforce Regulations and Rules	Interpret Rules and Regulations
Promote Safety	Provide Safe Working Conditions
Plan and Improve Work Methods	Use Improved Work Methods
Get Workers' Cooperation	Give Advice
Induct New Workers	Listen to His Suggestions and Problems
Represent Management to Worker	Provide Good Working Relations
	Be a Good Leader
	Plan His Work
	Consider Mental and Physical Ability

SUPERVISOR MUST KNOW:

Policies
Instruction
Job Management
Work Performance
Technical Skills
Personnel Relations
Rules and Regulations

Chart showing the typical duties of the first-line supervisor.

Police organizational units can be classified into three broad areas: functional areas, geographic units and chronological units.[9] The typical functional units of a police department include: the bureau, the division, the section, and the unit.

The **bureau** is generally the largest organizational subunit of the department. Bureaus are usually commanded by a deputy chief in large departments and captains or lieutenants in small departments. The function of the bureau is to supervise and administer the sub-units of the bureau. **Divisions** usually perform either general or specialized services. The commander of a division is usually a captain in large police departments. Common divisions include Uniform/Patrol, Traffic, and Investigative divisions. A **section** is a sub-division of a division and is generally responsible for certain types of activities common to the entire division. For example the homicide section of the Investigative Division would be responsible for investigating homicides. In large departments, the section chief is a lieutenant. In small departments that do not have sections, the functions are handled by the division. In addition to the above functional units, often task forces are used for unique problems that are of limited duration.

The **geographic units** are generally the area, the precinct, the sector, the beat, the route, and the post. The area is the largest and is usually used only in the larger departments. For example, the city may be divided into four areas. The precinct is the next largest in the major agencies and the largest in the smaller agencies. Patrol sectors are usually organized by precincts. The sectors usually are subdivisions of a precinct and contain several beats. The beat is the basic patrol unit. Posts are physical places where officers are assigned.

The **chronological units** of policing are the shifts and the platoon. The shift defines the time of day the officers work. The platoon refers generally to a group of officers assigned to one shift.

ADMINISTRATIVE PROCESSES

Administrative process refers to those interrelated means employed on a continuing basis by which an administrator achieves his or her organizational goals and objectives.[10] There are five generally accepted processes that apply to law enforcement agencies:

1) planning,

2) organizing,

3) applying resources,

4) direction, and

5) control.

Planning is the process of determining the objectives and goals of the agency. There are three basic steps in planning: formulation of objectives, assessment of the means to achieve the objectives, and the preparation of programs to accomplish the objectives. Planning should be considered an on going process to meet the constantly changing situations that affect a law enforcement agency. It is both long range and short range in nature and should relate both to policy and operations.

Organizing is the process by which group activities are structured and authority relationships are formalized. Organizing should permit the organization to accomplish its goals and objectives with the most efficient use of the total resources of the agency.

Staffing and **assembling resources** is the attempt of management to use its limited resources to accomplish its goals and objectives. Staffing is similar to organizing in that both are designed to make the most of limited resources. **Organizing** pertains to the design of the form of the organization; staffing refers to assigning personnel to the positions created by the organizing process.

The function of direction is to get personnel to accomplish their duties. Direction also involves the establishment of working relationships at each working level from top to bottom. Direction in law enforcement agencies is normally accomplished through orders, both oral and written.

Staff control is the process that measures existing job performances and corrects the performance of those whose performances are considered as lacking in one way or another. Control is also considered as the process of verifying whether performances occur in conformity with departmental plans and goals.

Organization

As noted earlier, police agencies are organized on a semi-military model. The typical organization of a police agency contains operating departments of patrol, investigation, service and administration. Other departments include training and special services. The agency using the bureaucracy organizational form has a clear chain of command and the departments within the agency also have their own chain of command. The organization of individual units within a department are discussed in Chapter 8.

Accreditation

Four law enforcement associations — International Association of Chiefs of Police (IACP), National Organization of Black Law Enforcement Executives (NOBLE), National Sheriffs' Association (NSA), and Police Executive Research Forum (PERF) — have combined to form the Commission on Accreditation for Law Enforcement Agencies (CALEA). The purpose of the commission is to establish and administer an accreditation process for law enforcement agencies. Accreditation is considered one method to professionalize the police and improve police services.

Presently, CALEA has researched, developed, and adopted over 900 standards. The standards are grouped into 48 chapters. Standards are also classified as either mandatory or non-mandatory standards. The standards cover five major subject areas: (1) the role, responsibilities, and relationship with other departments; (2) organization, management, and administration; (3) law enforcement operations, operation support, and traffic law enforcement; (4) prisoner and court-related services; and (5) auxiliary and technical services.[11]

Information Management

Information management in law enforcement has expanded beyond the use of three by five cards and a simple one minute briefing at roll call. The professional must understand the operation of modern computer systems. This requires more than a knowledge of word processing programs on a microcomputer. Computers are constantly evolving and offering more alternatives to the law enforcement community.

Basic law enforcement records may vary from jurisdiction to jurisdiction, but the principles behind their utilization will remain the same. There are two basic types of reports: operational and administrative. Each serves a vital purpose and to neglect one in favor of the other is to destroy the effectiveness of any records division and ultimately the operational capability of the agency. Operational reports refer to reports dealing with police actions involving the public, crime prevention, crime fighting, etc. Administrative reports are internal reports dealing with administrative matters of the department.

The use of computers has enhanced law enforcement's ability to obtain information. With advanced computer based systems, supervisors can observe the location and status of any patrol vehicle on a particular beat.

National and regional computerized information centers provide virtually instantaneous transmission of information for use by the officer on the street. As crime becomes more sophisticated and fiscal pressures increase, law enforcement agencies will look toward increased computerization to save costs and enhance service to the public.

Police Budgets

Few cities, counties and states are financially secure in this modern age. Taxpayer revolts which decry increasing property taxes, as well as escalating capital costs, have placed municipalities between the proverbial rock and hard place. As revenues shrink or remain static, and costs of operating municipal government increases, the budgetary process and knowledge of finances becomes an increasingly critical skill for the effective police administrator.

There are several different types of budgeting methods including ceiling budgets, line-budget items, performance budgets, program budgets and zero-based budgets. The budgets themselves and the method in which they are prepared is a mechanical process that can be memorized or understood depending on the jurisdiction in which the administrator is located.

In this era of tight budgets it is incumbent upon the police administrators to continually educate city managers and elected officials regarding the unique services and equipment necessary for an effective law enforcement operation. Part of this education involves clearly stating budgetary goals or objectives in a manner that can be understood, measured and evaluated. In evaluating the budget, the administrator must insure that bureaucratic "featherbedding" does not occur within the department. These tactics include padding, manipulation of data and inappropriate organizational dynamics.

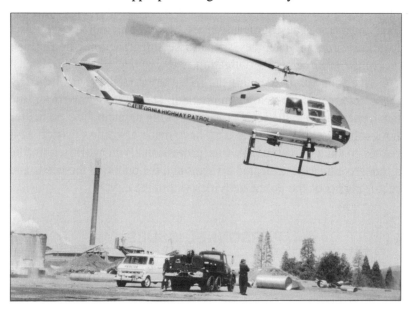

Modern day equipment and training costs are staggering to shrinking law enforcement budgets.

The source of funds for paying for law enforcement normally comes from the municipality's general fund, but law enforcement officials should consider other sources of revenue when evaluating their finances. These other sources of revenue include the asset forfeiture program, user fees, special assessments or taxes, and grants.

Law enforcement's obligation is to provide the best and most effective police services within the budgetary guidelines established by the elected officials. No administrator should pit himself or the department against the representatives of the municipality, no matter how vehemently he believes they have made a wrong decision as it relates to budget matters. A true professional will work within the system to educate the elected officials and the public to the needs and requirements of the police activities within the city.[12]

PERSONNEL ISSUES

Recruitment and Selection

As noted in earlier chapters, for many years police recruitment and selection was based on political connections. The reforms of the 1960s and 1970s and the recent social changes have resulted in more effective police recruitment and selection. Other factors that have influenced recruitment and selection include the depressed labor market, the reduced personnel demands of the military services, and the laws and court decisions regarding fair employment opportunities.

In recent years, the depressed labor market and the reduction in the number of young persons serving in the military have increased the attractiveness of a police career. In addition, the large number of students enrolled in criminal justice programs at colleges and universities helps provide a large pool of educated young people from which the police departments may choose.

Generally, police departments base their selection of recruits on a combination of written, physical, medical, and psychological examinations. Other factors include background investigations and strength requirements. Most police departments use polygraph examinations to screen applicants. Most will disqualify a candidate who has a prior criminal record involving substantial drug use or a felony conviction. Some departments also disqualify candidates who have been convicted of misdemeanors.

Law enforcement agencies have specific criteria for qualification of applicants and for the selection of candidates. As noted earlier, the law enforcement agencies use written and oral exams, psychological tests, physical fitness tests, and background investigations to select candidates for their agencies.

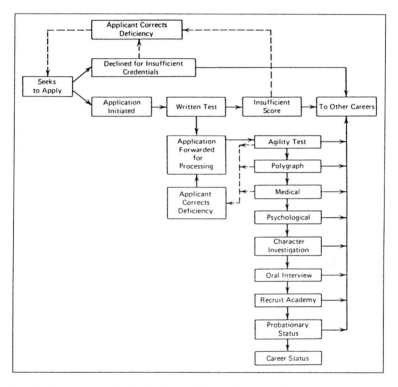

Flow chart for police applicants showing typical steps from application to career status.

The source of funds for paying for law enforcement normally comes from the municipality's general fund, but law enforcement officials should consider other sources of revenue when evaluating their finances. These other sources of revenue include the asset forfeiture program, user fees, special assessments or taxes, and grants.

Metropolitan police departments generally use written examinations as their primary screening device. Minority groups have contended that these tests are discriminatory and culturally biased against minority groups. There are also questions regarding the validity of the tests to predict effective performance as a police officer. To counter these criticisms many police departments are currently using tests that are designed to be more job-related and tests that will measure an applicants ability to take quick and reasonable actions under conditions of stress.

Since none of the standard tests have a high score for reliable prediction, many experts advocate the elimination of standard tests and the selection of candidates based on nonwritten objective measures such as: the verbal skills of the applicant, the ability to recall license numbers and to remember faces, and demonstrated past performance in school or work situations.

Federal civil rights statutes require the agencies to provide equal employment opportunities to potential candidates. The statutes prohibit discrimination of individuals based on race, sex, national origin, religion, and age unless there is a bona fide occupational qualification (BFOQ) that makes the discrimination unavoidable. The courts have stated that any discrimination affecting one of the above protected classes is considered suspect; that any agency attempting to justify the discriminatory requirement has the heavy burden of proving that the requirement is necessary; and that there are no reasonable alternatives to substitute for the requirement. The statutes prohibit indirect as well as direct discrimination. For example requiring police officers to be of certain height and weight may discriminate against women and some minority groups who tend to be of smaller stature than the average adult males.

Police departments have traditionally placed height, weight, and physical ability requirements on new applicants. These requirements included testing candidates on their ability to do certain physical activities such as a minimal number of push-ups, sit-ups, and running exercises. Court cases have held that such requirements are discriminatory toward women and certain minority groups. The present trend is to require candidates to have a height and weight proportional to their body frame and to meet physical agility tests that are based on objective minimum requirements. In addition, departments have attempted to develop physical ability tests that are more job-related than the traditional tests used in the past. For example, strength tests generally based on the typical arrestee's weight and the amount of resistance the arrestee usually gives the police are used in many departments.

Another trend of police departments in their selection process is the movement from the reliance on physical tests to an increased reliance on the use of personality and intelligence tests.

EXHIBIT 6-1

CONTEMPT OF COP

In some law enforcement agencies, the worst crime that a citizen can commit when stopped by a police officer is to treat the officer with contempt. This is often referred to as "Contempt of Cop."

Can you imagine committing "contempt of cop" against this officer?

On March 3, 1991, Rodney King was stopped by Los Angeles Police Officers after a chase involving the California Highway Patrol. After he was stopped, apparently he resisted the efforts of the police to handcuff him and he may have made several derogatory comments to the police officers. He was beaten by the officers including blows to the head with a baton and kicking. The beating was videotaped by a local citizen and made the national news. Four officers were charged and tried for assault. When a jury found the officers not guilty, rioting broke out which resulted in hundreds of millions of dollars in damage and more than fifty deaths. Later two of the officers were convicted in federal court of violating King's federal civil rights.

The King case is a symbol of some of the major problems facing modern police departments. This case points out that regardless of the attitude of an individual being arrested, the individual still has certain constitutional rights and the police must exercise restraint in the use of force. Shortly after the assaults of King were viewed on national television, the Gallop Poll results indicated that confidence in police had declined significantly. In addition, prior to the viewing only about 10 percent of the public believed that the police were brutal. After the viewing, approximately 30 percent of the public believed that the police were brutal. It will take the Los Angeles Police Department years to regain the level of trust they had with the community as the result of the conduct of several police officers. [*Note*: The police officers were tried twice for the same conduct. This didn't violate the protection against double jeopardy because in the first trial, they were tried for violations of state law and in the second for violations of federal law.]

Promotion

Generally police departments employ "time in rank" system for determining promotion eligibility. Under this system, each officer must spend a certain amount of time in one rank before he or she is eligible to advance to the next. An advantage of this system is that it helps eliminate favoritism and politics in the promotion process. A significant disadvantage is that time in rank often receives more weight than performance of duty. In addition, the system tends to restrict lateral transfers from other police agencies.

Career Development

In this section, the initial appointment of a recruit and the typical career development pattern for police officers will be examined. An officer's career is started by receiving an appointment. Normally after all testing phases are completed and the background investigations are completed, the candidates are listed in a designated order from which appointments are made. As vacancies occur, the candidates are appointed as recruits. The use of an eligibility list is common with most medium and large size departments. The list prevents the need to conduct a testing process each time that a vacancy occurs. It also provides a pool of eligible applicants to draw from.

After the applicant is accepted and appointed as a recruit, the individual is enrolled in a recruit academy. In some cases, the individuals attend the academy prior to appointment to enhance their eligibility as a police officer. The academy provides basic training in police related subjects such as criminal law, ethics, arrest techniques, pursuit driving, community relations, and basic investigation techniques. The length of police academies varies from five to 20 weeks.

At the academies, the recruits are not expected to achieve an advanced level of knowledge or experience in any one subject but to achieve a foundation to build on in later years. The academies are not identical; each academy reflects what the different agencies feel are the needs of the recruits and the functions of the departments. While the goal of an academy is to provide initial training for recruits, it has the secondary goal of permitting police supervisors to scrutinize recruits in a controlled environment. Recruits who do not meet the rigid standards set in the academies will find themselves screened-out before graduation.

The new officer is appointed as a probationary employee for a certain period of time. Generally a probationary employee has little job protection and his or her employment may be terminated on general grounds. The period of probation normally runs from six to 12 months and in the case of marginal performers, it may be extended for additional periods of time. After the probationary period is completed, the officer has extensive job protection and can generally only be terminated for cause.

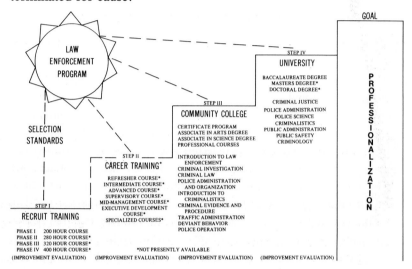

Example of a well planned law enforcement career development program. (Courtesy of the Florida Police Standards Board)

Career Paths

The most important aspect of career development is the provision of a career-path enhancement for officers. The career paths should include position enhancement, new assignments, and opportunities for promotion. The below example of a career path would be typical for an officer in a medium to large size department. The career path for officers in small offices is limited by the lack of flexibility which is available in larger departments.

Typical career path:

— initial training to include police academy and OJT for one year,

— assignment to patrol duties for about five years,

— assignment to specialist position or duties for about two years,

— promotion to sergeant and transferred back to patrol,

— first level supervision duties in patrol for about two years,

— transferred to detective unit for three years as an investigator,

— promoted to lieutenant and assigned training management duties for about two years,

— management position in patrol for about four years,

— additional assignments depending on abilities of officer and needs of the department.

Drug Testing

Should applicants and police officers be required to submit to a drug test? Many departments are facing this question. The issue is a sensitive one. Many object to drug testing as a violation of the personal rights and human dignity of the individual officers.

In view of the fact that there is a potential for corruption created by the use or dealing in illegal drugs, courts have upheld the right of law enforcement agencies to conduct random drug tests. The International Association of Chiefs of Police has adopted a "Model Drug Testing Policy."[13] The policy generally provides:

— that all applicants and recruits be tested for drug and narcotics use;

— current employees be tested when they are involved in the use of excessive force or suffer or cause to suffer on-duty injury; and

— all officers assigned to special "high-risk" areas such as narcotics and vice be routinely tested.

Moonlighting

Police officers often take second jobs (moonlighting) to supplement their pay . Moonlighting has both advantages and disadvantages to a law enforcement agency. One big advantage is that it puts police officers on the streets at critical times such as ballgames and other sporting events without cost to the public at large. In addition, the police officer working part-time security for a company generally provides a better trained person than would otherwise be available. For example, a bank that uses off-duty police officers as security guards generally has a better trained person to handle any attempted robberies, etc. One of the problems is the question of liability. Is the city liable for the actions of the officer in attempting to stop a bank robbery while the officer is working as a security guard during off-duty time? This is not an easy question to answer and generally depends on the state law, especially since the officer has a duty to the public to prevent crime even when off-duty. A second aspect of this problem is what happens when the police officer is permanently injured while working off-duty on an order maintenance function. If the injury is not permanent, should the officer be allowed to use sick leave from the department? These and similar questions often plague a law enforcement agency regarding the employment of off-duty officers.

It is difficult for a law enforcement agency to restrict officers from working during their off-duty hours. Agencies are, however, allowed to place reasonable restrictions on their off-duty employment. The agencies can also restrict the wearing of official uniforms while on off-duty employment.

Law enforcement agencies often take one of three management approaches to the private employment of their officers. The management approaches are the officer contract model, the union brokerage model, and department contract model.

1) Officer contract model — the individual officer finds a job and then applies to the agency for permission to accept the job. The hours of employment and terms of the employment are negotiated between the officer and the private employer, subject to approval by the law enforcement agency.

2) Union brokerage model — the union finds paid details or jobs for its member officers. The union negotiates the contract and conditions of employment, subject to approval by the agency.

3) Departmental contract model — the agency contracts with employers and assigns officers on a voluntary basis to the paid details or jobs. The private employer pays the agency who in turn pays the individual officers.

Employee Termination

Our expectations of a police officer's role includes, in many cases, his or her off-duty conduct. While in most cases an employee's social relationships and lifestyle preferences are of no concern to the employer, two federal courts of appeal held that police officers' private lives may be under scrutiny by their superiors. Accordingly, police officers have been fired for openly cohabiting outside of marriage and for having sexual relations with a minor prior to joining the force.[14] There are other cases that have held that the off-duty sexual conduct of police officers is not just cause for dismissal. In those cases where the courts have upheld dismissal, the courts based their decisions on the heightened visibility of law enforcement officers and the threat their off-duty behavior may pose to the police as a whole.[15]

In many jurisdictions, an officer has a right to a due process hearing before being terminated or demoted. The essential elements associated with a due process hearing include:

— timely and adequate notice of the alleged misconduct or grounds on which the action is based;

— opportunity to make an oral statement or argument during the hearing;

— a chance to present witnesses and evidence at the hearing;

— the right to confront adverse witnesses;

— the right to cross-exam adverse witnesses;

— the disclosure of all evidence that will be considered;

— right to be represented by an attorney;

— a statement of findings of fact;

— a statement of reasons for the opinion or a reasoned opinion; and

— a decision by an impartial hearing officer.

Everyone is concerned regarding the rights of defendants at criminal trials, seldom however, is the public concerned with the constitutional rights of a police officer. A difficult legal quandary is the extent to which a department may restrict the right of a police officer from participating in political activities. To what extent can the department restrict the right of an officer as to freedom of speech or right of association?

Most attempts to restrict police employees' First Amendment rights are struck down by the courts because the restrictions are too broad or the department cannot establish that the speech in question produced an adverse effect on its ability to perform. Federal and state laws prohibiting partisan political activity have been upheld if the prohibitions are not overly broad. The courts are less likely, however, to uphold restrictions on nonpartisan political activity.

In other areas covered by the First Amendment, the courts have permitted departments to ban the police from off-duty association with criminals or other undesirables. The courts have also upheld grooming standards as long as the standards are not racist or sexist.

DISCUSSION QUESTIONS

1. Can you explain this paradox? "The typical police department is a small agency— the typical police officer is employed by a large metropolitan police department."

2. Compare and contrast metropolitan police with rural law enforcement.

3. Explain the concept of "bureaucracy."

4. Why are police departments considered open systems?

ENDNOTES

[1] Henry L. Tosi, *Theories of Organization*, (Chicago: St. Clair Press, 1985), p. 32-34.
[2] Randy L. LaGrange, *Policing in America*, (New York: Nelson Hall, 1993).
[3] Francis X. Hartmann, "Debating the Evolution of American Policing," *Perspectives on Policing*, no. 5, (Washington D.C.: National Institute of Justice, November, 1988).
[4] James Q. Wilson, *Varieties of Police Behavior: The Management of Law and Order in Eight Communities*, (Cambridge: Harvard University, 1986).
[5] Randy L. LaGrange, *Policing in America*, (New York: Nelson-Hall, 1993).

[6] Ibid.

[7] Max Weber, *The Theory of Social and Economic Organization*, (New York: Oxford University, 1947).

[8] Bruce L. Heininger and Janine Urbanek, "Civilianization of American Police," *Journal of Police Science and Administration*, vol. II, no. 2, (1983), pp. 200-205.

[9] Brian A. Reaves, "Police Departments in Large Cities," *Bureau of Justice Statistics Special Report*, (Washington, D.C.: Government Printing Office, 1989).

[10] Donald O. Schultz and Erik Beckman, *Principles of American Law Enforcement*, 2nd ed., (Placerville, Ca.: Copperhouse Publishing Co. (Custom), 1992).

[11] Raymond E. Arthurs, Jr., "Accreditation: A Small Department's Experience," *FBI Law Enforcement Bulletin*, (August 1990), pp. 1-5.

[12] Harvey Wallace, Cliff Roberson and Craig Steckler, *Introduction to Police Administration*, (Englewood Cliffs, NJ: Prentice-Hall, 1993).

[13] National Institute of Justice, "Employee Drug Testing Policies in Police Departments," *National Institute of Justice Research*, (Washington D.C.: Department of Justice, 1986).

[14] *Shawgo v. Spradlin*, 701 F.2d. 470 (5th Cir, 1983); and *Andrade v. City of Phoenix*, 692 F. 2d 557 (9th Cir., 1982).

[15] John A. Fossum, *Employee and Labor Relations*, (Washington D.C.: BNA, 1990).

[16] Edward Davis and Anthony J. Pinizzotto, "Killed in the Line of Duty," *FBI, Uniform Crime Reporting Section*, (Washington D.C., 1993).

CRITICAL ISSUES FOR
LAW ENFORCEMENT
PERSONNEL

Most of us do not fully comprehend the implications of the awesome power that the police possess in their exercise of discretion to arrest. In a simple situation involving a defendant of modest means, arrest may cause loss of job, a period of detention, the indignities of being fingerprinted and photographed, immeasurable psychic pain, at least several court appearances — and finally the expenditure of many hundreds of dollars for bail and a lawyer.

I n this chapter, we will examine the role expectations and limitations placed on law enforcement personnel. The first expectation examined will be the role that courts have envisioned for the police. This role has been developed by the use of court decisions and constitutional limitations.

CONSTITUTIONAL PROVISIONS — EFFECTS OF LEGAL INTERPRETATIONS

Presently, the police are charged with the responsibility to:

1) protect life and property and safeguard individual liberties and

2) maintain order and prevent crime.

To accomplish these objectives, police officers are given certain powers. However, the police are restricted in carrying out their duties by the limitations placed on the police by court decisions. The most visible restrictions are those placed on the police by the U.S. Supreme Court in the court's interpretations of the individual rights guaranteed by the U.S. Constitution. There are 23 individual rights guaranteed to persons accused or suspected of criminal conduct in the U.S. Constitution. These individual rights are often collectively referred to as "due process." The most famous protections are those that restrict the right of police regarding searches and seizures under the Fourth Amendment of the U.S. Constitution and those regarding confessions under the Fifth Amendment.

The courts have used the constitution to place certain restrictions on the police. The restrictions are based on the courts' concept of the appropriate role of police in our society. The expected police role, as envisioned by the court, is that of a crime fighter who fights fair. Critics complain that the courts have cast the role of the police as a crime fighter with one arm tied behind his or her back.

"Listen kid, don't believe nothing people tell ya!"

EXHIBIT 7-1

Police Personality

Many experts believe that police officers develop a unique set of personality traits that make them different from the average person. The typical police personality is described as dogmatic, authoritarian, suspicious, racist, hostile, insecure, conservative, and cynical.[1] According to those researchers, throughout all stages of a police career cynicism is found at all levels of policing, including chiefs of police.

Probably the most well-known study of police personality was conducted by Arthur Niederhoffer.[2] Niederhoffer contends that most police officers develop into cynics as a function of their daily duties. According to him police officers develop the attitude that most people are out to break the law and will cause harm to the officer if necessary. His major findings include:

— police cynicism increases with length of service as a police officer,

— college educated police officers tend to become very cynical when they are denied promotion,

— military type police academies cause recruits to quickly become cynical.

The Exclusionary Rule

The exclusionary rule holds that evidence seized in violation of a person's constitutional rights may not be admitted in evidence against that person in a criminal case. The rule was first established by the U.S. Supreme Court in 1914 by the case *Weeks v. United States*. In that case, the court held that evidence obtained in violation of a person's Fourth Amendment rights could not be used in a federal criminal court against that person. The court in several companion cases, however, failed to require the state courts to follow the exclusionary rule until the case of *Mapp v. Ohio* in 1961.

The court stated that the purpose of the rule is to deter police misconduct. The rule is based on the principle that fruit (evidence) obtained from the poisoned tree (illegal search, seizure or confession) must be suppressed. In addition, any related evidence that was discovered as the result of the constitutional violation must also be suppressed. The exclusionary rule applies only to the individual whose rights were violated. For example if A, B, and C are tried for the possession of drugs and the court determines that the search violated only A's rights, the evidence may still be used against B and C because their rights were not violated.

There are several major exceptions to the exclusionary rule that allow certain evidence to be admitted despite the illegality of its taking. The chief exceptions are discussed below.

1. **Inevitable discovery**: This exception developed from the *Nix v. Williams* case in which the evidence was discovered as the result of illegal questioning by the police. At the time of the questioning, the police were searching along a highway for the victim's body. The court held that since the police would have discovered the evidence anyway without the constitutional violation, it was admissible in court.

2. **Purged taint**: The purged taint exception developed from the *Wong Sun v. United States* case in 1963. In that case, the defendant's house was illegally entered by the police and during that entry, the police obtained an unsigned confession from the accused. Wong Sun was released from custody. Several days later, he voluntarily returned to the police station and signed his confession. The court held that his voluntary return and signing of the confession purged the taint; therefore, the signed confession could be admitted into evidence.

3. **Foreign soil**: The foreign soil exception involved the illegal search of a Mexican national's home in Mexico. When the defendant was extradited to the U.S. and tried for murder, the court ruled that the evidence seized could be admitted against the defendant since the constitutional violation, if any, occurred in Mexico.

4. **Reasonable mistake**: The reasonable mistake exception has been limited to mistakes by judges in issuing warrants, not to mistakes by police officers. The court indicated that if the police were aware of the judge's mistake and failed to take action to correct the mistake, then the evidence could be excluded because of bad faith on the part of the police.

5. **Aerial surveillance**: The courts have allowed evidence derived from aerial surveillance to be admitted into evidence despite the fact that the police had no probable cause to conduct an aerial observation of the defendant's home and enclosed property.

6. **Satellite Surveillance**: With the increase of satellites and the enhancement of magnification resolution, use of this technology is becoming routine. Police may use historical review (events that took place in the past and were captured on film and archived) to help recreate a crime scene. Real time viewing (viewing events as they are unfolding) is useful, if not mandatory, for dealing with events like the Branch Davidians Compound (Waco, Texas) or the L.A. riots. Currently, the courts are allowing use of this evidence along the same guidelines as with aerial photography.

The major problem with the exclusionary rule was first noted by Supreme Court Justice Benjamin Cardozo who stated that the rule permitted the criminal to go free because the constable had blundered. The United States is probably the only country that punishes the police officer by turning loose the criminal.

Searches and Seizures

The Fourth Amendment to the U.S. Constitution provides:

"The right of the people to be secure in their persons, houses, papers, and effects, against unreasonable searches and seizures shall not be violated, and no warrants shall issue, but upon probable cause, supported by oath or affirmation, and particularly describing the place to be searched, and the persons or things to be seized."

Note that the above amendment protects only:

1) persons,

2) houses,

3) papers, and

4) effects

against unreasonable searches and seizures. To determine whether results of a search or seizure are admissible, the first question should be "Does the Fourth Amendment apply?" For example, open fields, parks, etc. are not protected by the Fourth Amendment since they do not fit within one of the four protections. Accordingly, the police do not need a warrant or probable cause to search a city park. If the Fourth Amendment does not apply, then the evidence is probably admissible. If the amendment applies, then the question that should be examined is "Has the Fourth Amendment been complied with?" This question will be discussed later in this chapter. The final question is if the Fourth Amendment applies and it has been violated, does the evidence fit within one of the exceptions noted earlier? [*Note*: The Fourth Amendment is a compound sentence dealing with unreasonable searches and seizures and the requirements for a warrant.] The amendment states that a warrant may be issued only if it meets the below requirements:

1) probable cause,

2) supported by oath or affirmation, and

3) particularly describing the place to be searched, and

4) the persons or things to be seized.

A search warrant must be issued by a neutral and detached magistrate. A neutral and detached magistrate is a judicial officer who has no involvement or stake in the case. For example, a city judge whose pay is based on a percentage of the fines collected is not a neutral magistrate since conviction of the suspect could increase the judge's salary. Also, the State Attorney General cannot issue a search warrant because as an attorney general he is responsible for supervising the criminal justice system and therefore is not neutral and detached.

Prior to issuing a warrant, the magistrate needs to have sufficient information to conclude that probable cause exists to issue the warrant. The Fourth Amendment requires that the information presented to the magistrate be supported by oath or affirmation. Normally this is accomplished by the police presenting a sworn affidavit to the judge. The affidavit must contain sufficient information for the judge to make the probable cause determination. In some cases, the courts have upheld telephonic warrants where the information is orally presented to the judge over the telephone after the judge has given an oath to the officers.

Probable cause is defined as:

1) information sufficient to cause a reasonable person to believe a crime has been committed or is being committed;

2) information sufficient to believe that the place or person to be searched or the person or thing to be seized is connected with the criminal conduct.

Probable cause can be based on hearsay or other evidence that does not meet the strict requirements of court admissible evidence. The probable cause must be based on timely information. For example, information that a defendant possessed drugs two years ago will not support a current warrant to search him.

General search warrants are unconstitutional. The warrant must particularly describe the place or person to be searched. Any search that exceeds the scope of the warrant is considered as a search without a warrant for the portion of the search that exceeds the warrant. For example a warrant that authorizes the police to search apartment 204 at 1234 Maple Lane does not authorize the police to search any other apartment at that location and any such search would be considered a warrantless search.

Scholars have debated for years whether a warrant is required for a search to be reasonable. The general rule based on numerous court decisions is that unless the search and seizure falls within one of the recognized exceptions discussed below, a warrant must be obtained. As one appellate judge stated: "You must get a warrant unless you can't." To encourage police to obtain warrants, the courts have adopted a rule of evidence that assumes that any search pursuant to a warrant is a valid search and any search without a warrant is an invalid search. For example, in a court case if a search was based on a warrant, it is assumed to be a valid search and the defendant has the burden of establishing that the search was unreasonable. If however, the search was without a warrant, the prosecution has the burden to establish that the search was legal.

The recognized exceptions to a search warrant requirement are as follows:

1. **Automobile** — The courts have upheld warrantless searches of automobiles based on the theory that the mobility of the vehicle makes the obtaining of a warrant difficult. A second rationale given is that there is less of an expectation of privacy in an automobile than in a home. [Note: Probable cause is still required.] The automobile exception only applies to automobiles on

public streets and parking lots. It does not apply to vehicles parked on private property.

2. **Incident to arrest** — If there is a valid arrest, the person arrested and the immediate area where the arrest occurred may be searched without a warrant and without probable cause to search. [*Note*: There must be probable cause to arrest, but probable cause is not needed to search incident to a lawful arrest. If the arrest is unlawful, then the fruits of the search will be excluded from evidence.]

3. **Exigent circumstances** — The exigent circumstances exception applies in those cases where because of the circumstances, the police do not have time to obtain a warrant. For example, the police hear gun fire from a house. They can immediately go into the house to investigate the situation. Exigent circumstances refers to emergency circumstances where there is not time to obtain a warrant.

4. **Hot pursuit** — If the police are in pursuit of a person and that person enters a private home, then the police may enter without a warrant to search the house for the person being pursued.

5. **Consent** — A person may waive their rights under the constitution. Accordingly, a person may consent to being searched. In this case, all the police need to establish is that the individual did consent to the search. No probable cause is needed in consent cases. [*Note*: The person giving consent must have the right to consent. For example if two people are living together, normally both may give consent to search their living spaces. A casual visitor, however, may not give consent to search the home.]

6. **Plain view** — Items in plain view may be viewed by the police as long as they are in a place where they may legally be. For example, the police have a search warrant to search for guns in a home. While searching for the guns, they see a television on a table. They may look at the television since it is in plain view. They may not, however, move the television in order to get its serial number. This latter restriction is based on the concept that the television's serial number is not in plain view.

7. **Open fields** — The amendment protects only persons, houses, papers, and effects; places such as open fields and other common areas are not protected by the constitution.

8. **Border Searches** — Traditionally, the courts have allowed customs officials and other federal agents to search persons and vehicles that are coming into the United States from a foreign country. Boats and ships may also be searched. Border searches require neither probable cause nor a warrant.

Arrest Warrants

Arrest warrants, like search warrants, are subject to the Fourth Amendment and must be issued by a neutral and detached magistrate. Unlike search warrants, however, an arrest warrant may be based on stale information. In addition, where search warrants have limited life, arrest warrants last until canceled. Another important difference between arrest and search warrants is that the courts have placed less emphasis on the need to obtain arrest warrants.

Interrogations

The courts have placed restrictions on the ability of police to interrogate suspects. The most famous is the *Miranda warning* requirement. Basically, before the police may interrogate a person being held in custody, the police must advise the person of his or her rights. The *Miranda warning* does not need to be given unless the person is in custody. The courts, however, have defined "**custody**" as any situation where the suspect has been detained or is not otherwise free to leave. When a person's liberty is restrained, the individual is considered in custody.

The *Miranda* case placed the following restrictions on police interrogations:

— Before questioning any suspects who are in custody, the suspects must be warned that they have a right to remain silent, that any statement made by them can be used against them, they have a right to have an attorney present during the interrogations, and if they cannot afford an attorney one will be appointed without cost.

— Any waiver of the suspect's rights must be knowingly and intelligently made.

— If the suspect indicates that he or she wishes an attorney or wishes to remain silent, the police must cease questioning and cannot resume questioning unless the suspect has either been provided with an attorney or indicates that he or she wishes to reopen questioning.

This section has discussed the role expectations of the police in regard to their crime fighting functions. While crime fighting is the most visible function of police work, it is not the one that receives the most police emphasis. As will be noted in the next section, the police place their emphasis on order maintenance functions.

EXHIBIT 7-2

Police Culture

Jerome Skolnick contends that there is a "working personality of police officers." He concludes that there is a police culture with its own customs, laws, and morality.[3] This personality is developed through a process of informal socialization starting when new officers attend the police academy and continues when the new officers begin to work with veteran police offices. According to Skolnick, the informal socialization process is far more important to the new officers than the formal police academy in shaping their later behavior as a police officer. The informal socialization is acquired generally from one's peers in settings such as the locker room, the squad car, or over a cup of coffee. During these settings, the new officer develops a shared view of policing that is often described as "streetwise." The officer learns just how acceptable various informal means of accomplishing the job will be to other officers.

EMPHASIS UPON ORDER MAINTENANCE

Large scale order maintenance is usually seen in the form of riot or protest control.

Kenneth C. Davis states that individual police officers choose which laws to enforce and which to overlook. His conclusions were based on his research involving the Chicago Police Department. During the period covered by his research, the department had a policy of full compliance with the law (to enforce all the laws). When he asked the officers which laws they enforced, their standard answer was "I enforce all the laws." Despite the policies and their statements, he concluded that individual officers make the decisions on which laws to enforce and which not to enforce. None of the officers enforced every law.[4]

Since the police respond to a variety of situations and are expected to immediately remedy the situation, the re-establishment of order tends to be the quick solution to most of the problems. Accordingly, there tends to be an emphasis on order maintenance rather than law enforcement or service functions.

Most police departments now use strategies that emphasize informal discretionary action in lieu of formal arrest, search, and interrogation. These strategies also tend to influence officers to focus on order maintenance rather than other functions. Numerous studies indicate that officers tend to spend less than ten percent of their time performing crime prevention or crime solving duties and a significantly higher portion merely maintaining order.

CIVIL LIABILITY

When police have departed from the role expectations that society places on them, frequently their conduct is the subject of legal action. There are three general theories under which a police employee or department can be the subject of civil litigation:

1) as the result of an action based on an intentional act, e.g., battery, assault, false arrest, infliction of mental distress, and conversion of property;

2) as the result of an action based on negligence, e.g., negligent driving, negligent discharge of a firearm, and negligence in the use of lawful force to affect an arrest; and

3) as the result of an action based on an infringement of a constitutional right, e.g., illegal search, denial of right to counsel, and illegally preventing a person from exercising a constitutional right.[5]

A majority of civil actions are based on violations of constitutional rights which are filed pursuant to Title 42, U.S. Code, Section 1983. Civil suits under Section 1983 are the most common federal civil rights actions brought against police officers and their employers. Many states have similar statutes. Section 1983 reads, in part, as follows:

> Every person who, under the color of any statute, ordinance, regulation, custom, or usage of any State... subjects or causes to be subjected any citizen... to the deprivation of any rights, privileges, or immunities secured by the Constitution and laws shall be liable to the party injured in an action at law....

Under Section 1983, any individual whose constitutional rights have been violated by a police officer may file an action against the officer for both compensatory damages (actual damages) and punitive damages. The types of actions that have been filed under Section 1983 include:

— false arrest;

— illegal search and seizure;

— verbal harassment;

— denial of right to counsel;

— denial of right of association under First Amendment;

— excessive use of force in effecting a legal arrest;

— retaliatory prosecution;

— denial of medical treatment by prisoner;

— denial of mail by a prisoner;

— destruction of private property;

— illegal interrogation;

— failure to provide police protection; and

— wrongful use of deadly force.

Federal law enforcement officers generally cannot be sued under Section 1983 since that section requires that the officers are acting under "color of state law." They may, however, be sued for violations of individual constitutional rights under the Bivens case.[6] The "Bivens" action is a judicially created counterpart to a Section 1983 action.[7]

Some general principles regarding Section 1983 actions include:

— Section 1983 does not create any substantive rights, but merely provides a remedy for violations of substantive rights created by the federal constitution or other federal laws.

— Section 1983 is available even if the conduct in question also violates state law.

— A plaintiff suing under Section 1983 need not bring separate state and federal actions. They can be combined in one action.

— Unlike the Federal Tort Claims Act and most state tort claims acts, there is no requirement that the plaintiff first submit an administrative claim. Also, there is no requirement for the individual to exhaust his or her state remedies prior to filing an action under 1983.

— The conduct complained of must have been taken under color of law or use of authority. An officer is acting under "color of law" if the officer uses his office to carry out the conduct in question.

— The complained conduct must have been the legal cause of the harm alleged by the plaintiff.

At common law, the government could not be sued because the "King could do no wrong." Thus, the sovereign (e.g., cities, counties, and states), were immune from civil suits for actions of its employees. Because of this lack of a common law right to sue the government, to hold a city or county liable for the actions of a police officer, there must be a statutory provision that permits the suit. In most cases, the provision is Section 1983 or a similar state statute.

In those cases where the local government can be sued, we must look to state law to determine whether the suit names the police department or the city as the defendant. In most states, the police departments are merely subdivisions of the city or municipality; therefore, the actual defendant is the city or municipality. In the vast majority of cases, the plaintiff sues the city, the department, and the individual involved to ensure that the right person or unity has been included in the suit.

The phrase "Seven Deadly Sins" is used to refer to a list of legal theories by which civil litigation may be instituted against a local government or a police supervisor. Each of the "sins" involve either negligence or lack of competence in management and administrative actions. The "sins" are as follows:

1) Negligent appointment of a police officer;

2) Negligent retention of a police officer;

3) Negligent assignment of a police officer;

4) Negligent entrustment of duties to a police officer;

5) Lack of adequate training of a police officer;

6) Failure to properly supervise a police officer; and

7) Failure to properly direct a police officer [8]

EXHIBIT 7-3

Police Brutality

The history of policing includes the numerous charges of police brutality. In 1920, the Wickersham Commission detailed numerous instances of police brutality. In the 1940s, the police were described as a "gestapo" after race riots in Detroit and other major cities. Similar charges were made after the 1968 Democratic National Convention in Chicago. The 1992 Rodney King incident in Los Angeles and similar incidents create the impression that police brutality is still a major concern for the citizens of our county.

In examining police brutality, two questions need to be considered:

1) Is the average police officer generally brutal, and

2) Are the police overzealous in their use of force?

Numerous research studies tend to indicate that police are not as brutal as isolated incidents seem to suggest. In one study, it appears that out of 5,360 observations, the police seemed to use excessive force in only 44 cases.[13]

POLICE ETHICS

We expect high ethical standards of our police officers. As noted earlier in this chapter, even when the police are dealing with child molesters and murders, we expect them to "fight fair." The high ethical standards expected of our police originate from the basis that we have entrusted them with the enforcement of the fundamental rules that guide our society. An officer's failure to meet those ethical standards is seen as a dishonor to our system of justice. The problem with the high ethical standards requirement is that our police officers are no more resistant to temptation than anyone else. Another problem in this area is the conflicting pressures that are often placed on the police officer. For example, they are expected to enforce parking and gambling laws, though most of the time we prefer that they do not. In some cases, there is strong public resistance to the enforcement of some of our laws such as speed limit restrictions on open highways. The third problem in this area is that the law enforcement profession affords many opportunities and temptations to become involved in illegal behavior such as bribery.

Types of Dishonesty

The types of dishonest and/or unethical behavior that police are involved in varies widely. The most common behaviors include accepting bribes for not enforcing the law, improper political influence, fixing traffic tickets, minor thefts, and burglaries. W. Clinton Terry uses the following terms to identify some of the various types of deviancy in which police may become involved.[9]

Mooching — The act of receiving free meals, etc. for possible future acts of favoritism.

Chiseling — The act of demanding free or reduced admission to entertainment events whether or not connected to police duty.

Favoritism — The practice of using license tabs, window tickets, bumper stickers, etc. to gain immunity from minor traffic violations.

Prejudice — The practice of treating certain groups of people, especially minorities, with less than impartial or neutral objective attention. In addition, this includes giving special privileges to those who have political influence.

Shopping — The practice of picking up small items from retail stores whose doors are found unlocked after business hours.

Extortion — Making demands for placing advertisements in police magazines or to purchase tickets to police functions.

Bribery — The acceptance of cash or gifts for past or future assistance or to avoid prosecution.

Shakedown — The practice of appropriating expensive items for personal use and attributing it to criminal activity when investigating a burglary or an unlocked door.

Perjury — The practice of presenting false testimony in order to convict a criminal or to give a fellow officer an alibi.

Premeditated theft — The planned burglary involving the use of keys, tools, etc. to gain entry or to prearrange plan for the unlawful acquisition of property.

Law Enforcement Code of Ethics

As a Law Enforcement Officer, my fundamental duty is to serve mankind; to safeguard lives and property; to protect the innocent against deception, the weak against oppression or intimidation, and the peaceful against violence or disorder; and to respect the Constitutional rights of all men to liberty, equality and justice.

I will keep my private life unsullied as an example to all; maintain courageous calm in the face of danger, scorn, or ridicule; develop self-restraint; and be constantly mindful of the welfare of others. Honest in thought and deed in both my personal and official life, I will be exemplary in obeying the laws of the land and the regulations of my department. Whatever I see or hear of a confidential nature or that is confided to me in my official capacity will be kept ever secret unless revelation is necessary in the performance of my duty.

I will never act officiously or permit personal feelings, prejudices, animosities, or friendships to influence my decisions. With no compromise for crime and with relentless prosecution of criminals, I will enforce the law courteously and appropriately without fear or favor, malice or ill will, never employing unnecessary force or violence and never accepting gratuities.

I recognize the badge of my office as a symbol of public faith, and I accept it as a public trust to be held so long as I am true to the ethics of the police service. I will constantly strive to achieve these objectives and ideals, dedicating myself before God to my chosen profession . . . law enforcement.

POLICE STRESS

Police work is considered one of the most "stressful" of all occupations and is often blamed for the high levels of suicide, alcohol and drug abuse, divorce and family problems, and poor job performance. Some of the factors associated with police work which may contribute to stress are potential physical danger, boredom, excitement, uncertainty, organizational demands, and shift work.[10]

EXHIBIT 7-4

COP-KILLERS

Two FBI researchers interviewed murderers who were responsible for the deaths of 54 law enforcement officers. While they were trying to identify potential cop-killers, they also discovered that there were many similarities between victims that could have contributed to their deaths. Their findings include:

— 39 percent of the slain officers were involved in an arrest or crime-in-progress call when they were killed. 17 percent died while responding to disturbance calls; 11 percent while handling or transporting prisoners; and seven percent while investigating suspicious situations.

— 58 percent of the killings took place at night, the fewest percentage took place in daylight hours.

— The victims had an average of 8 years of experience.

— 80 percent were assigned to vehicle patrol, and 70 percent were assigned to one—officer vehicles.

— Handguns were used in 72 percent of the killings. The most popular handgun was the .38 special.

— 76 percent of the killers had used drugs or alcohol shortly before the killings.

— Only 3 percent of the killers had no prior criminal record.

— 48 percent of the killers admitted that they had previously killed or attempted to kill someone.

Many of the slain officers were known as friendly, hard-working, service-oriented officers who were also considered "laid back" and "easy-going." The slain officers also had a tendency to use less force than other officers and often failed to follow departmental procedures. Slain officers were more service-oriented and tended to gravitate toward the public relations aspects of law enforcement. There was also a tendency to bend or disregard rules and procedures when making arrests, during confrontations with prisoners, or during traffic stops. The victims would often take actions without waiting for backup officers to arrive on the scene. The slain officers were often the type of people who would look for the good in others and felt that they could accurately "read" people and situations.

The researchers, however, found few similarities between the murderers. When asked what the officers could have done to prevent the killing, 47 percent of the murderers said that

...there was nothing the officers could have done to prevent the murder. The killers stated that the officers made mistakes or approached them in ways that made them easy prey.

The killers also noted that the victims often failed to conduct adequate body searches and frequently ignored the crotch area where many stated they had hidden their weapons or contraband.

The researchers concluded that to prevent killings of police, the police officers need to maintain their vigilance and follow good solid police practices which are taught by almost all law enforcement agencies.[16]

Stress can have either physiological, psychological or a combination of both effects on a person. Physiological stress deals with the biological effects on a person and includes heart disease, high blood pressure, ulcers, etc. Psychological stress deals with psychological changes that can occur such as increased anxiety. Psychological stress differs from physiological stress in that there are no physical signs or effects of the stress. It is often referred to as mental stress. There are four major dimensions of stress: hyperstress (overloaded with change); hypostress (underloaded with change); eustress (resulting from favorable or positive change); and distress (resulting form unfavorable or negative change).

For police officers, stress is an inevitable part of life and a certain amount can help to stimulate people to achieve their goals. Negative stress, however, inhibits achievement and produces health problems. Stress has been associated with coronary heart disease, skin irritation, nervous disorders, neurosis, alcoholism, drug abuse, and numerous other physical and mental disorders. Often, negative stress occurs when an individual feels inadequate about performance expectations or the surrounding working environment.

With this intersection flooded, these officers almost lost their lives—you don't expect to drown driving down a city street.

One widely held theory is that stress occurs in a three step process— alarm reaction, resistance, and exhaustion. The alarm reaction step refers to the physiological changes that the body undergoes in response to stress. If the stress producing situation continues, the alarm reaction stage is followed by the resistance stage. During the resistance stage, the body seems to develop a resistance to the situation and earlier symptoms may disappear. If the stress situation continues, the body's resistance cannot be maintained and the exhaustion stage is reached. Severe physiological and psychological problems can occur during the exhaustion stage.

The vulnerability to stress is different for each individual. Each person has a different threshold to stress. Accordingly, the level of stress that may overwhelm one person may not affect another. In addition, some individuals can handle intense stress for short periods of time and not handle low levels of stress over extended periods of time.

Policing has been ranked among the top ten most stress-producing occupations in the United States.[11] Four commonly recognized sources of police stress are listed below:

1) external stress — caused by the real dangers of responding to calls involving armed persons;

2) organizational stress — caused by the demands of police work and organizational requirements such as scheduling, paperwork and training requirements;

3) personal stress — generated by personal problems and interpersonal relationships among officers themselves; and

4) operational stress — caused by the need to daily confront the tragedies of urban life. [12]

DISCUSSION QUESTIONS

1. Explain how the courts attempt to control police actions.

2. Should the police have a right to use unethical tactics to catch criminals?

3. What is the purpose of the *Miranda warning* requirements?

4. Should the police be allowed to wear their uniforms when they are working at second jobs, such as traffic control at a ball game?

5. Why is police work a stressful occupation?

ENDNOTES

[1] Richard Lundman, *Police and Policing*, (New York: Holt, Rinehart & Winston, 1980).

[2] Arthur Niederhoffer, *Behind the Shield*, (Garden City, NY: Doubleday, 1967).

[3] Jerome H. Skolnick, *Justice Without Trial: Law Enforcement in a Democratic Society*, (New York: John Wiley, 1966).

[4] Kenneth C. Davis, *Police Discretion*, (St. Paul: West, 1975).

[5] *Police Supervision: A Manual for Police Supervisors*, (Arlington, Va.: IACP, 1985).

[6] *Bivens v. Six Unknown Named Federal Agents*, 403 U.S. 388 (1971). [The name of this case has also been a matter of numerous discussions. How can an unknown federal agent be "named?"]

[7] Isidor Silver, *Police Civil Liability*, (New York: 1991), p. 8.

[8] *Police Supervision: A Manual for Police Supervisors*, (Arlington, Va.: IACP, 1985), pp. 37-38.

[9] W. Clinton Terry, *Policing Society: An Occupational View*, (New York: Wiley, 1985), p. 242.

[10] Roy R. Roberg and Jack Kuykendall, *Police and Society*, (Belmont, Ca.: Wadsworth, 1993).

[11] "Stress on the Job," *Newsweek*, (April 25, 1988), p. 43.

[12] Joseph Victor, "Police Stress: Is Anybody Out There Listening?" *New York Law Enforcement Journal*, (June 1986): p. 20.

[13] Albert Reiss, *The Police and Public*, (New Haven: Yale University, 1972); and David Bayley and James Garofalo, "The Management of Violence," *Criminology*, vol. 27, (1989).

8

POLICE OPERATIONS

Hell, I thought Vietnam was bad. I came home and became a cop only to find out I'm right back in a war — a war fought on our streets everyday.

R esearch on police roles indicates that the police spend a preponderance of their time on non-crime related activities. Most of a police officer's time is spent handling minor disturbances, service calls, and administrative duties with little actual time spent on crime fighting efforts. It is estimated that only about 10 percent of an officer's time is spent on crime fighting, whereas social service and administrative tasks require over 50 percent of the officer's time.[1]

PATROL

The word "patrol" in early English meant to "walk or paddle in muddy water." There are several versions of how the word became associated with law enforcement. One popular version is that the police are "walking in muddy water" when they patrol the community looking for the dirty (criminal) aspects of its citizens. Patrolling is the most visible part of police work. Many of our opinions of the quality of the local police department are based on our observations of police patrols in the community.

The largest and most visible component of any municipal law enforcement agency is the patrol section. It consists of officers working in uniform twenty-four hours a day, 365 days a year. They handle calls for service from the public in motor vehicles, on horseback, or on foot. Patrol is the essence of the police mission.[2] Although all aspects of the police organization have the responsibility of meeting the organization's mission, patrol usually takes the lead in this effort due to its size and visibility.

In many organizations, patrol also accepts the responsibility for the functional supervision of other units of the department during non-traditional working hours. For example, supervision of the Communications Unit or Records Unit may be provided by patrol supervisors between midnight and eight in the morning or during weekends and holidays when police management personnel are not on duty.

An integral part of the patrol function is their response to noncriminal calls for service. Depending upon community expectations, noncriminal calls for service range from conducting vacant home checks while homeowners are on vacation to contacting homebound senior citizens daily to see if they are in need of assistance. Police will often respond to medical aid calls, even if a paramedic program is available. Traffic control can be provided for churches as well as security for high school sporting events and dances. However, with the advent of limited resources, it has become necessary for law enforcement to re-evaluate the role of patrol and streamline its functions in order to concentrate on their primary mission.

Generally we consider the major activities of police patrol to be law enforcement. Studies indicate, however, that the police officer on patrol averages less than one felony arrest a week. Most experts now agree that the great bulk of police patrol activities are devoted to order maintenance or peace keeping.

Studies indicate that the average patrol time is utilized as follows:

1) 25 percent responding to calls for service. This refers to the percentage of time that the officer assigned to patrol spends answering or responding to requests from citizens for help.

2) 40 percent on preventive patrol. This refers to the percentage of time that the officer spends on patrol while attempting to prevent crime.

3) 15 percent on officer-initiated activities. This refers to the percentage of time the officer is actively involved in officer initiated activities (i.e., stopping and talking to juveniles in the area).

4) 20 percent on administrative tasks. This is the time that the officer spends on completing reports and other administrative reports.[3]

Effectiveness of Patrolling

Preventive patrolling is based on two assumptions: (1) patrolling improves police response time and (2) improved response time will result in an increase in the number of crimes solved. A research study in Garden Grove, California indicated, however, that fast response time accounted for less than five percent of arrests for serious crimes and that the use of differential response (having different response standards for different situations) saved the department over $223,000 a year.[4]

For years, we considered preventive police patrols as one of the best deterrents of criminal behavior. The visible presence of police was viewed as an effective crime prevention technique. However, a Kansas City study seems to indicate that police patrols are not effective utilizations of the limited resources available. The Kansas City study divided the city into 15 districts. Five of the districts retained normal police patrols, five districts greatly increased the number of police patrols, and the final five used the reactive approach and responded only when called by citizens. The researchers concluded that the variations in police patrol techniques appeared to have little effect on citizen's attitudes toward the police, their satisfaction with the police, or their fear of crime. The researchers concluded that:

1) patrolling did not reduce crime,

2) it did not affect the rates of reporting crimes to the police,

3) it did not affect the effectiveness of the police, and

4) it had no significant effect on the citizen's opinion of the effectiveness of the police.[5]

While the study has been criticized because of its research design, it has greatly influenced the thinking of researchers on the effectiveness of police patrolling. As one expert noted, "it is about as rational for the police to patrol their jurisdiction hunting for crime as it for a fire-truck to patrol the neighborhood hunting for a fire."

Single Officer Patrols

Generally, a patrol vehicle occupied by one officer is more cost efficient than one occupied by two officers. From a cost standpoint, it is apparent that in most cases funding two officers in a vehicle is not economically practical. The debate between one-officer versus two-officer patrol techniques has always taken place within law enforcement agencies. Unions or associations, which represent the field officer, tend to support two-officer patrol vehicles. However, cost-conscious police administrators have generally favored the single-officer patrol vehicle concept.

Unions present the issue of officer safety in their argument. Their contention is that two officers riding together will provide immediate support to each other in a time of crisis — the alternative being a back-up unit, which is often delayed. The unions also argue that two officers can be watching for activity on both sides of the vehicle, making the patrol effort more effective.

Many police executives agree with the officer safety issue, particularly in certain cases. Some cities contain neighborhoods which are unsafe for a lone officer on patrol. Sections of the larger, older cities present a real danger to law enforcement officers. For example, New York, Philadelphia, Detroit, and Chicago have tremendous inner-city crime problems which require two-officer vehicles. Violent criminals are less likely to assault two police officers as opposed to a single officer.

Alternative Patrols

A number of alternatives are available to the most common patrol technique — random patrol in an automobile. Foot patrol is an example. Foot patrol was reintroduced to major population centers such as Newark, New Jersey and Houston, Texas which resulted in a number of findings:

1) With the presence of foot patrol in neighborhoods, fear levels decrease significantly;

2) Alternatively, with the withdrawal of foot patrol, fear levels increase significantly;

3) Citizen satisfaction with police increases with the presence of foot patrol in neighborhoods;

4) Police who patrol on foot have a greater appreciation for the values of the neighborhood residents than do police in automobiles;

5) Police who patrol on foot have greater job satisfaction, less fear, and higher morale than do officers who patrol in automobiles.[6]

TRAFFIC

Traffic control is another important contact the police have with the public. More citizens have contact or interaction with the police because of traffic control problems than any other reason. Why and how traffic laws are enforced can have a significant effect on how the community views the police. Since traffic control is a complex activity with thousands of contacts with the public, selective enforcement is necessary in the maintenance of traffic laws. It would be impossible to strictly enforce every traffic regulation or law.

Duties of a Traffic Officer

The duties of officers assigned to traffic include:

— obtaining the best possible movement of vehicles and pedestrians;

— ensuring compliance with various regulations and traffic laws from as many motorists and pedestrians as possible;

— assisting at traffic accidents;

— investigating the causes of traffic accidents;

— assisting lost or stranded motorists and pedestrians; and

— helping to educate the public regarding traffic laws and safety.

Accident Causing Violations

According to the National Safety Council certain traffic law violations are more likely to cause serious accidents. In most jurisdictions, the traffic officer is expected to concentrate on those violations. Those violations include:

— driving under the influence of drugs or alcohol;

— speeding;

— following too close to other vehicles;

— improper or unsafe passing of other vehicles;

— failure to stop at stop signs;

— failure to yield the right-of-way; and

— driving over center lines.

Speed Traps

One controversial issue in traffic is the use of "speed traps." A speed trap is a predetermined section of a public road that has been measured and marked by boundaries. This enables the police to determine the speed of a vehicle by timing how long it takes a vehicle to go from one boundary to the other. Several states, including California, do not allow evidence as to the speed of a vehicle based on a speed trap to be used in court. In a few states, communities use speed traps as a source of revenue.

Sobriety Tests

Traffic officers are expected to identify drivers who are driving under the influence of drugs or alcohol (DUI). Usually the first indication of DUI is slow or erratic driving. In addition, when investigating an accident, the officer may smell the presence of alcohol. In most cases, the officer conducts a field sobriety test as a screening test. If the driver fails the field test, one of three tests is normally given.

Breath test—This is the test most commonly given for measuring the amount of alcohol in the blood (blood-alcohol). Earlier models of the breath test were not very accurate. Later models, however, are more reliable and acceptable to the courts.

Blood test — This is the more accurate test, but the results are delayed because the blood sample must be sent to a laboratory for analysis.

Urine test—This test measures not only the alcohol in a person's blood but can also be used to test for the presence of drugs.

The amount of alcohol in a person's blood is expressed as a percentage of alcohol relative to blood volume. For example, a reading of .08 percent means that alcohol constitutes eight one-hundredths of the sample tested. Most DUI statutes prohibit both (1) a person from driving under the influence of alcohol or drugs and (2) driving with a blood alcohol content of a certain amount. Accordingly, in California, a person with a blood alcohol content greater than .08 but who is not under the influence of alcohol because of a high personal tolerance for alcohol would still be guilty of the statute prohibiting the driving of a vehicle with a blood alcohol content of .08 or greater.

CRIMINAL INVESTIGATIONS

The first detective bureau was established in 1841 by the London Metropolitan Police. We tend to see the police investigator as a romantic figure portrayed in movies and novels. The detective is usually pictured as a loner who often breaks departmental rules (e.g., Hunter, Columbo, and Dirty Harry). Unlike those portrayed in the movies, the criminal investigator is likely to be an experienced veteran civil servant who has worked his or her way up to the detective division. Detectives are usually considered the elite of the police department. They are paid more, wear civilian clothes, and have more freedom in accomplishing their duties.

The general duties of detectives are to investigate the causes of crime and attempt to identify the individuals responsible for committing particular crimes. They usually enter the case after patrol officers have made initial contacts. Often they investigate the cases on their own. In addition, they follow up on initial police reports by the use of leads and informants. Detective bureaus are generally sub-divided into sections or bureaus such as homicide, vice, robbery, rape, etc.

The general mission of an investigator is:

1) to establish that a crime has been committed,

2) to locate and take statements from witnesses,

3) to establish the identify and whereabouts of the offender,

4) to collect, preserve, and transport evidence, and

5) to testify at court.

The effectiveness of detectives has been the center of much debate. A study by the Rand Corporation concluded that a great deal of a detective's time was spent in nonproductive work and that a detective's expertise did little to solve cases. A similar study by the

Police Executive Research Forum (PERF) found that if a time lapse of more than 15 minutes occurs between when the crime is reported and the criminal is identified there is only a five percent chance of solving the crime. Accordingly, by the time that the case is transferred to an investigator there is only a five percent chance that the criminal will be identified and arrested. The PERF study did, however, conclude that detectives do make meaningful contributions to the solution of criminal cases.[7]

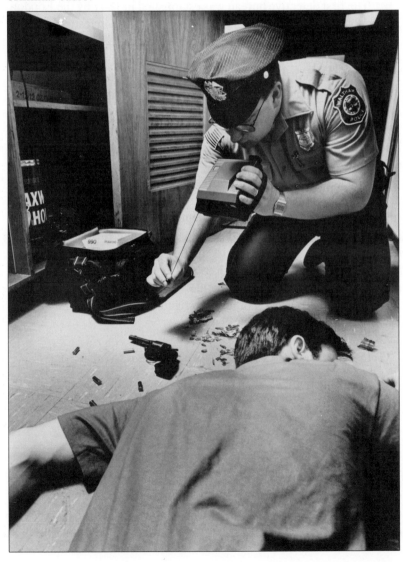

To increase the effectiveness of investigation efforts, the trend in most law enforcement agencies is to give patrol officers greater responsibilities to conduct on site investigations at the scene of the crime. Old-fashioned detective divisions have been replaced by specialized units. In addition, the use of technological advances in areas such as DNA and fingerprint identification has increased investigative effectiveness. Sophisticated computer identification systems are now being used to help witnesses identify suspects. These devices allow the investigator to develop computer-assisted drawings of the suspects. Other methods to improve investigative effectiveness include the careful screening of cases referred to the division, monitoring case flow and activity, and the use of targeted investigations in which focus is placed on certain individuals who are known to be engaged in criminal behavior on a continuing basis. Specialized investigations are discussed in the next section.

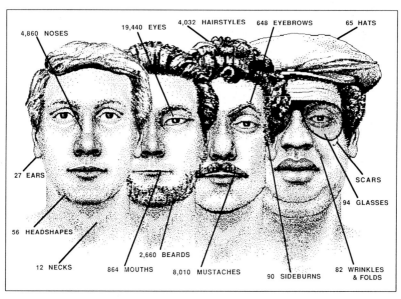

Compusketch feature library for computer generated composite sketches (Courtesy of VISATEX Corp.)

COMMUNITY POLICING

During the 1960s and 1970s many communities began to experiment with the concept of team policing. In team policing, teams of officers were assigned on a semi-permanent basis to particular neighborhoods. They were expected to become familiar with the local community and its problems. The members of a team were given considerable discretion in processing complaints received from local citizens. "Team policing" was based on the concept that the police team, as law enforcers, was responsible for the reduction of crime in that particular neighborhood. In the 1980s, community policing concepts developed in which the police were considered service providers, not enforcers. The mission of the police was to assist the community in resolving a vast array of problems which may or may not have been crime related.

Community policing starts with good community relations.

The community policing concept evolved from critical examinations of how police should respond to citizens and to the problems of crime, drug abuse, and disorder.[8] **Community policing** is based on the concept of proactive crime prevention. It involves the visible presence of police in neighborhoods conducting activities designed to solve crime-producing problems, arrest criminals, maintain order, and resolve disputes. It includes the concept of shared responsibility in that the police and the community work as partners in establishing and maintaining safe and peaceful neighborhoods.

Police presenting a Neighborhood Watch program.

According to the advocates of community policing, the advantages of community policing include:

— The police officer moves from a position of anonymity in the patrol car to direct engagement with the community. This gives the officer more immediate information and insight about neighborhood problems and possible solutions.

— The police officer is able to engage more directly in proactive crime by freeing the officer from the emergency response system.

— The concept makes policing operations more visible to the public and therefore increases public accountability of the police.

— It encourages the officers and the public to view themselves as partners.

— It moves the decision-making and discretion from the supervisory level to the patrol officer on the scene who typically is more familiar with the local community problems and expectations.

— It develops a relationship between the police and the community which encourages the public to take more initiative in preventing and solving crime.

Since community policing is more a *philosophy* than a *tactic*, different agencies are using different approaches to implementation. The most common approaches include increasing foot patrols, creating a visible police presence by attending community meetings and events, and opening storefront police offices in the neighborhoods.

In Madison, Wisconsin the police agency created an experimental police district. The area chosen to implement community policing on a trial basis was their south sector which has a wide diversity of cultural and ethnic groups. The area has 11 neighborhood associations and a better-than-average reputation of supporting the police. As part of the program, storefront substations were established and staffed by the best officers. The substations were located in or near community centers in the lower income housing complexes of the city's South Side. Neighborhood foot patrols were established in order for the officers to maintain close contact with the residents of the area in which they patrol. The substation hours were typically from noon to 8 p.m., Tuesday through Saturday with 24-hour telephone answering service available. The early conclusions of the experiment include:

— A substantial positive shift in the officers' attitudes toward their work and the work place.

— Improved perceptions and attitudes by the community toward the police.

— A significant reduction in reported burglaries in the experimental area.

EXHIBIT 8-1

A Community Police Officer's Day

The police officer involved in community policing, in addition to the traditional law enforcement activities, such as patrol and responding to calls for service, include:

— operating neighborhood substations

— meeting with local community groups

— analyzing neighborhood problems and attempting to assist in their resolution

— talking with students

— meeting local businesspersons

— conducting security checks

— dealing with disorderly people

In Oakland, California in evaluating their community policing efforts, research was conducted on the effects of foot patrols in reducing the community's fear of crime, citizen satisfaction with the police, and crime. Foot officers were observed and interviewed, and two-week activity statistics were obtained. The study found great diversity in the tactics foot officers used to keep drunks moving, rounding up truants, etc. Often the mere presence of the officer at a troubled street corner would restore order. Most of the activities of the foot officers were self-selected as opposed to a common standard of responding to assigned calls.

EXHIBIT 8-2

Critical Assumptions In Community Policing

1) The increased visibility of police in the community reduces the public's fear of crime.

2) The public's satisfaction or dissatisfaction with police can be easily measured.

3) The police should actively help define and shape community norms.

4) Public fears stem more from disorder than crime.

5) Signs of neglect and decay invite crime to a neighborhood.

6) Active involvement in community affairs will not violate the political neutrality of the police.

Problems With Community Policing

There are some problems with community policing. One chief complaint is that dividing the police into substations is not as efficient as the centralization of police resources. Another problem is the difficulty in defining the community. Often communities are defined based on political boundaries or existing police sectors rather than in terms of an ecological area which is defined by common norms and shared values. Defining the exact roles of police officers in community policing may also cause problems. How the community police agents integrate with the regular activities of the police department can also be an area of concern. Community policing assumes that the neighborhood actually wants increased police presence. This assumption ignores the unfortunate reality that citizens often fear the police as much as they fear crime. Since the role of the officer is different in community policing, it may be difficult to hire the right types of officers needed for community policing.

EXHIBIT 8-3

Neighborhood Safety

Neighborhoods provide easy targets for criminals in two respects: first, the intruder may find no one home and second, there are few passers-by who can spot intruders. The social changes in our neighborhoods have also made homes easier targets. For the first time in history, large numbers of dwellings are completely unattended for many hours each day. This is due to the increase in single-person households, generally smaller numbers in each family, and an increase in the number of two-wage earner families. In addition, high density neighborhoods are being replaced by lower density ones where individuals do not know or regularly talk with their neighbors.

To offset these problems, the police have instituted several programs designed to combat neighborhood crimes. The most popular programs include "Neighborhood Watch" and "Operation Identification."

The "Neighborhood Watch" program has been the major response by police to the problem of unprotected, low-density neighborhoods. This program encourages citizens to get to know their neighbors, to attend block meetings to discuss crime problems, and to call the police if they observe any suspicious activity in the neighborhood. Signs warning potential criminals that the area is protected by the program are posted in the neighborhood. The citizens may even go out on patrol on a regular basis, but they do not work directly with the police. The appeal of "Neighborhood Watch" is substantial. Approximately one-fifth of people responding to a national survey indicated that they participated in the program or a similar one.

The "Operation Identification" program is designed to encourage citizens to mark their property for easy identification, thus making it less inviting to steal. Usually the police set up booths or tables at local shopping centers and invite the public to bring their property to be marked.

PROBLEM-ORIENTED POLICING

Problem-oriented policing is closely associated with community policing. Problem-oriented policing embraces the concept that many crimes are caused by existing social conditions within the community.

Traditional police models are based on responding to calls for help in the fastest time possible, dealing with the situation, and returning to the patrol as soon as possible. This model usually results in a superficial relief to the immediate problem. In problem-oriented policing (POP) the police use a proactive orientation. Under this approach, the police identify long-term community problems and develop strategies to solve them. For example, if the neighborhood is being used by street level drug dealers to sell their products, the police, after identifying the problem (drug activity), devise a long-term plan to eliminate the problem. Accordingly, the police, under the POP model, are concentrating police resources on "hot spots of crime" in the communities.

Seattle, in its efforts to crack down on drugs, established a precinct Anti-crime Team (ACT) consisting of a sergeant, detective, and two uniform officers. Their goal was to use community support to disrupt or destroy drug operations. Other efforts in the area included changing pay telephones in areas with high drug use to a "call out status only." Accordingly, drug dealers could not use the telephones to receive messages. Citizens' complaints of drug activity received by the community hot-line or by other means were referred to the ACT. Property owners gave police advance permission to enter private property such as parking lots to investigate people loitering on them. Telephone hot-lines were established. An anti-graffiti program was started. Steps were taken to involve other city agencies in fighting the drug and crime problem.

As can be noted from the above examples, problem-oriented policing focuses on a particular problem and takes extraordinary steps to reduce or eliminate the problem. The actions taken are in addition to the standard police activities being utilized in the neighborhoods.

SUPPORT FUNCTIONS

All police departments must have units that handle the support functions of the department. The most common support functions include personnel, internal affairs, budget and finance, records, communications center, training, community relations, planning and research, property and equipment, and detention.

Personnel Unit

Most police departments have their own personnel unit that is responsible for the recruitment, selection, promotion, assignment, and separation of personnel. Each of these functions requires the advice and guidance of experts to comply with the many rules and regulations associated with the activities.

Budget and Finance

Generally police departments are responsible for the administration and control of their budgets. Included in this function is the administration of the payroll, purchasing, budget planning and auditing financial records.

Internal Affairs

Internal affairs units are normally charged with the goal of keeping the department free of corruption. They police the police. Any citizen complaints regarding police corruption are usually investigated by internal affairs. They also investigate the use of force by the police and police participation in actual criminal violations. Internal affairs is a controversial unit and its members are distrusted by other officers. In smaller departments, usually one officer is appointed by the chief to conduct internal affairs' business.

Community Relations

While building community relations is a function of all employees of a police department, the larger departments have special units that deal with the public and whose goals include the building of a positive police image in the community.

Planning and Research

In small departments, usually the duties of planning and research are the responsibility of the chief. In larger departments, generally there is a separate planning and research unit whose duties are to conduct long range planning and supervise applied research.

Records

Records units are used by police departments to maintain and disseminate information on wanted offenders, traffic violators, stolen merchandise, etc. The use of computers has allowed police departments to maintain highly sophisticated information.

Communications Center

The communication center helps in the effective and efficient dispatching of patrol cars. Modern computer technologies are being used to make the most of limited resources.

Training

Training units are generally responsible for entry level training, and also continuing in-service training. Entry level training is normally accomplished at police academies. Large departments usually operate their own academies whereas smaller departments may send their recruits to academies run by other departments or educational organizations. The average officer receives about 20 weeks of pre-service training which includes about 450 classroom hours and 200 hours of field training.

Firearms training is a continuing process where the officer must "qualify" several times a year.

The amount of pre-service training required by individual states varies greatly around the country. Pre-service training generally includes the nuts-and-bolts of police work, handling of weapons, first aid, community relations, patrol techniques, criminal law and procedure, use of deadly force, and crowd control. After this training the rookie officer is paired with a veteran officer for on-the-job training in the field.

Police officers spend numerous hours each year in training under continuing education programs or advanced officer training such as special weapons and tactics teams, hostage negotiation, command colleges, self defense tactics, new laws and procedure updates along with personal skills (i.e., report writing, computer training, court testimony, physical conditioning, stress reduction, etc.).

"One push of the button on the ACME training compliance unit and I guarantee you'll never screw up again."

Property

Police are required to handle evidence which includes weapons and narcotics. They are also required to safeguard property belonging to prisoners in detention, towed vehicles, abandoned cars, etc.

Generally, in large departments, there are separate units with the responsibility to handle the property or evidence. In smaller departments, the responsibility of handling property is frequently a subdivision of another operating unit.

Detention

Most law enforcement agencies operate detention facilities for the temporary custody of suspects who have been arrested. These facilities are normally used as holding cells until the arrestees can be transported to the county jail.

INNOVATIONS IN POLICE OPERATIONS

By the year 2000, many researchers predict that police departments will rely more heavily on new technologies for investigation efficiency. Computer-based record keeping and electronic surveillance devices will be commonly used by police units. In addition, it appears that the police will be more concerned with public well-being and security than with efforts to control crime. The police will be asked to do more with less resources.

The transfer of certain traditional police functions to private police should reduce the demand on law enforcement. For example, one proposal is to transfer burglar alarm response to the private sector. It is noted that the number of homes with private security systems has grown rapidly. It is estimated that by the year 2000, 30 percent of homes will have private security systems. There will also be an increase in the number of false alarms of these systems. It is estimated that about 30 percent of the current calls are false alarms.

Each year, more is expected of our police officers. The average police officer needs to be a sidewalk sociologist to fix community and individual problems. Police are no longer primarily crime fighters, but are civil problem solvers. This duty of solving civil problems has been placed by default on the police departments. The police are available 24 hours a day, seven days a week. No other social service is as readily available as the police. Many of the calls to the police for assistance have nothing to do with crime. For example, when a cat is stranded in a tree, the normal reaction is to call the police. If an elderly person has not been seen for several days, often the police will be contacted to check on that person.

DISCUSSION QUESTIONS

1. How effective are our present patrolling techniques?

2. Compare and contrast community policing with problem-oriented policing.

3. Why is it necessary to have an internal affairs unit?

4. Should police departments use one-man vehicle patrols?

5. What are the advantages of community policing compared to traditional policing?

ENDNOTES

[1] John Webster, "Police Task and Time Study," *Journal of Criminal Law, Criminology, and Police Science*, vol. 61, (1970): pp. 94-100.

[2] Charles D. Hale, "Patrol Administration," *Local Government Police Management*, (1982), p. 115.

[3] Stephen Schack, Theodore H. Schell, and William G. Gay, *Specialized Patrol: Improving Patrol Productivity*, vol. 2, (Washington D.C.: Government Printing Office, 1977).

[4] Michael F. Cahn and James Tiern, *An Alternate Approach in Police Response*, (Washington D.C.: National Institute of Justice, 1981).

[5] George Kelling et al. *The Kansas City Preventive Patrol Experiment: A Summary Report*, (Washington D.C.: Police Foundation, 1974).

[6] George Kelling, *Foot Patrol*, (Washington D.C.: National Institute of Justice, 1987).

[7] John Eck, *Solving Crimes*, (Washington D.C.: Police Executive Research Forum, 1984).

[8] National Institute of Justice, "Community Policing in the 1990s," *National Institute of Justice Journal*, (August, 1992): pp.2-15.

PART III

THE COURT SYSTEM

The Douglas County Courthouse built in 1880.

STRUCTURE AND ROLE
OF COURTS

How to win a case in court?
If the law is on your side, pound on the law.
If the facts are on your side, pound on the facts.
If neither are on your side, pound on the table.

—Anonymous

This chapter will examine the structure and role of our federal, state, and local criminal courts. Criminal courts are the heart of the criminal justice system. They have three primary missions:

1) to administer justice in a fair and impartial manner;

2) to protect the individual rights of persons accused of crimes; and

3) to provide an authority for controlling crime.

Courts are established by either the U.S.Constitution, state constitutions, or legislation. Courts that are established under a constitution are called constitutional courts. Those established by a state or federal statute are considered legislative courts.

The organization of the federal and state court systems is strikingly similar. The major problem facing both court systems is the sharply increasing caseload. This is especially true in state courts where the caseloads continue to climb and the resources to handle this increase are diminishing.

FEDERAL COURTS

The Articles of Confederation which governed our country from 1781 to 1789 did not provide for federal courts. Thus, the federal government was forced to use state courts, which proved to be unworkable. Hence, provisions in the U.S. Constitution that provided for a federal court system were accepted by the delegates at the Constitutional convention without debate.[1] The U.S. Constitution, Article III, Sections 1 and 2 provide for our federal court system.

Article III

Section 1. The Judicial Power of the United States shall be vested in one Supreme Court, and in such inferior Courts as the Congress may from time to time ordain and establish. The Judges, both of the supreme and inferior Courts, shall hold their Offices during good Behavior, and shall, at Times, receive for their Services, a Compensation, which shall not be diminished during their Continuance in Office.

Section 2. The judicial Power shall extend to all Cases, in Law and Equity, arising under the Constitution, the Laws of the United States, and Treaties made, or which shall be made, under their Authority; to all cases affecting Ambassadors, other public Ministers and Consuls; to all Cases of admiralty and maritime Jurisdiction; to Controversies to which the United States shall be a Party; between Citizens of different States; ....

In all Cases affecting Ambassadors, other public Ministers and Consuls, and those in which a state shall be a Party, the Supreme Court shall have original jurisdiction. In all other cases before mentioned, the supreme court shall have appellate jurisdiction, both as to Law and fact, with such exceptions, and under such regulations as the Congress shall make.

The Trial of all Crimes, except in Cases of Impeachment, shall be by Jury; and such Trial shall be held in the State where the said Crimes shall have been committed; but when not committed within any State, the Trail shall be as such place or places as the Congress by Law have directed.

Under the authority granted by the above two sections of the Constitution, the federal government has established a three-tiered hierarchy of court jurisdiction which consists of the U.S. District Courts, U.S. Courts of Appeal, and the U.S. Supreme Court. In addition to those courts, there are also federal courts that have limited jurisdiction over specific subject matter.

FEDERAL JUDICIAL SYSTEM

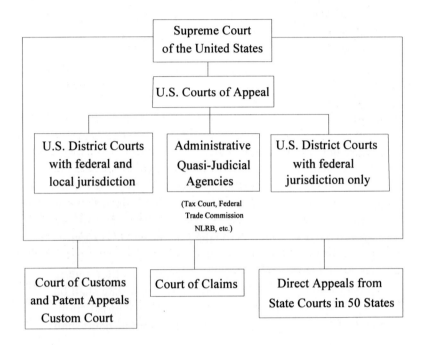

U.S. District Courts

The general trial courts in the federal system are the U.S. District Courts. These courts have jurisdiction over cases involving violations of federal law, including civil rights abuse, interstate transportation of stolen vehicles, and kidnapping. The district courts also have civil jurisdiction on questions involving citizenship rights, suits between citizens who reside in different states, when one state sues another state or a citizen who lives in another state, or where the federal government is a party to the suit.

The district courts were first created by the Judicial Act of 1789. Presently, there are 94 district courts in the United States. Each state has at least one district court. Several states, like New York and California, have four district courts. One district court is located in Washington, D.C. to handle the cases arising in Washington. Four district courts handle the U.S. Territories (i.e., Guam, Virgin Islands, and Northern Mariana Islands, etc.). The remaining 89 courts are within the 50 states.

While there are only 94 U.S. District Courts, there are almost 600 district court judges. Each district court has at least two judges assigned to it with each judge sitting as the judge of the district court. The busiest courts have many more judges assigned to them. For example, the U.S. District Court for the Southern District of New York located in Manhattan has 27 judges. In most cases, a single judge presides over each trial. In selected cases involving constitutional issues, a three-judge court may be convened.

The district courts handle thousands of criminal cases each year. Several of the courts are busier than others. For example, the district court judges in the Southern District of California were the busiest in the U.S. in 1987 and handled 134 criminal cases per judge. The district courts in California, Illinois, and New York process more criminal cases in any one year than does the rest of the federal judiciary combined. [*Note*: The average judge in a state criminal court may handle several thousand criminal cases each year. Only about 13 percent of all criminal cases are tried in federal courts and about 87 percent are tried in state courts.]

In all but the least populous western states and the small eastern states, federal judicial court districts are subdivided into sections. For example, in Alaska there is only one federal district court. It is designated as the U.S. District Court for Alaska. California, on the other hand, has four federal judicial districts. The federal court districts are labeled geographically. California's federal judicial districts are the U.S. District Courts for northern, central, southern, and eastern districts of California. In some states, like Louisiana, there are northern, southern and middle judicial districts.

Federal district courts are courts of general jurisdiction. The phrase "general jurisdiction" means that they are trial courts with the authority to handle all prosecutions for violations of federal law. In addition to having criminal and civil jurisdictions the district courts also serve as appellate courts for those matters tried before a U.S. Magistrate. In addition, they have appellate functions in dealing with certain writs of habeas corpus.

Writs of habeas corpus are writs brought before the court challenging the custody of a person. In a writ of habeas corpus the person filing the writ (normally a prisoner) is requesting the court to issue the writ requiring the person who is holding someone in custody to appear before the court and justify the legality of the confinement.

The principal aim of a writ of habeas corpus is to release a person from an unlawful confinement. Generally such writs are used to attack the constitutionality of a state criminal conviction. The person bringing the writ generally alleges that his or her conviction is illegal in that it violates the protections guaranteed by the U.S. Constitution or other federal statutes. (This writ will be discussed further in Chapter 11.)

Judges to the district courts are appointed by the President of the United States with the advice and consent of the senate. They are appointed for life and can be removed only by impeachment. While theoretically the judges are appointed by the president, the custom is that the senior senator of the state who is of the same party as the president controls the appointments in that state. Because of their lifetime appointment, federal judges tend to exhibit greater resistance to improper pressures and have higher legal competence than do state judges who are elected to office for limited terms. [*Note*: The federal courts in the three U.S. Territories (Guam, Virgin Islands, and Northern Mariana Islands) are considered legislative courts and their judges serve 10 year terms.]

There are approximately 45,000 criminal cases filed in federal district courts each year. See attached chart for a breakdown on various types of offenses handled by the district courts. Approximately 35,000 writs were filed in federal district courts in 1988 by state and federal prisoners. The writs consume an increasing larger portion of the federal courts' dockets each year.

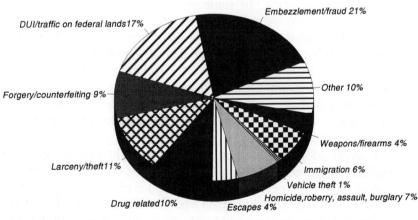

Cases Handled in Federal District Courts

percentage by type of offense

Embezzlement/fraud 21%

DUI/traffic on federal lands17%

Forgery/counterfeiting 9%

Other 10%

Weapons/firearms 4%

Larceny/theft11%

Immigration 6%

Vehicle theft 1%

Homicide,roberry, assault, burglary 7%

Drug related10%

Escapes 4%

Source: U. S. Dept. of Justice

Courts of Appeal

The courts of appeal consider only cases previously tried in trial courts. The courts of appeal were created by Congress in 1891 as the Circuit Courts of Appeal.

Appeals from federal district courts go to the U.S. Courts of Appeal. There are 13 U.S. Courts of Appeal. The country is divided into 11 circuits, the District of Columbia, and the courts of appeal for the federal circuit. Each court, except the Court of Appeal for the 13th Circuit, is located in a circuit. For example, the U.S. Court of Appeals for the Ninth Circuit is located in San Francisco and hears appeals of cases from the district courts located in California and other western states. The 13th Circuit Court was created in 1982 with national jurisdiction, but limited subject matter jurisdiction. It hears only appeals in patent questions, minor claims against the government, and appeals from the U.S. Claims Court and the U.S. Court of International Trade.

Each circuit has at least four judges. Circuits with a great deal of litigation have more than 20 appellate judges. The chief judge of each circuit has supervisory responsibilities for the circuit. Presently, there are 171 circuit court judges. Appellate cases are usually heard by panels of three judges. Important cases may be heard by all the appellate judges assigned to that circuit (referred to as "en banc").

The courts of appeal do not rule on the guilt or innocence of a criminal defendant. Their duties are to determine if the decisions of the trial court are legally correct. If the court of appeals determines that there are no prejudicial errors of law, then the court upholds (affirms) the decision. If the court of appeals finds prejudicial error the court normally returns the case to the trial court. The trial court can either retry the case or dismiss it. In most cases, the court of appeals will issue a written opinion regarding the law that was applied to the case.

Criminal appeals from district courts constitute a very small part of the work of the appeals courts. The criminal cases appealed most often involve drugs or fraud. Any person convicted by a federal district court has the right to appeal to the court of appeals. The appeals can be divided into three classes:

1) frivolous appeals which have little substance and no significant new issues;

2) ritualistic appeals which are brought primarily because of the demands of the litigants (appellants); and

3) nonconsensual appeals which involve significant questions of law and policy.

There is little chance of reversal for the first two types. These are usually disposed of quickly. There is a greater chance of reversal of the lower court decision for the third type. However, only about ten percent of all cases appealed are reversed. Decisions of the courts of appeal are final except for the few cases reviewed by the U.S. Supreme Court.

U.S. Supreme Court

The people can change Congress, but only God can change the Supreme Court.

—Senator George Norris

The U.S. Supreme Court is the highest appellate court and the court of last resort for all cases tried in the various federal and state courts. In the criminal area, the court sits only as an appellate court. The court is composed of nine justices— one chief justice and eight associate justices. Like other federal judges, the justices are appointed by the president with the advice and consent of the senate.

While the Court is provided for in the constitution, it is only in the briefest form. The Court was actually created by the Judiciary Act of 1789. When President Washington signed that act, he sent to the Senate for confirmation the names of the first chief justice and five associate justices. Of the five associate justices, one declined, another accepted but never attended. All had either resigned or died by 1799. The chief justice, John Jay spent most of his time in Europe and resigned in 1796. The Court did not gain its present stature until the appointment of John Marshall as chief justice. He was chief justice from 1801 to 1835. Two years after he assumed the chief justice position, the court issued the *Marbury v. Madison* case. In this case, the court claimed, exercised, and justified its authority to review and nullify acts of congress that are in conflict with the U.S. Constitution.

The *Marbury v. Madison* case decided in 1803 resulted from a dispute between congress and the president over the power of the president to appoint judges. As the result of the election of 1800, Thomas Jefferson was elected president by defeating John Adams. Adams' party, the Federalists, sought to entrench themselves in the federal judiciary. Just prior to leaving office, Adams approved legislation that created 16 new district courts and 42 justices of the peace. On his last night in office, Adams signed the commissions of the new judges and attempted to deliver the appointments. William Marbury's, an assistant to the secretary of the Navy, appointment was not delivered before Adams left office. Marbury asked the Supreme Court to issue a writ ordering Jefferson to deliver the appointment. The Judiciary Act of 1789 had authorized the court to issue such writs.

Chief Justice Marshall knew that if he ordered Jefferson to deliver the appointment, Jefferson would refuse to obey the order. The Court, under Marshall's leadership, held that congress had acted unconstitutionally and exceeded its power when it expanded the jurisdiction of the Court. In his opinion, he stressed the right of the Court to review legislation as to its constitutionality, and congress could not expand or contract the jurisdiction of the Court. This decision, by not requiring Jefferson to deliver the commissions, prevented a conflict between the Court and the president. The decision's most noteworthy effect, however, was the establishment of the Court's power to review acts of congress.

The Court has discretion over most of the cases it will consider and chooses only those cases that have important issues and are worthy of its attention. In most cases to obtain review by the Supreme Court, the person files a *writ of certiorari* which is a writ that requests that the court review the holdings of the lower appellate court. The Supreme Court must accept all cases in which:

— a federal court holds an act of congress to be unconstitutional;

— a U.S. Court of Appeals holds a state statute in violation of the federal constitution;

— a state's highest court holds a federal law to be invalid;

— an individual's challenge to a state statute on federal constitutional grounds is upheld by a state supreme court.

Currently approximately 5,000 requests for writs are submitted to the Supreme Court each year. The Court only accepts about 200. Most of the 200 will be civil cases. Generally the Court accepts only about 60 criminal cases a year for review.

When the Court issues a decision on a case, the Court either affirms, reverses, or remands a case. If the Court affirms a criminal conviction from the lower court, the conviction remains in force. If the Court reverses it, the conviction is overturned and the case is returned to the lower court. The Court may also remand a case to a lower court for further proceeding not inconsistent with the guidelines set forth in the Court's decision.

The Court has developed several ground rules to govern the review of cases.

— It will not accept a case unless there is an adversarial dispute regarding the case. It does not provide advisory opinions.

— The Court will not anticipate a question of constitutional law in advance of the necessity for deciding it.

— If the case can be decided on non-constitutional grounds or on constitutional grounds, the court will choose the non-constitutional grounds.

— The Court will not formulate a constitutional rule of law that is broader than is required by the facts of the case.

— When possible, the Court will avoid deciding the validity of an act of congress.

EXHIBIT 9-1

Summary of Supreme Court Jurisdiction

Original Jurisdiction

Mandatory cases (must be heard by the Court):
(1) Disputes between the states.

Discretionary cases (the Court may accept, but not required to):

(1) Cases brought by a state.

(2) Disputes between a state and a foreign government.

(3) Cases involving a foreign, diplomatic person.

Appellate Jurisdiction

Mandatory cases:

(1) Cases in which a federal court has declared an act of congress unconstitutional and the federal government is a party.

(2) Any case in which a state supreme court has held an act of congress unconstitutional.

(3) Cases where the state law conflicts with the Constitution or federal law.

Discretionary cases:

(1) All decisions of federal courts of appeal except those in mandatory category

(2) All decisions of the state's highest court involving a federal issue except those in mandatory category.

In its first five years of existence, the Court ruled only on four matters. Now the Court receives at least 70 petitions each week. The very nature of the caseload permits the Court to do little more than formulate general policy. When the Court issues a major decision such as *Mapp v. Ohio* (the exclusionary rule), it lacks the time to rule on all the corollary principles that may derive from a major decision. Accordingly, it may take years before a new rule and its corollary principles are clearly defined. For example, after the *Mapp v. Ohio* decision was announced, it was unclear whether the decision would apply to cases that have already been tried or only on cases yet to be tried. What exceptions should be made to the rule also needed to be decided. Studies of the impact of Supreme Court decisions indicate that in the field of criminal law, each major decision issued by the Supreme Court creates more legal questions that the decision answered.[2]

Each year, the Court begins a new term on the first Monday in October. The Court will then give full consideration to approximately 200 cases before it recesses for the summer. Most petitions filed with the Court are disposed of by denying review. To accept a case for review, normally four justices must vote to review the case. Over 80 percent of the writs filed with the Court are denied.

EXHIBIT 9-2

Justices of the U.S. Supreme Court 1994

Justice	Date Sworn In	Nominated By	Views
Chief Justice William H. Rehnquist	Jan. 1972	Nixon	Very conservative
Harry A. Blackmun	June 1970	Nixon	Usually liberal
John Paul Stevens	Dec. 1975	Ford	Moderate to liberal
Sandra Day O'Connor	Sept. 1981	Reagan	Conservative
Antonin Scalia	Sept. 1986	Reagan	Very conservative
Anthony Kennedy	Feb. 1988	Reagan	Conservative
David H. Souter	July 1990	Bush	Very conservative
Clarence Thomas	Oct. 1991	Bush	Very conservative
Ruth Ginsburg	Aug. 1993	Clinton	Moderate to liberal

STATE COURTS

While no two state systems are exactly alike, there are striking similarities. Most states have a three-tiered system with courts of (1) limited jurisdiction, (2) general jurisdiction, and (3) appellate courts. In each state there are major trial courts. In California, they are called superior courts; in Texas its the district court; and in New York, they are called supreme courts. The major trial courts are also courts of general jurisdiction like the federal district courts. All states also have lower courts which are generally courts with limited jurisdiction and a system of appellate courts.

California Court System

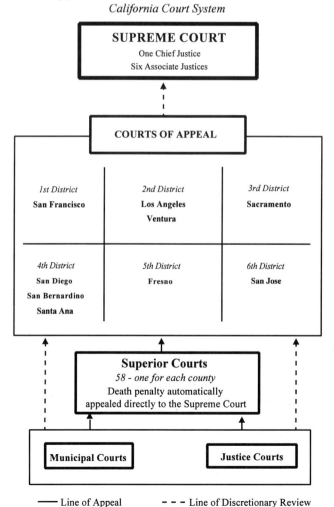

SUPREME COURT
One Chief Justice
Six Associate Justices

COURTS OF APPEAL

1st District	*2nd District*	*3rd District*
San Francisco	Los Angeles	Sacramento
	Ventura	

4th District	*5th District*	*6th District*
San Diego	Fresno	San Jose
San Bernardino		
Santa Ana		

Superior Courts
58 - one for each county
Death penalty automatically
appealed directly to the Supreme Court

Municipal Courts   Justice Courts

——— Line of Appeal   - - - Line of Discretionary Review

Lower Courts

There are approximately 13,000 lower courts in the United States. They are called municipal, county, or justice courts. They handle misdemeanor criminal cases, traffic violations, and preliminary proceedings in felony cases. While defendants generally have the same rights in the lower courts as they do in the major trial courts, the judges try the cases in a more informal manner. Most lower courts are not courts of record and therefore do not keep written records of the proceedings.

Since the number of traffic, petty and misdemeanor crimes far outnumber felonies, the lower courts constitute the first and, in most instances, the only contact that most citizens have with the criminal court system. Lower courts vary across the U.S. and often within a single state. These courts are also more of a reflection of the community and community standards than any other type of court.

In criminal cases tried before a lower court, the appeal is to the court of general jurisdiction or major trial court. In most states, if the criminal case is appealed the case is tried "de novo" in superior or district court. In a trial de novo, the case is completely retried as if it were a new case.

The lower criminal courts generally conduct the first appearance of the accused in felony trials. At the first appearance, the accused is advised of the charges against him or her, assigned an attorney if the defendant does not already have one, and bail is set.

In those states, like California, where a grand jury is not used, the lower court (justice or municipal) conducts a preliminary hearing. The purpose of a preliminary hearing is to determine if there is probable cause to require the accused to stand trial. At the preliminary hearing, the judge may dismiss the charges, reduce them to a lower level, or order the accused to stand trial before the superior or district court. If the judge dismisses the charges, it is "without prejudice" (the prosecutor may refile the charges if additional evidence is discovered).

In most states, the lower court judges are elected. In some states, they are appointed by the governor subject to voter confirmation at the next general election. In those states where they are appointed by the governor, normally they must also be confirmed by a judicial appointment committee which contains representatives from the state legislatures and the judiciary. A few states permit the appointment or election of non-lawyers as judges. In *North v. Russell*, the U.S. Supreme Court held that misdemeanor criminal trials before non-lawyer judges did not violate the concept of due-process and was therefore legal. In that case, the accused was tried in a Kentucky court and sentenced to a jail term by a judge with no legal training or education.[3]

Major Trial Courts

The major trial courts are more formal in their proceedings than the lower courts. They are courts of record in that a record is made of their proceedings. They are also courts of general jurisdiction in that they have the authority to hear and determine all criminal cases. The major trial courts usually have exclusive jurisdiction over felonies; they are the only court which has the authority to try felony cases. All states require that the judges of the major trial courts be lawyers.

Appellate Courts

Appellate courts hear and decide appeals from trial courts. All states have appellate courts to appeal criminal convictions. Thirty-nine states have a two-tiered appellate system with an intermediate court of appeals (generally referred to as the court of appeals) and a court of last resort (the state supreme court). The remaining states have only one level of appeals for criminal cases.

The appellate courts have the responsibility to review cases to determine whether the state has reached its burden of proving all elements of the crimes charged beyond a reasonable doubt, correctness of the judges rulings and instructions to the jury, and whether the defendant has carried his or her burden in establishing affirmative defenses. Most appeals from the trial courts are based on irregular proceedings in the trial court, whether the accused was provided his or her procedural guarantees, or the ineffectiveness of defense counsel. As noted earlier, less than 10 percent of the cases are reversed on appeal. In most states, the accused has an automatic right of appeal to the intermediate appellate court. In death penalty cases, the accused has the right to appeal to the state supreme court or other court of last resort.

The accused is not present when his or her case is presented to an appellate court. The court looks only at the record of trial, the appellate briefs submitted by each side, and argument of counsel.

California
TRIAL COURTS

Superior Courts

58 courts with a total of 408 judges.

Jurisdiction

Civil - Over $25,000.00

Criminal - Felonies and misdemeanors not otherwise provided for

Appeals - Go to Courts of Appeal applicable to the district,
or Supreme Court, depending on appellate jurisdiction

Municipal Courts

74 courts with a total of 305 judges.

Jurisdiction

Civil - $25,000.00 or less

Small Claims

Criminal - Misdemeanors

Appeals - Go to appellate department of Superior Court

Justice Courts

245 courts with a total of 245 judges

Jurisdiction

Civil - $25,000.00 or less

Small Claims

Criminal - Minor Misdemeanors

Appeals - Go to the appellate department of Superior Court

While there is a presumption of not guilty when the accused is tried in a trial court, no such presumption exists in the appellate proceedings. In fact, there is a presumption that the trial court's actions and findings are correct in law and fact.

Caseload

As noted earlier, one of the major problems with the courts, both state and federal, is the increasing caseload. It is estimated that state courts alone process over 90 million civil, traffic and criminal cases each year. Federal courts hear approximately 30,000 criminal and 220,000 civil cases each year. The overloaded court dockets have resulted in the charges of assembly-line justice. The only reason that our criminal courts are able to function is the high percentage of guilty pleas. If every defendant pled not guilty and demanded a jury trial, the system would probably collapse. In 1993, the county of Los Angeles considered and partially adopted the practice of not trying misdemeanor crimes in an effort to reduce caseloads.

Budget restraints often prevent the establishing of additional courts and the hiring personnel to handle new cases. Other methods used in an attempt to reduce the overload problem include the use of diversion programs where the defendant is diverted out of the criminal justice program into a treatment program, decriminalization of certain crimes, and bail reform.

Court Reform

Court reform is seen as a method to make the processing of cases more efficient and to reduce the budgetary requirements of the court system. One method, according to many researchers, is to unify the court system. Unification is the merging of the lower courts with the major trial courts to have only one level of trial courts. Several states, including California, have taken steps to study the feasibility of such a merger.

The court mergers are also referred to as the unification of the courts. The recommendations by various court reformers as to unification of state courts include the following:

— unifying felony and misdemeanor courts into one criminal court;

— creating a single, unified state court system for both civil and criminal courts;

— centralizing the administrative responsibility of the courts;

— improving physical facilities of the courts;

— increasing the number of trial courts and judicial personnel;

— abolishing the justice of peace courts; and

— having a uniform appeal procedure for all courts.

Presently, some unification has taken place in Arizona, Illinois, North Carolina, Oklahoma, and Washington. It is being considered in other states, but any decision in this regard is likely to encounter strong political opposition from various pressure groups.

Other possible reforms include the creation of professional court administrators and other assistants to remove some of the duties from the judges. Limiting the right of an accused to appeal his or her conviction also has been advanced as a method of reducing court overloads.

The costs of the court systems have placed heavy burdens on the counties. To save money many courts have even stopped providing free lunches and coffee to juries. The budget problems will continue to plague the courts. Accordingly, it appears that most court reforms will be motivated by the desire to save money.

DISCUSSION QUESTIONS

1. How do state and federal appellate courts differ?

2. What is the impact of the caseload in our criminal courts?

3. How should our courts be reformed to handle the ever increasing workload?

4. Compare and explain the functions of the major trial courts with those of the lower courts.

ENDNOTES

[1] Mary Ann Harrell and Burnett Anderson, *Equal Justice Under Law: The Supreme Court in American Life*, rev. ed., (Washington D.C.: National Geographic Society for the Supreme Court Historical Society, 1982).

[2] Alan Blumberg, *Criminal Justice: Issues and Ironies*, (New York: New Viewpoints, 1979).

[3] *North v. Russell*, 427 U.S. 328 (1976).

PLAINTIFF

SAMUEL B. TAYLOR, Jr.
JUDGE

ROLES IN THE COURT SYSTEM

The prosecutor has absolute and unrestricted discretion to choose who is prosecuted and who is not.

—Anonymous

This chapter will examine the various roles of the persons involved in our court system. In addition, some of the key problems of the system will also be examined, including the two biggest dilemmas — the volume of cases and plea bargaining.

The principle roles in our court system, judges and counsel, are staffed by attorneys.[1] Under the court system, the defense counsel and the prosecutors are considered adversaries and the judge the referee. We often fail to realize, however, that as attorneys, these individuals have more in common with each other than with the other persons involved in the court system (i.e., the police, corrections and the accused). Thus, while the prosecutor and the police may be on the same side and the defendant and the accused on the other side, the key players in the system have more in common with the opposition than with other individuals on their own side.

The education and training of judges and counsel are similar, yet very different from the others involved in the court system. Almost all judges have participated in court as either prosecutor or defense counsel. Many counsel have also participated as both prosecutor and defense counsel.

The judges and counsel are law school graduates. Law school is more than an educational experience. It is an introduction to a philosophy of human experiences and an orientation to a lifestyle.[2] Law school is also a rite of passage for lawyers, much the same as the police academy is a rite of passage for police officers. In addition, the judges and counsel have all "passed the bar." It is only after passing the state bar examination, that they are admitted to practice law. The judges and counsel are also members of the local bar association and frequently attend social functions together.

One of the most important roles in the system is that of the prosecutor, especially the U.S. Attorney. This is the individual who is charged with the responsibility of filing criminal cases. Until the case is filed, it does not become a part of the court system.

COURTHOUSE WORK GROUP

The major organizational goal of criminal courts is the efficient disposition of cases filed in that court. Accordingly, harmony within the organization is promoted by discretion and negotiation by the "courthouse work group." The courthouse work group is a term used to describe judge, prosecutors, and defense attorneys who regularly work in a court. These individuals have similar educational backgrounds, work closely with each other, and have similar career goals. Case disposition takes place by this group during informal discussions.

For example, in one typical jurisdiction all the prosecutors and defense counsel who are on that day's trial docket meet in the judge's office with the judge prior to court convening. These meetings are generally very informal with the judge calling the docket of cases and asking what is happening in each case. In one case, the defense may indicate that they are going to request a delay and provide reasons for the delay. The judge will indicate how he or she will probably rule on the request. In another case, the prosecutor may indicate that there is a plea bargain and then inform the judge of the details of the bargain. At this time the judge indicates whether or not he or she will approve the plea bargain and accept the guilty plea. In other cases, the counsel may indicate that the case is a "go." This means that the case will be tried and that both sides are ready for trial.

After each case is discussed, the meeting dissolves and the counsel return to the court room. Later the judge enters the court and calls the docket (convenes court). The informal agreements made in the judge's office are then made formally in open court. If the judge has indicated that a certain request (e.g., a request for a delay) will not be granted, rarely will the counsel make the request on the record in open court.[3]

While these informal meetings are not provided for in the rules and laws governing criminal procedures, they exist in most jurisdictions and are invaluable in keeping the flow of cases moving. The "justice" negotiated in the judge's chambers overshadows the formal trial in open court. It is important, however, to maintain a smooth functioning organization; this type of "informal justice" provides efficiency to the overall system.

Members of the work group have a mutual understanding as to the roles of each member of the group. Only rarely do the members of the work group question the guilt of the defendant. It is assumed by the work group that in the majority of cases the defendant is guilty. The members do not oppose each other in competition for the truth, they are in effect a team, negotiating the best settlement possible with minimal dispute and maximum justice.[4]

Does the defense counsel do a disservice to his or her client by being a member of the courthouse work group? As one researcher stated: "Negotiation and settlement doesn't indicate an injustice, but the best resolution to a complex problem."[5] Courts are bureaucratic organizations and thus place a high value on efficiency, economy and speed in disposing of cases. The defense counsel as a member of the work group understands the bureaucratic pressures and makes them work to his or her advantage in getting the best deal for the defendant. In those cases where the defense counsel believes that the defendant is not guilty, the judge and prosecutor are more likely to be influenced to drop the case by a counsel who is a member of the group.

Defendants are not a part of this work group and are alien even to their counsel. While the judge and counsel have clearly delineated roles, the expected role of the defendant is not as clear. Without a defendant, there would be no criminal case. In most cases, however, the defendant is, in effect, an invisible person in the proceedings.

PROSECUTORS

We often think that the prosecutor's role is to convict the defendant. This is erroneous. The prosecutor has the duty to ensure justice, not merely to convict. Accordingly, if the prosecutor has a reasonable basis for believing that the defendant is not guilty, the prosecutor should not attempt to obtain a conviction. In such a case, if the prosecutor is the decision maker (e.g., district attorney), then the prosecutor should request that the case be dismissed. If the prosecutor is not the decision maker (e.g., an assistant district attorney), the prosecutor should present the facts to the district attorney and request either that he or she be relieved from the case or that the case be dismissed. It would be unethical for an attorney to attempt to convict an innocent person.

The American Bar Association's Code of Professional Responsibility, Canon 7-103 provides:

7-103: Performing the Duty of Public Prosecutor or Other Government Counsel

A. A public prosecutor or other government lawyer shall not institute or cause to be instituted criminal charges when he knows or it is obvious that the charges are not supported by probable cause.

B. A public prosecutor or other government lawyer in criminal litigation shall make timely disclosure to counsel for the defendant, or to the defendant if the defendant does not have counsel, of the existence of evidence, known to the prosecutor or other government lawyer, that tends to negate the guilt of the accused, mitigates the degree of the offense, or reduces the punishment.

Duties of Prosecutor

As noted earlier, the prosecutor in federal court is the U.S. Attorney or Assistant U.S. Attorney, probably the latter. In state courts, he or she is the district attorney, state's attorney, commonwealth's attorney, or county attorney. As reflected in the above, American Bar Canons of Professional Responsibility, the prosecutor's primary duty is not to convict, but to seek justice. If the prosecutor believes that the defendant is guilty and there is sufficient evidence to support the charges, then, and only then, is the prosecutor under a duty to enforce the criminal charge against the defendant.

Often, young prosecutors forget this and attempt to obtain as many convictions as possible to build a reputation as a "tough" prosecutor on crime. This conflict can lead to prosecutorial misconduct. Since appellate courts generally uphold convictions in those cases where the misconduct is not serious, some prosecutors who are overzealous or motivated by personal or political gain attempt to prosecute using questionable tactics that are marginally acceptable.

The prosecutor is also sometimes known as the plaintiff.

Under our adversarial system, only the prosecutor has the authority to refer charges to the courts. A case does not begin until the prosecutor files the charges or grand jury indictment with the court. In most jurisdictions, if the prosecutor refuses to prosecute, the only remedy is to remove the prosecutor for misconduct or elect a new one. The courts will refuse to order a prosecutor to prosecute a case. Prosecutors do not have sufficient assets to prosecute all cases. Accordingly, they select those cases to prosecute and not to prosecute. Prosecutors tend to focus on certain types of crimes in deciding which crimes to prosecute. Often the decisions are made based on the personal behavioral norms of the elected district attorney. The prosecutor cannot, however, forget that he or she may soon be up for re-election and may have to answer to the voters for his or her actions.

In the above paragraphs, the reference to prosecutor has generally been to the elected or appointed prosecutor. In most jurisdictions this individual as the head of the prosecutor's office makes policy decisions and rarely tries a case in trial court. Most cases are tried, however, by the assistant district attorneys or assistant state's attorneys. There are approximately 2,300 chief prosecutors in the United States. They employ about 20,000 assistants. About 97 percent of the chief prosecutors are elected to office. The others are usually appointed by the governor.

The general duties of an assistant district attorney or assistant state's attorney include:

— helping investigate possible violations of the law;

— cooperating with police in investigating crimes;

— interviewing witnesses;

— subpoenaing witnesses to appear in court;

— plea bargaining in accordance with policy directions from the elected prosecutor;

— trying the cases in court;

— recommending sentences to the court; and

— representing the government in appeals.

Assistants need to make many decisions regarding the processing and prosecution of cases. Often there is neither time nor the opportunity to check with the elected prosecutor regarding decisions. The elected prosecutor is, however, held responsible for decisions made by his or her assistants. In most prosecutors' offices, the elected prosecutor provides detailed guidelines or standards for the assistant prosecutors to follow in making decisions. For example, in most offices there are specific guidelines regarding plea bargaining.

Management of Cases

To combat the high volume of cases, prosecutors' offices are organized by one of three methods: horizontal, vertical, and mixed. The most predominate in large offices is the horizontal method. It is similar to an assembly line. Under this method, each assistant prosecutor is assigned to handle a different phase of the trial. For example, one team of prosecutors handles the intake and screening phase, another team handles the initial appearance, another team handles the arraignments, and a different team handles the actual trials. If there is an appeal, yet another team handles the appeals. The horizontal method permits a high volume of cases to be handled in an impartial method. The biggest problem with this method is that victims or complaining witnesses are required to deal with different prosecutors at each phase in the trial. Another disadvantage of this system is that often a prosecutor first sees the case on the day it is scheduled for trial.

Vertical prosecution is where teams of prosecutors are assigned the case and at least one member of that team follows the case to its conclusion. This method of prosecution is more costly than the horizontal method. For example, if a scheduled case is not tried, under the horizontal method, the prosecutor just takes the next case. Under the vertical method, the prosecutor usually does not have another case scheduled for trial that day. Another disadvantage of the vertical method is that cases need be scheduled according to the day the prosecutor will be available, whereas under the horizontal method a prosecutor is always available. The chief advantage of vertical prosecution is that the prosecutor becomes more familiar with the case, the victims, and witnesses.

Under the mixed method, some cases are tried by the vertical method and the remainder by the horizontal method. For example, rape and child abuse cases may be tried under the vertical method and the rest of the cases by the horizontal method. The mixed method is a compromise between the need to handle large caseloads as efficiently as possible and the need to give special attention to certain sensitive types of cases.

Training and Education of Prosecutors

Until the 1980s, assistant prosecutors were young lawyers who came to the prosecutor's office directly from law school. They worked for a couple of years in the DA's office to gain trial experience and then would typically go to work for a major law firm. For years, the assistants' pay was typically lower than attorneys with similar experiences in law firms, but the heavy trial experience would allow the assistants to gain invaluable experience that would serve them as they sought employment later with major law firms. During the 1980s, because of the changing job market and the upgrading of assistant prosecutors' positions, career patterns for assistant prosecutors were developed. Now many assistants see their positions as career positions, not merely a stepping stone to a civil law career.

Most prosecutor offices need to improve the training of prosecutors. For the most part, the only special training that an assistant receives after law school is on-the-job training. In recent years, state bar associations have provided seminars and short courses for both young prosecutors and defense counsel. The National College of District Attorneys was founded in the 1970s to provide formal training for prosecutors. The College is located at the University of Houston Law Center and provides training for the new prosecutor, career prosecutors, and the executive course for the elected or appointed district attorney. The college is non-profit and is partially funded by the American Bar Association, National Association of District Attorneys, and grants from major corporations. Because of the expenses involved in sending prosecutors to the college, however, it trains only a small percentage of prosecutors.

Part-time Prosecutors

Another problem with prosecutors is the high number of part-time prosecutors in small jurisdictions. Many states, like California, have taken steps to consolidate the prosecutors' offices in order to eliminate the need for part-time prosecutors. The part-time prosecutor generally practices law to supplement his or her income. Conflicts often arise when the prosecutor is also a part-time civil attorney. In addition, most part-time prosecutors receive little or no formal training to handle the complex duties of prosecutor.

U.S. ATTORNEY-EXPANDED FEDERAL ROLE

Justice George Sutherland described the role of the U.S. attorney as follows:

The United States attorney is the representative not of an ordinary party to a controversy, but of a sovereignty whose obligation to govern impartially is as compelling as its obligation to govern at all; and whose interest, therefore, in a criminal prosecution is not that it shall win a case, but that Justice shall be done. As, such, he is in a peculiar and very definite sense the servant of the law, the twofold aim of which is that the guilty shall not escape or innocence suffer. He may prosecute with earnestness and vigor—indeed, he should do so. But while he may strike foul ones, it is as much his duty to refrain from improper methods calculated to produce wrongful conviction as it is to use ever legitimate means to bring about a just one.[6]

Sutherland as reflected in the above court decision sees the U.S. attorney as:

— a representative of the sovereign,

— whose interest is not to win, but to do justice, and

— to use every legitimate means to obtain a just decision.

The U.S. attorney is the prosecutor or district attorney in the federal system. There is a U.S. attorney for each federal district court. They are appointed by the president and serve at the pleasure of the president. It is customary for every new president to request the resignation of all U.S. attorneys at the start of a new administration.

The U.S. attorneys, therefore, tend to have the same political outlook as the president and probably support the president during the election process. Accordingly, to some extent, the U.S. attorney is a political person.

As the chief federal prosecutor for the district court, the U.S. attorney determines which federal crimes will be prosecuted and which will not be. The new federal court sentencing guidelines, however, limit to some extent the plea bargaining that the U.S. attorney may do.

EXHIBIT 10-1

Power to Dismiss

In *United States v. Cowen*, the U.S. attorney entered into a plea bargain with the defendant that if the accused would plead guilty to one charge of bribery and cooperate with the Watergate investigation, the U.S. attorney would dismiss another indictment pending in a Texas case. The accused conformed to the bargain. The U.S. attorney then made a motion in a U.S. District Court in Texas to dismiss the indictment. The judge refused to. The case was appealed to the Fifth Circuit Court of Appeals. The appellate court held that until the conviction is final, a prosecutor has an absolute power to dismiss an indictment.[7]

DEFENSE COUNSEL

Defending people accused of a crime is the most distasteful function performed by lawyers.

—F. Lee Bailey

At a trial in Leningrad, USSR in 1974, the first thing that the accused's attorney did was to apologize to the court for defending "an enemy of the people." This would never happen in our courts. Under our system of justice, the accused has the right to a counsel whose duty is to serve the interests of the accused. While the defense counsel is an officer of the court, he or she is also the representative of the defendant in our adversarial process. The Sixth Amendment provides that in all criminal cases the accused shall have the right to the assistance of counsel. As a member of the courthouse work group, the defense counsel should represent the interests of the accused.

Right to Assistance of Counsel

... in all criminal prosecutions, the accused shall enjoy the right...to have the assistance of counsel for his defense.

—Sixth Amendment, U.S. Constitution

The Sixth Amendment, U.S. Constitution guarantees that the accused shall have the right to the assistance of counsel in all criminal cases. This means that no matter how petty the offense, the accused has the right to assistance of counsel. This issue has never been seriously questioned. The controversial issue is "When the accused cannot afford an attorney, when is the government required to provide the accused with counsel?"

As a general rule, the accused is entitled to the appointment of a counsel any time that the accused is subject to punishment which may include jail or prison time and the accused cannot afford to retain an attorney.[8] [*Note*: If the accused can afford counsel, he or she has the right to counsel in all criminal proceedings.] Typically, the indigent accused has the right to counsel at every significant phase of the trial. Generally, the counsel is not appointed until arraignment. See Exhibit 10-2 regarding the indigent accused's rights to counsel.

EXHIBIT 10-2

Sixth Amendment Right to Counsel

Federal Trials: The indigent accused has the right to assigned counsel in all federal criminal trials, *Johnson v. Zerbst*, 304 U.S. 458 (1938).

Capital Cases: Under *Powell v. Alabama*, 287 U.S. 45 (1932) an indigent accused has the right to assigned counsel.

During Arraignment: An indigent accused has the right to appointed counsel during arraignment, *Hamilton v. Alabama*, 368 U.S. 52 (1961).

Prior to Plea: The judge must inform the defendant of his or her right to counsel prior to accepting the defendant's guilty plea, *Carnley v. Cochran*, 369 U.S. 506 (1962).

Felony Offenses: An indigent defendant has the right to appointed counsel in all felony cases, *Gideon v. Wainwright*, 372 U.S. 355 (1963).

Imprisonment: An indigent defendant has the right to the appointment of counsel if there is a possibility that the accused may be confined as the result of the charges. *Argersinger v. Hamlin*, 407 U.S. 25 (1972).

Indictment: The right to counsel in federal cases becomes applicable upon indictment, *Massiah v. United States*, 377 U.S. 201 (1964).

Interrogation: The defendant has the right to counsel during any police interrogation after charges have been filed and a suspect has the right to counsel during any in custody police interrogation. *Escobedo v. Illinois*, 378 U.S. 478 (1964) and *Miranda v. Arizona*, 384 U.S. 694 (1966).

Line-ups: The defendant has a right to presence of counsel at any line-up conducted after the defendant has been indicted or "other adversary criminal proceedings." *Gilbert v. California*, 388 U.S. 263 (1967) and *Kirby v. Illinois*, 406 U.S. 682 (1972).

Adversary Proceedings: Once any adversary proceedings have begun against the defendant, the defendant has the right to the assistance of counsel.

Another problem in our system is that of providing counsel in those cases where the accused cannot afford an attorney. States and the federal government use several different methods. The three methods generally used are: public defender, assigned counsel, and contract counsel.

Public Defender

The first public defender's office was established in Los Angeles County, California in 1914. Thirty states and the federal government use a public defender system to provide legal services to indigent defendants. The public defender is an attorney who is employed by the state or federal government to serve as counsel for indigent defendants. In those jurisdictions using a public defender, generally when the trial judge conducts arraignments a public defender will be available in court to be appointed as counsel for the accused.

EXHIBIT 10-3

Who is the Public Defender?

The author was attending a hearing in Louisiana on the delivery of defense services for the state of Louisiana. Discussion focused on whether the state should have a public defender system. A prosecutor objected to the use of the term "public defender" in describing the attorney appointed to defend the accused. The prosecutor stated that the attorney was only an individual appointed to represent criminals, and that he as a prosecutor was the individual charged with protecting the public. Accordingly, he proposed that the prosecutor's title be changed to that of public defender and that the individual appointed to represent the accused be entitled "counsel for the accused." His suggestions did not receive much support. The state adopted a public defender system.

In some jurisdictions, the public defenders receive less pay than the prosecutors and their positions are considered less prestigious than those of the prosecutors. Most states have corrected this situation and have attempted to make public defenders' positions as prestigious as that of the assistant prosecutors.

Most public defenders' offices are struggling under a massive caseload and often the attorneys do not have the luxury to spend sufficient time on particular cases. There are often frequent criticisms regarding the quality of services provided by public defenders. It appears that public defender offices, like other state agencies, vary in the quality of services provided. In each office you are likely to encounter individuals who fail to adequately perform their assigned duties as counsel. But, however, you also find many well-qualified and highly competent counsel. In both the public defender and the assigned counsel systems, attorneys may be found who do not wish to anger judges through the use of extensive motions, arguments, demands for jury trials, etc. It appears that the quality of service provided by public defenders is very similar to that provided by individual attorneys who have been selected and hired by the defendant. In both situations, you find good attorneys and bad ones.

Assigned Counsel

Most jurisdictions which do not have a public defender system normally assign individual attorneys to represent indigent defendants. Judges use several methods to decide which attorney should be appointed. The most common is the use of a list of all attorneys practicing in the local court. From this list, the judge appoints the next available attorney to defend the accused. Assigned counsel generally receives a small fee from the state for the representation of the defendant.

The assigned counsel system is the oldest and, until recently, the most widely used method for providing representation to indigent defendants in criminal cases. There are many problems with this system. The problems include:

— in many jurisdictions only new and inexperienced counsel are assigned;

— in some jurisdictions "has beens" are assigned as a supplement to their retirement income;

— in those jurisdictions that use all members of the local bar, frequently counsel will be assigned who do not normally practice criminal law;

— for those counsel assigned, the pay is substantially lower than the counsel would make on a non-assigned case and most of their out of pocket expenses are not paid, accordingly, this discourages attorneys from accepting appointments;

— seldom are additional funds available to hire investigators, etc. to assist in the cases;

— the few attorneys who are financially dependent upon the assignments will be hesitant to vigorously defend the cases for fear of angering the judge.

Despite the above problems, there are some definite advantages of using the assigned counsel system. They include:

— counsel may bring a different perspective to the case since counsel is not a part of the courthouse work group;

— the accused generally feel more comfortable when represented by a private attorney rather than a public defender.

Contract System

Presently, six states exclusively use the contract system, and several other states use the contract system to supplement the public defender system. It is the newest system, but appears to be growing as more states attempt to obtain more for their limited resources. Under the contract system, the jurisdiction publishes "request for proposals" (RFPs). An RFP invites private law firms to bid for the services. The law firms submit proposals on establishing a defender system and the costs involved. The government then selects the firm with the best bid. That firm is responsible for providing indigent defendants with representation in court.

Quality of Representation

The most popular grounds for appeal in criminal courts is that of ineffective assistance of counsel. The appellate courts generally require not only that the defendant establish that his or her counsel made errors at trial, but also that the errors prejudiced the defendant. The courts are hesitant to engage in second guessing trial counsel (Monday morning quarterbacking). In addition, a defendant who is represented by a retained attorney (one hired by the defendant) has a more difficult time in establishing ineffective assistance of counsel. The rationale for the latter rule is that the accused should not be rewarded for poorly selecting an attorney.

Counsel on Appeal

As noted earlier, an indigent defendant has the right to appointed counsel at trial if the accused is subject to possible jail or prison time. Many question when an indigent defendant has a right to appointed counsel to appeal his or her case. The U.S. Supreme Court stated in *Douglas v. California* that an indigent defendant has the right to appointed counsel, if requested, on the first appeal following conviction if state appellate review is statutorily required. If the appeal is discretionary with the courts (the courts do not have to accept the case for review), then the accused has no right to an appointed counsel.

Duties of Defense Counsel

Would you defend a person who rapes an eight year old girl? How could you defend a person who has committed murder? No one person has a more demanding and more misunderstood role than that of the defense counsel. Too often we associate the defense counsel with the person he or she represents.

Questions like the above are commonly asked of attorneys. The people who ask those types of questions fail to realize that under our adversarial system of justice, the accused has the right to have a counsel appear on his or her behalf and the counsel owes a duty to represent the accused within legally permissible bounds. Even if the accused has admitted his or her guilt to the defense attorney, the attorney has the right to force the government to prove the accused's guilt beyond a reasonable doubt. The defense attorney's role is to be the spokesperson and representative for the accused. If the attorney can legally prevent the state from proving the accused's guilt, the attorney must do so.

The defense attorney is an officer of the court, and, as such, he or she cannot present false evidence, allow perjury to be committed or break the law in defending the accused. The defense attorney, however, is required to use any legal method to prevent the accused's conviction or in the case of conviction to obtain the lightest sentence possible for the accused. It is not the attorney's duty to determine what sentence is best for the accused; its his or her duty to obtain the lightest sentence unless requested otherwise by the defendant. An undecided issue in this regard is the defense counsel's duty to fight the death penalty or to attempt to ensure that the death penalty is imposed when the accused is being tried for a capital offense and requests the death penalty.

You are representing an accused. Prior to trial, the accused tells you he is going to commit perjury at trial. What do you do? As noted earlier, the defense counsel cannot violate the law in defending the accused. If, for example, the accused tells the counsel that he is going to testify falsely at the trial, the counsel should encourage the accused not to. If the accused insists on testifying and indicates that he will commit perjury, the defense counsel should request that the judge relieve the counsel from the duties to represent the accused before the accused testifies. The problem in this case, is that the counsel cannot tell the judge why he or she wants to be relieved due to the rules of confidentiality. All the counsel can tell the judge is that there is a conflict between the accused and counsel. This problem could last indefinitely, because when new counsel is appointed, if the accused tells the new counsel that he intends to commit perjury, the new counsel should also be excused. What normally happens, however, is once a counsel has been excused, the accused realizes the problem and doesn't tell all to the new counsel.

A young girl is missing, the girl's parents offer a reward for information regarding the missing girl's whereabouts. You are defending an accused on an unrelated murder charge. He informs you that he killed the young girl and buried her body in the local cemetery. If the police find the body, evidence on the body will lead the police to your client. What do you do?[9]

Information that an attorney receives from his or her client is privileged and cannot be divulged without the client's consent. Accordingly, if an accused tells his attorney that he committed a murder, the attorney cannot divulge this information without the client's consent. This privileged communication is based on the theory that the accused needs to be able to communicate with his or her attorney without fear of the communications being used against him or her. In the above situation, the New York Bar Association ruled that the communication was privileged and the attorney should not have revealed the information regarding the girl's death.

In one Virginia case, the accused told his counsel that the money from a bank robbery was in a locker in a bus station. The counsel advised the accused to hide the money elsewhere. The attorney was convicted of being an accessory after the fact. While the communications as to the location of the money was privileged, the attorney went beyond that when he advised the accused to hide the money in a different location. This conversation was overheard by a nosey telephone operator who reported it to the police. [*Note*: The privileged communication extends to the attorney, attorney's secretary and paralegal, but not to a third person such as a telephone operator who overhears the conversation.]

The courts have recognized that there is an important relationship between the accused and his or her counsel. Accordingly, an accused has the right to refuse a counsel, and, in turn, counsel has a right to refuse to represent any accused. When the accused is assigned a counsel at government expense, and the accused does not like his or her attorney, a problem occurs. As a general rule when dealing with "appointed" counsel, the judge will allow the defendant to "fire" one attorney, but will require reasons before allowing the defendant to fire the second attorney. Normally a defendant can fire his or her "retained" counsel at any time. The judge, however, may decide not to delay a scheduled trial or other court appearance to allow the defendant time to obtain new retained counsel. [*Note*: "Appointed counsel" is one provided by the government to indigent defendants. "Retained counsel" is a counsel that has been hired and paid by the defendant.]

Waiver of Counsel

In the above sections, we have discussed the accused's right to counsel and the obligations of the government to provide the accused with counsel when the accused cannot afford to retain an attorney. However, the accused has the right to refuse an attorney.

The U.S. Supreme Court faced this issue in *Faretta v. California*. This case, decided by a six to three vote, held that an accused has a constitutional right to self-representation. In this case, Anthony Faretta was charged with grand theft. A public defender was assigned to represent him at his arraignment. He requested the right to defend himself. The judge, after warning the accused that he was making a mistake, approved the defendant's request. Several weeks into the trial, the judge questioned Faretta regarding his ability to defend himself and appointed a public defender to represent him. The court ruled that the defendant cannot be forced to accept an attorney. The court stated that the right to defend is given directly to the accused; for it is he who suffers the consequences if the defense fails.[10]

JUDGES

The judges are the weakest link in our system of justice, and they are also the most protected.

—Alan M. Dershowitz

EXHIBIT 10-4

Functions of the Trial Judge

The American Bar Association Standards for Criminal Justice makes the below statement regarding the responsibility of the trial judge.

1. General responsibility of the trial judge.

(a) The trial judge has the responsibility for safeguarding both the rights of the accused and the interests of the public in the administration of criminal justice. The adversarial nature of the proceedings does not relieve the trial judge of the obligations of raising on his own initiative, at all appropriate times and in an appropriate manner, matters which may significantly promote a just determination of the trial. The only purpose of a criminal trial is to determine whether the prosecution has established the guilt of the accused as required by law, and the trial judge should not allow the proceedings to be used for any other purpose.[11]

Trial Judges

The trial judge is an officer of the court. It would be more accurate to describe him or her as the "master of the court." The trial judge's duties are varied and far more extensive than would appear on the surface. During the trial, judges rule on appropriateness of the conduct of all others involved in the court process including spectators. Judges determine what evidence is admissible and, during jury trials, which instructions of law the juries will receive. Any motions, questions of law, objections, and, in most states, the sentence to impose are questions decided only by the judges. The senior judge in any one court or the presiding judge is responsible for the docketing (scheduling) of cases, motions, etc. Judges also have extensive control over probation officers, the court clerks and indirectly, to some extent, the police.

Appellate Judges

The duties and responsibilities of an appellate judge are very different from those of a trial judge. The responsibilities of an appellate judge include:

1) examining the record of trial, trial brief, notice of appeal, and other matter submitted with the appeal to determine if the appeal is properly presented and the appropriate issues are properly before the court;

2) presiding over oral arguments;

3) negotiating a decision among the justices considering the appeal; and

4) writing an opinion that explains the logic and reasons for the decision.

The appellate justice's work is largely confined to reviewing cases tried by trial judges. Instead of the noisy, crowded trial court with numerous distractions, the appellate justice deals mainly with paperwork (e.g., briefs, records of trial, and research regarding prior court decisions).

Selection of Judges

There are approximately 26,000 judges in the United States. The vast majority of them are lower court judges. Most states now require that a judge have a law degree and be licensed to practice law in the jurisdiction. Many states like California, Florida, and New Jersey require the judges to be admitted to practice in that jurisdiction and at least "learned in the law." There are still, however, a number of lower court judges who do not have formal legal training.

While judges have the most important role in the judicial process, the current methods used to select judges do not guarantee that the best fitted and best trained persons are appointed as judges. Judges are selected by one of three methods: popular election, appointment, or merit plan. Thirty-two states elect their judges. Some elections are partisan (candidates run as members of a political party) and some are nonpartisan (candidates run without a party designation). Some states and the federal system appoint their judges. Other states use a form of merit system or the Missouri Plan.

The **Missouri Plan** was created in the 1940s to overcome the widespread use of political patronage in the appointment of judges.Under the Missouri Plan, the judges are selected based on their records of achievement in the legal field. After serving an initial term of office, the judge is then on the ballot for confirmation. When the judge's confirmation is presented to the voters, it is normally on a yes or no vote.

California elects its judges. However, in most situations in California, when a vacancy occurs the governor appoints a new judge. At the next election, the judge stands for election. In 1992, 88 percent of the trial court judges in California were placed on the bench initially by gubernatorial appointments to fill vacancies. In states using nonpartisan elections only 43 percent of the judges were initially elected, the majority were initially appointed by the governor.[12]

In most states, like California, it is rare that a sitting judge is defeated by an opponent. An exception to this is Texas. In Texas, the judges are elected in partisan elections and the judicial races are very political in nature. A problem with the partisan election of judges is illustrated in a Texas case. In the 1970s, Texas elected an individual to the state supreme court who was being investigated for criminal homicide in another state and had little prior legal experience. This individual's last name was very similar to that of a popular politician in the state and it is assumed that many voters thought they were voting for the politician. [*Note*: This individual resigned from the state supreme court as part of a criminal plea bargain.]

A few states, like New York, use a variety of methods for selecting judges. Appellate court judges are appointed by the governor from a group of candidates selected by a judicial nominating commission and approved by the state senate. Partisan elections are used to select major court trial judges. Municipal judges in New York City are appointed by the mayor of New York City.

Removal of Judges

As noted earlier, federal judges in constitutional courts hold office "during good behavior" for life. In most states, the judges serve terms of four to seven years. The most common method of removing judges is the failure to re-elect a judge when his or her term expires. In those states, like California, where judges are subject to being removed by a "fail-to-retain" vote, they can be removed by a negative vote. The opportunity to remove by failing to retain or not re-electing the judge occurs only when the judge's term is expiring.

In some states, the judges are subject to being recalled. The general recall procedures are: a recall petition with a sufficient percentage of voter signatures is filed with the state election commission; the recall question is then placed on the next general election ballot; a majority vote at the recall election will remove the judge. This process is time consuming and expensive.

Federal judges and some state judges may be removed by impeachment. The U.S. Constitution provides, in part, that any civil officer of the U.S. (including judges) may be removed by impeachment for crimes of "treason, bribery, or other high crimes and misdemeanors."[13] In federal cases, the House of Representatives must vote on the articles of impeachment which is an accusation of criminal wrongdoing. The actual trial occurs before the senate. Two-thirds vote of the senate is required before the judge is removed from office. Like recall procedures, impeachment is time consuming and expensive.

The most workable method of judicial removal is by use of the "Judicial Conduct Commission." In 1960, California was the first state to establish a judicial conduct commission. Now all states have some form of judicial removal commission. The judicial commission normally consists of judges, non-lawyer citizens, and attorneys. For example, Florida's commission has 13 members. Six are judges (two from circuits courts, two from county courts, and two from the district courts of appeal), two attorneys appointed by the state bar, and five non-lawyer citizens appointed by the governor. The members serve staggered six-year terms. The Florida commission is empowered to deal with charges of misconduct, persistent failure to perform judicial duties, and any physical or mental disability that interferes with the performance of duties.

EXHIBIT 10-5

The Removal of a Judge

In California, the nine member commission voted six to three to remove a municipal judge who was found to have:

— conducted "bargain days" (days on which defendants received only one-half the customary sentence for pleading guilty),

— held hearings when prosecutor and defense counsel were not present,

— sexually harassed a court reporter,

— left the bench during a criminal trial and instructed attorneys to record their objections in his absence in writing so he could rule on them later,

— made racial remarks toward a Mexican-American and an Asian-American.

The California Supreme Court subsequently removed the judge.[15]

The National Advisory Commission on Criminal Justice Standards and Goals makes the following recommendation regarding judicial conduct commissions:

A judicial conduct commission should be created, composed of judges elected by the judicial conference, lawyers elected by the bar, and at least two laymen of different political persuasions appointed by the governor. Whatever the size of the commission, no more than one-third should be members of the judiciary. The commission should be empowered to investigate charges bearing on judges' competence to continue on the bench, and should be empowered to take appropriate action regarding their conduct.[14]

In most states, the commission investigates and, in appropriate cases, recommends removal of judges. The state legislatures generally are required to approve the report before the removal is effective. In some states, the approval is left to the State Supreme Court.

Federal Court Judges

Generally, federal court judges hold their offices for life "during good behavior." The judges are nominated by the president and confirmed by the senate. In most cases, the president nominates judges of the same political party as the president. In fact, of the 107 Supreme Court justices, only 12 were not of the same party as the president. This power to nominate federal judges is an important political power. Especially since the judges appointed by a president generally serve in his or her office years after the president's term has expired. Accordingly, a president's influence will be present for many years after the president has been replaced.

For many years, the president appointed his friends or political supporters to the courts. President Reagan, however, changed this practice. He started the trend that has been followed by both Bush and Clinton, to appoint judges that seemed most ideologically suited to the president's agenda. In addition, Reagan started the trend of appointing younger judges who would most likely serve longer terms of office.

The practice of selecting judges based on their ideology has had the effect of making the appointments more controversial and more difficult to achieve senate confirmation. Previously, most presidential appointments were quickly approved by the senate. Now, the confirmation hearings are more adversarial in nature and the candidates face an in-depth examination regarding their past career activities and personal conduct.

Federal Magistrates

U.S. Commissioners for many years served the same functions that justices of the peace served for state courts. Commissioners had the authority to issue search and arrest warrants, arraign defendants, hold preliminary hearings, and try cases involving petty offenses. In 1967, the President's Commission on Law Enforcement and Administration of Justice noted that 30 percent of the commissioners were not lawyers and all but 7 of the 700 commissioners had other jobs. The president's commission recommended that the system be either eliminated or reformed. As the result of the recommendations, Congress established the federal magistrate system and provided for a three year phasing out of the commissioners.

Federal magistrates are appointed to assist district courts. There are presently 452 federal magistrates. Magistrates are lawyers appointed by district court judges for eight year terms. Part-time magistrates are appointed for four year terms. The Federal Magistrates Act of 1968 empowers them to issue search warrants, hear preliminary stages of felony cases, set bail, and try misdemeanor cases.[16] In 1976, the magistrates were given the authority to review civil rights and habeas corpus petitions and make recommendations regarding them to the district court judges.

It is estimated that magistrates perform about 475,000 separate tasks a year for the federal districts. Misdemeanor and petty offense trials account for 20 percent of the magistrates time. About 30 percent of their time is involved with preliminary proceedings in criminal cases, 40 percent involves the disposition of motions and pretrial conferences, and the remaining 10 percent in miscellaneous duties.[17]

OTHER COURT PERSONNEL

Court Administrator

In most of the large judicial districts, a professional court administrator is used to take charge of the difficult tasks of managing the court system. The administrator's functions include personnel, financial, and records. The administrator keeps the court records in order, assigns trial schedules, tracks complex cases and coordinates computerized information. These functions were previously managed by the chief judge of the circuit or district.

Court Clerk

The clerk administers the oath to jurors and witnesses. He marks the evidence and keeps a log of what exhibits have been admitted. The clerk also assists the judge by performing administrative duties for the judge. The Clerk of the Court is the official records keeper of the court and, thus, is responsible as custodian for all legal documents filed with the court.

Bailiff

The bailiff's duties are to keep order in the courtroom, to call witnesses, and to take charge of the jury when the jury is not in the courtroom. The bailiff is also responsible to insure that no outside influences are brought to bear on the jury. In many cases, the bailiff is an uniformed "go-fer" for the judge and jury.

Court Reporter

The reporter's duties are to record all the trial, including the testimony of witnesses, oral arguments, instructions and any words spoken during the court proceedings. In cases where there is no court clerk, the reporter lists, for identification purposes, all exhibits offered into evidence.

Through the continued pursuit of court efficiency and/or cost reduction, audio and video taping of court procedures as a means of eliminating court reporters is being given serious consideration. Replacing, usually highly paid, court reporters with video equipment operated by a lower paid and skilled video technician seems to be a viable alternative.

California's State Judicial Council estimated that using recording equipment in 75 courtrooms during pilot testing resulted in an annual savings of over $28,000 per court. The council contends the use of this equipment should be allowed when court reporters are either not available or the court lacks the funds to pay for a reporter.

Unfortunately, groups, such as the California Court Reporters Association with 3,200 members, are suing to not allow only video and audio recording of trials. They see no reason why equipment cannot augment their personnel, but they argue that such equipment cannot replace court reporters.

Here again, efficiency results in a reduction of personnel which typically sparks a lawsuit to block such action. Since this above use of recording equipment was to have begun in January 1994 and the subsequent legal challenge was filed in late December 1993, it will take some time for this issue to work its way through the court system. In the interim, court reporters will still be holding their jobs, and courts will have to spend an average of $28,000 per year more for the privilege of having a court reporter personally record what transpires in court.

A video technician recording a trial.

CASELOADS AND PLEA BARGAINING

As noted in Chapter 9, overwhelming caseloads are one of the biggest problems facing our justice system. The caseloads also contribute to prosecution problems and make plea bargaining a necessity. Often, defendants are induced to plea bargain to get the case over with quickly. Many persons object to the morality of plea bargaining. Their contention is that the government should not stoop to bargain (enter into a contract with a criminal).

Plea bargaining is considered a necessary evil in our justice system. It has been described as the exchange of prosecutorial and judicial concessions in return for a plea of guilty. The plea bargain may be structured in the following ways:

— for a reduction in sentence;

— for the dropping of other charges;

— for reducing the charged crime to a lessor included crime;

— for the promise to recommend a lenient sentence by the prosecutor; or

— for the deleting of aggravating factors considered (e.g., striking allegations of prior convictions or allegations of armed weapon).

The advantages of plea bargaining for the government include:
— reduction in the overall financial costs of trying cases;

— improvement in the efficiency of the courts by disposing of many cases with guilty pleas; and

— conservation of the resources of the prosecutor's office.

The advantages for an accused to enter into a plea bargain include:

— reduction in the length of time the accused will be detained in pretrial confinement;

— an increase in the potential for a reduced sentence; and

— a decrease in the cost of legal representation.

One of the most controversial issues in the plea bargaining process is the role that judges should play. Some judges refuse to take part in the bargaining process. Other judges take an active part in plea bargaining and pressure participants to facilitate the bargaining process. Some judges not only take part in the bargaining process but also make specific suggestions as to the terms of the bargain. Scholars disagree as to which role a judge should take in this process. Those who advocate that the judge should not take a part in the process base their position on the need for the judge to remain fair and impartial. Those who advocate the opposite role contend that the judge, as an experienced judicial officer, can take an active part in the plea bargaining process and still remain fair and impartial.

Many researchers have criticized plea bargaining as being very informal, discretionary in nature, and lacking definite guidelines; and thus, it is subject to abuse.

DISCUSSION QUESTIONS

1. Compare and contrast the roles of the defense counsel and the prosecutor.

2. Why doesn't the prosecutor always have a duty to convict?

3. Name the key players in the court system and compare their roles.

4. What are the advantages and disadvantages of plea bargaining?

5. Who profits most by plea bargaining?

6. Would you defend an individual accused of murder if you knew that he was guilty?

ENDNOTES

[1] Counsel includes both prosecutors and defense counsel.

[2] Howard Abadinsky and L. Thomas Winfree, Jr. *Crime and Justice*, 2nd ed., (New York: Nelson-Hall, 1992), p. 374.

[3] The informal meetings described in this section are based on the personal experiences of the author, for a similar description of such meetings in the Chicago criminal courts see: Paul B. Wice, *Chaos in the Courthouse*, (New York: Praeger, 1985).

[4] Joel Samaha, *Criminal Justice*, (St. Paul: West, 1991).

[5] Peter Nardulli, *The Courtroom Elite*, (Cambridge, Ma: Ballinger, 1978).

[6] *Berger v. United States*, 295 U.S. 78 (1935).

[7] *United States v. Cowen*, 524 F. 2d. 785 (1975).

[8] *Argersinger v. Hamlin*, 407 U.S. 25 (1972).

[9] This was an actual case that occurred in the 1970s in Buffalo, New York.

[10] 422 U.S. 806 (1975).

[11] American Bar Association, *Standards for Criminal Justice*, approved draft, (1972).

[12] N.Gary Holten and Lawson L. Lamar, *The Criminal Courts*, (New York: McGraw-Hill, 1991), p. 96.

[13] U.S. Constitution, Article II.

[14] National Advisory Committee on Criminal Justice Standards and Goals, *Courts*, (1973), p. 153.

[15] Wallace Turner, "Coast Panel Urges Removal of Judge," *The New York Times*, (May 8, 1982): p. 24.

[16] 28 U.S.C. 636 (b).

[17] Administrative Office of the United States Courts, *The United States Courts*, (Washington D.C.: Government Printing Office, 1989).

Courtroom of the future at McGeorge School of Law.

PRETRIAL AND TRIAL
PROCESS

Justice, though due to the accused, is due to the accuser also. The concept of fairness must not be strained till it is narrowed to a filament. We are to keep the balance true.

—Justice Cordozo in Snyder v. Massachusetts,
291 U.S. 97 (1034)

PRETRIAL PROCEDURES

A s noted in Chapter 10, the decision to prosecute is a function of the prosecutor and is generally not reviewable. In many states and the federal government, before the prosecutor may file felony charges with a court, he or she must obtain a grand jury indictment. In other states, the prosecutor files an "information" with the lower court.

Decision to Prosecute

Generally, after an arrest or on the completion of an investigation, the case is referred to the prosecutor's office. In some jurisdictions, however, the case is not referred until after the accused has made an initial appearance in court. When the case is received in the prosecutor's office, it is reviewed to determine if the case merits prosecution. Due to a lack of resources, prosecutors cannot try all cases referred to their offices.

Additional reasons that prosecution may be declined in a case include:

— insufficient evidence;

— witness problems;

— interests of justice;

— defendant pleas in another case;

— pretrial diversion;

— referral to another jurisdiction for prosecution;

— due process problems (e.g., questionable search); and

— referral to treatment programs (e.g., alcohol rehabilitation programs).

The prosecutor may also reduce the charge to a misdemeanor. Of the above reasons for declining prosecution, insufficient evidence is the most common reason for rejection. For example, approximately one half of all drug cases in which prosecution is declined were based on insufficient evidence. The second most common reason involved witness problems, in that the witnesses were unavailable or unwilling to be involved.[1]

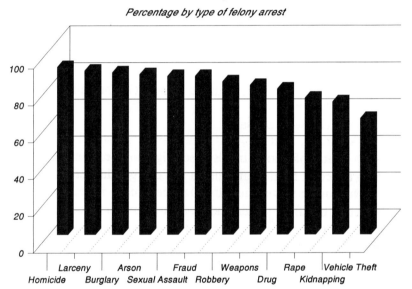

Likelihood of Being Prosecuted

Percentage by type of felony arrest

Source: U.S. Dept. of Justice

Bail

Traditionally the bail system required the defendant to guarantee his or her appearance at trial by posting a money bond. This money would be forfeited should the defendant fail to appear in court for trial. The Eighth Amendment of the U.S. Constitution states that excessive bail shall not be required. While the amendment does not grant the right to bail in all cases, all states and the federal government give the defendant the right to bail except in limited situations.

The traditional bail system discriminates against the poor who cannot afford bail. Accordingly, alternatives to the bail system include release on recognizance, conditional release, third-party custody, and citation release.

EXHIBIT 11-1

Pretrial Releases

Traditional Bail Bond

In this situation, the defendant, or someone on the defendant's behalf, posts the full amount of the bail.

Privately Secured Bail

A professional bondsperson signs a promissory note to the court for the bail amount and charges the defendant a fee for the service (usually 10 percent of the face amount of the bond). If the defendant fails to appear in court as required, the bondsperson may be required to pay the court the full amount of the bond. Frequently, a bondsperson will require the accused or the accused's family to post collateral in addition to the fee. If the accused fails to appear, the accused owes the bondsperson the amount of money that the bondsperson has to pay the court. This amount is in addition to the 10 percent fee already paid by the accused for bail services.

Deposit Bond

The courts, in many states, allow the defendant to post a deposit, usually 10 percent of the full bail with the court. This is also frequently referred to as the "10 percent Bail" program. If the defendant fails to appear, he or she owes the full amount of the bond to the court. If the defendant appears, most of the deposit is returned. Generally the courts keep one percent of the bond amount for administrative costs.

Unsecured Bail

In this situation, the defendant pays no money to the court, but is liable for the full amount of the bail if the accused fails to appear.

Release on Recognizance (ROR)

In this situation, the court releases the defendant on the defendant's promise to appear in court as required.

Conditional Release

The court releases the defendant subject to the defendant agreeing to follow certain specified conditions. For example, the judge may release a defendant providing he or she will not leave the city, or bother the witnesses.

Third Party Custody

The defendant is released to the custody of a third person who promises to assure the accused's presence in court. No monetary transactions are involved in this type of release. This type of release is very common with juvenile defendants released into the custody of their guardians.

Citation Release

The defendant is released pending the first court appearance by signing a citation issued by a law enforcement person. Normally the citation release is used only in traffic cases and cases involving minor offenses.

The U.S. Supreme Court made it clear in 1950 that the purpose of bail was "to assure the defendant's attendance in court when his presence is required."[2] Accordingly, we assume that any bail higher than that necessary to ensure the accused's presence at trial is excessive and, thus, unconstitutional.

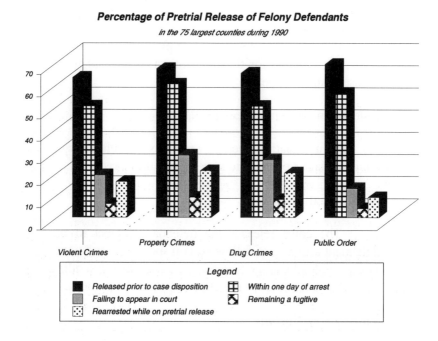

Percentage of Pretrial Release of Felony Defendants

in the 75 largest counties during 1990

Source: U.S. Dept. of Justice

The U.S. Bail Reform Act of 1984 added the duty to consider the safety of the community when making the pretrial release decision. The act provided that bail could be refused in those cases where the accused is charged with a violent offense, has a serious criminal record and is considered a danger to the community or is a flight risk.

Other key features of the act were its establishment of a "no-bail" presumption for certain types of cases. Many scholars thought that the "no-bail" presumption denied the accused due process since it authorized punishment before trial. The U.S. Supreme Court in upholding the constitutionality of the Bail Reform Act stated: "The legislative history clearly shows that Congress formulated the Bail Reform Act to prevent danger to the community— a legitimate regulatory goal — not to punish dangerous individuals.[3]

When the U.S. Supreme Court held this act constitutional, most states enacted similar statutes. Accordingly, now in determining whether to release a defendant from custody prior to the trial, the judge must consider both (1) the likelihood the accused will be present for trial and (2) the safety of the community.

Grand Jury

The grand jury originated in England in 1166, when King Henry II required all knights and other freemen drawn from rural neighborhoods to file accusations of felonies with the court. As the common law developed, the grand jury was limited in number to 23 citizens with a minimum of 12 present. Similar to the present grand jury, the grand jury heard accusations of crimes from witnesses and returned indictments. The grand jury could initiate criminal investigations.

Today, the grand jury is a group of citizens selected by the presiding judge of the superior or district court. Generally, there are 23 citizens assigned to each grand jury and the jury usually meets several days a week for about six months. Unlike a trial jury, the grand jury has accusatory and investigative functions. The grand jury hears evidence presented by the prosecutor. The jury can also call their own witnesses and question them. The function of a grand jury is to determine if an individual should be tried for a felony. In making this determination, the grand jury may use inadmissible evidence including hearsay. If the required number of jury members agree, usually 12, the jury issues a "bill of indictment." If sufficient members do not agree, then the jury issues a "no bill," and no indictment is issued.

If a grand jury fails to indict an individual, double jeopardy does not apply, and a different grand jury may issue an indictment based on the same evidence. For example in a 1993 Texas case, the first grand jury refused to indict an individual accused of rape because the victim had requested that the rapist use a condom. The jury members indicated that in requesting that the rapist use a condom, the victim had consented to the sex act. The case was then referred to a second grand jury who indicted the individual. He was then tried, convicted and received a forty year sentence for rape.

Prosecutors have wide discretion in presenting evidence to the grand jury. As noted earlier, hearsay and other inadmissible evidence may be present. As noted in one case, the prosecutor may introduce any evidence to support his or her theory of the case. The court stated, however, that the grand jury may not indict solely on rumors.[4] In one famous case involving gangster Frank Costello, the court held that an indictment could be based solely on hearsay information.[5]

Many critics of the grand jury procedures contend that the grand jury is a rubber stamp for the prosecutor. It appears that in most cases where the prosecutor requests an indictment, the grand jury issues an indictment. Many researchers contend that a grand jury should be used only in those cases where a community voice is needed. For example, in many cities when there is a situation where the police have killed someone, the prosecutor presents the facts to the grand jury and allows the grand jury to decide on the legality of the police officer's conduct.

Other criticisms of the grand jury include:

— the failure to provide the accused with due process;

— the grand jury takes testimony in private and its proceedings are secret;

— in most cases, the accused is not present and doesn't have the opportunity to present evidence in one's own defense; and

— the defense counsel has no right to be present during the questioning of a witness whom the jury is considering indicting.

The American Bar Association has the following recommendations regarding reform of the grand jury system. The key recommendations are as follows:

— witnesses should be allowed to have their own attorneys in the hearing room when the witnesses are testifying;

— prosecutors should be charged with the duty to also present evidence that may indicate a suspect is innocent;

— witnesses before a grand jury should be granted protection against self-incrimination; and

— grand jurors should be instructed as to the elements of each crime being presented against a person.[6]

Misdemeanor Procedures

Laws are a dead letter without courts to expound and define their true meaning and operation.

—Alexander Hamilton

Generally misdemeanor procedures are more informal than those observed in felony courts. In most cases, misdemeanor prosecution is based on a formal complaint or information filed by the prosecutor. The **complaint** is a sworn written document that identifies the accused, lists the criminal charge or charges, and states the date, time, and place where offenses are alleged to have occurred. Usually a police officer, who is familiar with the facts of the case, signs the complaint under oath. The complaint normally orders the accused to appear before a judge at an initial hearing. At the initial hearing, the accused is formally advised of his or her rights, the charges against the defendant, his or her rights to counsel, and asked to enter a plea. Most misdemeanor cases are disposed of at the initial hearing with a plea by the defendant. If the defendant enters a not guilty plea, the judge sets a trial date. Frequently during the period between the initial hearing and the trial date, the accused will withdraw the not guilty plea and enter a plea of guilty as the result of a plea bargain agreement. Defendants in misdemeanor cases are usually released on bail or on their own recognizance while awaiting trial.

Felony Cases

The task of the trial court is to reconstruct the past from what are, at best, second-hand reports of the facts.

—Justice Jerome Frank, U.S. Court of Appeals

Felony cases are processed either by indictment or appearance before a preliminary hearing. In those states that require indictments by a grand jury, the case is normally presented to the grand jury by the prosecutor. If the grand jury returns an indictment, the indictment is then filed with the superior or district court.

In states, like California, that do not require an indictment by grand jury, an **information** is presented to a lower court (justice or municipal). The information is a charging document similar to the complaint in a misdemeanor case. The information is presented to the municipal or justice court where a preliminary hearing is held. About half the states use preliminary hearings rather than grand juries. The purpose of the preliminary hearing is to determine if there is probable cause to have the defendant answer to the charge in a felony court. At the preliminary hearing, the judge can dismiss the charges, reduce the charge to a misdemeanor and try the case, or order the defendant to be bound over for trial in felony court.

After the indictment is filed or the accused is bound over by the municipal or justice court on an information, the accused is arraigned before the trial court. In some states, the arraignment may be before the lower court. At the arraignment, the accused is informed of the charge(s) against him or her, advised of the right to counsel, and a plea is entered. In addition, the judge must decide whether the accused should be released on bail or some other form of release while awaiting trial.

At the preliminary hearing, the prosecution presents its evidence including witnesses to the judge. The defense counsel may also present evidence favorable to the accused. At this hearing, the judge determines whether probable cause indicates that the accused has committed a felony.

The accused may plea guilty, not guilty, or *nolo contendere* when asked to plead. A plea of *nolo contendere* means that the accused does not contest the charges. It is treated as if the accused entered a plea of guilty. If the accused enters a guilty plea he or she admits all of the elements of the offense charged. If the accused enters a plea of not guilty, the case is set for trial. Normally both a trial date and a date for pre-trial motions are set by the judge after the judge accepts the not guilty plea. At the pre-trial motion date, the counsel are afforded an opportunity to present motions. Typical motions include: motion to suppress certain items of evidence, motion for speedy trial, and motion for dismissal of charges.

EXHIBIT 11-2

PLEAS

Plea of Not Guilty

A plea of not guilty denies placing the burden of proving guilt beyond a reasonable doubt on the prosecution. If the defendant stands mute and refuses to enter any plea, a plea of not guilty will be entered on the defendant's behalf by the judge. [*Note*: An accused has a constitutional right to be assumed innocent until proven guilty beyond a reasonable doubt.]

Guilty Plea

A guilty plea is not only an admission of guilt but is also a waiver of the right to jury, the right to remain silent, the right to confront the witnesses against you, and the right to require the prosecution to establish guilt beyond a reasonable doubt by admissible evidence. While an accused has a right to plead guilty, the trial judge is not required to accept this plea. If the judge feels that the accused's plea is not providently entered, the judge can enter a plea of not guilty for the accused. In addition, in capital cases the accused cannot enter a plea of guilty if the state is requesting the death penalty. The rationale for this rule is to allow the accused to plea guilty in a death penalty case would be the same as allowing the accused to commit suicide.

Nolo Contendere

This is a plea of "no contest." It is essentially a guilty plea. By entering a nolo plea, the accused waives the above rights, the same as if he or she had plead guilty. Often the *nolo contendere* plea is used in those cases where the accused is also liable in civil court. By pleading nolo, the accused does not admit commission of the act in question. The accused does not have a right to plead *"nolo contendere."* This form of plea is acceptable in only about one half of the states and the federal government.

Not Guilty by Reasons of Insanity

In most states, the accused may plea not guilty by reasons of insanity. In states that do not allow the accused to plead insanity, the accused must plead not guilty and raise the issue of insanity as an affirmative (acceptable) defense. The normal plea in insanity cases is "not guilty and not guilty by reasons of insanity." This plea requires that the government prove the defendant committed the offense, then the issue of the accused's sanity is determined. In all states and the federal government, insanity is an affirmative defense, so the burden of producing evidence as to the sanity or insanity of the accused is first upon the defense. If no evidence is entered at trial regarding the sanity of the accused, it is assumed that the accused is sane.

Statute of Limitations or Double Jeopardy

In most states, before the accused enters a plea as to his or her guilt, the defense of statute of limitations or double jeopardy must be pled. In most cases, if these defenses are not pled before the guilty or not guilty plea, these defenses are relinquished.

Pretrial Motions

As discussed earlier, when an accused has entered a plea of not guilty, the judge sets both a trial date and a date to hear motions. The hearing on motions will generally be two or three weeks prior to the trial date. A motion is a formal application or request to the court for some ruling. The purpose of a motion is to gain some advantage by the party making the motion. Often, the plea of the accused is determined by the court's rulings on the motions. The common motions include: motion for discovery, motion for severance of charges or defendants, motion for suppression of evidence, motion to limit, and motion for change of venue.

A **motion for discovery** is a request by one side, usually the defense, to see the evidence against the accused and to discover the names of witnesses that the government or defendant plans to present at trial. Each state has various rules regarding the extent of the discovery allowed. California, for example, allows extensive discovery by the defendant. Oklahoma, however, allows the defendant only limited discovery. The U.S. Supreme Court has held that a prosecutor has a duty to disclose any evidence that is favorable to the defendant when requested by the defense.[7] The Supreme Court has also ruled that there was no constitutional requirement for the prosecution to fully disclose its entire case file to the defense.[8]

A **motion to suppress evidence** is normally used when there is a question regarding the legality of the search. If the court sustains (approves the motion), the evidence cannot be used at trial. If the court denies the motion, the evidence may be admitted. In many cases, the ruling on this motion will determine whether the accused pleads guilty or the case is dismissed. If the evidence is suppressed, the government may not have sufficient other evidence to go to trial. If the evidence is admitted, the accused may change his or her plea and enter a guilty plea.

A **motion for severance of charges** normally occurs when the defendant has been arrested for several charges and the defense attempts to have the charges severed and thus tried in different cases. This could occur when the accused wishes to use different tactics to defend different offenses. A motion for severance of defendants occurs when more than one accused is scheduled to be tried together. There are times when it will be prejudicial for one defendant to be tried with another defendant. For example, if one defendant wants a jury trial and the other wishes a trial by judge alone. If one defendant has confessed to the crime, it would be unfair to the other defendants to be tried with him. Another situation where severance is considered necessary is when one defendant intends to blame the other defendants for the criminal misbehavior.

The defendant has a right to be tried in the district or county in which the crime occurred. If, however, the defendant feels that he or she cannot receive a fair trial in that location, the defendant may make a **motion for change of venue**. The defendant, by this motion, is requesting that the trial be conducted in a different location. For example, in 1992 defendant Howard killed a state highway patrol officer after listening to rap music. The killing occurred in a small town on the Texas Gulf Coast. At Officer Davidson's funeral (the victim) over 1,000 people from the local community attended. When defendant Howard was arraigned, his counsel requested that the trial be held in a different location because the feelings of the local community would prevent the accused from receiving a fair and impartial trial. The case was tried in a different part of Texas. The accused received, however, the death penalty.

A **motion for a continuance** is a request for delay in the start of the trial. There are also a number of grounds that can be used to make a motion for dismissal. A **motion for dismissal** is a request that the judge dismiss the charges. Grounds for dismissal include lack of a speedy trial, improper grand jury indictment, defective information, and violation of certain constitutional rights.

Speedy Trial

In all criminal prosecutions, the accused shall enjoy the right to a speedy and public trial....

—Sixth Amendment, U.S. Constitution

There are two separate speedy trial issues. First, the Sixth Amendment of the U.S. Constitution gives the accused a constitutional right to a speedy trial. Second, most states and the federal government provide a statutory right to speedy trial. The constitutional right is based on a standard of reasonableness. To determine if the accused's constitutional right to a speedy trial has been violated, the court looks at:

— length of the delay,

— reason for the delay,

— prejudice to the accused because of the delay, and

—whether or not the accused has asserted his or her right to a speedy trial.

The U.S. Supreme Court in *Klopfer v. North Carolina* applied the constitutional right to a speedy trial to the states. This case involved Professor Klopfer who was a professor of zoology at Duke University. He had been indicted by a grand jury for criminal trespass as the result of a sit-in demonstration at a segregated motel and restaurant. At the first trial, the jury failed to agree on a verdict and the judge granted a mis-trial. After a year had passed with no action by the prosecutor, the defendant demanded either to be tried or his charges dismissed. The prosecutor then requested that the judge place the case on the inactive trial docket. The judge granted the prosecutor's request and the defendant appealed the decision. The U.S. Supreme Court, in striking down the North Carolina law that allowed a judge to place a case on the inactive docket, held that the North Carolina procedure clearly denied the petitioner (defendant) the right to a speedy trial under the Sixth Amendment. The court stated that the right to a speedy trial was a fundamental right that is secured by the Sixth Amendment.[9]

The statutory rights to a speedy trial are based on state statutes modeled after the federal Speedy Trial Act of 1974. For example, under the federal statute, there is a 100-day deadline between arrest and trial unless the accused waives his or her right to a speedy trial. In California, under their state statute, the time period between arraignment and trial must not exceed 56 days unless time is waived by the defendant. The difference being that the constitutional right is based on the concept of reasonableness and the statutory right is based on definite time limitations.

The only remedy for violation of an accused's right to a speedy trial is to dismiss the charges. In most cases, a speedy trial does not help the defendant. In fact, the longer a defendant delays going to trial the greater the likelihood that the prosecution's witnesses will disappear, die, forget the facts, etc. Accordingly, except in those cases where the accused is confined, generally the accused waives his or her right to a speedy trial.

Right to a Public Trial

The Sixth Amendment also provides that the accused shall have the right to a public trial. The right to a public trial originated in England as a guarantee against proceedings being carried out in secrecy in the Star Chamber court. Secret trials were also used in Spain and France. A study of our history indicates a strong distrust for secret proceedings. Accordingly, the right to a public trial is a fundamental right and applies to both the states and the federal government. Under certain circumstances if the accused does not object, a judge may close the court. Only under rare occasions can a trial be closed over the objections of the defendant.

One rationale for the fundamental right to a public trial is that the government will be more forthright and above reproach if their actions are openly viewed by the public. In addition, by having an open trial, witnesses are less likely to lie about the accused since their conduct is under the scrutiny of the public.

Right to Confront Witnesses

The Sixth Amendment also provides the accused with a right to be confronted with the witnesses against him. This is known as the confrontation clause and it is considered essential to a fair trial. It restricts and controls the admissibility of hearsay evidence and it requires the witnesses to testify in open court while facing the accused. The theory is that the witnesses are less likely to give false testimony if they are required to face the accused during the testimony. The defense can also cross-examine the witnesses, determine their biases, and attempt to determine their veracity.

The courts have insisted that the accused be afforded the right to confrontation and cross-examination as essential to a fair trial. In *Coy v. Iowa*, the trial court had allowed two young girls to testify from behind a screen that separated them from the defendant. The U.S. Supreme Court ruled that the screen between the accused and the witnesses violated the accused's right to confront the witnesses against him.[10] In *Maryland v. Craig*, the U.S. Supreme Court indicated, however, that in certain circumstances the defendant's right to confront the witness may be limited in order to obtain a definite social objective. In this case, the court allowed a child sex abuse victim to testify via closed-circuit television.[11] The trial court in the *Craig* case determined that face-to-face confrontation would cause trauma to the victims. The Supreme Court considered that the circumstances in this case overrode the defendant's right to confront the witnesses. It appears that only in those cases involving child sexual abuse will the court allow the defendant's confrontation rights to be limited and only in those cases where face-to-face testimony would be harmful to a child victim.

THE JURY

Even though most cases are handled with a guilty plea and only a few cases are tried by a jury, the jury is the focal point of the criminal justice system. The Sixth Amendment also guarantees the accused the right to trial by jury. The two major issues regarding the right to a jury trial are:

1) whether all offenders, including those being tried on minor offenses, have a right to jury trial;

2) the size of the jury; and

3) whether the jury verdict must be unanimous.

Right to a Jury Trial

In felony cases, there has never been a question regarding the right to a jury trial. Prior to 1970, the general rule for state criminal trials was that in serious crimes the accused had a right to a jury trial but not in minor offenses. In *Baldwin v. New York*, the court moved away from the serious-minor classification and established the rule that if the accused was facing a possible sentence of six months or more in jail, the accused had a right to a jury trial.[12] If the accused is facing a possible sentence of less than six months, then the accused has no right to a jury trial unless provided by state statute. Many states, like California, provide the right to a jury trial any time the accused faces a possible jail sentence.

The U.S. Supreme Court discussed this issue again in *Blanton v. North Las Vegas*. The issue in this case was whether the accused had a right to a jury trial in cases involving driving under the influence (DUI). The court stated that if the state considered the offense a petty offense, the accused has no right to a jury trial. If the state, however, treats the crime as a serious crime then the accused has a right to a speedy trial. [*Note*: Nevada had a statute that classified DUI as a petty offense unless aggravating circumstances were present.[13]]

Jury Size

A related issue is whether the accused has a right to a trial by a jury consisting of at least 12 jurors. Historically, trial juries have consisted of 12 jurors. As the results of *Williams v. Florida*, the U.S. Supreme Court has approved trial by a six person jury. The court stated:

We conclude, in short, as we began: the fact that a jury at common law was composed of precisely 12 is a historical accident, unnecessary to effect the purposes of the jury system and wholly without significance....[14]

After the *Williams* case, many states adopted the six person jury for misdemeanor cases. In some states, like Florida, a six person jury may be used in felony cases. The U.S. Supreme Court has set six as the minimum size for a jury.

A related issue is the requirement for unanimous verdicts in jury cases. The Supreme Court has ruled that in trials with six person juries, the verdict must be unanimous. The court has approved statutes that allow less than unanimous verdicts in cases with 12 person juries. In *Apodica v. Oregon*, the court approved a state statute that allowed conviction based on the vote of 10 jury members in a 12 person jury.[15] The Supreme Court has never approved a less than unanimous verdict in cases with less than 12 jurors.

Jury Selection

The Sixth Amendment guarantees a defendant the right to an impartial jury. In addition, the due process clause of the Fifth and 14th Amendments prohibits juries that exclude members of the defendant's racial, gender, ethnic, religious, or similar groups. To ensure an impartial jury, states and the federal government require that the jury panel (potential members of the jury) be selected from a fair cross-section of the community wherein the court convenes. Most jurisdictions randomly select the jury panel from the local census, tax rolls, city directories, telephone books, drivers' license lists, etc.

After the jury panel is selected, they are directed to appear at a certain time and place. It is from the jury panel that the actual jury is selected. The principle method used by the counsel to ensure that the jury is impartial is the *"voir dire"* of the jury. *Voir dire* is the questioning of the prospective jury members about matters that could influence their ability to serve on a jury. In some jurisdictions, counsel submit their questions to the judge who then asks the questions to the individual jury members. In other jurisdictions, both counsel have the opportunity to question the prospective jurors. Counsel can then challenge the prospective jury members. If the counsel's challenge is sustained by the judge (approved), the prospective jury member is excused.

There are two types of challenges — challenges for cause and peremptory challenges. A **challenge for cause** is based on something that indicates that the person would not be an impartial juror or would not follow the judge's instructions. Both sides have unlimited challenges for cause, but the judge may overrule the challenge (disapprove). An example of a challenge for cause would be where a juror indicates that he was the victim of a robbery and therefore would be prejudiced against the defendant who is charged with robbery.

Each party to a jury trial has a certain number of peremptory challenges, normally about 10 in felony cases. **Peremptory challenges** may be used for any legal reason to excuse a prospective juror. The judge cannot overrule a peremptory challenge. [*Note*: Peremptory challenges cannot be used to exclude members solely on the basis of race.[16]]

In capital cases, we often talk about a "death qualified" jury. This refers to the fact that all the members selected for the jury have indicated that in the appropriate circumstances they would vote for the death penalty. The prosecutor asking for the death penalty has the right to challenge for cause any prospective juror who indicates that under no circumstances would the juror vote for the death penalty.

EXHIBIT 11-3

Fair and Impartial Jury?

The prospective juror stated that he was a retired banker. He was immediately peremptorily challenged. The defense attorney was later asked why he challenged the banker. The answer was that bankers, especially retired ones, tended to be very conservative and thus tended to support "law and order" over individual rights. The experienced defense attorney stated that his purpose in conducting *voir dire* and in challenging perspective jurors was not to obtain a fair and impartial jury, but a jury that was inclined to vote for his client? Is this ethical? If not, how is it prevented?

After the *voir dire* is completed and the jury has been selected, they are impaneled (sworn in). The judge then gives preliminary instructions to the jury. The jurors are instructed that they are not to talk to others about the case, to read the papers, or decide on the case until all the evidence has been submitted and the jury has received their instructions from the judge.

TRIAL PROCEEDINGS

A criminal trial is a highly complex and very formal method of establishing the guilt or absence of guilt of the accused. Less than five percent of cases go to trial. The remaining cases are disposed of by guilty pleas, diversion out of the court system, or by dismissal.

To obtain a guilty verdict, the prosecutor must establish the accused's guilt to each and every element of the offense. The guilt must be established "beyond a reasonable doubt." The concept of proof beyond a reasonable doubt is hard to explain. Some common attempts include:

— a doubt that would cause prudent persons to hesitate before acting in a matter of importance to themselves;

— not frivolous or fanciful doubt;

— a doubt based on reason and common sense; and

— persuasion to a moral certainty.

After preliminary matters have been disposed of, the jury is seated in the jury box. The prosecutor has the opportunity to make an opening statement. This statement is not evidence but may be used to inform the jury of the direction that the prosecutor is attempting to go. The defense counsel may make his or her opening statement immediately after the prosecution finishes or the defense may wait until the defense presents its case.

The prosecutor having the burden of proof begins the trial. Witnesses are called and evidence is presented. After the prosecution rests its case, the defense presents its case. Then, the prosecution may present evidence in rebuttal to counter the defense.

After both sides have rested, the prosecution presents its closing argument. The defense then presents its closing argument. Finally, the prosecution may present an argument in rebuttal to the defense's closing argument. The reason that the prosecutor goes first and is afforded the last word is based on the concept that the side with the burden of proof has the right to open and close the case. In the arguments presented by counsel, it is unethical for counsel to indicate a personal belief on whether or not the accused is guilty. For example, the prosecutor may argue that the government has proven the guilt of the defendant beyond a reasonable doubt. It is unethical for the prosecutor, however, to state that he or she believes that the defendant is guilty.

After argument has been completed, the judge gives instructions to the jury. This is also called charging the jury. The instructions are used to explain the law of the case to the jurors. The subjects covered in the instructions include burden of proof, the elements of the offense, voting procedures to be used by the jury, etc.

Typical jury room—where jury retires to confer about verdict.

Generally in jury trials, the jury makes the findings of guilty or not guilty. After a guilty finding, the judge sets the sentencing. Sentencing will be discussed in Chapter 12. If the jury is unable to reach a verdict, the jury is considered a "hung jury." In cases involving a hung jury, the jury is excused. The prosecution either retries the case or the charges are dismissed.

Although there are no provisions for it in the statutes, juries have nullification power. The nullification process occurs when the jury brings in a verdict of not guilty despite the fact that the evidence established the guilt of the accused. When jury nullification occurs, the accused cannot be re-tried for that offense. The power of nullification is a common law right that juries have. It is based on the concept that the jury is not required to explain any findings of not guilty.

Before the death penalty may be imposed by a judge, the jury must not only find that the accused is guilty but also that the special circumstances that allow the imposition of the death penalty exist. Death penalty cases are generally bifurcated trials (in two parts). The first part deals with the question of guilt and the second part deals with the question of whether special circumstances are present which would allow the death sentence.

Fair Trial

One method used to ensure that the accused receives a fair trial is the selection of an impartial jury. The accused has a right to be tried in the district in which the crime occurred. This right may be waived by the accused when necessary to receive a fair trial. For example if the local newspapers contain rumors regarding the accused's guilt, the accused may request a **change of venue**. This is a request that the trial judge move the location of the trial to a different site in an attempt to receive a fair trial. Only the defense may make a motion for change of venue.

Another method that a judge may use to help the accused obtain a fair trial is to sequester the jury. When a judge sequesters the jury, they are placed in isolation so that jury members will not be inappropriately influenced by information other than that given in court (i.e., newspaper accounts, talking with others about the case, and television accounts).

Admissible Evidence

In order to convict a defendant, the prosecution must establish guilt beyond a reasonable doubt by admissible evidence. The admissibility of evidence is determined by the rules of evidence. The types of evidence normally presented at a trial include oral testimony of witnesses, documentary evidence, physical evidence (the gun or drugs), and scientific evidence. Scientific evidence refers to the results of tests such as drug analysis and ballistics tests.

Reasons that evidence may be excluded from trial (not considered by the jury) include:

— the defendant's constitutional rights were violated when the evidence was seized by the police;

— the evidence is not relevant to the issues before the jury;

— the evidence does not meet the reliability tests required for admission; and

— the inflammatory nature of the evidence outweighs its probative value.

Under the exclusionary rule, any evidence that was seized in violation of the accused's constitutional rights cannot be used against the accused (the evidence is excluded). Accordingly, any evidence discovered by the police during a search may not be used against the defendant if the police violated the accused's rights against unreasonable searches and seizure. In many cases, when the results of the search are excluded, the prosecutor does not have a case against the defendant, especially in a case involving the possession of illegal drugs. If the drugs are excluded for evidence, the prosecutor generally dismisses the case. The purpose of the exclusionary rule as set forth in *Mapp v. Ohio* is to deter police misconduct.[17] The rule has been criticized for allowing the criminal to go free when the police officer makes an innocent or unknowing mistake.

When the prosecution attempts to enter a confession or other statement made by the accused, the prosecutor must establish that the statement was voluntarily made and that the accused's rights were not violated when the statement or confession was taken. Most of the issues involving the admissability of confessions are based on the *Miranda v. Arizona* case.[18] In the *Miranda* case, the U.S. Supreme Court held that before the police could conduct in-custody interrogation, the police must advise the accused of his or her rights in this area. These warnings are now popularly known as the *"Miranda"* warnings.

Appeals

In most cases, the defendant, if convicted, has the right to appeal the conviction. At the original trial, the accused is presumed to be not guilty. At the appellate stage, however, there is a presumption that the trial court's decision was correct. The appellate court looks only for errors of law in determining whether the trial verdict should be sustained (approved).

DISCUSSION QUESTIONS

1. Explain the role and function of the jury.

2. Why does the prosecution have the burden of proof in criminal cases?

3. Why are pretrial motions important to counsel?

4. Explain the process of selecting jurors.

5. Would you qualify for a "death qualified jury"?

ENDNOTES

[1] Bureau of Justice Statistics Study, "Felony Arrests," (1987).
[2] 342 U.S. 1 (1951).
[3] *U.S. v. Salerno*, 55 USLW 4663 (1987).
[4] *Hale v. Henkel*, 201 U.S. 43 (1906).
[5] *Costello v. United States*, 350 U.S. 359 (1956).
[6] American Bar Association, *Grand Jury Policy and Model Act*, (Chicago: ABA, 1982).
[7] *Brady v. Maryland*, 363 U.S. 83 (1963).
[8] *Moore v. Illinois*, 408 U.S. 786 (1972).
[9] 386 U.S. 213 (1967).
[10] 487 U.S. 1012 (1988).
[11] 497 U.S. 836 (1990).
[12] 399 U.S. 66 (1970).
[13] 489 U.S. 538 (1989).
[14] 399 U.S. 78, 90 (1970).
[15] 406 U.S. 404 (1972).
[16] *Taylor v. Louisiana*, 419 U.S. 522 (1975).
[17] 367 U.S. 643 (1961).
[18] 384 U.S. 436 (1966).

Early use of the Pillory for punishment.

SENTENCING

The sword of human justice is about to fall upon your guilty head.

—Isaac C. Parke
Federal District Court Judge, 1876

In this chapter, we will examine the types of punishment, the philosophy, constitutional restraints, and the considerations involved in the sentencing process.

Under our justice system, once a defendant has been found guilty of a criminal offense, the state has a right to inflict punishment in the form of a *sentence* on the accused. The concept of punishing criminals is one of the most complex and controversial issues in the criminal justice system. Early in our history, punishment was seen as a spectacle used to teach moral lessons. It was believed that the more gruesome the punishment the public observed, the more punishment would serve as a deterrent to crime. Punishments, through the centuries, have considerably changed due to the maturing of our customs, economic conditions, religious beliefs, and political ideals. Throughout time sentencing concepts have tended to directly reflect current customs, ideals, and conditions.

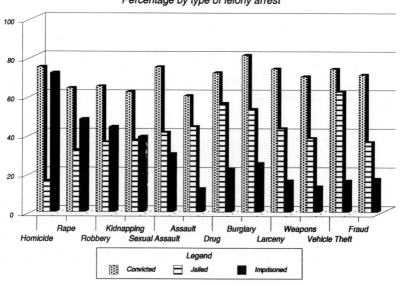

Likelihood of Conviction and Sentencing

Percentage by type of felony arrest

Legend: Convicted, Jailed, Imprisoned

Source: U.S. Dept. of Justice

TYPES OF PUNISHMENT

There are four basic types of punishment (sanctions) that may be imposed by the court after the defendant has been convicted: a fine, incarceration, probation, and the death penalty.

The proper *sanction* for a particular criminal is rarely individually rationalized. Our courts focus primarily on the crime committed and not the criminal committing the crime. If the system were to attempt sanctions based on the individuality of each criminal the courts would not only grind to a halt from the time incurred to evaluate each criminal (what sanction or combination of sanctions would best punish this individual) but also from the issues raised by sentencing disparities for like crimes. This is not to say that our present system does not take into consideration the criminal. We tend to deal with the individuality of a criminal by generalizing with classifications such as "first time offender" and "habitual criminal."

In addition, there is little coordination of sentencing between judges. Although ranges or specific sanctions for a particular crime exist, the presiding judge has flexibility in handing-down a particular sentence. Therefore, like crimes will be punished equitably but not identically. Hence, endearing terms are often heard for judges such as "soft" or "hanging."

The death penalty is reserved for aggravated criminal homicides. It is clearly the most controversial and most regulated type of punishment in our system. On any given day, there are approximately 1,500 prisoners on death row awaiting execution. On average it takes about 10 years from the date the accused is sentenced to death until the actual execution. This delay is the subject of considerable debate. The death penalty is discussed in detail later in this chapter along with alternate punishments.

Fines

Fines are usually the sole punishment in minor cases. In serious cases, especially those involving financial gain, the courts will often impose a large fine in addition to either probation or incarceration. In most cases, the only guidance given judges regarding the imposition of fines is the statutory maximum fine allowable for the offense committed.

Research has failed to establish the effectiveness of fines in controlling human behavior. Often the fines imposed by the courts have little relationship to the crimes committed or the need to rehabilitate the offenders. Take, for example, Michael Milken who was found to have bilked investors out of approximately 1.4 billion dollars through junk bond sales, yet his fine was only 600 million dollars and a few years in a minimum security prison. He was out of the "country club" prison in approximately two years and allowed to keep an 800 million dollar fortune. Although this was a record fine, was it an effective deterrent?

Fines are the most common punishment imposed by the lower courts. The primary sanction for those who do not pay their fine is imprisonment. Currently there are thousands of people confined in local jails because they failed to pay their fines. In *Tate v. Short*, the U.S. Supreme Court held that imprisoning a person for failure to pay a fine discriminates against the poor.[1] The courts avoid this problem by typically allowing the defendant at sentencing a choice of either paying the imposed fine or electing to spend a certain amount of time in jail.

Probation

Probation is the most common sentence handed-down in major trial courts. Under probation, the defendant is permitted to live in the community subject to restrictions placed by the courts. The courts are given wide discretion in imposing special conditions on the defendant when sentencing the individual to probation. Probation is discussed in detail in Chapter 14.

Incarceration

Prior to the 17th century, incarceration as a form of punishment was not used. About that same time it was common for English judges to spare the lives of certain criminals if they would agree to be transported to the colonies. Those that were transported were sold to the highest bidder in order to pay for their transportation.[2] After they were sold, they became indentured servants. Transportation to the

colonies quickly became the most popular sentence for common
thieves.

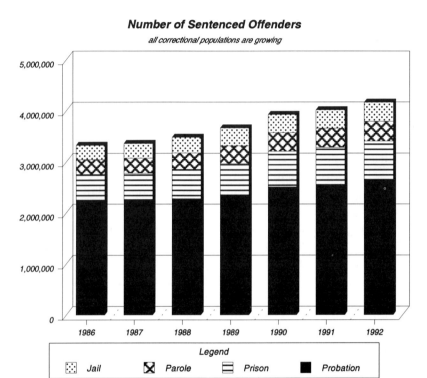

Number of Sentenced Offenders

all correctional populations are growing

Legend

▦ Jail   ☒ Parole   ☰ Prison   ■ Probation

Source: U.S. Dept. of Justice

After the American Revolution, Australia became the destination
for most transported convicts. The inmates shipped to Australia served
as indentured servants in the plantations, mines, and sheep ranches. In
the 1850s serious opposition developed in England regarding the
practice of transporting prisoners. The Society for the Improvement of
Prison Discipline asked reformer Alexander Maconochie to investigate and report on the conditions of these indentured servants in
Australia. As the result of his reports, the British Parliament passed the
English Penal Servitude Act of 1853. This act eventually ended
transportation and substituted imprisonment as a form of punishment.

Incarceration, as a form of punishment, was first used in the United States in the 18th century to replace physical torture and capital punishment. In theory, incarceration is to be imposed when the courts consider it necessary to confine the defendant to protect the public from future criminal conduct by this individual. Incarceration is also imposed in those cases where the legislature has mandated that all persons convicted of certain crimes be given a jail or prison sentence. The incarceration may be in a local jail or a state correctional institution. This form of specific deterrence is discussed later in this chapter.

Today incarceration sentences are based on one of three models: legislative, judicial, and administrative.

The **legislative model** involves a definite sentence having been established by the legislature for all persons convicted of a particular crime. Specific sanctions, including terms of confinement are detailed. For example, in some states the defendant on the third conviction for driving under the influence (DUI) must be sentenced to 90 days in jail.

In the **judicial model**, the judge is given a general range in which the defendant may be sentenced. The defendant may be sentenced from three to ten years for robbery. It is the judge in these situations who determines the length of the defendant's actual sentence.

In the **administrative model**, while the judge may sentence the individual to prison, an administrative agency determines the actual length of the imprisonment. The administrative model is currently not used in any state. Prior to 1978, it was used in California. Currently, most states use the judicial model, although there is an increasing trend to use the legislative model.

Sentences are given by the judge in most states, even in those cases where the jury made the determination of guilt. In cases involving incarceration, the judge is normally restricted as to the range of sentencing which may be imposed. In felony cases, the judge normally delays the sentencing until receipt of a pre-sentencing report by the probation department regarding the social and personal history of the defendant. The pre-sentencing report will also contain a recommendation by the probation department as to the sentence that will best "assist" in the rehabilitation of the defendant. Typically, the defense attorneys are allowed to submit material to the probation department for inclusion in the pre-sentencing report. By submitting favorable material, the defense counsel is attempting to obtain a favorable recommendation from probation (i.e., a more lenient sentence).

Under our trial system, the accused has a "right of allocution" which means that the accused has a right to address the court before the sentence is announced. The defense often uses this right to ask permission of the court to present an alternative presentencing report. In recent years, the trend for defense counsels to hire professionals with correctional or probational experience to prepare alternative presentencing reports has increased. These reports are professionally prepared by an individual who can devote more time to the report than can the usually overworked probation officer who has many such reports to complete. If allowed by the judge, the defense's alternative presentencing reports are then submitted for review and can then be weighed against the assessments in the probation department's report.

When defendants are convicted of more than one charge, they are normally sentenced on each charge. In cases involving multiple charges and imprisonment, the defendant can be ordered to serve the sentences either concurrently or consecutively. A *concurrent sentence* is one where the defendant is serving time on all the charges at the same time. A *consecutive sentence* is where the accused serves time on one offense and when the first sentence is completed, the accused serves time on the next sentence. For example, the defendant is convicted of two charges of battery. He is given three years on the first and two years on the second. If he serves the sentences concurrently, the maximum he will serve is three years. If he serves them consecutively, he could serve three years on the first sentence and then two years on the second, for a total of five years. In most cases, the court allows the defendant to serve the sentences concurrently. Consecutive sentences are usually reserved for the most serious and uncooperative defendants.

Good Time Credits

One of the factors influencing the length of time that a prisoner serves is the use of "good time." The "good time" credit is used to control and discipline a prisoner. An inmate can have his or her sentence reduced by obeying prison rules, donating blood, being involved in work or educational programs, etc. The statutes in each state regulate the amount of good time that may be given and the factors that may be used in awarding good time. The statutes also provide situations in which good time may be withheld from a prisoner. Some states credit good time on a flat basis per month (e.g., six days per month). Other states grant good time credit on an increasing rate with each additional year served (e.g., one month for the first year, two months for the second and third years, and three months for the fourth year).

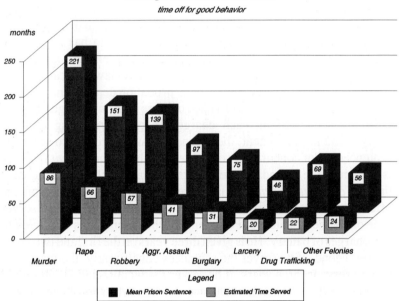

Average Time Served in Prison
time off for good behavior

Source: *U.S. Dept. of Justice*

Often an inmate may have his or her sentence reduced by as much as one-half with the use of good time. In 23 jurisdictions and the federal government, good time may be deducted only from the maximum term. In other states where the inmate has a minimum and a maximum term, the good time is deducted from both the minimum and the maximum terms.

Conversely, good time may also be taken away from a prisoner. State and federal statutes on good time contain provisions governing the number of days that may be lost or forfeited, the reasons the credits may be lost, and the methods or procedures necessary for forfeiture of the good time credit. Most states require that before good time may be taken away from an inmate, the inmate has a right to a hearing and an appeal regarding the loss of good time. In addition, in most states the warden has the right to restore good time credit that has been forfeited.

Indeterminate/Determinate Sentencing

In the early 1900s, prison reformers called for the imposition of **indeterminate sentences**. The belief was that prison sentences should be tailored to fit the individual needs of the defendant and that offenders should only be kept in confinement until they are rehabilitated. Under the general concept of indeterminate sentencing, the defendant is sentenced to both a minimum and a maximum number of years of confinement. After the defendant has served the minimum, and an administrative board has determined that the defendant has been rehabilitated, he or she is released.

Prior to the 1970s, the indeterminate sentencing concept was adopted by at least 41 states. In the 1960s and 70s, however, there was a growing movement against the indeterminate sentencing approach. Many reformers felt that too many criminals were being released into society without paying the penalty for their crimes and that a *price tag* should be placed on criminal behavior. The price tag would be set penalties for each crime. Under the "price tag" argument, a criminal would know before he commits a particular crime what he will pay as a penalty. This classical approach to sentencing assumes that the criminal is a rational person and has free will.

Starting in the late 1970s, many of the states abolished indeterminate sentencing and adopted determinate sentencing. A **determinate sentence** is where the judge imposes a flat or fixed sentence. In some jurisdictions, the defendant must serve the entire sentence, except for good time, before the defendant is released. In others, the prisoner is eligible for parole after serving a minimum period of time, usually about one-third of the sentence.

Mandatory sentences and presumptive sentences are variations of the determinate sentencing concept are . A **mandatory sentence** is one established by the legislatures to limit judicial discretion in certain crimes. Many states have adopted mandatory sentences for crimes involving the use of a firearm, rape, arson, and driving under the influence.

Presumptive Sentencing

The *presumptive sentencing* approach is where the legislature sets suggested terms for particular crimes. Offenders convicted of the violation of one of the crimes with a presumptive sentence would normally be sentenced to the presumptive sentence unless the judge finds that the circumstances of the particular case warrant a more or less severe punishment. In most states using this approach, the factors that the judge may consider to vary the presumptive sentence are carefully spelled out in the statutes. The purpose of the presumptive sentence approach is to:

1) reduce sentencing disparity,

2) limit judicial discretion, and

3) impose sentences that the defendants will be required to serve.

California's Determinate Sentencing Act of 1978 is an example of the presumptive sentencing approach. This act allows the judges to give a short, middle, or long term sentence for each offense. The judges are required to use the middle sentence unless mitigating circumstances indicate that the short term would be more appropriate or aggravating factors indicate that the long term is appropriate. Judges must explain, on record, why they departed from the presumptive sentence (middle term). A formal fact-finding hearing must be held before the long term sentence can be imposed. At the fact-finding hearing, the judge must find as a fact that one or more aggravating circumstances exist. Typical aggravating circumstances include: the use of a weapon in committing the crime, a prior criminal record, or the degree of harm inflicted on the victim.

Similar to the presumptive sentencing approach is the *structured sentencing approach* currently being used in Delaware and Maryland. In those states, a sentencing commission established "rational sentences" for the commission of certain offenses along with the presence of certain factors. The judges are then requested, but not required, to use the rational sentences.

Sentencing In Federal Court

Sentencing in federal courts changed substantially after the Sentencing Reform Act of 1984.[3] This act established the U.S. Sentencing Commission and empowered the commission to develop guidelines which scale punishments according to the gravity of the offense and the offender's past criminal record. The guidelines developed by the commission apply to all federal defendants who committed their crimes after November 1, 1987.

One of the stated purposes of the reform act was to introduce a "truth in sentencing" approach to federal criminal procedure. Under the guidelines, federal prisoners may no longer be released from prison and placed on parole by the parole commission. Instead, the sentences imposed by judges are served in full except for time off for good behavior. Offenders are supervised after their release only if a judge makes the supervision a part of their original sentence.

A review of the federal sentencing patterns prior to the act and after the act indicates:

— after implementing the act, the percentage of defendants convicted of felonies receiving prison sentences rose from 52 percent to 60 percent;

— the average length of sentences of incarceration decreased, however, for all but drug offenders; and

— the average prisoner now serves 29 percent more actual incarceration time than those sentenced prior to the effective date of the act.

The sentencing guidelines are computed for a variety of offenses and offenders. The following table of the Minnesota guidelines indicates how the guidelines work. The federal table is very similar. Such tables are designed and updated by sentencing commissions.

One of the biggest criticisms of the use of guidelines is that they reduce the individualization of sentences— judges cannot tailor sentences as necessary in an attempt to rehabilitate a defendant. For example, under the table, an individual with an IQ of 70 would be sentenced to the same sentence as an individual with an IQ of 140. One of the factors that prompted the imposition of sentencing guidelines was the desire to remove racial and cultural considerations from the sentencing decision. Research, however, indicates that blacks and the poor are still more likely to receive prison terms than whites and the rich.

Severity Levels of Conviction Offense		Criminal History Score						
		0	1	2	3	4	5	6 or more
Sale of a Simulated Controlled Substance	I	12*	12*	12*	13	15	17	18-20
Theft Related Crimes ($2,500 or less)	II	12*	12*	13	15	17	19	20-22
Theft Crimes ($2,500 or less)	III	12*	13	15	17	18-20	21-23	24-26
Nonresidential Burglary Theft Crimes (over $2,500)	IV	12*	15	18	21	24-26	30-34	37-45
Residential Burglary Simple Robbery	V	18	23	27	29-31	36-40	43-49	50-58
Criminal Sexual Conduct 2nd Degree (a) & (b)	VI	21	26	30	33-35	42-46	50-58	60-70
Aggravated Robbery	VII	44-52	54-62	64-72	74-82	84-92	94-102	104-112
Criminal Sexual Conduct, 1st Degree Assault, 1st Degree	VIII	81-91	93-103	105-115	117-127	129-139	141-151	153-163
Felony Murder, 3rd Degree Felony Murder, 2nd Degree	IX	144-156	159-171	174-186	189-201	204-216	219-231	234-246
Murder, 2nd Degree (with intent)	X	299-313	319-333	339-353	359-373	379-393	399-413	419-433

Minnesota Guideline Grid, Presumptive Sentence Lengths in Months

☐ Presumptive commitment to state imprisonment.

*One year and one day

Sentencing Practices

Mandatory Sentencing

What kind of sentence can a defendant expect upon conviction? Michael Tonry reviewed the research on mandatory sentencing and made the following conclusions:
— Lawyers and judges will take steps to avoid application of sentencing laws that they consider unduly harsh.

— Dismissal rates are higher in the early stages of the criminal justice process after implementation of mandatory sentencing laws.

— In states with mandatory sentencing laws, defendants who are not diverted or dismissed make more vigorous efforts to avoid conviction.

— Defendants who are convicted under mandatory sentencing laws spend longer in prison than they would in absence of the mandatory laws.[4]

Non-Mandatory Sentencing

The Bureau of Justice Statistics evaluated approximately 15,000 cases in 18 different states to ascertain sentencing practices in the U.S.[5] Their conclusions are as follows:
— Forty-five percent of defendants convicted of a felony were given prison sentences, 26 percent went to jail, and 29 percent received probation.

— Defendants convicted of homicide are more likely than other defendants to go to prison (85 percent). Those convicted of drug offenses were least likely (23 percent).

— Eighty-five percent of the convicted defendants were convicted on the highest original charge. Fifteen percent were convicted on a lesser charge.

— Defendants who pled guilty received shorter sentences than defendants who pled not guilty. In addition, those pleading guilty were less likely to go to prison that those pleading not guilty.

Felon Sentencing

by state court in 1992

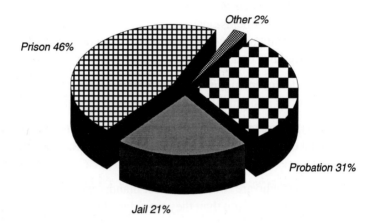

Other 2%

Prison 46%

Probation 31%

Jail 21%

Source: U.S. Dept. of Justice

Habitual Criminal Statutes

Habitual criminal statutes mandate that individuals who have served time for multiple felony offenses receive either enhanced punishment or mandatory life imprisonment sentences. Habitual criminal statutes are an attempt to incapacitate those individuals who perpetually commit criminal misconduct. The general approach is as follows: if the defendant has two or more serious felony convictions, the prosecution can seek to have the defendant declared a habitual offender. If the court agrees, the individual may be sentenced to life imprisonment. The U.S. Supreme Court approved the use of habitual criminal statutes in the case of *Rummel v. Estelle*.[6] In the *Rummel* case, the defendant was convicted of obtaining $120.00 through false pretenses and had two prior convictions. [Note: In this case, Rummel could be released by establishing that he had rehabilitated.] In a similar case, *Solem v. Helm*, the Supreme Court held that it was cruel and unusual to sentence a person to life imprisonment without the possibility of parole for writing a "no account" check. This case is further discussed later in this chapter. Recent cases indicate that the court is more willing to approve life sentences for chronic offenders who have not committed life-threatening crimes.[7]

Extralegal Factors

Certain extralegal factors such as race, gender, or wealth should not be considered in determining the appropriate sentence to impose on a convicted defendant. Any such consideration would be a violation of the concept of due process. Unfortunately, it appears that in the past, many of those factors were considered by the courts.

It appears from an examination of sentencing practices, that there is a definite gender bias in sentencing. Women are far less likely to receive sentences involving incarceration than men. In addition, it appears that females are more likely to be granted pretrial release than men.[8]

Evidence is clear that there is an association between social class and sentencing outcomes. Rich defendants are far less likely to go to prison or jail than poor defendants. The differences could be explained, however, by the fact that rich defendants can obtain better legal representation. Research also indicates that judges are more lenient toward elderly defendants and are less likely to send them to incarceration than younger defendants.

PRINCIPLES OF PUNISHMENT

Sentencing has two domains— the purposes that justify punishment and the concept of proportionality (referring to the nature and amount of punishment in relation to the person and the criminal conduct being punished).[9]

There are two common justifications for punishment— retribution and prevention. Prevention is subdivided into the categories of general deterrence, specific deterrence, and rehabilitation.

Retribution

Retribution is based on the concept that it is right to punish the wicked. As Sir James F. Stephen, an English 19th century judge stated:

The infliction of punishment by law gives definite expression and a solemn ratification and justification to the hatred which is excited by the commission of the offense. The criminal law thus proceeds upon the principle that it is morally right to hate criminals, and it confirms and justifies that sentiment by inflicting on criminals punishments which express it.[10]

Included within the retribution justification is the principle of culpability. **Culpability** refers to the concept that criminals are responsible for their criminal conduct and therefore must pay the consequences of their misconduct. Another version of retribution is the principle of "just desserts." This principle refers to the concept that the criminals have committed a crime against society and therefore owe a debt to society. The punishment that criminals receive is what they deserve for the debt. Reduced to its basic theme, retribution can be stated as: "You hurt us, therefore, we have a right to hurt you."

EXHIBIT 12-1

An American Indian Precept

According to an American Indian precept, if the child is naughty do not hit it. Make the child fast. When the child is hungry, it will remember its past misconduct. Beating a child makes it more naughty.

Do you agree with this precept? Why?

Prevention

Prevention justifies punishment. Punishment can be seen as necessary in order to deter others from committing crimes. Two types of deterrence can be classified under prevention — general deterrence and specific deterrence.

General Deterrence

General deterrence refers to actions designed to prevent others from committing crimes. An example of a general deterrent action is the passing of statutes mandating prison terms for individuals who use firearms in committing their crimes. These statutes are designed to discourage anyone from using a firearm during the commission of a crime.

General deterrence as a justification for punishment was first advocated in the 18th century by Cesare Beccaria and Jeremy Bentham, founders of the classical school of criminology.[11] They contended that the only purpose of punishment was to protect society. The concept of crime prevention, as we know it today, was nonexistent. Their concept of justice included an exact scale of punishments for acts without reference to the criminal's circumstances. According to them, the criminal takes a variety of factors into account before freely choosing to commit a criminal act. Therefore, the criminal should be held responsible for his or her behavior.

Both Beccaria and Bentham contended that punishment should be only as severe as is necessary to deter crime. Punishment is considered a deterrent only if it is perceived as fair and in proportion to the crime committed. If the punishments are too severe, they cause people to commit other criminal acts solely to avoid punishment.

Beccaria and Bentham were firm in their belief that punishment should be determined by legislatures, not judges. They reacted against the widespread practice of their day in which judges were autonomous and did what they pleased. Judges could augment statutory punishments with whatever they saw fit at the time. The concept of "due process" did not exist. The status, money and power of the accused often affected sentencing. Punishments were arbitrary and inconsistent.

Beccaria was opposed to capital punishment except in two instances. The two exceptions are:

1) in the case of an imprisoned individual who could endanger the security of the nation, and

2) in the case of an imprisoned individual who could still cause other serious crimes to be committed while imprisoned.

The main points of the classical school are as follows:

— The doctrine of "free will" is used to explain human behavior. Free will refers to the concept that criminals freely choose to commit the criminal behavior in question.

— Criminals are responsible for their behavior.

— Crime reduction can be accomplished by inflicting a sufficient amount of pain upon the offender.

— The purposes of punishment should be to deter others from committing criminal acts.

— The type and amount of pain to impose on the offender should be determined by focusing only on the crime itself.

— Punishment to be effective should be prompt, certain and serve a useful function.[12]

EXHIBIT 12-2

A Chinese Proverb

There is an old Chinese proverb that states:

"It is better to hang the wrong fellow, rather than no fellow."

This is based on the classical concept that certainty of punishment is an important variable in reducing crime.

Accordingly, if a crime has occurred, punish the person most likely to have committed it.

Would this practice reduce crime? How does it conflict with our requirement of establishing the criminal's guilt beyond a reasonable doubt?

Specific Deterrence

Specific deterrence refers to actions designed to prevent a specific individual from committing crimes. For example, sending a bank robber to prison deters that individual from robbing other banks during the time incarcerated in prison.

Rehabilitation

Rehabilitation is based on the concept that we should rehabilitate the criminal rather than punish him or her.

The positivists emphasized not the *crime* (as had the classical thinkers) but the *criminal* as an individual. The central theme of positivism is determinism and not "free will." They believe that the criminal is not a rational person, but is for some reason mentally, morally, or physically defective. Where the classical theorist stated that the criminal by use of his or her "free will" made a voluntary choice to commit the criminal act, the positivist contended that because of determinism the criminal had no choice in the crime decision. Only by treating the criminal could the "illness" of crime be eliminated.

The positivists contend that punishment should be directed toward preventing the defendant from committing any additional crimes. Punishment should, therefore, be based on the needs of the individual rather than the crime the individual committed.

Proportionality

The Eighth Amendment to the U.S. Constitution provides that excessive bail shall not be required, or excessive fines imposed, nor cruel and unusual punishments inflicted. The Supreme Court has held that this amendment not only bars barbaric punishments, but also sentences that are disproportionate to the crimes committed.[13] In *Robinson v. California*, the Court stated that one day in prison would be cruel and unusual punishment for the "crime" of having a common cold. In that case, the individual was being punished because of his status as a drug addict.[14]

In *Solem v. Helm*, the accused was found guilty of uttering (attempting to cash) a "no account" check. Because he had three prior felony convictions, he was sentenced as a recidivist and received life imprisonment. The court indicated that no penalty is per se constitutional. The courts must look at the gravity of the offense, the sentences imposed by other courts for the same offense, and sentences imposed on other criminals within the same jurisdiction. The Court held that life imprisonment without the possibility of parole for uttering a "no account" check was cruel and unusual.

The majority of cases involving the concept of proportionality are capital cases. They are discussed in the next section.

DEATH PENALTY

In 1993, approximately 77 percent of the people in the United States supported the use of the death penalty. The Death Information Penalty Center, however, contends that when the public is provided with alternative sentences such as life imprisonment without any possibility of parole that only a minority of people support the death penalty. The center contends that one reason the majority of the public supports the death penalty is the erroneous belief that criminals sentenced to life in prison are released after several years. According to the center, 33 states can impose life sentences without parole and in all other states those who are sentenced to life are required to serve at least 20 years.[4] It appears that the strongest argument used by persons opposed to the death penalty is the prospect that innocent people may be executed. Other objections to the use of the death penalty include moral reasons, the argument that the death penalty is used arbitrarily, and that it is imposed in a racially discriminatory manner.

State death penalty executions in 1990

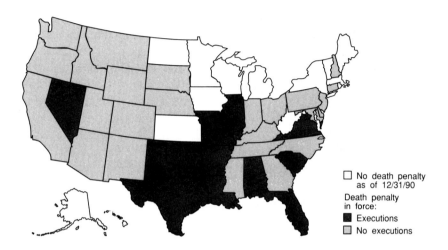

☐ No death penalty
as of 12/31/90

Death penalty
in force:

■ Executions

☐ No executions

Source: U.S. Dept. of Justice

EXHIBIT 12-2

Michael Owen Perry

On April 1, 1993, there were 2,676 people on death row awaiting execution in the United States. Eventually most will be executed. Michael Owen Perry is one of those who will probably never be executed. He is insane. In 1990, the U.S. Supreme Court ruled that the state could not execute him until he regained his sanity and could therefore understand the nature and gravity of his punishment. In October, 1992, the Louisiana Supreme Court ruled that the state could not forcibly-medicate him in order to assist him in regaining his sanity for the purposes of killing him.

Perry was convicted of killing five members of his family on July 17, 1983. Apparently Perry went to his grandmother's house and calmly blew the heads off of his two cousins who were sleeping. He then walked across the backyard to his parents' house where he killed his mother and two other people. At his trial, the issue of insanity was not raised. He was found guilty and sentenced to death.

His appeal to the U.S. Supreme Court was based on the issue of whether it was cruel and unusual punishment and a violation of the Eighth Amendment to medicate a prisoner in order to execute him ("medicate to execute"). The court never answered this question. The Louisiana Supreme Court, however, held that it was a violation of the Amendment.

The U.S. Supreme Court has had a tortured experiment in the constitutional regulation of the death penalty.[15] Prior to 1972, the Supreme Court placed virtually no constitutional restrictions on the imposition of the death penalty. Most state legislatures had rejected the automatic death penalty statutes. The juries were generally instructed that if they found the defendant guilty of a capital crime, they must then decide between death and life imprisonment. The juries had virtually unguided discretion. In most cases, little information regarding the defendant's character, background, and previous criminal record was presented.

In 1972, the U.S. Supreme Court decided *Furman v. Georgia*.[16] This case held by a 5-4 decision that the capital punishment statute in Georgia was unconstitutional. All nine justices wrote separate opinions. Each of the opinions concluded that juries should not be given unguided discretion in imposing the death penalty. The decision while providing no guidance regarding the use of the death penalty clearly established that all states' death penalty statutes were unconstitutional.

In 1976, the majority members of the Supreme Court concluded in *Greg v. Georgia*, that the authors of the cruel and unusual punishment clause did not intend to forbid capital punishment. They only intended to prohibit punishments not officially authorized by statute or not lying within the sentencing court's jurisdiction and any torture or brutal, gratuitously painful methods of execution.[17]

Electric chairs, such as this, are used along with lethal injection, gas chambers and firing squads to execute prisoners.

As the result of the death penalty cases decided by the Court during the 1970s, the following guidelines or actions are considered necessary before a sentence involving the death penalty will be approved by the Court:

— The trial must be tried in separate phases. First, the question of the defendant's guilt must be established;

— At the same time guilt is established, the jury is also required to determine the existence of any special circumstances necessary for the imposition of the death penalty (e.g., murder for hire, murder committed to prevent arrest, prior conviction of murder, murder of a victim, and torture murder);

— If the defendant is found guilty of murder and one or more of the required special circumstances are determined to be present, further proceedings are held on the question of the penalty to be imposed.

Generally special proceedings determine whether the defendant shall be sentenced to death or life imprisonment. After hearing the evidence at the special proceedings, the jury must weigh the evidence and determine if the mitigating circumstances outweigh the aggravating circumstances. If so, life imprisonment rather than the death penalty shall be imposed. In most states with the death penalty, the decision by the jury must be unanimous. If the jury fails to reach a decision, then life imprisonment is given. **Mitigating circumstances** are those circumstances that tend to reduce the severity of the crime (i.e., cooperation with the investigating authority, surrender, good character), whereas **aggravating circumstances** are those circumstances that tend to make the crime more serious (i.e., use of a deadly weapon, committing an offense against a law enforcement officer, taking advantage of a position of trust to commit an offense, etc.).

Those who contend that the death penalty is unconstitutional typically base their legal argument on the "cruel and unusual punishment" clause of the Eighth Amendment to the U.S. Constitution. Those who support the death penalty point out that the due process clauses of the Fifth and Fourteenth Amendments state: "...no person shall be deprived of life...without due process of law." Thus, the two amendments imply that the constitution does not forbid the death penalty.

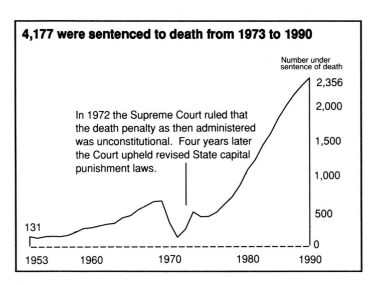

4,177 were sentenced to death from 1973 to 1990

Number under sentence of death

In 1972 the Supreme Court ruled that the death penalty as then administered was unconstitutional. Four years later the Court upheld revised State capital punishment laws.

2,356
2,000
1,500
1,000
500
0

131

1953 1960 1970 1980 1990

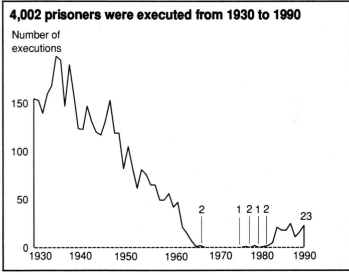

4,002 prisoners were executed from 1930 to 1990

Number of executions

150

100

50

2   1 2 1 2   23

0

1930 1940 1950 1960 1970 1980 1990

Source: U.S. Dept. of Justice

The most common arguments for retaining the death penalty are as follows:

Incapacitation — Supporters of the death penalty contend that the potential for recidivism is serious enough to require the ultimate incapacitation.

Deterrent — Supporters argue that the death penalty serves as a strong deterrent to keep individuals from committing serious crimes. [*Note*: Opponents argue that the death penalty is not a deterrent, since murder is not a crime normally committed by rational people.]

Proportional — Punishing criminals with the death penalty conforms to the requirement that the penalty be proportional to the crime.

Public Opinion — Supporters contend that the majority of the public supports the death penalty.

Those who argue against the death penalty use the following arguments to support their views:

Possibility of Error — There is a possibility of error and an innocent person will be executed.

Cruel and Unusual — The death penalty is a barbaric punishment and there is no place for it in modern society.

Discriminatory — The death penalty is most often used against minorities.

No Deterrent — The opponents argue that the death penalty does not deter others from committing serious criminal acts.

Rehabilitation — There is always the chance that a person might be rehabilitated.

ALTERNATIVE SENTENCING

Each year, the problem of prison overcrowding continues to grow and take a larger portion of states' resources. As prison populations continue to increase, alternative sentencing options will become increasingly popular. Some of the facts that have forced the states to consider alternative sentencing include:

— Nationwide, about one in every 50 persons is under the control of correctional authorities.

— In the 1980s, per capita expenditures grew 21 percent overall while correctional expenditures grew 65 percent.

— The nation's prison population doubled during the 1980s and currently is more than 650,000 people.

— The growth of our prison population is over 10 times the growth rate of the general population.[18]

A problem exists in selling alternative sentencing to the public. Many questions regarding alternative sentencing remain unanswered as to the safety and management of these programs. The public tends to assume that anything less than complete incarceration for all criminals will endanger public safety.

Forms of alternative punishments include restitution, diversion, shock probation, community service, house arrest, electronic monitoring, and education or treatment programs. These options have advantages to the public as well as to the offender. They are less expensive to operate than incarceration, and they help keep the offender in the community so as to prevent the breakup of the family and continue income.

The concept behind restitution is that the criminal should be required to compensate the victim for the victim's injuries. In many states, the statutes require restitution as a part of any sentence involving probation. Diversion refers to the practice of referring defendants out of the criminal justice system into treatment programs or educational programs. Shock probation is where the individual is sentenced to prison for a short period of time and then placed on probation. The purpose of the short confinement is to impress on the defendant the pains of imprisonment and then allow him or her to serve the remainder of his or her time on probation under the threat of re-imprisonment.

Alternative forms of sentencing are discussed in detail in Chapter 14 along with discussions on probation.

DISCUSSION QUESTIONS

1. Explain the principle of proportionality in sentencing. What guidelines should the courts use in applying this principle to a particular case?

2. What are the requirements before the death penalty may be imposed?

3. Explain the differences between general deterrence and specific deterrence.

4. What justifications can you provide for the imposition of punishment?

ENDNOTES

[1] 401 U.S. 395 (1971).
[2] Samuel Walker, *Popular Justice*, (New York:Oxford University Press, 1980).
[3] Public Law 98-143, 98 Stat. 1837 (1984).
[4] Michael Tonry, *Sentencing Reform Impacts*, (Washington, D.C.: Government Printing Office, 1987).
[5] Bureau of Justice Statistics, *Felony Sentencing in 18 Local Jurisdictions*, (Washington, D.C.: Government Printing Office, 1985).
[6] 445 U.S. 263 (1980).
[7] *Harmelin v. Michigan*, 111 S. Ct. 2680 (1991).
[8] Ellen Hochstedler Steury and Nancy Frank, "Gender Bias and Pretrial Release," *Journal of Criminal Justice*, vol. 18, (1990): pp. 87-101.
[9] Joel Samaha, *Criminal Law*, 4th ed., (St. Paul: West, 1991), p. 52.
[10] *A History of the Criminal Law of England*, vol. 3, (London: Macmillan, 1883), p. 82.
[11] Coleman Phillipson, *Three Criminal Law Reformers*, (London: Dutton, 1923).
[12] Jeremy Bentham, *An Introduction to the Principles of Morals and Legislation*, ed. by John Bowring, (New York: Russell & Russell, 1962).
[13] *Solem v. Helm*, 463 U.S. 277 (1982).
[14] *Robinson v. California*, 370 U.S. 660 (1962).
[15] Robert Weisberg, "Capital Punishment," in Wayne LaFave ed., *Criminal Justice and the Supreme Court*, (New York: Macmillan, 1990), p. 351.
[16] *Furman v. Georgia*, 408 U.S. 238 (1972).
[17] 428 U.S. 123 (1976). See also Weisberg, (1990), p. 352.
[18] Charles B. DeWitt, "Alternative Sentencing, A Special Report," *National Institute of Justice*, (Sept. 1991).

PART IV

CORRECTIONS

Inside the famous "Rock". The nickname for the federal prison at Alcatraz.

STRUCTURE AND PURPOSE OF THE CORRECTIONAL SYSTEM

In a free society you have to take some risks. If you lock everybody up, or even if you lock up everybody you think might commit a crime, you'll be pretty safe, but you won't be free.

—Senator Sam Ervin

The correctional system comprises the entire range of punish-ment and treatment programs used by the government. The system includes jails, prisons, community treatment programs, refor-matories, correctional institutions, probation, and parole. Probation and parole are discussed in Chapter 14.

CONTEMPORARY CORRECTIONAL PHILOSOPHY

There are two basic correctional philosophies used to justify the imprisonment of inmates. First, the rehabilitative philosophy which contends that the purpose of confinement is to rehabilitate the inmate into a useful member of society. This philosophy is also referred to as a "corrective" or "treatment" orientation. The second philosophy holds that prisons exist to punish offenders and to prevent them from committing crimes against the public by locking them up. This is known as the "just deserts" philosophy.

While there is significant controversy regarding the correctional system, most people agree that, presently, the system does not "correct" or rehabilitate criminals. It is estimated that one third of all inmates released from prison will be back in prison within three years. Despite the apparent lack of success, the debate continues over the future of our correctional system.

One of the major debates concerns the conflicting goals of our correctional system. The most commonly stated goal is that of "correcting" or rehabilitating the criminal. Others contend that the function of our correctional system should not be to rehabilitate or treat criminals, but to keep dangerous criminals apart from society and to give them their "just deserts" for their criminal misconduct. This latter approach also argues that during the time that inmates are confined, they are not out in society committing crimes on innocent victims. Accordingly, we should measure the success of the system by factors such as the security of our institutions of imprisonment and reduction in crime rates while offenders are incarcerated and thus, incapacitated. Since the 1980s, it appears that the "just deserts" philosophy has dominated our courts and correctional systems. This philosophy supports the assumption that our prisons' primary goal is to incapacitate offenders who would otherwise be harming innocent citizens. While this conservative tide dominates our correctional system, there are still many penal experts who maintain that institutions can be useful in offender rehabilitation. Many examples of the treatment philosophy exist in our prisons today such as: educational programs, which exist in all institutions; vocational training that provides inmates with job skills and further prepares them for eventual release; and substance abuse programs which are also present in many institutions. In addition, every state maintains some type of early-release and community correctional programs.

HISTORY OF CORRECTIONS

In ancient times, the most common punishment for crimes was banishment or exile. Physical punishment was reserved for slaves. About the 11th century, the forfeiture of land and property became a common punishment for individuals who violated the law or failed in their duties to the feudal lords. The word "felony" was adopted to describe those crimes for which on conviction carried the forfeiture of land and property. The term "felonia" from which felony came, actually refers to a breach of faith with one's feudal lord.

The early penal institutions were created for the purposes of detaining individuals awaiting trial and those waiting for their punishments to be carried out. The concept of incarceration as a punishment did not begin until much later. At that time, the standard punishments included the death penalty, transportation to distant lands, and physical beatings. For relatively minor offenses, often the individuals were retained in confinement at night while they worked to pay off their debts to society. The first penal institutions were hideous places devoid of proper food, hygiene, and medical treatment. Most often the jailor was a "shire reeve" (sheriff). The jailor was paid a fee for each prisoner under a fee system. In many cases, the inmates were forced to pay for their own food and those who could not pay were forced to eat scraps.

In the 1700s, jail conditions in England were deplorable. Many inmates were being transported to North America. As the number of inmates grew, it was impossible to transport all of them to America. By the 1770s, inmates were being kept in abandoned ships anchored in the English harbors. Sheriff John Howard of Bedfordshire was appalled at the conditions that existed in the English jails. In 1777, he published his famous book, *The State of Prisons* which condemned the lack of basic humane care provided for English prisoners. His writings led to the reform of the English system.

The first American jail was built in James City, Virginia in the early 17th century. Pennsylvania, however, is considered the origin of the American correctional system. William Penn revised the Pennsylvania criminal statutes to forbid torture and the capricious use of mutilation and physical punishment. Under the revised statutes, these penalties were replaced with the use of imprisonment, limited flogging, fines, and forfeitures of goods and property.

Penn also established a victim's restitution program. All property belonging to the offender was used to make restitution to the victim, with restitution being limited to twice the value of the damages. Inmates who owned no property were required to work in the prison workhouse until the victim had been duly compensated. After Penn's death in 1718, the Pennsylvania criminal code was changed back to harsh physical punishment conducted in public places.

There is a dispute as to which was the first American prison. Many contend that the first was the Newgate Prison in Connecticut which opened in 1773 on the site of an abandoned copper mine. Newgate closed in 1823. The Castle Island Prison is also considered by many as the first American prison. This Massachusetts' prison opened in 1785 and closed in 1800.

In 1776, Pennsylvania again adopted William Penn's criminal code. In 1787, Dr. Benjamin Rush and a group of Quakers formed the Philadelphia Society for Alleviating the Miseries of Public Prisons. At that time, the only custodial institutions in the state were the local county jails. All inmates (men, women, and children) were frequently placed in one dingy room. As the results of the pressures of the Quakers, the Pennsylvania State Legislature in 1790 passed statutes reforming the system. As a direct result, a separate wing of the Walnut

Street Jail in Philadelphia was renovated and reserved for prisoners serving long term sentences of imprisonment. Many consider this the first state prison in the United States.

The separate wing of the Walnut Street Jail had individual solitary cells where the prisoners were kept. This wing was called a penitentiary house. The prisoners were to be kept in isolation and provided "an opportunity to reflect on their misconduct." The inmates were seldom allowed to leave their cells. Food was taken to them and they were not allowed to talk to each other. The silence rule prompted the prisoners to develop a crude system of sign language. Unfortunately, overcrowding undermined the goals of solitary confinement when more than one inmate was placed in each cell. It is interesting to note that overcrowding has been one of the major problems of our correctional system since 1800.

The Auburn System

By 1800, the current systems operating in both New York and Pennsylvania were having difficulties handling the ever-increasing numbers of inmates. To reduce the problem, the use of pardons, relaxing prison discipline, and limiting supervision were used. In 1816, New York built the Auburn Prison in Auburn. This prison, unlike the earlier prisons, was designed on the tier system. The cells were built vertically on five floors. Prisoners were divided into three classes: one group was placed continually in solitary confinement; another group was allowed labor as a form of recreation; the third group (the largest) was separated only at night.

There was little privacy for the prisoners. The prisoners were also required to eat and work in groups. The philosophy of the Auburn system was to control the inmates through fear of punishment and silent confinement. By 1823, the silence requirement had been abolished and was replaced by whipping with a raw-hide whip for violation of the prison rules.

Pennsylvania System

In 1818, Pennsylvania built a new state penitentiary near Pittsburgh named the Western Penitentiary. Each inmate in this prison was placed in a single cell for the duration of his confinement. Classifications were abolished and each cell was a miniature prison designed to prevent the inmates from contaminating each other. The prison was designed in a semicircle with the cells positioned along its circumference. The cells were built back to back with some facing the outside wall and the others facing inward. This new Pennsylvania concept was centered on the penitentiary as a place to do penance. By removing the sinner from society and requiring him to undergo a period of isolation in which to reflect on the evils of his ways, the inmate would reform.

Since prisoners were isolated from each other, inmates could not collectively plan escapes or get into fights. Accordingly, this eliminated the need for large numbers of guards. If, however, discipline was a problem, the whip was not spared.

There were many heated debates between those who supported the Auburn system and those who supported the Pennsylvania system. The Pennsylvania system was criticized as cruel and inhumane. The supporters of the Pennsylvania system contended that their system was efficient, humane, well-ordered and provided the ultimate climate to rehabilitate the criminals. The Auburn system was accused of being a breeding ground for criminal associations. [*Note*: These arguments sound very similar to those of today. Most prisons in the United States today are built on the Auburn concept.]

Civil War Era

The most remarkable aspect of the prisons built during the civil war era is the fact that they are very similar to the prisons of today. The Auburn system was adopted in all states except Pennsylvania. The prisons experienced overcrowding and cells built to house one prisoner often contained as many as four. Prison industry developed and the practice of hiring the prisoners out as contract laborers became common. The prison industry and contract labor practices resulted in abuse of inmates who were, in many cases, forced to work for dishonest businessmen for little or no wages. During this era, the prisons became major manufacturers of shoes, clothing, and furniture. Prison manufacturing was so successful that by the 1880s, labor unions obtained federal legislation to keep prison made goods out of interstate commerce.

Penologists Enoch Wines and Theodore Dwight formed the National Congress of Penitentiary and Reformatory Discipline held in

Cincinnati, Ohio in 1870. At this congress, Z.R. Brockway, the warden at the Elmira Reformatory in New York, advocated the individualized treatment of prisoners, indeterminate sentencing, and parole. Brockway had instituted vocational and college training courses at his industrial prison. While he proclaimed that the Elmira Reformatory was an ideal reformatory, most penologists conclude that his achievements were limited. His most significant accomplishment was the injection of some humanitarianism into the industrial prisons of that era. As the result of his claims, many institutions were constructed under the label of reformatories. Most of them were, however, only prisons oriented toward industry.

Age of Progress

The early part of the 20th Century was an era of contrast for our prison systems. The prison wardens and administrators, along with many politicians, advocated stern discipline to control the dangerous criminals that were in our prisons. In contrast, there were the prison reformers, like the Mutual Welfare League who pushed for an end to harsh corporal punishments and for the creation of education and training programs for prisoners.

Entrance to Folsom Prison, CA.

By 1930, many of the harsh rules for prisoners were relaxed and prisoners were given benefits of mail privileges, visitation, and the ability to mingle in the exercise yard for several hours each day. Some prisoners were even allowed to listen to radios.

During this era, the development of specialized prisons started. San Quentin was built in California to house inmates considered salvageable and Folsom Prison was built to house those considered hard-core offenders. Organized labor was successful in ending the contract labor practice in prisons and in placing restrictions on the growth of prison industries. Despite the changes, the inmates were still subject to severe discipline, harsh rules, and solitary confinement.

Modern Era

The modern area has been a period of turmoil for our correctional systems. There have been three distinct trends:

1) the prisoners' rights movement,

2) concern for violence within the system, and

3) the failure of rehabilitation efforts.

During the period from 1960 to 1980, the federal courts ruled that prisoners have a limited right to free speech, the rights to freedom of religion, medical care, proper living conditions, and procedural due process in prison discipline cases. These rights were unheard of prior to the 1960s. The violent riots that occurred in Attica Prison in New York and the New Mexico State Penitentiary drew the public's attention to the potential for violence and death in our institutions. The two opposing reactions to those riots were (1) a call for the improvement of living conditions in our institutions and (2) a call for more discipline and the building of new prisons to hold these dangerous criminals.

The failure of our prisons to rehabilitate prisoners has led to the development of alternatives to incarceration for the less violent and increased efforts to incarcerate dangerous criminals for greater lengths of time. The latter efforts have included a get-tough policy on judicial and legislative sentencing practices and policies. As a result, the number of persons in our institutions has skyrocketed.

Old Folsom Prison

Modern Folsom Prison

INSTITUTIONS

In this section, the most prominent types of current correctional facilities will be examined. While prisons, as institutions, are only about two hundred years old, jails date back to ancient times.

The new Sacramento County jail built downtown and designed to fit in with the highrise/business look of the city.

Jails are generally locally controlled places of confinement, whereas prisons are institutions under the control of the states or federal government. In addition, jails are used for confinement in cases where the punishment is one year or less. Prisons are used to confine felony offenders whose sentences are in excess of one year. Jails are also used to hold persons awaiting trial. Prisons generally cannot be used to confine a person unless that person has been convicted of a felony.

Jails

Jails were originally designed to hold persons awaiting trial. Presently, our jails have four common purposes:

— To hold persons awaiting trial that do not qualify for pretrial release;

— To hold convicted defendants who have not yet been sentenced;

— To punish offenders who have been convicted and sentenced to time in jail; and

— To hold convicted felony offenders who have been sentenced to imprisonment until they can be transported to a state institution.

Interior view of a modern jail.

Jails are also used to hold state prisoners when the state institutions are over their capacity. Jails have traditionally been used as the holding pen for our undesirables. In many cases, they are also used to house persons who have no other place to be held (e.g., indigents, looking for a place out of the winter's harsh elements and drunks until they are sobered up).

Jails are clearly the low-priority units in our criminal justice system. Since they are generally regulated at the local or county level, they, until recently, were not sufficiently regulated. Most states now, however, have jail standards commissions to regulate county and municipal jails. These commissions develop minimum standards for the jails and then monitor the jails to ensure that the jails are in compliance with the standards.

An enclosed exercise yard at a modern jail.

According to recent studies, about 45 percent of the people in jail are awaiting trial. There are approximately 3,400 jails in the United States. County sheriffs run 2,900 of them. Most of the remainder are municipal jails. Several states are considering the development of state jails to handle non-violent offenders and to relieve the overcrowding in our state institutions. On any given day, there are approximately 400,000 individuals confined in jails in the United States. In 1978, the figure was less than 200,000. Approximately 6,000 of these inmates are under the age of 17 years. Annually there are almost 10 million people booked into the jails. Since the 1980s, the number of women in jail has increased by approximately 145 percent, about twice the growth rate for males.

Prisons

The state institutions for the confinement of inmates are called prisons, penitentiaries, correctional institutions, and reformatories. Often the only difference between the institutions are their names. Most institutions are classified as either maximum, medium, or minimum security institutions.

The maximum security institutions are probably the most familiar to the public. They include such places as Sing Sing, Joliet, Folsom, Attica, San Quentin and the Huntsville State Prison in Texas. These institutions are generally built like a fortress with inter and outer walls. Inside, the inmates live in metal-barred cells that contain their own plumbing and sanitary facilities. The inmates are generally under close supervision at all times.

The next most secure institution is the medium security prison. They are similar in appearance to the maximum security institutions, but the security and atmosphere are generally more relaxed. In addition, medium security prisons offer more privileges to the inmates such as more relaxed visitor privileges.

Mule Creek Prison (medium security).

Minimum security facilities often use dormitories to house the inmates. The security is more relaxed than at the other types of institutions. Often the prisons are constructed in compounds surrounded by cyclone-type fences. The prisoner dress code is more relaxed, and, in many, work furloughs and educational releases are available to inmates. Minimum security facilities are often criticized by the public for being too much like country clubs.

Farms and Camps

Prison farms and camps are used as an extension of the institutions. In most cases, the farms and camps are an extension of minimum security facilities. In other situations, they are separate institutions. Farms and camps are found primarily in the South and the West. The camps are generally in forests where the prisoners work on conservation projects. The farms generally focus on the production of dairy products and vegetable crops. In several states, there are road camps where prisoners are held while they are doing road construction for the state.

Hidden Valley Ranch—a privately operated minimum security facility for 60 inmates.

Boot camps are used in many states as shock treatment for young offenders. The defendants are sentenced to boot camp for about six months and then placed on probation. If the defendant does not complete boot camp, then he or she is subject to being confined in a closed institution. While at the boot camps, the inmates receive counseling, confidence building training, and other treatment programs. While the daily cost of keeping a young prisoner in boot camp is higher in general than in a minimum security prison, the shorter average sentences provide long-term savings. Until recently, boot camps were available only to male inmates. Several federal courts of appeals cases have held that the states must make the same type facilities available to its female defendants.

Coed Prisons

There has been a trend since the 1970s to construct prisons that house both men and women. In 1990, there were 35 minimum security coed prisons in the United States. At the coed prisons, inmates usually share food services, recreational facilities, educational programs, medical facilities, and jobs. The major advantages of the coed prisons are the expanded programs available for women prisoners. This occurs because of the joint participation, greater flexibility in staffing, and a more normal environment produced by heterosexual contact. The disadvantages include the opportunity for the development of illicit relationships and increased disciplinary problems.

Community Facilities

One often stated goal of corrections is to reintegrate the individual back into society as a productive member. To accomplish this, community facilities are used to help inmates adjust to life outside of prison and therefore ease their transition back into society. Many of the facilities are "half-way" houses which are used to help the inmates bridge the gap between prison and the community. There is a lot of controversy regarding the effectiveness of community facilities. Most of the controversy concerns the perceived "coddling of criminals who should be in prison" and the perceived "high recidivism rates" for individuals assigned to these programs. In addition, most of the facilities are located in decrepit neighborhoods and therefore are not conducive to establishing a positive self-image in the individuals being reintegrated into society.

There are also community facilities that serve as alternate places of commitment for persons who would otherwise be confined in a closed institution. For example, many first time defendants are given the option to take treatment programs in community facilities in lieu of commitment to an institution. The programs at these facilities normally focus on drug and alcohol abuse treatment programs.

Private Institutions

To offset the high cost of running correctional institutions, many states have experimented with the use of private institutions. Private institutions are prisons built and operated on a contract basis by private companies for profit. It is interesting to note that originally most of our jails were private institutions operated on a similar fee system. Along this line, the federal government has used private companies to run detention centers for illegal aliens. In 1986, the state of Kentucky opened the first private 370 bed minimum security state prison at Marion. Presently, there are over 20 private corporations attempting to obtain permission and contracts from various states to open private prisons. Supporters of the private institutions claim that private companies can provide better service at a lower cost to the state.

Private institutions tend to be newer facilities and incorporate modern designs. The photo above depicts a modern cell wing command center. All doors, lights, windows, entries and exits are controlled and monitored from this location using closed circuit television.

PRISONERS' RIGHTS

As noted earlier, during the period 1960 to 1980 prisoners gained substantial rights. Prior to 1960, the courts were reluctant to intervene with an administrative branch of the government, into prison activities. This judicial policy was often referred to as the "hands off" doctrine. Accordingly, unless the circumstances of the case clearly violated the Eighth Amendment, the courts would apply the hands off doctrine. The courts used three common justifications for the hands off doctrine:

1) Correctional administration was a technical matter best left to the experts.

2) Society in general was apathetic to the field of corrections.

3) Prisoners' complaints involved privileges rather than rights.[1]

In the 1960s, the NAACP Legal Defense Fund and the American Civil Liberties Union's National Prison Project used the Federal Civil Rights Act to question the treatment of prisoners.[2] Section 1983 of that act reads as follows:

Every person who, under color of any statute, ordinance, regulation, custom, or usage of any State or Territory subjects, or causes to be subjected, any citizen of the United States or other person within the jurisdiction thereof to the deprivation of any rights, privileges, or immunities secured by the Constitution and laws shall be liable to the party injured in an action at law, suit in equity, or other proper proceedings for redress.

In the 1964 case of *Cooper v. Pate*, the U.S. Supreme Court recognized the right of prisoners to bring an action under section 1983 if they were being denied a right.[3] In this case, the prisoners were being denied their right to practice their religion. This case which involved the issue of freedom of religion, opened the door for providing other prisoners' rights.

Right to Legal Services

In 1941, the Supreme Court recognized the right of prisoners to have access to the courts. The writ of *habeas corpus* is the most typical document and simply states that the person detaining this particular prisoner is doing so unlawfully and the prisoner and the detainer must be brought before the court to determine the lawfulness of the detention. Because most prisoners did not have the legal expertise to prepare such writs, often this was a hollow right. Additionally, prison authorities used harsh disciplinary measures to prevent other inmates from assisting a prisoner in preparing a writ. In 1971, the Supreme Court in *Johnson v. Avery* held that unless the states could provide some reasonable alternative to inmates in the preparation of petitions and writs, a "jailhouse lawyer" must be permitted to assist illiterate inmates in preparing legal papers.[4] A "jailhouse lawyer" is an inmate who possesses some legal skills and who offers to aid other inmates. The court did not address the issue of determining what a reasonable alternative is in allowing prisoners to use "jailhouse lawyers."

In *Bounds v. Smith*, the court held that the prisoners must be provided with adequate law libraries or with the help of legally trained persons.[5] Listed below are several other issues in regards to legal rights that were decided by the courts.

— Inmates have a right to the assistance of "jailhouse lawyers" when filing a civil rights action against prison officials.

— Assigning only two attorneys to a prison having more than 13,000 inmates is not a reasonable alternative to a "jailhouse lawyer."

— Courts must review prisoners' petitions even if they have only limited merit.

The expansion of prisoners' access to the courts was limited by the conservative Burger court in 1982. That year, the court in *Rose v. Lundy* held that before a federal court can review a prisoner's petition, the inmate must have exhausted all legal avenues open to the inmate in state courts.[6]

Freedom of Expression

Freedom of expression is a right guaranteed by the First Amendment. Prior to 1960, many persons contended that an inmate lost his or her First Amendment rights while confined in a penal institution. Four cases decided by the courts clarify prisoners' rights regarding freedom of speech and freedom of expression.

> *Safley v. Turner* held that prisoners have a right to receive mail from one another. That inmate to inmate mail is not presumptively dangerous nor inconsistent with penalogical principles.[7]

> *Gregory v. Auger* held that prison officials can restrict mail to those in temporary detention as a means of increasing the deterrent value of disciplinary detention.[8]

> *Ramous v. Lamm* held that the refusal to deliver mail written in a language other than English was unconstitutional.[9]

> *Procunier v. Martinez* concerned the right of prisoners to correspond and the right of the administration to censor mail. California law allowed prison officials to censor letters that they considered to be "lewd, obscene, or defamatory" and those which expressed "inflammatory political, racial, religious or other views." The U.S. Supreme Court ruled that prison censorship of mails is permissible only in cases where (1) deemed necessary for prison security and (2) the restrictions are limited to only that which is reasonably necessary. Other cases have upheld the right of prisoners to correspond with the media and the right to publish prison newspapers.

Freedom of Religion

Freedom of religion is a fundamental right guaranteed to prisoners by the First Amendment. This clause has two prongs. First, it protects an individual's rights to freely practice the religion of his or her choice. Second, it prohibits the government from forcing religion on a person. Courts have held that prisoners have the right to be free from religious discrimination, to hold religious services, have access to clergy, to correspond with religious leaders, and to wear religious metals and crosses. Some of the related religious issues include:

— Prison officials can refuse to use an inmate's religious name on official records.

— Prisoners have a right to a diet that will keep them in good health without violating their religious beliefs unless the government can establish that this is impractical.

— Buddhist prisoners have the same rights to practice their religious services as do prisoners with more conventional religious practices.

— A prisoner cannot be disciplined for refusing to handle pork, if the handling would violate his or her religious beliefs.

— An individual has the right to wear long hair if it is a requirement of his sincere religious beliefs.

Many states hold that before the warden may restrict a prisoner's right to religious freedom, the restriction must be the "least restrictive" means of achieving the goal desired. For example, religious freedom may also include the types of clothes that prisoners are allowed to wear. San Quentin banned the wearing of certain types of clothes on the grounds that such clothes facilitated escape plans. The inmates challenged this restriction in the California state courts and won. The prisoners' success was based on a finding by the court that the regulation was not the least restrictive means of achieving the goal of preventing escapes.[10]

An employment case seemingly having nothing to do with prisoners' freedom of religion may eventually have significant impact in this area. The case, *Employment Division v. Smith* was decided by the U.S. Supreme Court in 1990.[11] In that case, the court held that laws that impose a burden on religious conduct do not violate the First Amendment's guarantee of free exercise of religion as long as the laws are fashioned in an even handed manner and have a secular purpose. Legislation is pending in the U.S. Congress to override that court case.

The legislation, Religious Freedom Restoration Act (RFRA), if enacted, will also apply to prisoners and will place a burden on states to establish that any restriction on a prisoner's freedom of religion is necessary. The legislation will abolish the current test for establishing the validity of any prison-related regulation and will replace it with a new test requiring prison administrators to prove that there is a "compelling state interest" in the regulation and that the proposed regulation is the "least restrictive means" available to achieve the intended results. In August, 1993, 26 state attorney generals asked Congress to exempt prisons from the act. [*Note*: Many states, like California, already use the above test.]

Medical Rights

In one case, *Newman v. Alabama*, a court ruled that all the medical facilities in the Alabama state prisons were inadequate.[12] In another case, the Supreme Court ruled that the guarantee against cruel and unusual punishment established the government's obligation to provide adequate medical care for those whom it is punishing.[13] The judgings of complaints regarding medical care are decided by the courts on a case by case basis using the "deliberate indifference" standard. This standard was set forth in the *Estelle v. Gamble* case.

Deliberate indifference to serious medical needs of prisoners constitutes the "unnecessary and wanton infliction of pain"...proscribed by the Eighth Amendment. This is true whether the indifference is manifested by prison doctors in their response to the prisoner's needs or by prison guards in intentionally denying or delaying access to medical care or intentionally interfering with the treatment once prescribed.

It is apparent that courts cannot close their judicial eyes to prison conditions which present a grave and immediate threat to the health or physical well-being of prisoners...Practices which result in deprivation of basic elements of adequate medical treatment...would be equally vulnerable.[14]

Overcrowding

In at least 37 states and the District of Columbia, our jails and prisons are overcrowded. In addition, large numbers of prisoners are being held in local jails because there is no room for them in state institutions. Between 1980 and 1990, the incarceration rate increased nearly 100 percent. Many penal experts attribute this growth rate to the increasing belief that incarcerating predatory criminals can bring crime rates down. The standard answer to overcrowding has been to build new prisons. Budget cutbacks and belt-tightening, however, may halt the expansion of institutions.

Inmate Populations

1992 for all facilities

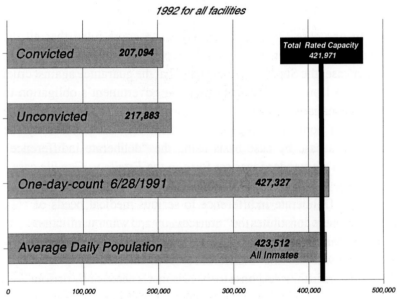

Source: U.S. Dept. of Justice

Overcrowding is not limited to our prisons, it is also one of the most critical problems facing our jails. Approximately 40 percent of our largest jails have or have had recent court orders mandating the reduction of jail populations. In many cases, innovative ways are being used to overcome the problem. For example, New York City recently purchased river barges to house jail overflow.

Alien Prisoners

about 1 in 23 inmates are not U.S. citizens

over 31,000 inmates

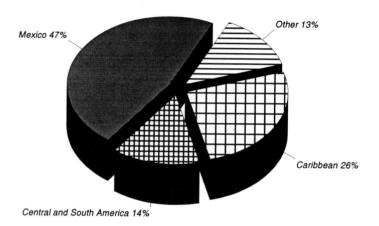

Mexico 47%

Other 13%

Caribbean 26%

Central and South America 14%

Source: U.S. Dept. of Justice

Many experts have linked overcrowding with prison violence. For example, data from the Texas prisons indicates that large increases in prison population without increases in prison space caused an increase in prisoner suicides, killings of other prisoners, and a significant rise in disciplinary action rates.[15] In addition, many prison rights groups contend that overcrowding is a violation of the Eighth Amendment's prohibition on cruel and unusual punishment.

Overcrowding has resulted in many inmates being paroled. Parole is often seen as a desirable low-cost method to reduce inmate population. Many states have release programs such as the Emergency Powers Act which allows the governor to establish early release programs when the prison population reaches a certain limit. Generally, governors tend to order the parole boards to advance either the parole dates of inmates or order the mandatory release of certain categories of prisoners. For example, in 1983, in Texas over 1,000 non-violent prisoners were released early when the state prison system reached it capacity. In addition other inmates were given 21 months additional credit on their sentences.

The parole boards also appear to be more apt to release a prisoner on parole because of overcrowding. For example, in 1980 only about 32 percent of eligible prisoners were released on parole compared to about 72 percent in 1992.

LIFE IN PRISON

Treatment Programs

All institutions maintain some types of treatment programs for inmates. Often, budget restrictions dedicate which types of treatment programs an institution may implement. The most common type and cheapest is group counseling.

The general goals of prison counseling programs are to help the prisoners adjust to prison life and assist them in preparing for eventual release into society. While individual counseling is probably more effective than group counseling, it uses more of the limited resources of the prison. The number of clinically trained counselors is generally inadequate to carry out satisfactory counseling programs. Accordingly, many counseling programs are lead by nonclinical personnel as group leaders.

Some institutions have the necessary resources to employ a variety of more intensive individual and group techniques such as behavior modification, aversive therapy, reality therapy, and transactional analysis. In a few institutions new therapy techniques are being tried, such as the "living skills" program. The living skills programs are designed to assist inmates in improving interpersonal skills in such areas as parenting, anger management, budgeting, work relations, and personal health.

Recently, prisons have recognized the need for treating "special needs" inmates. These are inmates who have a variety of emotional problems but are in prison because they are not considered "insane." Special treatment programs have been designed to treat these individuals. Other special needs inmates include those with drug-dependence and AIDS-infected inmates. Many of the prisons have implemented comprehensive drug abuse treatment programs in their facilities. Correctional authorities have found it difficult to develop effective policies to handle the AIDS infected inmates.

Inmate Culture

Inmates in correctional institutions are segregated from the outside world, kept under close scrutiny, and forced to obey strict rules.

The daily cell search being performed.

Inmates personal possessions are restricted. Many have no choice regarding the clothes they wear. Their mail is censored and sometimes destroyed. They have only limited access to visitors. Despite the above, most inmates quickly adapt to the prison routine. They learn to deal with confinement as a daily fact of life. In addition, they learn to handle the predominant emotion of boredom.

Positive Drug Tests While Incarcerated

percentage of adults by security of facility

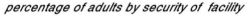
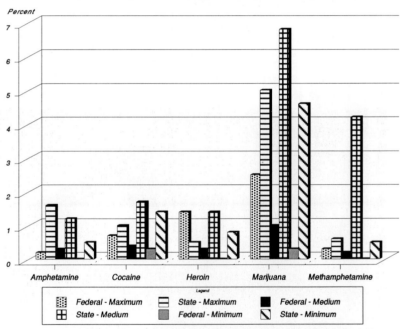

Source: U.S. Dept. of Justice

In adapting to prison, inmates become a part of the prison culture. It is a unique sub-culture of our society. Inmates become familiar with and generally participate in the black market (the hidden economy of the prison) and the hustle. Hustling involves the sales of illegal commodities such as drugs and alcohol. Inmates also learn to deal with prison gangs which are generally divided along racial lines. A significant aspect of prison culture is the inmate social code. This social code contains unwritten guidelines that express the values, attitudes, and forms of social behavior that are considered acceptable conduct by other inmates. This social code tends to be passed on from one generation of inmates to the next.

Some of the important principles that have been noted regarding the social code include:

1) Don't interfere with other inmates' interests.

2) Don't lose your "cool."

3) Don't exploit other inmates.

4) Don't lose your dignity.

5) Be tough.

6) Don't be a sucker.[16]

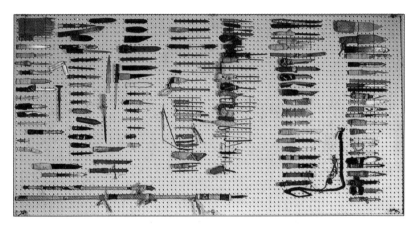

Typical assortment of weapons confiscated from maximum security prisoners.

Inmates quickly learn that, for the most part, heterosexual relationships are a thing of the past. Often heterosexuals will turn to homosexual relationships when faced with long sentences. Researchers have found complex sexual relationships in prisons between inmates; inmates tend to group themselves into cliques on the basis of sexual preferences.

DISCUSSION QUESTIONS

1. What should be the philosophy of our corrections system?

2. Should inmates retain their constitutional rights while being punished by imprisonment?

3. If you were governor, how would you solve the overcrowding problem?

4. Why have our institutions always had an overcrowding problem?

5. How do you measure the success of a correctional system?

ENDNOTES

[1] *Siegel v. Ragen*, 88 F. Supp. 996 (N.D.Ill., 1949)
[2] 42 U.S.C. (1983).
[3] 378 U.S. 546 (1964).
[4] 409 U.S.968 (1971).
[5] 430 U.S. 817 (1977).
[6] 455 U.S. 509 (1982).
[7] 777 F.2d. 1307 (8th Cir., 1985).
[8] 768 F.2d. 287 (8th Cir., 1985).
[9] 639 F. 2d. 559 (10th Cir., 1980).
[10] *The Texas Lawyer*, (July 5, 1993), p. 18.
[11] 494 U.S. 872 (1990).
[12] 349 F.Supp. 278 (M.D. Ala., 1972).
[13] *Estelle v. Gamble*, 429 U.S. 97 (1976).
[14] 460 F.2d. 765 (5th Cir., 1972) at 578.
[15] G. McCain, V. Cox, and Paul Paulus, *The Effect of Crowding on Inmate Behavior*, (Washington D.C.: Government Printing Office, 1981), p. vi.
[16] Gresham Sykes and Sheldon Messinger, "The Inmate Social Code," *The Sociology of Punishment and Corrections*, ed. Norman Johnson, (New York: Wiley, 1970), p. 404.

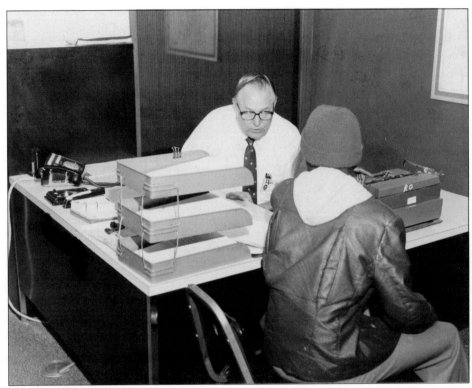

A "client" checks in with his parole agent.

COMMUNITY
CORRECTIONS

*Community corrections was officially a good
idea, but if you made enough noise, you didn't
have to have it in your neighborhood.*

—Robert Bright

C ommunity corrections have traditionally emphasized rehabilitation while maintaining the offender in the community.
Community corrections include probation, parole, and residential
programs. Probation is the conditional release of a convicted person.
Parole is the early release of a prisoner from imprisonment. Probation
and parole differ in that usually with probation, the individual does not
go to prison and with parole the individual is conditionally released
from prison before the completion of his or her sentence. In addition,
in many states, probation is administered by the individual counties or
major trial courts and parole is administrated by the state.

Involvement in treatment programs is normally included as a
condition of probation and parole. The most common treatment
programs are directed toward the areas of alcohol and substance abuse
and behavior modification. The types of treatment programs and
organizations offering those programs vary greatly across the nation.

PROBATION

Probation can be traced to the common law practice of "judicial
reprieve." Under judicial reprieve, a judge would suspend punishment
so that the convicted person could demonstrate that he or she had
reformed his or her behavior. The practice of "recognizance" was also
used to enable offenders to remain free if they agreed to pay the state
a sum of money in lieu of punishment. Often the debt was structured
so that the defendant was required to pay it only if he or she was
determined to be engaged in subsequent criminal conduct. In some
cases, before the judge would accept the defendant's recognizance
contract, sureties were required. The sureties (person(s) other than the
defendant) were responsible for the behaviors of the defendant after
they were released.

John Augustus of Boston is considered the originator of the concept of probation. As early as 1841, Augustus, a private citizen, requested that Boston judges release defendants under his supervision. It is estimated that over an 18 year period he supervised about 2,000 individuals on probation. He helped them get jobs and re-establish them in the community. Only a few of the individuals under his supervision became involved in subsequent criminal behavior.

Augustus's work inspired the Massachusetts legislature to authorize the hiring of a paid probation officer for Boston. By 1880, probation was extended to other jurisdictions within the state. Missouri and Vermont soon copied the Massachusetts procedures. The federal government established a probation system in 1925. By that date, most other states had also adopted similar systems.

EXHIBIT 14-1

Position Description for Probation Officer

The following position description for probation officers is currently being used in the Harris County Probation Department in Houston, Texas. (Reprinted with their permission.)

Adult Probation Officer

I. Minimum Qualifications

A. Bachelors degree in criminology, corrections, counseling, law, social work, psychology, sociology, or a related field; or

B. One year of graduate study in one of the above fields; or

C. One year experience in full-time casework, counseling, or community or group work that has been approved by the Director;

D. Not presently employed as a peace officer;

E. Not currently on probation or parole or serving a sentence for any criminal offense and never have been convicted of a felony.

II. Essential Functions

A. Ability to supervise felony and misdemeanor probationers according to state and departmental standards;

B. Ability to write Pre-Sentence Investigations according to state and departmental standards;

C. Ability to collect, count, reconcile, and safeguard court ordered monies encumbered by the department;

D. Ability to successfully complete forty hours of professional training per year;

E. Ability to work with others, manage a changing work schedule and stressful situations in the office and in the field;

F. Ability to use good judgments in making decisions;

G. Ability to make field visits.

H. Ability to work with minimal supervision.

III. Marginal Functions

A. Assess probationer risks/needs and develop, implement, and evaluate direct treatment/supervision plans on an ongoing basis;

B. Monitor compliance with court ordered Conditions of Probation and provide guidance to assist probationer in meeting requirements of probationary term;

C. Maintain confidentiality of all departmental and client records according to federal, state and local departmental regulations;

D. Ensure that all case file documentation is legible and written in the proper format;

E. Ensure that all case files are in proper order as per departmental standards and filed in alphabetical order in the appropriate file cabinet;

F. Maintain knowledge and understanding of department policies, state standards, correctional law, and probation supervision techniques;

G. Staff all violations, pre-sentence investigations, probation orders, and client transports with the Director, Assistant Director or their designee prior to taking action on a given case;

H. Keep supervisor informed of any problems with a probationer, office staff, or other agencies;

I. Ability to perform other duties not listed, to be determined and assigned as needed by the Director or Assistant Director.

Probation, as noted earlier, refers to a conditional release of a convicted person. Probation can have several different meanings within our present criminal justice system. Probation can be used to describe a sentence that has been given to a defendant where the defendant is placed and maintained in the community under the supervision of an agent of the criminal court. Probation refers to a status or class (i.e., he is on probation and thus subject to certain rules and conditions that must be followed in order to avoid the serving of a sentence). Probation also refers to an organization (i.e., the county probation department).

Probation is based on the philosophy that the average defendant is not a violent dangerous criminal, but one that needs additional guidance in order to conform to society's demands. Probation generally involves the replacing of a part of a defendant's sentence of confinement with a conditional release. Probation is essentially a contract between the defendant and the court. If the probationer complies with certain orders of the court (conditions of probation), the court will not require the defendant to serve a certain sentence (normally a sentence to confinement). If the defendant later violates the terms of the contract, the court is no longer restricted by the contract and may sentence the defendant to serve a stated punishment.

Probation Outcomes

for 100 felons 1986-1989

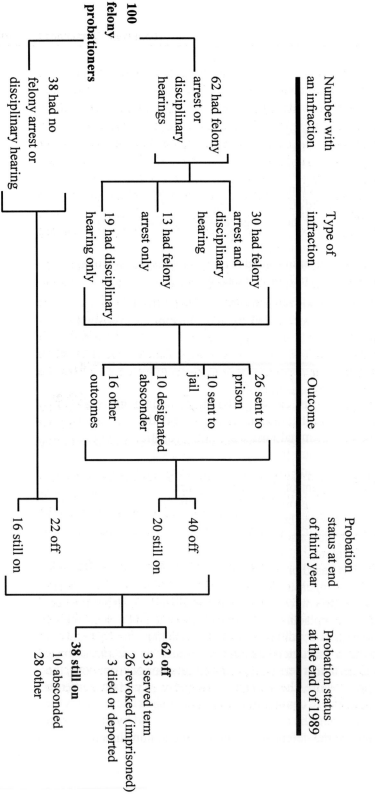

Number with an infraction	Type of infraction	Outcome	Probation status at end of third year	Probation status at the end of 1989

100 felony probationers

62 had felony arrest or disciplinary hearings

- 30 had felony arrest and disciplinary hearing
  - 26 sent to prison
  - 10 sent to jail
  - 10 designated absconder
  - 16 other outcomes
- 13 had felony arrest only
- 19 had disciplinary hearing only

40 off
20 still on

38 had no felony arrest or disciplinary hearing

- 22 off
- 16 still on

62 off
33 served term
26 revoked (imprisoned)
3 died or deported

38 still on
10 absconded
28 other

In some states, the defendant at the time he or she is placed on probation is informed as to the terms of the sentence being probated. For example, a defendant may be sentenced to prison for a term of three years with the actual serving of the time probated for five years. If the defendant stays out of trouble for five years, then the sentence is never served. If the defendant's probation is revoked, then the defendant serves three years from the time the probation was revoked.

In other states, the defendant is placed on probation for a certain period of time. If the probation is revoked, then the defendant receives a sentence the length of which is determined at a sentencing hearing after the probation is revoked.

Probation is the most popular sentence given in felony cases. In some states, the juries may recommend probation. However, even in those states where the juries may decide the punishment (i.e., Texas) only the judge may grant probation. Most states have restrictions on the granting of probation for certain serious crimes. In addition, it appears that the death penalty may not be probated. This is based on the fact that the death penalty is limited to those cases where the defendant is beyond rehabilitation.

The length of the probation period may vary. A five year period appears to be a common one for felony cases. In fact, the Federal Criminal Code recommends that federal probation periods last for five years.

In some cases, the judge grants probation only if the defendant agrees to serve a period of local time (jail). For example, one judge as a matter of policy will not grant probation in felony cases unless the accused does at least thirty days time in the local jail. This practice is known as "split sentencing."

Shock probation is frequently used in the case of first time offenders. In these cases, the judge grants probation only after the accused has sampled prison life. Shock probation is designed to give defendants a "taste of the bars" before placing them on probation. Evaluations of shock probation have indicated that shock probation's rate of effectiveness may be as high as 78 percent.[1] Critics of shock probation claim that even a brief period of incarceration can reduce the effectiveness of probation which is designed to provide the offender with nonstigmatized community-based treatment.

Extent of Probation

There are approximately 1,900 probation agencies in the United States. About half are associated with a state-level agency and the remaining with county or city governments. Approximately 30 states have combined probation and parole agencies. While prison populations have been increasing at a rapid rate in the past twenty years, it appears that the number of persons on probation has been increasing at an even faster rate. On any given day, there are approximately 1.8 million individuals in the United States on probation. One of the reasons for the popularity of probation is its low cost. It costs only about $3.00 per day to maintain an offender on probation.

EXHIBIT 14-2

Criteria for Granting Probation

Listed below is the recommended criteria for granting probation developed by the American Law Institute's Model Penal Code:

1. The court shall deal with a person who has been convicted of a crime without imposing sentence of imprisonment unless, having regard to the nature and circumstances of the crime and the history, character and condition of the defendant, it is of the opinion that his imprisonment is necessary for protection of the public because:

   a. there is undue risk that during the period of a suspended sentence or probation the defendant will commit another crime; or

   b. the defendant is in need of correctional treatment that can be provided most effectively by his commitment to an institution; or

   c. a lesser sentence will depreciate the seriousness of the defendant's crime.

2. The following grounds, while not controlling the direction of the court, shall be accorded weight in favor of withholding sentence of imprisonment:

  a. the defendant's criminal conduct neither caused nor threatened serious harm;

  b. the defendant did not contemplate that his criminal conduct would cause or threaten serious harm;

  c. the defendant acted under a strong provocation;

  d. there were substantial grounds tending to excuse or justify the defendant's criminal conduct, though failing to establish a defense;

  e. the victim of the defendant's criminal conduct induced or facilitated its commission;

  f. the defendant has compensated or will compensate the victim of his criminal conduct for the damage or injury that he sustained;

  g. the defendant has no history of prior delinquency or criminal activity or has led a law-abiding life for a substantial period of time before the commission of the present crime;

  h. the defendant's criminal conduct was the result of circumstances unlikely to recur;

  i. the character and attitudes of the defendant indicate that he is unlikely to commit another crime;

  j. the defendant is particularly likely to respond affirmatively to probationary treatment;

  k. the imprisonment of the defendant would entail excessive hardship to himself or his dependents.

3. When a person has been convicted of a crime and is not sentenced to imprisonment, the court shall place him on probation if he is in need of the supervision, guidance, assistance or direction that the probation service can provide.

Conditions of Probation

A probated sentence is an act of clemency on the part of the court. Accordingly, in most states the court may place conditions that restrict an individual's constitutional rights. For example, a judge may require that the defendant voluntarily submit to searches and/or drug testing when requested by the probation officer. Generally, there are two sets of conditions that are imposed on a probationer: standard conditions that are imposed on every probationer, and special conditions designed for a particular defendant. Exhibit 14-3 sets forth the standard rules used in the State of Texas, these are very similar to those used in other states.

EXHIBIT 14-3

Standard Probation Rules for the State of Texas

(Texas Code of Criminal Procedure, Article 42.12)[2]

1. Commit no offense against the laws of the state of Texas or of any other state or of the United States.

2. Avoid injurious or vicious habits.

3. Avoid persons or places of disreputable or harmful character.

4. Report to the probation officer as directed.

5. Permit the probation officer to visit him at his home or elsewhere.

6. Work faithfully at suitable employment as far as possible.

7. Remain within the county unless travel outside the county is approved by probation officer.

8. Pay any fines imposed and make restitution or reparation in any sum that the Court deems proper.

9. Support your dependents.

10. Participate in any community-based program as directed by the court or probation officer.

11. Reimburse the county for any compensation paid to appointed defense counsel.

12. Compensate the victim for any property damage or medical expense sustained by the victim as a direct result of the commission of the offense.

Administration

Generally there is a probation office for each felony court. In large urban areas, the probation offices of several courts may be merged into one office. The individual in charge of a probation office is normally called the "chief probation officer" (CPO). It is the duties of the CPO to carry out policy and to supervise the probation officers. Probation officers (POs) are generally charged with four primary tasks: investigations, intake, diagnosis, and treatment supervision.

The investigation functions are usually related to the pre-sentence investigation that the court uses in deciding on the appropriate sentence. The intake task refers to the process by which probation officers interview individuals regarding cases that have been scheduled in court for the initial appearance. Intake is normally used only in minor cases and is directed toward the possibility that the case may be settled without further court action.

The probation officer's analysis of the defendant's personality and the development of a personality profile of the defendant occurs during the diagnosis functions. Diagnosis also involves the formulation of the treatment necessary to rehabilitate the defendant (i.e., the PO diagnoses that the defendant has a drinking problem). The treatment supervision refers to the duties of the PO after the defendant has been placed on probation. During the treatment supervision phase, the PO should evaluate the effectiveness of the treatment programs ordered by the court.

Probationer's Rights

The courts have ruled that probationers (those on probation) have fewer constitutional rights than other citizens. The theory is that probation is an act of mercy by the courts, and therefore certain conditions can be placed on individuals accepting probation. The three major issues in probationers' rights are:

1) search and seizure,

2) right of confidentiality, and

3) revocation rights.

The courts have held that probationers' homes may be searched without a warrant. The courts have also indicated that probationers may be required to consent to future searches as a condition of probation.[3] The courts have held that the probation officer-client relationship is not a confidential relationship and therefore, the probation officer may testify as to matters related to him or her in confidence by the probationer.[4]

Before probation may be revoked, the probationer has certain procedural due process rights. Generally, when the probation officer makes the decision to revoke probation, the offender is notified and a formal hearing is scheduled. Generally, the rules for revoking probation and parole are the same. There are three major U.S. Supreme Court decisions in this area.

Mempa v. Rhay decided by the court in 1967 held that a probationer was constitutionally entitled to counsel in a revocation of probation hearing where the imposition of the sentence had been suspended.[5] Most lower courts interpreted this case to apply only in those situations that involved deferred sentencing and not in those cases where the probationer was sentenced at the time of trial. Accordingly, some jurisdictions provide counsel at revocation hearings and other jurisdictions do not.

The Supreme Court in *Morrissey v. Brewer* required an informal hearing to determine if there is probable cause to believe that an individual on parole had violated the terms of his parole. If the informal hearing establishes probable cause of a parole violation, then a formal hearing needs to be held to determine if parole should be revoked. At the formal hearing, the parolee has procedural due process rights.[6] The lower courts have applied the *Brewer* case to probation revocations.

In *Gagnon v. Scarpelli*, the Supreme Court held that both probationers and parolees have a constitutionally limited right to counsel in revocation proceedings.[7]

Future of Probation

Many individuals have voiced concerns regarding the placing of criminals on probation. Despite this, it appears that probation will continue as the most popular form of alternative sentencing available to judges. Part of the appeal of probation is based on its low cost and its flexibility. There appears to be a trend to use probation in conjunction with community treatment programs.

PAROLE

Most inmates are eventually released from prison. For most inmates, their reintegration into society is accomplished through parole. Parole is the early conditional release of prisoners. The term "parole" is French meaning "to promise." It was first used to refer to the practice of releasing enemy soldiers if they promised not to fight again. When released, the soldiers were informed that if they were captured again, they would be executed.[8]

The Penal Servitude Act, discussed in Chapter 12, also made possible the granting of a "ticket to leave" for those prisoners who had served a significant portion of their sentence. This was a conditional release which permitted the former convicts to be at large in certain areas. They were required to carry a "license" which contained the conditions of their release. The usual conditions were the requirements to work hard, stay sober, and maintain lawful behavior. In Ireland, Sir Walter Crofton instituted a mark system for the Irish prisons. Prisoners could earn marks for good conduct and hard work. When the prisoners earned sufficient number of marks, they were conditionally released from prison.[9]

Prison and Parole Increases

Rate per 100,000 population

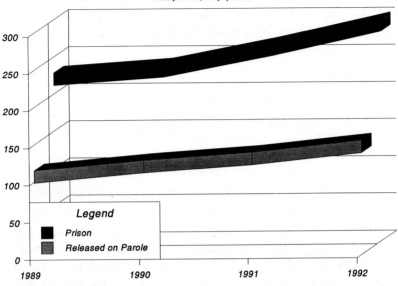

300			
250			
200			
150			
100			
50			
0			
1989	1990	1991	1992

Legend

■ Prison

▨ Released on Parole

Source: U.S. Dept. of Justice

Parole developments in the United States are traced to the New York practice of allowing prisoners to be released early under their "good time law." Early release for good time was first used in New York in 1817 and is now being used in all states. The first parole agency was established in Ohio in 1884. By 1927 only three states did not have parole agencies. Presently, parole is the primary method of release for prison inmates. Over half of all inmates released from prison each year are released on parole. With prison overcrowding problems, the practice of releasing prisoners prior to the expiration of their prison terms will probably continue.

Parole is a method of completing a prison sentence in the community under the supervision of a parole officer. Parolees are subject to detailed rules, standards, and guidelines designed to help them return to society. Parole is generally considered a privilege and not a right. Accordingly, the courts permit more regulation of parolees' conduct than other individuals.

Parole Board

The authority to grant discretionary parole is generally vested in an administrative board (the parole board). The American Correctional Association lists four primary functions of a state parole board:

— grant parole to prisoners,

— supervise control of parolees,

— discharge individuals from parole, and

— make parole revocation decisions.

Generally the boards are independent administrative agencies and are not part of the state department of corrections. In a few states, like Ohio, they are a part of the correctional agency. Some argue that the boards should be independent of the correctional administration so that they are not under the influence of prison administrators. Those arguing in favor of having the boards included in the correctional administration believe the boards will have better communications and coordination with the correctional administration. Most of the state boards are relatively small, usually with less than 10 members in addition to the associated staffs.

Appointment of board members differs in each state. In most states, board members are freely appointed by the governor or are chosen from a list submitted by the state legislature. In other states, they are chosen from a list of civil service employees. Often the appointment to the board is a political reward for persons who have served the governor. The length of the board member's term also varies by state. In four states, the members are appointed for life, but it is more common to be appointed for terms of two to six years.

The actual parole decisions are made at parole board hearings. In some of the larger states, the parole boards sub-divide into panels of three or more members to hear cases and make decisions. In several states, individual parole board members investigate assigned candidates for parole and make recommendations to the board regarding the "candidates" for parole.

Most candidates for parole are chosen because of required statutory eligibility guidelines for parole. In rare cases, the prison administration may request the board to consider certain inmates. In those emergency overcrowding situations where the prisons are forced to reduce their populations, the governor may order the board to consider certain classes of prisoners for early release.

A contemporary parole board meeting in casual surroundings.

In making the decision on whether to grant parole to an inmate, the boards consider whether there is a reasonable probability of the inmate succeeding outside prison. In making the decision, the boards generally examine the records of the inmate while in prison, the number and types of crimes convicted of, and recommendations of the prison counselors and administrators. In most states, the candidates for parole appear before the board or panel and are allowed to present materials in support of the granting of parole.

There is no uniform method used to inform candidates for parole as to the decisions of the parole board. In most cases, they are either informed by letter of the board's decision or are informed by the prison administration. There is an increasing trend for parole boards to make a decision immediately after the hearing and then to recall the candidate and notify the candidate at that time of the board's decision.

The rights of a candidate during the parole decision also vary in each state. In about 20 states, the inmate is permitted to have counsel present during the parole hearing. In about half of the states, the candidate is allowed to present witnesses on his or her behalf. Almost all states require the parole board to state reasons for their decisions in granting or denying parole. In some states written justification of the decision is required.

Presumptive Parole Dates

A recent trend in many states is to establish the concept of a *presumptive parole date* for inmates. The presumptive date is based on information such as the seriousness of the offense, the risk of recidivism, and possibility of good time. The inmate is then paroled on the presumptive date, unless there is cause to delay the parole.

About 15 states have established parole guidelines that institute presumptive parole dates. Under the guidelines, the offenses committed are scored based on their severity; the offender's personal characteristics believed related to the chances of success on parole are also scored. The total score determines the presumptive release date of the inmate.

Due Process Rights

For the most part, the U.S. Supreme Court considers parole an act of clemency, not a right. If however, the state statutes indicate that the inmate will receive parole at a given time except for good cause, the courts have been more likely to require procedural due process rights in the decisional process. For example, a state statute that ordered the parole of inmates at a set time except for those who violated prison rules was held to create a right to parole and thus required the state to comply with procedural due process rights before denying an inmate parole.[10] In a Connecticut case, the court ruled that the practice of the board in granting 75 percent of the applications did not create a "liberty interest" and didn't entitle the inmate to written reasons for the denial of his parole. [*Note*: At that time Connecticut did not require boards to provide reasons for denials of parole.][11]

Parole Rules

As with probation, parolees must agree to abide by certain rules and regulations. Generally the rules curtail or prohibit certain behavior while encouraging or demanding others. In many cases, the rules limit the social life of a parolee by restricting the places the individual can go and who he or she can associate with. In addition to the general rules that every parolee in the state must agree to, there are also individual rules designed for each parolee.

Many reformers have argued that parole rules are too restrictive and too vague and are designed to provide the parole officer with discretion in dealing with individual parolees. Others contend that parole rules and conditions are often vestiges of prior attempts to demean and shackle parolees. For example, Virginia has a rule that a prisoner must learn to read before he or she may be paroled. This "no-read-no-parole" rule is currently being challenged in court as discriminatory toward minorities based on the fact that a higher percentage of minorities cannot read. Other common parole rules include prohibitions against the use of alcohol, marriage without parole permission, limited or no driving privileges, and restrictions on borrowing money.

Parole Supervision

Once released to the community, the parolee is under the supervision of a parole agent or parole officer. Like probation offices, parole agencies are under-staffed and under-funded. Accordingly, meaningful supervision is almost non-existent. Parole officers tend to deal with more difficult cases than probation officers because the parolee has been institutionalized for an extended period of time and must be reintegrated into society. The stigma of being an "ex-con" is also present with parolees. In addition, it is more likely that a parolee has a prior record for criminal behavior than a probationer.

Some parolees need greater supervision than others. Accordingly, the supervision plan needs to be flexible enough to provide individualization for each parolee. To aid in developing supervision plans, California is using a point system that classifies the parolees into various classes. These are: 1) control cases needing close surveillance, 2) service cases needing social service rather than surveillance, and 3) minimum supervision for those individuals needing only limited supervision. Parole officers assigned to control cases have fewer parolees to supervise than those assigned to other cases. Often parolees assigned to the minimum classification are monitored only by follow up telephone contacts. It appears that more states are tending towards the California system.

Individual parole officers have a variety of styles of parole supervision very similar to the different styles of management noted in other occupations. A few experts contend that the typical parole officer is more concerned with the agency he or she works for and with improving his or her own career than with the welfare of clients.[13] Researchers have developed four typologies of parole supervision:

Punitive officer — The punitive parole officer is a guardian of law and order. He or she attempts to coerce the parolee into conformity and stresses protection of the community.

Protective agent — The protective parole officer vacillates between protecting the public and the offender. This type is ambivalent emotionally and shifts back and forth in taking sides with the offender and the community.

Welfare worker — The welfare type parole officer acts more like a welfare worker than a parole officer. This individual becomes very involved in the parolee's needs and situations.

Political opportunist — This individual is not really interested in the welfare of the parolee or the safety of the community. He or she is using the position as a stepping stone for career advancement.[14]

Revocation of Parole

Parole revocation proceedings are similar to those for the revocation of probation. In most states, the parole board makes the determination to revoke parole. The procedure is usually started by the recommendation of the parole agent. The procedural due process rights, discussed in probation revocation, usually apply in parole revocation hearings. Generally, the parolee has a right to advance written notice of the alleged facts and grounds for the revocation, right to call witnesses, and a hearing before a neutral and detached individual or board.

When a parolee's parole is revoked and he or she is returned to prison, the parolee may receive credit for the time spent in the community toward the sentence. This credit depends on state law. In *Harris v. Day*, a federal court of appeals ruled that a parole commission is not required to give the parolee credit for time spent in the community.[15]

Effectiveness of Parole

Experts disagree regarding the effectiveness of parole. Standard estimates range from a 70 percent success rate to a 70 percent failure rate. Often the determination as to the effectiveness of parole depends on the methods used to measure failure. For example, if rearrest is used as the measure of failure, it is noted that 42 percent of parolees are rearrested within six years. If return to prison is used as the measure, it is noted that the failure rate goes down since only about 19 percent are returned to prison.[16]

Abolish Parole?

There is a general public belief that parole is not effective and that parole, by releasing prisoners before they complete their sentences, creates a "myth of sentencing." The myth refers to the fact that the overwhelming majority of defendants do not serve all the time imposed by courts. To combat this, many people advocate that we should return to a "truth in sentencing" concept. By "truth in sentencing" it is meant that if a prisoner receives a four year sentence, he or she will serve four years except for time off for good time. This concept was discussed in Chapter 12 under Federal Sentencing Practices.

The general criticisms against parole include:

1. The rules and conditions which control parole are vague and do not conform to constitutional due process requirements. Some inmates are therefore unfairly denied parole.

2. It is unjust to decide whether to release a prisoner based on what that person is expected to do in the future.

3. The parole boards and prison administrators do not have the capacity to predict with any certainty whether an inmate can make a successful adjustment on parole.

4. There is no effective method to monitor a parolee's conduct while on parole.

The above criticisms can be reduced to two reasons for abolishing parole — uncertainty and disparity. With the use of detailed release guidelines, presumptive release dates, and procedural due process much of the uncertainty and disparity can be eliminated. In addition, it appears that corrections are heading in the direction of regulation and away from unlimited discretion. Since prison overcrowding is an accepted fact of life, it would appear that parole is necessary. The success or failure of the federal government's attempt to abolish parole should provide additional insight in this area.

EXHIBIT 14-4

Is Our Probation System Bankrupt?

The Probation Department of Fresno County, California has only 10 adult probation officers to supervise more than 18,000 cases which include about 5,000 adult felons. Similar conditions exist in their juvenile probation offices where a staff of six officers are required to supervise 2,500 juveniles.[12] The massive caseloads of the Fresno, California probation offices are very similar to those experienced in most probation offices throughout the United States.

ELECTRONIC MONITORING

Electronic monitoring seems to be the answer to the problem of huge numbers of clients in probation and parole and the overcrowding of our jails. With electronic monitoring the client is tracked and allowed to function under certain guidelines established by the court as a condition of sentencing, probation, or parole. If the offender fails

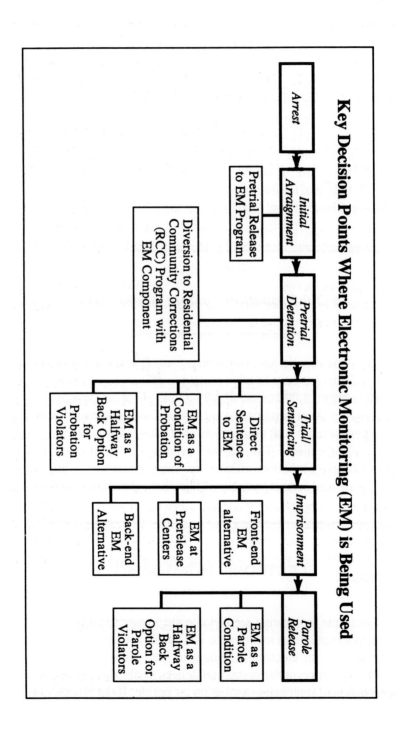

Key Decision Points Where Electronic Monitoring (EM) is Being Used

to comply with the obligations to this type of sentencing, then further jail, prison, or intensive parole/probation supervision will result.

The use of such monitoring devices enhances offender control within a community. The degree of control expected by the use of signaling devices is generally defined as follows:

Curfew: A curfew program includes home confinement during limited and specified hours, usually at night. Curfew is a characteristic component of intensive supervision and jail work-release programs.

Home Detention: A detention program is more restrictive than curfew. It requires the offender to remain at home at all times except for employment, education, treatment or other specifically preapproved and defined purposes.

Home Incarceration: In this type of program offenders are restricted to the home at all times except for very limited activities, such as religious worship or medical treatment.

The way most electronic monitoring devices work is the offender wears a wrist or ankle bracelet with a signalling device imbedded that produces a unique signature tone/code. This code is detected by a device within the home. The offender must "check-in" via telephone at predetermined times. The check-in establishes that the offender has met his conditions by downloading information from the monitoring device in the residence. There are also other forms of verification such as: pagers, voice verification, visual verification and continuous signaling systems. All produce the same effect — to establish the whereabouts of the offender at a certain time. In additon, the offender usually pays for the cost of electronic monitoring. The costs vary depending on the type of monitoring used and the intensity of the monitoring.

POST CONVICTION RESTRICTIONS

In early America, when an individual was sentenced to prison, the individual lost his or her civil rights and was considered "civilly dead."

Reformers have contended that one reason it is so difficult for ex-cons to reform is because of the legal restrictions that are placed on them by the fact of conviction. The practice of penalizing people after they have suffered a felony conviction can be traced to the Middle Ages. In early England, convicts forfeited their property and suffered "corruption of blood" which prevented them from willing their land to their heirs.

Presently, there are still civil disabilities associated with a felony conviction. The types and degrees of disabilities vary from state to state. Several states, like Hawaii, now prohibit the discrimination against an individual solely because of a felony conviction except in limited situations. The list of rights that ex-cons have lost in some states include:

— the right to vote,

— the right to hold certain public offices,

— the right to practice certain professions,

— the right to public employment,

— the right to serve on a jury, and

— the right to adopt children.

DISCUSSION QUESTIONS

1. Compare and contrast probation and parole.

2. What process rights do parolees have in any revocation proceedings in your state?

3. What is the role of a parole board?

4. Should parole be abolished? Justify your opinion.

5. What reforms are needed in the areas of probation and parole?

ENDNOTES

[1] Harry Allen, Chris Eskridge, Edward Latessa, and Gennaro Vito, *Probation and Parole in America*, (New York: Free Press, 1985), pp. 88-90.

[2] Note: Several of the conditions have been re-worded to enhance student understanding of them.

[3] *Griffin v. Wisconsin*, 483 U.S. 868 (1987).

[4] *Minnesota v. Murphy*, 465 U.S. 420 (1984)

[5] 389 U.S. 128 (1967).

[6] 408 U.S. 471 (1972).

[7] 411 U.S. 778 (1973).

[8] David Duffee, *Corrections: Practice and Police*, (New York: Random House, 1989), pp. 110-112.

[9] Gray Cavender, *Parole: A Critical Analysis*, (Port Washington, NY: Kennikat Press, 1982).

[10] Barbara Stone-Meierhoefer, "The Effect of Presumptive Parole Dates on Institutionalized Behavior," *Journal of Criminal Justice*, vol. 7, (1979): pp. 283-92.

[11] *Dumschat v. Connecticut*, 101 S. Ct. 2464 (1981).

[12] Fresno Bee, (July 18, 1993), p. 1.

[13] Richard McCleary, *Dangerous Men: The Sociology of Parole*, (Beverly Hills, Ca.: Sage, 1976).

[14] Daniel Glasser, *The Effectiveness of a Prison and Parole System*, (Indianapolis: Bobbs-Merrill, 1969), p. 290-293.

[15] 369 F. 2d. 755 (10th Cir., 1981).

[16] Peter Hoffman and Barbara Stone-Meierhoefer, "Reporting on Recidivism Rates," *Journal of Criminal Justice*, vol.8, (1980): pp. 53-60.

PART V

SPECIAL TOPICS

A twelve year-old boy is the victim of a gang shoot-out.

JUVENILE JUSTICE

*I went to where two guys shot it out in the street
and they both ended up killing each other. That
bothered me —seeing the blood and seeing the
holes and seeing these teenagers—two dead
teenagers.*

—A Cop

The components of the juvenile justice system include: the police, juvenile court, and juvenile corrections. The reformation of our juvenile justice system has been a long sought after goal. Many issues regarding the treatment of juveniles have been debated since the 19th century.

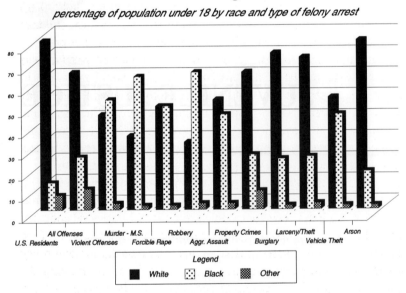

Likelihood of Being Arrested

percentage of population under 18 by race and type of felony arrest

Source: U.S. Dept. of Justice

The primary issues in juvenile justice which are feverishly debated today include:

— whether the juvenile's needs or rights are paramount to society's needs for security;

— the proper scope of authority for juvenile justice;

— processes used to adjudicate and make disposition of juvenile offenders; and

— reforms necessary to improve juvenile justice.

HISTORY OF JUVENILE JUSTICE

At common law, children over 14 years of age were treated as if they were adults. Children under the age of seven were considered incapable of committing crimes. Children between the ages of seven and 14, were *presumed* incapable of committing crimes; however the state could, by establishing the maturity of the child, hold them accountable as an adult. Even when formally treated as adults, children were rarely punished as harshly as adults by the criminal courts.

In early English history the doctrine of *parens patriae* was developed. According to this doctrine, the king could intervene in family life to protect the child's estate from dishonest parents or guardians. *"Parens patriae"* can be roughly defined as the duty of the state to act as a parent in the interest of the child. This principle expanded and now includes the right of the state to intervene to protect child welfare against parental neglect, incompetency and abuse.[1]

The Reform Movement of the 19th Century also developed a concern for children in general. A "child saving" movement which was directed at children in need or trouble grew out of this general concern. The child savers attempted to save children by using houses of refuge and reform schools. These institutions were based on the contemporary idea that children's environments made them "bad." Removing the youths from "poor" homes and "unhealthy" associations and placing them in special homes, houses of refuge or schools would cause the children to give up their bad and evil habits and would in fact reform the children.[2]

Establishment of the Juvenile Court

The influence of the child savers prompted the development of the first juvenile court in Cook County, Illinois in 1899. The Illinois Juvenile Court Act set up an independent court to handle criminal law violations by children under 16 years of age. The court was also given responsibility for supervising care of neglected, dependent and wayward youths. The Juvenile Court Act also set up a probation department to monitor youths in the community and it directed juvenile court judges to place serious offenders in secured training schools for boys and industrial schools for girls. The purpose of the Act was to separate juveniles from adult offenders and to provide a legal framework in which juveniles could get proper care and custody.

By 1940, every state in the United States had established a juvenile justice system. The juvenile justice systems were normally created as a division of family court. As the juvenile court movement spread throughout the United States it provided for the use of a quasi legal type of justice. The main concern of the juvenile courts was: "the best interests of the child." Accordingly, the courts did not adhere strictly to legal doctrine, protect constitutional rights, nor conduct their proceedings according to due process requirements. The general theory was that since these were not criminal courts, the youths did not have rights as if they were being tried in an adult criminal court.

Delinquency Case Rates by Age at Referral

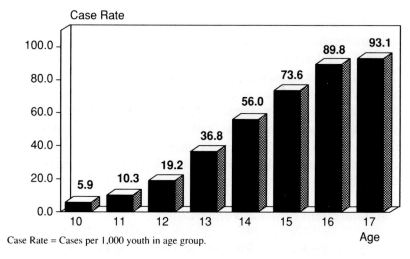

Case Rate = Cases per 1,000 youth in age group.

Source: U. S. Dept. of Justice

For many years, the stated goals of the juvenile justice system were to prevent juvenile crime and to rehabilitate juvenile offenders. In the 1980's, an additional goal—to protect society—was also imposed on the juvenile courts.

Our early reform schools were generally very punitive in nature and were based on the concept that rehabilitation could only be achieved through hard work. By 1950, group counseling techniques were standard procedures in the vast majority of juvenile institutions. Later, in the 1950's, the influence of therapists such as Carl Rogers promoted the introduction of psychological treatment in the juvenile corrections.

Just as the due process revolution affected prisoners' rights and defendants' rights, the U.S. Supreme Court also drastically altered the juvenile justice system. In a series of cases it was established that juvenile delinquents are protected under the due process clause of the Constitution, and, therefore, have constitutional rights in juvenile proceedings.

As a result of the influence of constitutional requirements in juvenile proceedings, the distinctions between adult and criminal juvenile justice systems are much less now than they were 40 years ago.

EXHIBIT 15-1

In Re Gault

FACTS: Jerry Gault, a 15 year old boy, was taken into custody by the sheriff of Gila County, Arizona. He was arrested based on a complaint of a woman who said that Jerry and another boy had made an obscene telephone call to her. At the time, Jerry was on a six month probation as a result of having previously been declared a delinquent for stealing a wallet.

Based on the verbal complaint, Jerry was taken from the children's home. His parents were not informed that he was taken into custody. When his mother appeared in the evening, she was told by the superintendent that a hearing would be held in juvenile court the following day.

The next day, a police officer, who had taken Jerry into custody, filed a petition alleging his delinquency. Jerry, his mother and the police officer appeared at a judicial hearing before a judge in his chambers. Mrs. Cook, the complaining witness, was not at the hearing. Jerry was questioned about the telephone calls, sent back to the detention home and then released a few days later.

On the day of Jerry's release, his mother received a letter indicating that a hearing would be held on his delinquency status in the next few days. When the hearing was held, the complainant, Mrs. Cook, was still not present. There was no transcript or recording of the proceedings. At the hearing, the juvenile officer stated that Jerry had admitted making the lewd telephone calls. Neither the boy nor his parents were advised of any of his rights including the right to be silent, the right to be represented by counsel, or the right to a due process hearing. At the conclusion of the hearing, the juvenile court committed Jerry as a juvenile delinquent to the state's industrial school in Arizona for the period of his minority (six years).[3]

This, in effect, meant that Jerry got six years for making an obscene phone call. Had he been an adult and convicted of the same crime, the maximum punishment would have been no more than a $50.00 fine and/or 60 days in jail.

Attorneys on behalf of Jerry filed a writ of *habeas corpus* with the Superior Court for the state of Arizona. The request for the writ was denied. The decision was appealed to the Arizona Supreme Court and that was denied. The denial by the Arizona Supreme Court was then appealed to the U.S. Supreme Court. The U.S. Supreme Court in a far reaching decision agreed that Jerry's constitutional rights were violated. The Supreme Court indicated that, at a very minimum, notice of charges is an essential right of the due process of law as is the right to confront witnesses and to cross-examine them, the right to counsel, and the privilege against self-incrimination.

Some items not answered by the court in reversing Arizona's determination of delinquency were whether Jerry had a right to a transcript and whether there was a right to an appellant review.

The significance of the *Gault* case was that it established that a child in delinquency adjudication proceedings has procedural due process constitutional rights as set forth in the constitution. [*Note*: This case was confined to rulings at the adjudication stage of the judicial process.]

Our juvenile justice system is independent, yet interrelated with the adult criminal justice system. The juvenile court system developed on the concept of *"parens patriae."* Starting in the 1960s, the concept was modified to one of procedural due process and in the 1980s to one of controlling chronically delinquent youths. It appears that the juvenile system will continue to evolve as we hunt for a more efficient system.

The present role of our juvenile justice system is to:

1) provide a social welfare program designed to assist and act as the "wise parent";

2) protect the constitutional rights of children;

3) act as a treatment agency to rehabilitate delinquents; and

4) protect society from violent youths.

JUVENILE COURT JURISDICTION

The modern juvenile justice court is a specialized court for children. It is more criminal in nature than civil. In most states, it is organized as an independent statewide court system or as a special session of either a family court or a lower court. Juvenile courts are normally authorized by state legislation and exercise jurisdiction over three distinct categories of juveniles: delinquent children, children in need of supervision, and children who have been neglected or abused.

Today most juvenile court systems embody both a rehabilitative and legalistic orientation. Rehabilitative orientation refers to the fact that the juvenile courts are charged with the responsibility of determining what is best for the child rather than punishing the child. The legalistic orientation is based on the concept that children have certain due process rights.

The administrative structure of the juvenile court revolves around a diverse group of persons (i.e., the juvenile court judge, the probation staff, the social workers, government prosecutors and counsel for the juveniles).

Generally, juvenile court jurisdiction is established by state statute and is based on two factors: the age of the child at the time the hearing is held, and the type of crime. For example, most juvenile courts are limited to children under the age of 17 and are limited as to subject jurisdiction regarding the type of crime committed. For example, premeditated murder is, in most states, not within juvenile court jurisdiction. There is a recent trend by state statutes to exclude certain serious offenses from the court's considerations. In regards to jurisdiction, once the court has obtained jurisdiction over a child the court ordinarily retains the jurisdiction until the child reaches the age of majority.

Source of Referral of Delinquency Cases by Offense

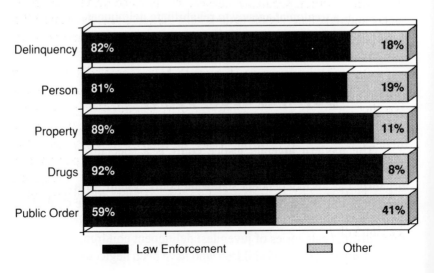

Source: U.S. Dept. of Justice

POLICE AND THE JUVENILE OFFENDER

Approximately 200,000 juveniles under the age of 18 are arrested each year. When a juvenile is found to have been engaged in criminal behavior, police agencies are charged with the decision to either release the child, detain him temporarily, or detain him and refer him to juvenile court. This discretionary decision to release or to detain depends on a list of factors such as: the type and seriousness of the child's offense; the ability of the parents to be of assistance in disciplining the child; the past record of the child as far as contacts with the police; the degree of cooperation from the child and the parents; and the demeanor, attitude and personal characteristics of both the child and parents toward the police.

When a child is taken into custody, the police officer must make the determination that probable cause to arrest exists. And once the juvenile is taken into custody, the juvenile has the same Fourth Amendment rights to be free from unreasonable searches and seizures as does an adult. Accordingly, one of the common legal procedures in juvenile hearings is an attempt to exclude any incriminating evidence that was taken as a result of a questionable search.

Another issue is whether or not the child taken into custody has rights to the *Miranda* warning and benefits of the *Miranda* decision. The U.S. Supreme Court has never directly ruled on this, but most states and appellate courts assume that the child has the same Fifth Amendment rights against self-incrimination as existed and were set forth in the *Miranda v. Arizona* case.[4]

One of biggest questions that courts have attempted to answer, in regards to the Fifth Amendment rights against self-incrimination, is whether a child under the age of majority can affectively waive his constitutional rights against self-incrimination. In our society, a child under the age of 18 generally lacks the capacity to enter into valid contracts. Accordingly, if the child is not old enough to purchase an automobile, is he or she old enough to waive his or her protection against self-incrimination. While this question has troubled the courts, most courts now allow the child to waive the right against self-incrimination.

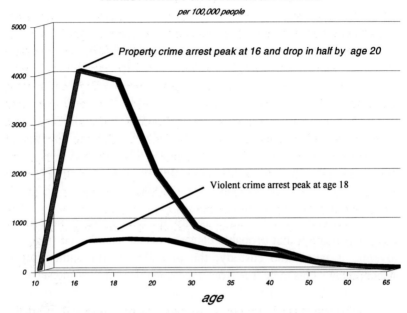

ARREST RATES FOR JUVENILE OFFENDERS
per 100,000 people

Property crime arrest peak at 16 and drop in half by age 20

Violent crime arrest peak at age 18

age

Source: U. S. Dept. of Justice

JUVENILE COURT

Differences Between Juvenile and Adult Justice Systems

The purpose of juvenile procedure is the protection and treatment of the child. With adults, the primary purpose is the punishment and/ or the rehabilitation of the guilty. The jurisdiction of the juvenile court is determined chiefly by age. In the adult system, jurisdiction is determined primarily by the nature of the offense committed.

Juveniles can be held responsible for acts that would not be criminal if they were committed by an adult (i.e., status offenses — truancy, vagrancy, incorrigibility and running away from home). Also, juvenile proceedings are generally more informal and private than those of adult courts which are formal and open to the public. The court has a duty to release certain information in the trial of adult offenders but are restricted in releasing information to the press regarding juvenile offenders. Juveniles do not have a right to bail, but are generally released in parental custody while adults are generally given the opportunity for bail or released on their own recognizance.

Plea bargaining occurs in most adult courts while juvenile court cases are settled by an admission as to the truth of the petition in open court. Juveniles' disposition is normally based on indeterminate terms whereas an adult sentence normally includes definite lengths of punishments and types of punishment. A juvenile has a right to treatment under the Fourteenth Amendment. No such right has been recognized as to adult offenders. In addition, a juvenile's record is sealed when the juvenile reaches the age of majority in most states. The records of an adult are an open record and may be looked at by the public except in unusual cases.

Pre-trial

After arrest and before trial, the juvenile is processed through the pre-trial stage of the juvenile adjudication process. The first stage is the intake. The intake process consists of the screening of the case by the police and the determination that the child needs to be referred to juvenile court. The intake stage is the stage where the police have great discretion as to the handling of the case. It also is the stage that represents an opportunity for the child to be placed in informal programs within the community. More than half the cases considered during the intake process never go beyond this stage. The juvenile court intake also seeks to screen out cases not within the court's jurisdiction nor serious enough for the court's intervention.

After the juvenile is taken into custody, during the intake processing the issue of detention of the juvenile must be decided. If it is determined that the child is to be retained in custody while awaiting trial, the child has a right to a hearing, a right to counsel and such other procedural safeguards including the privilege against self-incrimination. The general criteria used to support a decision to detain a child include: the need to protect the child, whether the child represents a serious danger to the public, and the likelihood that the child will return to court for adjudication. [*Note*: The latter two are very similar to those

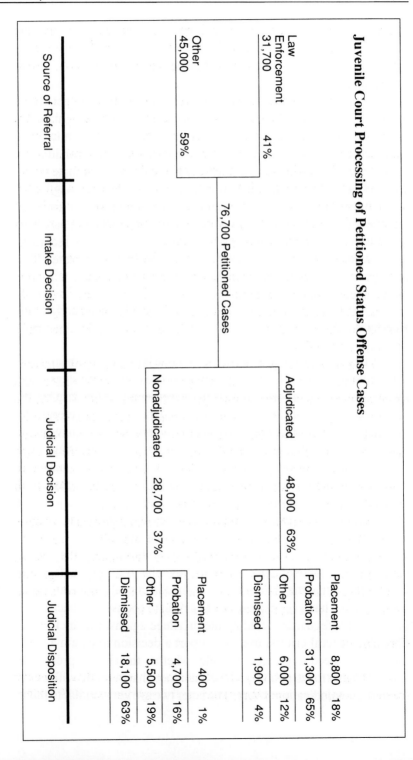

Juvenile Court Processing of Petitioned Status Offense Cases

considered in adult criminal court.] There is a presumption that the child should not be detained awaiting the adjudication. If, however, a valid reason for the child's detention exists then the court must note that in the records.

There are several issues involved in juvenile detention. One question is whether "delinquents" should be locked up with status offenders. **Status offenders** are those juveniles who committed conduct that would *not* be criminal had they been an adult; "delinquents" are those who have committed criminal misconduct. A second issue in juvenile detention is the removing of youths from adult jails. In many rural counties in which there are no adequate facilities for juvenile offenders, frequently juveniles who are picked up for serious offenses are detained in county jails with adults.

If the child is not detained, one of the decisions involved is whether or not a child should be required to establish bail. Only a few states allow juveniles to be released on cash bond. Many have code provisions that authorize the child to be released in the custody of the parents. In this regard, it is noted that there is no constitutional right to bail for juveniles.

In most juvenile justice courts, plea bargaining is not a matter. The child may admit or deny the allegations on the petition. As with adult criminal court, before a judge can take the admissions of the juvenile, the judge must follow the procedural safeguards in determining that the child knows of the right to a trial, that the plea or admission has to be made voluntarily, and that the child understands the charges and the consequences of the plea. This is based on the fact that an admission as to the truth of the petition is a waiver of the juvenile's Fifth Amendment right to privilege against self-incrimination.

It is the general belief that little plea bargaining exists in juvenile court. Generally, the juvenile court's statutes and rules of procedure do not provide rules that govern the plea bargaining process. In addition, the *parens patriae* philosophy of the court, the general availability of pre-trial social services, and the flexibility of juvenile court act to discourage the use of plea bargaining.

Diversion

The most common way of screening out juveniles after they have been processed into the court system is through the use of diversion.

Diversion is very popular in the juvenile justice system since it was recommended by the President's Commission on Crime in 1967. Several reasons for the growing popularity of diversion are:

1) it helps to reduce the increasing caseload;

2) it provides more flexibility than the juvenile justice treatment programs currently in existence; and

3) it costs less per capita than the use of institutionalization of juveniles.

Waiver of Juvenile Court Jurisdiction

Prior to the first juvenile court established in Illinois in 1899, juveniles were tried for violations of law in adult criminal courts. Today, most statutes provide that juvenile courts have primary jurisdiction over children under the age of 17. There are provisions in all state statutes, however, where juvenile court can waive jurisdiction in cases involving serious crimes and allow the juvenile to be tried in adult criminal court . The transfer of juveniles to criminal court is often based on statutory criteria. The two major criteria for waivers are the age of the child and the type of the offense alleged in the petition. For example, many jurisdictions require the child to be at least 15 before he/she may be tried as an adult.

The nature and effect of the waiver is significant to the juvenile. Accordingly, the United States Supreme Court has imposed several procedural protections for juveniles in the waiver process. The first major Court decision in this area was that of *Kent v. United States*.[5] This case challenged the provisions of the District Court of Columbia which stated that juvenile court could waive jurisdiction after a full investigation. The Supreme Court, in that case, held that the waiver proceedings are a critically important stage in the juvenile process, and therefore, juveniles must be afforded minimum requirements of due process of law.

Consistent with the minimal requirements, the following conditions are considered necessary before a valid waiver may occur.

1) A hearing must be held on the motion to waiver.

2) The child is entitled to be represented by counsel at the hearing.

3) The attorney representing the juvenile must be given access to all records and reports considered by the court in reaching a waiver decision.

4) The court must provide a written statement of the reasons for the waiver decision.

Prior to 1975, the procedure in most states was that when a juvenile was charged with a serious offense, there would be an adjudication hearing to determine whether or not the juvenile had committed the offense. If the court found that the juvenile committed the offense, there would be a hearing to determine whether or not a waiver of juvenile court jurisdiction should be entered and the juvenile, therefore, tried as an adult in adult criminal court. In 1975, the case of *Breed v. Jones* held that jeopardy attaches when the juvenile court begins to hear evidence as to whether the juvenile committed the offense, therefore, if an adjudication hearing is held prior to the waiver hearing, the juvenile cannot be waived to adult criminal court because that would constitute double jeopardy.[6] After the *Breed v. Jones* case, the courts were modified to establish a waiver hearing. If it was determined that the juvenile should be retained in the juvenile court system, a hearing on the adjudication phase would proceed.

Juvenile Trial

Juvenile courts dispose of about 1.5 million delinquency cases each year. The trial process in juvenile court is referred to as the adjudicatory hearing. It is in this hearing that the court determines whether or not the juvenile committed the offenses alleged in the petition. During the adjudication process, the juvenile has the constitutional right to a fair notice of the charges, the right to be represented by counsel, the right to be confronted by and cross examine witnesses, and the privilege against self-incrimination. In addition, the juvenile court, in making a determination in adjudicating the juvenile a "delinquent," must use the standard of proof beyond a reasonable doubt.

At the conclusion of the adjudicatory hearing the court is required to enter a judgment either sustaining the petition, (finding that the accused committed the crimes alleged in the petition) or dismissing the petition. Once the juvenile has been adjudicated a delinquent, the court must make a determination as to the disposition of the child.

Disposition

At a separate disposition hearing the juvenile court should look at the record of the delinquent, the family background, and the needs of the accused and the safety of the public. A juvenile court judge has broad discretion in determining the disposition of the juvenile. Some of the standard dispositions are dismissal of the petition, suspended judgment, probation, placement in a community treatment program, or commitment to a state agency that is responsible for juvenile institutional care. This latter disposition is basically a commitment to a reformatory or other state institution for juveniles. In addition, the court has the power to place the child with parents or relatives under extensive supervision or moderate supervision. It can make dispositional arrangements with private youth serving agencies, or it can have the child committed to a mental institution.

How are juvenile drug cases processed?

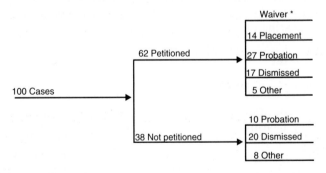

*Less than one case per 100.
Note: Detail may not add to totals because of rounding.
Source: Melissa Sickmund, *Juvenile court drug and alcohol cases, 1985-88* (Pittsburgh: National Center for Juvenile Justice, September 1990).

As with adult criminal court, probation is the most commonly used formal sentence for juvenile offenders. In fact, many states require that before a youth is sent to an institution, the youth must have failed on probation unless the juvenile has been charged with a serious felony.

Probation may include placing the child under the supervision of the juvenile probation department for the purposes of community treatment. The conditions of the probations are normally spelled out in the state court's order. There are general conditions from which all delinquents are required to obey (i.e., obey the law, stay away from other delinquents, attend school, etc.). There are also special conditions of probation which require each individual child to participate in certain training, treatment, and/or education programs.

Institutionalization

The most severe disposition that a judge may hand down at a juvenile court hearing is the institutionalization of the juvenile. In most states, this means that the child can be committed up until the child is 21 years of age. [*Note*: The disposition of commitment to an institution is an indeterminate sentence unlike that of most adult courts.]

Many persons involved in delinquency and juvenile law have questioned the practice of committing juveniles to institutions. De-institutionalization of juveniles has been attempted by using small residential facilities operated by juvenile care agencies to replace the larger state schools. There has been mixed reaction as to the success of de-institutionalization of juveniles.

The Right to Treatment

The right to treatment issue generally involves questions as to whether the juvenile has a right to psychological counseling or other types of special psychological treatments. While not directly stating that juveniles have a *right* to treatment while incarcerated, it appears that the Supreme Court is leaning in that direction. The Court of Appeals for the Seventh Circuit indicates that *Nelson v. Heyne* upheld the constitutional right to treatment for institutionalized juveniles under the Fourteenth Amendment and recent decisions by the U.S. Supreme Court seem to indicate that juveniles do have a right to receive treatment if committed to a juvenile institution.[7]

Types of Cases Handled by the Juvenile Courts

Violent Youth

Violent youth represent only about seven percent of juvenile court caseloads. However, they account for 11 percent of the detentions, 12 percent of the out-of-home placements, and 27 percent of the transfers to adult criminal courts.[8] The courts are more likely to file petitions in cases involving violent offenses than in any other types of cases.

Property Cases

Property offenses are a major part of the juvenile crime problem. Approximately 30 percent of all juvenile arrests are based on property offenses. Shoplifting was the most common offense for youths under the age of 15. Burglary was the most common property offense for older youths. Female offenders are more likely to be involved in shoplifting and male youths are more likely to be involved in burglary.[9] Approximately 25 percent of the youths arrested for property offenses are detained. Juveniles involved with motor vehicle thefts were the ones most likely to be detained awaiting disposition of the case.

JUVENILE GANGS

No discussion of the juvenile justice system is complete without an examination of the juvenile gang problem. The problem of youth gangs is both a long-standing and costly one. First, there is the direct cost to individual victims resulting from drive-by shootings, assaults, property damage, and robberies. Second, the community, as a whole, pays significantly for gang related activities, cost of law enforcement, trials and other judicial proceedings. It is estimated that correctional costs, which occur as the direct result of gang-related crime, are in the tens of millions of dollars each year in the United States. No one can place a dollar amount on the loss of life and the physical and emotional suffering experienced by their victims. In addition, there is a loss to society of the youths' potential skills and contributions due to their gang involvement.

Female gang members are increasing in number.

The magnitude of the gang problem is difficult to quantify. Chicago, for example, has experienced a significant increase in the number of youth gangs. One survey of Chicago public schools reported that nearly 40,000 school children had been attacked or threatened some time by gang members.[10] Cities in other parts of the United States (e.g., South Texas, New York, Florida, and Southern California) are also experiencing significant increases in youth gangs and gang related violence. One disturbing aspect of the increased gang activity is that the gangs are now recruiting seven and eight year olds as new members.

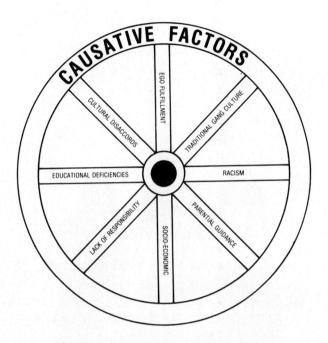

Why street gangs exist.

While juvenile gangs have been an inner-city phenomenon for years, they are now also spreading into rural areas. In addition, gang activity today differs significantly from gang activity in early decades. Whereas the earlier gangs tended to provide some sense of personal identity for their members in the cultural heterogeneity of the immigrant's world, most of today's youth gangs are financial enterprises. Their activities deal with drug trafficking and the acquisition and sale of stolen property. In addition, the gangs are ruthlessly violent in protecting their financial opportunities.

Gang Categories

Many experts state that gangs tend to stick to their own race and color and bond in their neighborhood. Some of the predominate gang categories include:

School in gang area.

White Supremist:

This is typically a drug abusing and racially motivated gang that is also frequently involved in satanic worship and practice in the occult. Some of the white gangs are called "skin heads." They are repeatedly involved in hate crimes against minorities.

African American:

The two prominent gangs are the Crips and the Bloods. These gangs are identified by the colors they wear. They are rival gangs originally from Southern California and are connected with drugs, robberies, and street violence.

Hispanic:

These gangs tend to be territorial, turf and neighborhood based street families. They tend to stress extreme loyalty and machismo. They are known to commit burglaries and crimes involving street violence. They also deal in drugs.

Typical gang mural found in Hispanic area.

Asian:

Asian gangs are harder to identify since they don't have a particular dress code. They tend to be violent and prey on their own culture, especially new immigrants.

Multi-racial:

In recent years, there appears to be an increase in multi-racial gangs that tend to be neighborhood-based in poor communities.

EXHIBIT 15-2

What Constitutes a Gang?

Accordingly to Professor R.J. Fox, West Virginia University, everyone has their own definition of gangs. It depends on who you talk to.

A Reno police officer: "Basically, a gang is a group of individuals two or more who have an identifiable gang name; they may or may not have a certain turf, but meet frequently.

A social worker in Southern California: "A group of people that form an allegiance for a common purpose and engage in unlawful behavior."

A California police detective in summing up the state's two-page definition: "Three or more who join, act in consort, find a gang name, find a gang territory, commit criminal acts for the further enhancement of anti-social behavior. It is the criminal acts that separate many gangs from youth groups."

EXHIBIT 15-3

Size of the Gang Problem

Nationwide in 1992

Gangs: 4,881
Gang Members: 249,324
Gang-related homocides (1991): 1,051
Gang-related incidents reported to police: 46,359

DISCUSSION QUESTIONS

1. What are the differences between an adult criminal court and a juvenile court?

2. Should your state retain a separate juvenile court system?

3. What can be done to improve the juvenile justice system?

4. Should juveniles have the same constitutional rights as adults?

5. What steps may be taken to reduce the juvenile gang problem?

6. What is the importance of the *Gault* case?

7. When should a juvenile court waive jurisdiction and refer the case to the adult criminal court system?

ENDNOTES

[1] Ralph Weisheit and Diane Alexander, "Juvenile Justice Philosophy and Demise of *Parens Patriae*," *Federal Probation*, (December, 1988): p. 56.
[2] Anthony Platt, *The Child Savers*, (Chicago: University of Chicago Press, 1969).
[3] *In re Gault*, 387 U.S. 1, (1967).
[4] 384 U.S. 436 (1966).
[5] 383 U.S. 541 (1966).
[6] 421 U.S. 519 (1975).
[7] 491 F.2d 1430 (7th Cir., 1974).
[8] Jeffery Butts and D.J. Connors-Beatty, "Juvenile Court's Response to Violent Offenders," *U.S. Department of Justice, Office of Juvenile Justice and Delinquency Prevention, Special Report*, (April, 1993).
[9] Ellen H. Nimick, "Juvenile Court Property Cases," *U.S. Department of Justice, Office of Juvenile Justice and Delinquency Prevention, Special Report*, (November, 1990).
[10] David W. Thompson and Leonard A. Jason, "Street Gangs and Preventative Interventions," *Criminal Justice Concepts and Issues*, (Los Angeles: Roxbury, 1993).
[11] Source: National Youth Gang Information Center and the California Gang Investigators Association.

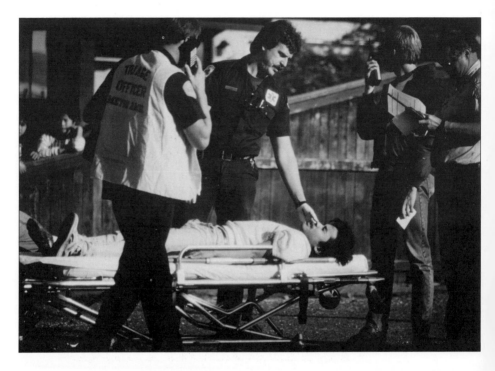

An innocent victim of a drive-by shooting.

CRIMINAL
VICTIMOLOGY AND
VICTIMS' RIGHTS

*For me, as a matter of fact, this was the most
notable quality of his confession—that Gary
White, who had brutally assaulted and murdered
Theresa Dunn a few hours after meeting her in
a Manhatten singles spot called Mr. Goodbar,
had a very clear sense of himself as the victim of
the woman he had murdered...*[1]

—Judith Rossner

The concept of "victim" can be traced to the ancient cultures. Its roots apparently lie in the religious notion of sacrifice.[2] As we discussed earlier, at one time the victim was a key actor in the criminal justice system and often the *de facto* prosecutor. With the emergence of public prosecutors, victims were reduced to mere witnesses. The present victims' rights movement started during the 1960s when society's attention was focused on domestic problems which included crime. From this period, the discipline of victimology developed.

Victimology is concerned with both the plight of victims and the roles that victims play in crimes. The branch that was concerned with the plight of victims began in the 1970s. This concern for the rights of victims developed into the victims' rights movement as we know it today.

CRIMINAL VICTIMOLOGY AND FEAR OF CRIME

In this section, we will explore the concept of victimology, victim's assistance programs, and the "fear of crime."

Victimology

Victimology is the study of crime from the victim's viewpoint, with emphasis on the relationship between the victim and the offender. Research indicates that the victim plays a significant role in the crime causation process in many crimes. Historically, we have been quick to blame the rape victim for being raped, but have largely ignored the victim's part in other crimes. [*Note*: It appears that in most cases, the rape victim is less involved, if involved at all, in the causation process than the victim is in the majority of other crimes.]

Mendelsohn, a Rumanian barrister, claims to have made the first in-depth criminological study of the victim and the victim-offender relationship. He used the term "penal-couple" to describe the relationship between the victim and the criminal. At the time he coined the term, Mendelsohn was a practicing attorney. He required his clients in criminal cases to answer some 300 or more questions regarding the crime and the victim. As the result of his study, he concluded that a "parallelity" exists between the bio-psychosocial personality of the offender and that of the victim. He viewed the total set of criminal factors as one set which includes the victim. Mendelsohn established "potential of victimal receptivity" to measure an individual's unconscious aptitude for being victimized.[3]

The essence of Mendlesohn's studies was the realization of the value of looking at the crime problem from a new direction by focusing on the victim and his relationship with the offender. Thus, Mendlesohn's perspective involves looking at familiar facts from an unfamiliar perspective.

Victimization trends, 1973-90

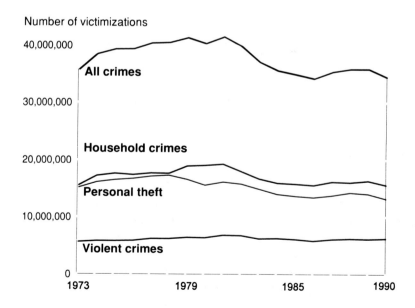

Number of victimizations

Source: U.S. Dept. of Justice

Hans Von Hentig, published a victim-centered study of crime in which he concluded that in many respects the victim shapes and molds the criminal and the crime. He concluded that there were four categories of individuals who make perfect murder victims: the depressive type, the greedy person, the wanton type, and the tormentor. He determined that the depressive type is at the top of the list. He sees the depressive type as dominated by a secret desire to be annihilated, and states that a study of accidents would reveal that many depressive persons are killed in accidents. In addition, he determined that the depressive person's instinct for self-preservation is weakened.

Who They Victimized

percent of violent inmates

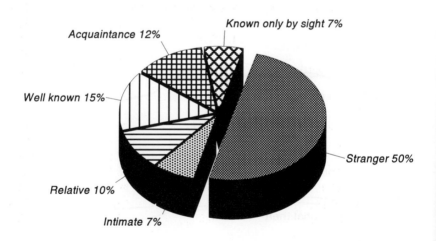

Source: U. S. Dept. of Justice

The depressed, according to Von Hentig, are not bold, but simply unsuspecting and careless. He points out that melancholy murderers are caught with less trouble by the police, and are more easily induced to plead guilty. Von Hentig also noted that the greedy person shows an inclination to be victimized and that the expectation of easy money

Race, sex, and age	Total population	Rate per 1,000 persons in each age group	
		Crimes of violence	Crimes of theft
White			
Male			
12-15	5,460,220	81.8	95.3
16-19	5,784,600	95.1	129.9
20-24	7,472,220	72.1	124.2
25-34	18,361,580	39.7	84.2
35-49	21,456,920	22.7	62.0
50-64	13,779,670	9.7	43.1
65 and over	11,033,720	5.3	21.6
Female			
12-15	5,201,740	46.7	107.9
16-19	5,685,620	52.5	117.5
20-24	7,604,240	46.3	115.0
25-34	18,119,260	27.2	83.4
35-49	21,692,220	17.9	66.8
50-64	14,950,500	6.0	38.3
65 and over	15,459,420	2.9	18.7
Black			
Male			
12-15	1,060,280	81.5	114.0
16-19	1,124,120	82.0	92.5
20-24	1,093,390	78.9	138.6
25-34	2,484,780	56.3	103.1
35-49	2,436,060	39.8	75.1
50-64	1,487,780	14.3	55.1
65 and over	996,000	8.7	12.7
Female			
12-15	1,040,170	31.2	54.5
16-19	1,117,150	68.0	57.9
20-24	1,324,420	36.0	78.8
25-34	2,930,640	34.1	68.8
35-49	2,963,080	15.3	62.7
50-64	1,840,260	5.1	33.6
65 and over	1,480,000	0.0	18.8

Victimization rates for persons 12 and over, by race, sex, and age of victim and type of crime. Source: U.S. Dept. of Justice.

affects some individuals like drugs, removing their normal inhibitions and deadening any well-founded suspicions. As to the wanton type, Von Hentig sees this type as victims not only to an aggressor but also to their own special conditions. For example, he notes a number of cases involving youthful victims and middle-aged women victims, who, approaching the climacteric period, fall victims to aggressors and their "own critical conditions". By "critical conditions," Von Hentig is referring to the situational stresses that are normally present during critical times of a person's life, (e.g., approaching old age).

The tormentor-type was his final class of perfect murder victims. In these cases, when some form of oppression, whether parental, marital, etc. has existed for some time, the oppression becomes tyrannical and insufferable. At this point, in many cases, a final explosion occurs with the tormentor becoming the victim as in the case where the wife-beating husband is killed by his wife, e.g., "the burning bed syndrome."[4]

Weapons Used While Committing Crime
percent of violent inmates

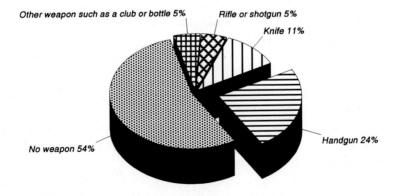

Other weapon such as a club or bottle 5%   Rifle or shotgun 5%

Knife 11%

Handgun 24%

No weapon 54%

Source: U. S. Dept. of Justice

Marvin Wolfgang conducted a study of criminal homicides in Philadelphia. One part of the study considered victim-precipitated homicides. Wolfgang stated that Hentig's concept of the "duet frame of crime" provided the basis for his analysis of the victim-prone relationship. He noted the importance of the social interaction concept of crime in his studies. Wolfgang concluded that a number of would-be murderers became victims. In many cases, the victim had the same major characteristics as the offender, e.g., socioeconomic standing in the community and prior criminal records. Wolfgang also concluded, in an article published eleven years after his original study, that many victim-precipitated homicides were, in fact, caused by the subconscious desire of the victims to commit suicide.[5]

Wolfgang's study was partially replicated by Pokorny for criminal homicides occurring in Houston, Texas; by Voss and Hepburn for criminal homicides occurring in Chicago; and by Roberson for criminal homicides occurring in San Francisco. Their findings support Wolfgang's conclusion that in many criminal homicides the victim plays a significant role in the causation process.

Victim Assistance Programs

The general feeling of being a living victim or victim-survivor is one of an outcast. Ostracized from society, forgotten by family, friends, and fellow workers. No one, or very few, bring the subject up.

—A Victim

When a person is the victim of a violent crime, the consequences can be grave. A victim rarely expects to be a victim, and therefore is not prepared for it. Often the victim does not know where to go for assistance and if the victim ends up in the hospital, he/she is often required to pay for the medical treatment.

Unfortunately, the effects of crime are not limited to the victim. The victim's family is often devastated, and the psychological trauma spreads to almost everyone closely connected to the victim. Some of the emotional scars last for years after the event. Until recently, the criminal justice system was an uncaring system for the victims.[6]

Rights of Texas Crime Victims

1.   The right to protection from threats of harm arising from cooperating with prosecution efforts.

2.   The right to have your safety and that of your family taken into consideration when bail is being considered.

3.   If you so request, the right to be informed about court proceedings, including whether or not they have been canceled or rescheduled.

4.   If you so request, the right to information about procedures in the criminal investigation of your case by law enforcement and about general procedures in the criminal justice system, including plea bargaining, from the prosecutor's office.

5.   The right to receive information about the Texas Crime Victim Compensation Fund, which provides financial assistance to victims of violent crimes and, if you so request, to referral to available social service agencies that may provide additional help.

6.   The right to provide information to a probation department conducting a presentence investigation about the impact of the crime.

7.   If you so request, the right to be notified of parole proceedings by the Board of pardons and Paroles, to participate in the parole process, and to be notified of the defendant's release.

8.   The right to be present at all public court proceedings, if the presiding judge permits.

9.   The right to be provided with a safe waiting area before and during court proceedings.

10.   The right to prompt return of any property no longer required as evidence.

11.   If you so request, the right to have the prosecutor notify your employer of the necessity of your testimony that may involve your absence from work.

12.   The right to complete a Victim Impact Statement, detailing the emotional, physical, and financial impact that the crime has had on you and your family, and to have that statement considered by the judge at sentencing and by the parole board prior to taking any parole action.

Victim assistance programs were first developed as a concern for restitution to be paid to a victim. Restitution for criminal acts has a long history dating back to the Middle Ages. In the United States, however, the victim was a forgotten person in the process until the 1960s. California, in 1965, became the first state to develop victim compensation programs. New York, Hawaii, Maryland, Massachusetts, and New Jersey quickly followed. Today all states have some form of victim compensation program.

In 1974, the Law Enforcement Assistance Administration contributed $50 million to victim witness programs. During the 1980s, however, federal funding for victims programs declined. With reduced funding, many programs were required to curtail services. Other programs obtained local funding and many programs looked to private funding.

In 1982, the U.S. Congress passed the Federal Victim and Witness Protection Act (PL 97-291) which was designed to protect and assist victims and witnesses of federal crimes. Also in 1982, the Presidential Task Force on the Victims of Crime was formed. This task force advocated better treatment of victims, fundamental changes in the judicial system including the abolition of the exclusionary rule, the abolition of parole, and reduction of good time credit that prisoners earn. In 1984, the Federal Victims of Crime Act was passed which committed the federal government to promote state and local victim compensation programs. To be eligible for federal funds under this act, state programs must include compensation for survivors of victims of drunk drivers and domestic violence. Many local programs had previously excluded these two groups of victims from the compensation programs.

The victims' rights movement also included the right of the victim to participate in any plea bargaining and the right to make a victim's impact statement during the sentencing phase of a criminal trial. For example, California's Proposition 8, the Victim's Bill of Rights, which includes Penal Code section 1191.9 provides:

The victim or next of kin has the right to appear, personally or by counsel, at the sentencing proceeding and to reasonably express his or her views concerning the crime, the person responsible, and the need for restitution. The court, in imposing sentence, shall consider the statements of victims and next of kin... and shall state on the record its conclusion concerning whether the person would pose a threat to public safety if granted probation...

Fear of Crime

The fear of crime is often out of proportion to the likelihood of criminal victimization. As noted below, the chance of accidental injury at work or at home is far greater than the chance of being a victim of a violent criminal act. Research indicates that women make more modifications in the way they live than do men because of the fear of crime. They are increasingly careful where they travel and the times of the day they leave their homes. Women are victimized, however, far less frequently than are men in all major crime categories except rape. Women and the elderly report the greatest fear of crime and young men the least fear. Young males, however, face the greatest chance of being a victim of a violent criminal act.[7]

Attitudes toward walking alone at night and safety at home
By demographic characteristics, 1992

	Percent Afraid to walk alone at night		Percent that feel safe at home	
	Yes	No	Yes	No
National	43	57	90	10
Sex				
Male	25	75	94	6
Female	59	41	86	14
Age				
18 to 29 years	45	55	89	11
30 to 49 years	32	68	91	9
50 years and older	52	48	89	11

Results of survey regarding feelings of personal safety. Source: U.S. Department of Justice.

Source: U. S. Dept. of Justice

VICTIMS' RIGHTS MOVEMENT

The neglect of crime victims is a national disgrace....If we take the justice out of the criminal justice system we leave behind a system that serves only the criminal.[8]

—Lois Herrington

Legislation to provide governmental compensation for victims was enacted in England in 1963. In 1965, California became the first state to provide governmental compensation for victims of crime. Next came New York and Hawaii. By 1983, 38 states had adopted some form of victim compensation. In addition, direct restitution by criminals to victims was revived in many jurisdictions. In most states today, restitution is required as a condition of probation.

Traditionally, we have thought of the victim as someone else. Each of us, however, is potentially a crime victim. One of every four U.S. households has been victimized by personal or property crime. At some point in time, crime will affect us, the lives of our relatives or close friends. The consequences of crime can involve financial loss, property damage, physical injury and even death. Victims often share a justified apprehension that they and their family members will be threatened or harassed as the direct result of their testimony against a violent criminal.

There has been a great deal of research on criminal victimization. It is only in recent years, however, that the victim's role in the criminal justice system has been acknowledged and considered. While victims have always been key persons in the system, more often than not they were kept at the periphery. They have often been referred to as the "forgotten persons" of the criminal justice system.[9] It also appears that the typical response of criminal justice personnel is regarded as having a negative impact on the emotional problems of victims. In some cases, the victims have been treated with less respect and dignity than the offender.

Task Force on Victims of Crime

The victims' movement has resulted in the criminal justice system taking a second look at victims, how they are treated, and their role in society. The report of the President's Task Force on Victims of Crime, which was published in 1982, has been used by the victims' movement as their call to action.

The Task Force submitted the following recommendations for federal and state action:

1) Legislation should be proposed and enacted to ensure that addresses of victims and witnesses are not made public or available to the defense absent a clear need as determined by the court.

2) Legislation should be proposed and enacted to ensure that hearsay is admissible and sufficient in preliminary hearings, so that victims need not testify in person.

3) Legislation should be proposed and enacted to ensure that designated victim counseling is legally privileged and not subject to defense discovery or subpoena.

4) Legislation should be proposed and enacted to amend the bail laws to accomplish the following:

   a. Allow courts to deny bail to persons found by clear and convincing evidence to present a danger to the community;

   b. Give the prosecution the right to expedited appeal of adverse bail determinations, analogous to the right presently held by the defendant;

   c. Codify existing case law defining the authority of the court to detain defendants as to whom no conditions of release are adequate to ensure appearance at trial;

   d. Reverse, in the case of serious crimes, any standard that presumptively favors release of convicted persons awaiting sentence or appealing their convictions;

   e. Require defendants to refrain from criminal activity as a mandatory condition of release; and

f. Provide penalties for failing to appear while released on bond or personal recognizance that are more closely proportionate to the penalties for the offense with which the defendant was originally charged....

5) Legislation should be proposed and enacted to abolish the exclusionary rule as it applies to Fourth Amendment issues.

6) Legislation should be proposed and enacted to open parole release hearings to the public.

7) Legislation should be proposed and enacted to abolish parole and limit judicial discretion in sentencing.

8) Legislation should be proposed and enacted to require that school officials report violent offenses against students or teachers, or the possession of weapons or narcotics on school grounds....[10]

A review of the above recommendations reflects that the victims' movement is similar in some of its proposals to many of those recommended by "law and order" movements; many of the recommendations will limit the individual rights of persons charged with criminal offenses. It is an accepted fact that the victim has been a forgotten person in our system and that reform in this area is greatly needed. The "law and order" orientation has caused many people to object to certain aspects of the victims' movement and has detracted from its effectiveness. For example, the proposal to eliminate the exclusionary rule is a recommendation that has caused considerable controversy which has detracted from the effectiveness of the victims' movement and has only limited relevance to victims' rights.

Most state statutes on victims' rights are patterned after the California statutes. The legal rights and entitlement of crime victims are emphasized in the statutes. By giving victims legal rights, victims can now look to the legal system to identify and enforce those rights.[11]

Both federal and state task forces on victims' rights have resulted in the passing of legislation that has reduced the pressures of testifying for victims. The efforts to reduce the pressures include establishment of special waiting rooms, procedures to limit long waits, changes in statutes to limit the need to attend pre-trial procedures, and escort and babysitting services.

By the time the Task Force report was published, the voters of California had already enacted legislation giving victims the right to allocution at felony sentencing hearings, i.e., the right to speak. Proposition 8, California's Victim's Bill of Rights, includes Penal Code Section 1191.1, which specifies the following:

> The victim of any crime, or the next of kin of the victim if the victim has died, has the right to attend all sentencing proceedings under this chapter and shall be given adequate notice by the probation officer of all sentencing proceedings concerning the person who committed the crime.
>
> The victim or next of kin has the right to appear, personally or by counsel, at the sentencing proceeding and to reasonably express his or her views concerning the crime, the person responsible, and the need for restitution. The court in imposing sentence shall consider the statements of victims and next of kin made pursuant to this section and shall state on the record its conclusion concerning whether the person would pose a threat to public safety if granted probation....

When asked whether the right was "effective," 81 percent of probation officers answered "minimally or not al all" (often because of the role of victim impact statements) compared with 69 percent of judges and 48 percent of prosecutors; less than 2 percent indicated that the right had been very successful. Sixty-six percent of district attorneys, compared with 40 percent of judges, thought that victim appearances increased the amount (as opposed to the frequency) of restitution awarded.

Judges indicated that, while the actual appearances had little overall impact on the sentences, they believed the right had benefits:

> It does allow the victims to air their grievances or "get it off their chest." To this extent they may feel the system is paying more attention to them.

> Prop. 8 has been a real significant step toward victim recognition and awareness. It is as important as a public statement as it is as a court tool.

Prosecutors wrote:

Judges are constrained by law, logic, and justice. In a majority of cases nothing the victim says is really going to impact.

Members of the judiciary who were responsive to victims' rights before, continue to be so, and others who place defendant's rights paramount...also continue.

RIGHT TO BE HEARD

Should the victim of a crime be given the right to initiate or intervene in a criminal prosecution? According to Professor Abraham S. Goldstein of Yale Law School:

The victim deserves a voice in our criminal justice system, not only in hearings on the amount of restitution to be paid him but also on the offenses to be used as the basis for such restitution....The victim should have a right to participate in hearings before the court on dismissals, guilty pleas, and sentences....

The Final Report of the President's Task Force on Victims of Crime recommended that the U.S. Constitution be amended to give the victim a "right to be present and to be heard at all critical stages of the judicial proceedings." The Report also recommended greater involvement of the victim in the sentencing phase of the trial. As stated in the Report:

Judges should allow for and give weight to input at sentencing for victims of violent crime...Every victim must be allowed to speak at the time of sentencing. The victim, no less that the defendant comes to court seeking justice. When the court hears as it may, from the defendant, his lawyer, his family and friends, his minister, and others, simple fairness dictates that the person who has borne the brunt of the defendant's crime be allowed to speak....Defendants speak and are spoken for often at great length, before sentence is imposed. It is outrageous that the system should contend it is too busy to hear from the victim.[12]

As the results of the task force, most states have enacted legislation that provides for the victim to have a right to participate in the sentencing process. The participation is limited to speaking and presenting a "victim's impact" statement. The voters in California passed Proposition Eight which included, among other provisions, the right of victims to speak at both felony sentencing and parole hearings.

Often, however, the right to speak at the sentencing hearing is of little importance unless the victim has a right to participate in the earlier critical stages of the trial. The decisions made at the earlier stages may have a greater role in the defendant's sentence than those made at the sentencing hearing. For example, the right to speak at sentencing may have no effect if the defendant has a plea bargain that guarantees him or her a light sentence or no imprisonment.

NOVA (National Organization for Victim Assistance) has long advocated a new amendment to the U.S. Constitution which would give the victim a constitutional right to be present and participate in all critical stages of the federal and state criminal justice processes.

Bail Decisions

Presently, most states do not provide for the right of victims to participate directly in bail decisions. The victims, however, can bring information to the prosecutor who can present that information to the judge. The prosecutors now often check with victims to see if there is any information that the prosecutor may use to prevent bail being granted.

Plea Bargaining

Plea bargaining takes place at various stages of the process. The general time for plea bargaining varies from court to court and county to county. Accordingly, it is difficult to ensure that the victim has materially participated in the plea bargaining process. To offset this in some states, like California, there are limits on plea bargaining in certain types of cases. Often, however, the limitations are avoided. Generally, victims have no rights to participate directly in plea bargaining. Some judges, though, require that the prosecutor check with the victims before the judges will accept plea bargains.

Victim Impact Statement

As discussed earlier, in felony cases there is a separate sentencing hearing. At the hearing, the judge considers a pre-sentence report normally prepared by the probation office. The pre-sentence report includes information concerning the circumstances of the crime and the prior history of the accused. In most cases, the probation office includes a recommendation for sentence in the report. Traditionally, the judge places great weight on the pre-sentence report in determining the appropriate sentence. Most states now require that the pre-sentence report contain a **victim impact statement**. The victim impact statement may be prepared by the victim or victim's counsel. If the victim does not submit an impact statement, usually the officer preparing the pre-sentencing report is required to include information regarding the effects of the crime on the victim and victim's family. In addition, the officer must include in the report a description of the financial or property losses suffered by the victim.

In most victim impact statements, a statement is included regarding the victim's views of the criminal and any sentencing recommendations that the victim may have. In most states, the victim has a right to know the recommendations for sentencing that are contained in the pre-sentencing report prepared by the probation department.

Victim impact statements may not be read to or given to the jury in a death penalty case. The U.S. Supreme Court ruled in *Booth v. Maryland*:[13]

> Death is a punishment different from all other sanctions...therefore considerations that inform the sentencing decisions in death penalty cases may be different from those that might be relevant to other ... punishment determinations.

The Court in this case said that the focus of victim impact evidence on the character and reputation of the victim and the effect on the victim's family may be wholly unrelated to the blame-worthiness of a particular defendant. It appears that the *Booth* case will apply only to capital cases and will have no effect on other felony cases. Some states still allow victim impact statements in capital cases as long as the statements are focused on the individual activities of the defendant.

Generally, the victim has only limited rights to participate in lower court trials. For cases tried in municipal or county courts, there is no separate pre-sentencing report or separate sentencing hearing. Accordingly, there is only limited opportunity for the victim to participate in the hearings. In some cases, the victims' views are presented to the court by the prosecutor. But in most cases, because of the summary type proceedings and the case loads, the prosecutor is not aware of any special victim considerations at the time the case is tried.

Parole

Generally, states provide the victim with a right to present information regarding the granting of parole for a defendant. In most cases, victims who speak at parole hearings are the next of kin of murder victims. Typically, at these hearings the victims are required to expend their own funds to travel to the prisons and are not paid for their time. The victims are normally not allowed to ask questions of the defendant, but must address their remarks to the members of the parole panel. Because of the difficulties of attending these hearings, most victims send letters stating their feelings regarding the granting of parole to be considered by the parole board. In a few cases, victims hire counsel to make appearances at the hearing and present their side of the case. Victims have a right, in most states, to be notified of the results of the parole decision. In addition, victims have a right to be notified when an inmate is released or has escaped from prison.

Juvenile Cases

The problem in juvenile cases is that juvenile courts have traditionally kept their proceedings confidential to protect the juvenile. Accordingly, there is a direct conflict between the confidentiality of juveniles and the victim's right to know. The trend is to relax the rules of confidentiality in order to provide the victim with information. In some states, like California, the victim has a right to attend the disposition (sentencing) phase of the juvenile trial. In addition, the probation department must provide the victim with information regarding the specifics of any orders regarding the juvenile, including information regarding the potential release of the juvenile. However, the general rule that juvenile records are permanently sealed to the public, including the victims, remains unchanged.

CIVIL LIABILITY

One aspect of the victims' movement has been the filing of civil lawsuits against businesses to force them to take steps to prevent crime. The movement involves lawsuits that seek large monetary judgments for victims of crime from businesses whose lax security contributed to the occurrence of the crime (i.e., forcing hotels to provide better security services or face civil liability when hotel guests are injured as the result of inadequate security precautions).

Another aspect of the victims' movement has been the emergence of volunteer groups to provide peer counseling and other valuable services to victims. For example, Mothers Against Drunk Drivers (MADD) has established education programs designed to assist victims of drunk drivers.

VICTIM COMPENSATION

As noted earlier, California was the first state to provide for victim compensation from public funds. Now all states have some form of victim compensation programs. Victim compensation, as discussed in this section, does not include restitution or civil suits against the defendant. In most cases, restitution or civil suits against the defendant are not fruitful because the defendants do not have the financial resources to pay even when ordered to do so by a court.

The general rules of victim compensation statutes are that the victim is compensated for medical expenses, loss of income, etc. that are not covered by insurance or other reimbursement programs. Usually, victims are not allowed to be reimbursed for property damages unless the property is necessary for the victim's livelihood. The general rules are as follows:

— Anyone who sustains injury, as a direct result of crime, who is legally dependent for support by a primary victim, any family member who was present during the commission of a crime is eligible for compensation.

— The victim or person applying for compensation must not have been an aggressor or participant in the crime.

— Pecuniary losses (out of pocket expenses) for which the victim has not and will not be reimbursed for and which causes an unnecessary financial hardship on the victim or person applying for compensation will be considered.

Crime victim funds are primarily from three sources:

1) assessments imposed by courts on all criminal defendants,

2) fines collected from certain crimes, and

3) public funds.

THE FUTURE OF VICTIMS' RIGHTS

Many people in the criminal justice system feel that the victims' rights movement has reached its peak and that the victim will once again be the forgotten person in the system. To justify their opinions, they point to the fact that with increasing caseloads the pressure to dispose of cases will cause the courts and the prosecutors to ignore the victims in their rush to close cases. In addition, they point out that federal, state, and local officials are under increased pressures to reduce governmental spending. These people fail to realize that special interest groups like Mothers Against Drunk Drivers (MADD) and the

National Organization for Victim's Assistance (NOVA) are stronger than ever and will increasingly place pressure on officials in the criminal justice system to "remember the victim." In addition, many states, like Texas, have established victim's information clearing houses to provide information centers that promote victim assistance programs.

Edwin Villmoare and Virginia V. Neto work as project director and project coordinator, respectively, for Victim Appearances at Sentencing Hearings Under the California Victims' Bill of Rights. Here is what they have to say in conclusion to their recent grant study on this subject.

Allocution at sentencing will be a modest right wherever it is established because plea bargaining effectively resolves the vast majority of all sentences before the victim can have a say. In fact, since plea bargaining may result in the dismissal of criminal charges, plea bargaining deprives some victims of the right to allocution altogether. If the intent behind the allocution right is to give victims an opportunity to comment on and influence the sentences for the crimes committed against them, victim participation must exist at earlier stages in the prosecution of cases. This is particularly true within a determinate sentencing system.

There is no doubt that victims deserve much greater attention and assistance than they have received in the past or are currently receiving. Victim participation in the prosecution of crimes raises complex legal and social issues. If victim participation is to be more than symbolic, additional resources will have to be invested in the criminal justice system and a number of existing procedures changed. Victims' rights cannot be grafted onto the existing system without generally remaining simply cosmetic, nor can they be made potent without creating profound changes throughout the entire system.

The question remains as to whether society is prepared to embark upon a process so potentially complex, expensive, and unpredictable.

DISCUSSION QUESTIONS

1. What accounts for the re-emergence of the victim in our criminal justice system?

2. What can be done to ensure that victims continue to have their rights protected in our system?

3. What expenses should victims be allowed to obtain payment for under victim compensation programs? Should reimbursement be based on need?

4. Discuss the conflicts between the rights of juvenile defendants and the victims' rights movement.

5. What is the importance of the victim-impact statement?

6. What victim compensation programs are available in your area? How can they be improved?

ENDNOTES

[1] Judith Rossner, *Looking for Mr. Goodbar*, (New York: Simon and Schuster, 1975).

[2] Andrew Karmen, *Crime Victims*, (Belmont, Ca.: Brooks-Cole, 1984), p. 1.

[3] B. Mendelsohn, "The Origin of Victimology," *Excerpta Criminologica*, vol. 3, Fall 1963, pp. 239-256.

[4] Hans Von Hentig, *The Criminal and His Victim*, (New Haven, Conn.: Yale Univ. Press, 1948).

[5] Marvin Wolfgang, *Patterns in Criminal Homicide*, (Philadelphia: Univ. of Pennsylvania Press, 1958).

[6] *Figgie Report on Crime*, (New York: Figgie Foundation, 1982).

[7] U.S. Department of Justice, *Reactions to Crime Projects: Executive Summary*, (Washington D.C.: Government Printing Office, 1982).

[8] Lois Herrington, Chairperson, President's Task Force on Victims of Crime, (1982), p. 2.

[9] Arthur J. Lurigio, Wesley G. Skogan, and Robert C. Davis, *Victims of Crime*, (Newbury Park, Ca.: Sage, 1990).

[10] Note: the above recommendations were summarized.

[11] Edwin Villmoare and Jeanne Benvenuti, *California Victims of Crime Handbook*, (Sacramento: McGeorge School of Law, 1992).

[12] Final Report, p. 77.

[13] 107 U.S. 2529 (1987).

DRUG ABUSE AND THE CRIMINAL JUSTICE SYSTEM

If only one thing is evident, it is that neither the nation's drug problem or its crime problem exists independently in America today.

D rug abuse and its associated problems have created a major impact on our criminal justice system. As noted earlier, many people consider our criminal justice system to be a drug driven system. In this chapter, we will explore the nature and extent of drug abuse in the United States.[1] The link between drug use and crime is complex. Crimes that do not seem to involve drugs may be the direct result of illegal drug use or distribution. Drugs may be indirectly related to crime in that many drug users involve themselves in crime in order to obtain money to sustain their drug habits. In many ways, drugs and crime are closely related to each other. Using or distributing some drugs is illegal and violators are subject to criminal sanctions.

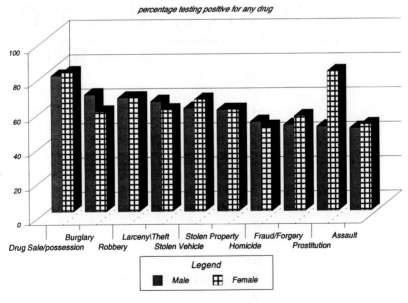

Prevelance of Drug Use Among Arrestees

percentage testing positive for any drug

Legend: ■ Male   ⊞ Female

Source: U.S. Dept. of Justice

FACTORS THAT INFLUENCE DRUG USE

Research indicates that drug use by friends is the strongest predictor of a person's involvement in drug abuse. Drug use usually begins and continues largely because youths have contact with peers who are also involved in drugs. Family influences are probably the second most important factor in predicting drug use. Families with inconsistent discipline, drug using parents or poor relationships between parents and children appear to foster drug use. It appears that family structure is less an important predictor of drug use than is the attachment of the children to their parents. Apparently, the more important the family factors are to a person, the less likely the individual is to become involved in illegal drug use.

Personality traits such as rebelliousness, orientation toward independence, low self-concept and alienation all appear to influence an individual to an orientation of risk taking and a high-tolerance for deviance and, thus, drug abuse. In addition, a lack of commitment to conventional values may also be related to drug use. Childhood anti-social behaviors are also highly predictive of drug use in adulthood. Other factors associated with drug abuse include poor school performance, involvement in delinquent activity, parents who have very little control over their children and are unsupportive, and children who place less values on traditional goals.

Most people who use illegal drugs have used or abused alcohol, tobacco, and legal drugs before becoming involved in drug abuse. Studies have shown that people generally begin to use legal drugs such as cigarettes and alcohol before they begin to use marijuana, and marijuana is used before other illicit drugs.

The average age that drug abusers first use illicit drugs is between the mid-teens and the early twenties. However, of those persons confined to state penal institutions, it appears that the average age of first use of illicit drugs is much younger than that of the average person in the general population.[2]

How Many People Use Illicit Drugs?

Eighty percent of prison inmates stated that they used drugs within the past year prior to incarceration; 52 percent said they had

The proportion of drug users varies across different populations

Survey and population	Percent of population who used illicit drugs	
	Ever	In the past month
National Household Survey on Drug Abuse — conducted periodically since 1972, now an annual survey that interviews a random sample of people living in households and in certain group residences the U.S. In 1991, 32,594 people were interviewed in their homes. Population excludes residents of some institutions and transient populations.	37%	6%
High School Senior Survey — also known as *Monitoring the Future* — is an annual survey conducted since 1975. In 1991, about 15,700 seniors in public and private high schools were surveyed. Dropouts and absent students are excluded. College students and young adults are also surveyed to provide comparative data.	44	16
Worldwide Survey of Substance Abuse and Health Behaviors Among Military Personnel — conducted four times since 1980. In 1988, 19,000 active duty military personnel were surveyed at U.S. military installations across the world.	—	5
Survey of Jail Inmates* — an interview survey of local jail inmates awaiting trial or sentencing or serving their sentence in a local jail conducted four times since 1978. In 1989, a representative sample of 5,675 inmates in 424 jails were surveyed.	78	44**
Survey of State Prison Inmates — an interview survey of State prison inmates conducted every 5 to 7 years (three times since 1974). In 1986, about 14,000 inmates in 275 facilities were interviewed.	80	52**

— Data not available.
*Percents for convicted inmates only.
**Use in the month prior to the offense that resulted in incarceration.
Sources: NIDA, 1991 National Household Survey on Drug Abuse and 1991 National High School Senior Survey; DoD, 1988 Worldwide Survey on Substance Abuse and Health Behaviors Among Military Personnel; BJS, 1989 Survey of Inmates in Local Jails and 1986 Survey of Inmates of State Correctional Facilities.

used it within the past month before incarceration. Generally, it is estimated that more than 75 million persons in the United States have used illegal drugs. According to a 1991 survey of high school seniors, about 44 percent of high school seniors across the nation admitted to the use of illegal drugs; 29 percent had "used" in the past year. Another survey found that 50 percent of college students had used illicit drugs.

The most commonly used illicit drug is marijuana. The next most commonly used illicit drugs are inhalants, stimulants, hallucinogens, and cocaine. A Bureau of Justice Science Statistic's study indicated, "That a third of the adult population knows someone who regularly uses cocaine or crack."

How Big is the Illegal Drug Business?

Americans spend vast sums of money for illegal drugs. For example, it is estimated that in 1990, Americans spent $18 billion for cocaine, $12 billion for heroin, $9 billion for marijuana, and $2 billion for other drugs. One report stated that illegal drug traffic employs a great many people and is a significant industry within the U.S. today.

SOURCES OF ILLEGAL DRUGS

Marijuana, cocaine and opium are made from agricultural crops. The main sources of these drugs are Central and South America, Southeast and Southwest Asia, and the Middle East. The opium based drugs consumed in the U.S. come primarily from Southeast and Southwest Asia and Mexico. Southeast Asia is the source of almost three-fourths of the estimated world poppy supply. Coca, the primary base plant for cocaine, is grown principally in South America. Most of the marijuana consumed in the United States is from other countries. However, the U.S. supplies a significant portion of its own marijuana market.[3]

Organization of Illegal Drug Business

It appears that organized crime in the U.S. is primarily involved in drug trafficking and distribution. A statement that is heard quite frequently is that drug trafficking is "organized crime." The term "organized crime" has been traditionally used to refer to groups such as the Mafia or La Cosa Nostra. These groups have great stability and longevity, and therefore are able to be very active in drug trafficking. There is also the Medellin and Cali Cartels in Columbia which are organized crime groups dealing primarily in drugs. It is estimated that these two cartels control up to 90 percent of the world's cocaine traffic. However, there are many domestic drug trafficking groups that are not very highly organized including many of our street gangs.

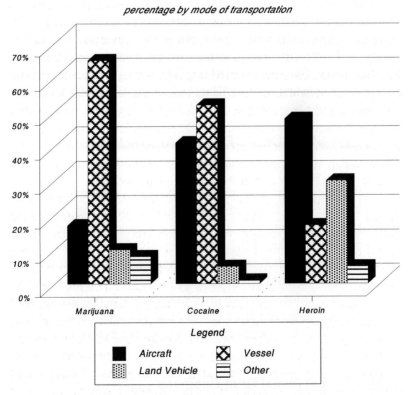

How Drugs are Smuggled into the U.S.
percentage by mode of transportation

Source: U.S. Dept. of Justice

In the 1960's and 1970's in New York City, for example, one of the first places in the U.S. to have widespread heroin and cocaine use, the marketplace for buying and selling illegal drugs could be described as free-lance with only a loose cooperation among wholesalers, dealers and street sellers. A street seller, for example, may deal with different suppliers each week and vice versa, and there is no commitment for transactions by either party. Drug sellers typically work independently, bearing alone the full risk of being arrested.

Since the 1970's, drug distribution has become more vertically integrated. In the legitimate business world such integration occurs when one firm merges with either a firm from which it purchases an input or a firm to which it sells output. Vertically organized selling groups in the illegal drug market maintain operations in several stages, such as regional distribution and street sales. These organizations have become more popular with the spread of crack cocaine. A vertically integrated illegal drug organization that is carefully controlled makes it more difficult for the police to arrest sellers with standard buy-and-bust techniques. Each person in the organization has a specific role and everyone works as a team. One person will lookout, another seeks new customers, another stores the drugs for upcoming sales, and another collects payment from the buyers. In the present day, a retail seller and his team typically work in a given location for a specific time, turn over all the money to someone at a higher level in the organization and are paid at the end of the day in drugs, money or both.

The illegal drug production is also becoming vertically integrated. It is estimated that cocaine production and distribution is the most vertically integrated of the drug markets. It is difficult in the illegal drug market to tell where one organization ends and another begins, but it is clear that there is a high level of cooperation in the processing of coca paste into cocaine and its distribution into the U.S.

The cocaine cartels yield extraordinary economic and political power. They employ thousands including many with expertise in law, finance, government, chemistry and distribution. For much of the 1980's, the two cartels agreed to divide much of the lucrative U.S. market. In 1993, evidence indicated that there was a head-to-head competition which suggested that the agreement was no longer in force. However, with the death of the head of the Medellin cartel in late 1993, a significant shift in the cartel's impact on drug trafficking is expected.

Cocaine trafficking to the U.S. originates in the Western Hemisphere.

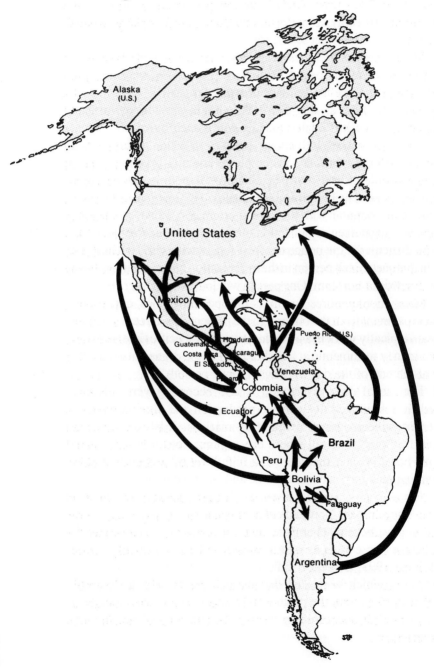

The famous French Connection about which a movie in the 1970's was made, operated between the 1950's and the 1970's in the heroin trade. This was Turkish heroin processed in France and transported by the Sicilian mafia to New York and other places in North America.

More recently, the Pizza Connection has distributed a large share of heroin consumed in the U.S. This is a loosely affiliated combination of Sicilian and American organized crime families who arrange the shipment of heroin to the U.S. and use pizza parlors in the U.S. to shield heroin operations and related financial transactions.

Like other social groups, drug selling groups tend to be made up of individuals who share similar backgrounds and experience to facilitate communications and trust. These groups tend to be racial, ethnic, and sometimes national such as the black, Hispanic or Jamaican groups. Unlike traditional organized crime groups, drug trafficking groups are seldom based on extended family ties. The Chinese, Thai and Sicilian groups have controlled a large segment of wholesale heroin distribution in the U.S. in recent years, and Mexican nationals have distributed heroin throughout the United States.

Members of youth gangs often engage in delinquent and criminal behavior including drug use and sales, and some observers believe that, as a group, youth gangs are heavily involved in distributing drugs. This view is most common for the Crips and Bloods, gangs that originated in Los Angeles. These gangs are described as having established drug trafficking operations in other parts of the country. However, research completed to date gives a much more ambiguous picture, suggesting that drug distribution is not usually an organized activity of youth gangs. Many law enforcement officials would disagree, finding youth gangs to be heavily involved in drug trafficking in many areas.

Pre-teen aged juveniles are sometimes recruited to serve as lookouts or other roles in support of trafficking. A major reason for recruiting youths to work in the drug trade is that they come under the jurisdiction of the juvenile justice system and are not usually subject to adult criminal penalties.

The number of juvenile drug arrests in the District of Columbia rose from 279 in 1986 to 1,550 in 1987 when the law was changed to increase the difference between sentence lengths for adult and juvenile drug offenders.

Many adults who distribute drugs are also drug users. Approximately 65 percent of those arrested for selling drugs were found to be regular drug users. One of the major reasons for being a distributor is to support one's own use and to assure an access to the drug supply. A study in New York City found that frequent heroin users were more likely than less frequent users to sell and engage in a high number of transactions. One study found that most juvenile drug dealers work strictly for money and are not frequent users. This is also likely to be true of retail drug distribution bosses and dealers above the street level. Studies suggest that some dealers know that their own drug use places them in a high risk of apprehension, reduces profit and may lead to personal deterioration that will make them unable to function efficiently.

A few drug dealers make a large amount of money, but most do not. The wholesale and mid-level dealers often make hundreds of thousands or millions of dollars. One study indicates that they are also able to escape detection. The lower-level dealers, especially the ones who are heavy drug users, usually operate on a smaller scale. Drug using retail sellers accumulate little wealth because their profits are often used to support drug use; the drug business is a fragile enterprise subject to disruption by law enforcement efforts; their involvement in drug sales is sporadic; and the earnings tend to be spent for expensive cars, gold jewelry and other consumer goods. And many retail dealers spend a substantial portion of their time in jail or prison. A Washington D.C. study estimated that a typical retail dealer's gross earnings at approximately $15,000.00 per year.

Drug Revenues

One of the problems for wholesale dealers is the fact that drug trafficking generates vast amounts of cash. At every point in the distribution chain drug transactions are conducted in cash. Illegal transactions involving cash do not leave a paper trail. However, the cash poses problems for drug traffickers because it is heavy and bulky. For example, one million dollars in $20 dollar bills weighs over 100 pounds. It is easily stolen because its ownership is not traceable and is easily exchanged. Cash is also not income producing until it is put into a bank or other investments are made with it.

Cash is also very conspicuous and easily detectable because of its bulk. For example, in 1990, the U.S. Customs Service announced that it had seized $22 million dollars in proceeds from drug sales in one seizure. The cash weighed about 3,000 pounds. In addition to being bulky, cash used in drug transactions often comes in contact with the drugs, thus making the cash detectable to drug sniffing dogs used by law enforcement and to forensic analysis.

To combat this problem cash transactions since 1970 in the amount of $10,000.00 or more must be reported to the Internal Revenue Service. This act also required that persons transmitting more than $10,000.00 across U.S. borders file a report with U.S. Custom Services. Therefore, illegitimate drug traffickers find it difficult to use legitimate financial systems without revealing their ownership of the cash. Subsequently, they resort to money laundering.

Money laundering is the concealment of income and the conversion of other assets in order to disguise its illegal source or use. At the most basic level money laundering involves three steps.

A. Placement—Physically getting the cash into the financial system including the conversion of the cash into other types of negotiable instruments such as money orders and cashiers checks.

B. The layering — Separating the proceeds of the source through layers of transactions such as wire transfers.

C. Integration — Providing an apparent legitimate explanation for the illicit proceeds.

More complex money laundering schemes involve multiple transactions with foreign banks and a variety of instruments. While money laundering is not new, since it has previously been used by tax evaders and corporations setting up slush funds for bribes and kick backs, it has grown to new heights of importance in combatting drug traffic.

Legitimate businesses are often used to launder illegal drug money. Businesses offer a cover for the introduction of cash into the legal financial system. Launderers often buy businesses such as bars, restaurants, entertainment establishments, jewelry stores and grocery stores that transact much of their business in cash. For example, the

La Mina, The Mine, reportedly laundered $1.2 billion for the Colombian cartels over a 2-year period

Currency from selling cocaine was packed in boxes labeled jewelry and sent by armored car to Ropex, a jewelry maker in Los Angeles.

↓

The cash was counted and deposited in banks that filed the CTRs, but few suspicions were raised because the gold business is based on cash.

↓

Ropex then wire transferred the money to New York banks in payment for fictitious gold purchased from Ronel, allegedly a gold bullion business.

↓

Ronel shipped Ropex bars of lead painted gold to complete the fake transaction. Ropex used the alleged sale of this gold to other jewelry businesses to cover further currency conversions.

↓

Ronel then transferred the funds from American banks to South American banks where the Colombian cartel could gain access to them.

Source: "Getting banks to just say 'no'," *Business Week*, April 17, 1989, 17 and Maggie Mahar, "Dirty Money: It triggers a bold new attack in the war on drugs," *Barron's*, June 1989, 69(26):6-38, 7.

Bandidos motorcycle gang invested in a string of after hours night clubs in Arkansas that laundered drug money and acted as fronts for the gang's drug and prostitution businesses. Receipts must be falsified to support the deposits of illegally generated cash. The legitimate business then pays taxes and avoids detection. Such businesses also provide legitimate employment opportunity for criminals.

There are three types of money laundering specialists:

1) The couriers who arrange for the transport and exchange of currency for monetary instruments.

2) The currency exchangers who receive cash as deposit in one country's currency and issue monetary instruments such as money orders in another country's currency.

3) The white collar professionals including lawyers, accountants, stockbrokers who provide financial services ranging from investment counseling to the incorporation of dummy businesses.

It is interesting to note that most people arrested for money laundering by the DEA did not have prior criminal records.

DRUG CONTROL

Historically, drug control efforts have been aimed at both the supply of and the demand for drugs. The supply reduction programs were aimed to lower drug use by making drugs more expensive and more difficult to obtain whether for the casual user or the addicts. They have also focused on limiting the availability of illegal drugs within the U.S. through the eradication of crops, disrupting smuggling routes into the country, and the interdiction or seizing of drugs at our border and in our territorial waters.

A Comprehensive Approach

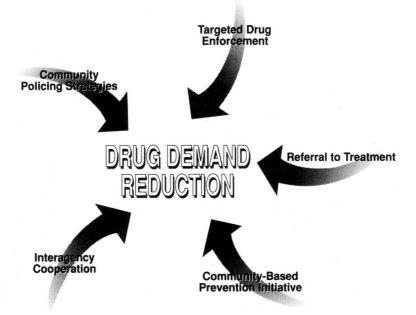

The demand reduction programs have been directly aimed at lower drug use by changing the behavior of current and potential drug users and by focusing on reducing the consumption of drugs through education about the consequences of illegal drug use and drug abuse treatment. These programs are designed to avert the onset of drug use and to treat people who are addicted to or dependent on drugs.

The criminal justice programs influence demand as well as supply; while prevention education efforts reduce supply as well as demand. For example, when the police make it difficult for drug users to find a seller, users, particularly casual users, cannot satisfy their demand for drugs. Also when users successfully end drug use because the criminal justice system required them to seek and complete a treatment program, the demand is reduced. When prevention programs are successful at preventing the onset of use, the future market of illegal drug businesses is effected since there is one less potential purchaser making drug dealing less profitable and therefore, less appealing.

Local Law Enforcement Strategies Against Drugs

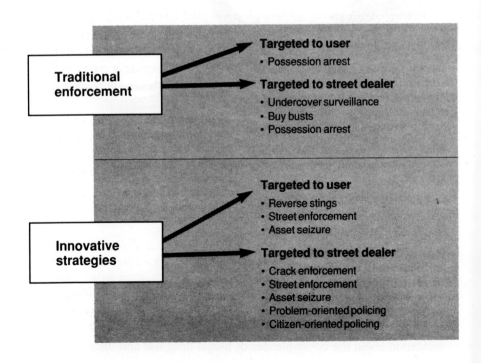

Legislation and national strategies have tended to blur the supply-demand dichotomy. For example, laws that punish drug use serve educational and prevention ends by shaping public opinion as to the dangers of drug use, thus diminishing its demand. Recent national drug control strategies have merged supply and demand efforts at the community level forging partnerships of educators, law enforcement officials and health treatment providers.

Drug Testing

Researchers have concluded that drug testing during the Vietnam War could have been a deterrent to using drugs at least when detection was linked to a sanction. Accordingly, when the Department of Defense began testing troops returning from Vietnam about five percent of the tests were confirmed as positive even though the troops knew that they would be tested and that a positive test would delay their departure for home. This rate dropped to two percent at the end of six months of testing.

Defendants and other drug abusers may be tested for drug use at all stages in the criminal justice process— arrest, incarceration, and supervised release such as probation or parole. The purpose of testing is to reduce criminal behavior by detecting current drug users and deterring their drug use. Many jurisdictions test offenders for drugs at one or more stages in the criminal justice process.

Drug testing in the workplace is also popular. In many cases, transportation workers and armed security guards are frequently tested as they pose a hazard or threat to the public if drug impaired. Secondary goals of workplace testing include reducing drug users' illegal activities, identifying drug users and referring them to treatment, and fostering public trust. A 1988 Gallop survey found that 54 percent of American corporations conducted drug testing.

As of 1991, 11 states had laws regulating the confidentiality and accuracy of workplace drug testing programs. Seven states regulate who can be tested and under what circumstances, and 14 more states have introduced legislation of which most regulate testing procedures but not the circumstances under which employers may require testing.

Criminal justice employees are generally subject to drug testing to insure public safety and public confidence. Police administrators give two central reasons for testing officers for drugs: the need to maintain public trust in the integrity and the professionalism of their department and concerns about public safety. Prison administrators cite public concerns about drug use generally as well as problems with contraband and work performance to justify drug testing of prison employees. An increasing number of police agencies and prison systems now test their employees and/or applicants, but most administrators do not believe that drug use among their officers is a major problem.

A 1990 survey of state and local police agencies found that 29 percent of local police agencies had policies authorizing the testing of applicants; 16 percent authorized testing of regular field officers; and 14 percent authorized testing of officers in drug related positions.

Local jurisdictions of more than 250,000 are more likely to have policies authorizing drug testing than the smaller jurisdictions. In state and local police agencies, applicants for employment are more likely to be tested under a mandatory program while sworn officers are usually tested only when suspected of drug use.[4]

A recent survey of state prison systems found that prison systems were more likely to test employees than applicants, usually testing only those suspected of drug use. Several states, like Georgia, limit its random testing program to only maximum security prisons.[5]

In the federal government, drug testing is a part of the Drug Free Federal Workplace Program that aims to improve the productivity and the safety of the federal workplace and to maintain public confidence in federal public employees.[6]

MODEL DRUG TESTING POLICY

(International Association of Chiefs of Police)

The International Association of Chiefs of Police (IACP) has developed a model drug testing policy. The policy recommends:

— The testing of all applicants for drugs and narcotics use.

— Testing present employees who are having performance difficulties or other indications of a potential drug problem.

— Testing employees when involved in the use of excessive force, suffer or cause on-duty injury.

— Routine testing of all employees assigned to "high-risk" assignments such as narcotics and vice. [7]

Legality of Drug Testing

The courts have ruled that drug testing implicates the Fourth Amendment protection against unreasonable searches and seizures. The courts have concluded that urine testing by the government for a criminal or non-criminal proceeding impinges upon the reasonable expectations of privacy protected by the Fourth Amendment and is therefore a search. This right of privacy covers the collection of the sample and the personal information which results from the testing of one's bodily fluids. Each of these steps in the process constitutes a search and seizure. Therefore, agencies may test if they can show that performing such tests and the procedures used in their performance are constitutionally reasonable. [8]

In the decisions on the reasonableness of the workplace testing programs, courts have tended implicitly or explicitly to apply a balancing test that weighs the employer's interest in drug testing against the employee's right and protection of privacy. The U.S. Supreme Court and other courts have used the law enforcement justification as a special form of safety justification to uphold the testing of law enforcement officers who carry firearms. This justification is stronger when the officers are involved in drug interdiction. Because courts balance employee versus employer interest on a case-by-case basis, mandatory employee testing is still evolving.

In two recent decisions reported in 1989, the U.S. Supreme Court upheld post-accident-testing of railroad employees after major train accidents and/or incidents and of the U.S. Customs employees seeking transfer or promotion to sensitive jobs directly involved in drug interdiction or requiring the carrying of firearms. An issue that has divided lower courts is whether public employee drug testing was ever permissible without individualized suspicion of drug use or impairment. The rulings have made clear that such suspicion is not always required at least in those cases where there is a compelling government interest in safety.

There appears to be different rights protecting different categories of employees in the workplace. For example, employees of federal, state and local governments are protected by the U.S. Constitution and/or state constitution which constrain government actions. Thus, government workers are protected against unreasonable search and seizures by the Fourth Amendment to the Constitution and by the due process clause of the Fourteenth Amendment. Private sector employees are subject to testing by government regulations and have the same constitutional protection as government workers. For example, agencies of the U.S. Department of Transportation that regulate private sector operations have mandated the testing of truck drivers, railroad employees, airline flight crews and mechanics and other transportation workers.

Federal Spending on the Drug Problem

State and local assistance from the U.S. government has increased by 37 times since 1981. In 1981, federal assistance to states and local governments totaled approximately $28 million. In 1991, that total reached approximately $1.016 billion. Additionally, state and local justice systems spend in excess of $5 billion per year to combat drug use. It is estimated that $5 billion of correctional system costs for handling drug offenders constitutes 60 percent of the budget used by state and local justice systems for the control of illegal drugs. To diagnose, treat and rehabilitate illegal drug users costs more than $2.5 billion per year. Research has established that illegal drug users are more prone than non-drug users to occupational accidents. A recent workplace study found that illegal drug users were 3.6 times more likely to be in an accident and five times more likely than their drug-free counterpart to file a workers compensation claim. A similar study found that workers who use cocaine were 1.5 times more likely to have had an accident, nearly twice as likely to be injured, and more than twice as likely to be absent from work for significant periods of time.

Asset Forfeitures

One method law enforcement officials have used to try and suppress illegal drug traffic is the taking away of the primary motivation for selling drugs — profit. This is done in the form of asset forfeiture. Forfeiture is a loss ownership of property derived from or used in criminal activity that has been seized by the government. Forfeiture of assets aims not only at reducing the profitability of illegal activities but of permanently curtailing the financial ability of criminal organizations to control illegal operations. There are two types of forfeitures — civil and criminal.

Civil forfeiture is a proceeding against property used in criminal activity. This was originally authorized by the First Congress of the United States allowing the forfeiture of vessels smuggling contraband into the U. S. Property subject to civil forfeiture. It often includes vehicles used to transport contraband, equipment used to manufacture illegal drugs, cash used in illicit transactions and property used or purchased with the proceeds of the crime. Under civil forfeiture, the government is required to notify registered owners and post notice of the proceedings so that any party who has an interest in the property may contest the forfeiture. If no claims are made on the property, it is automatically forfeited. If a claim is made on the property, the case is heard in civil court. No finding of guilt is required to forfeit the property.

Criminal forfeiture takes place as a part of the criminal action against the defendant accused of racketeering, drug trafficking or money laundering. The forfeiture is a sanction imposed upon conviction that requires the defendant to forfeit various property rights and interest in relation to the violation. Criminal forfeiture was first authorized in 1970 under the Racketeers Influence and Corrupt Organization Statutes (RICO).

Most state forfeiture procedures appear in control substance or RICO laws. Nine states permit administrative forfeitures and all but one state has provisions for civil forfeitures; eight states permit criminal forfeitures.

Originally, most forfeiture provisions were aimed to cover the seizure of contraband or modes of transporting or facilitating the distribution of such material. Common provisions permit seizure of conveyances such as airplanes, boats or cars, raw material products and equipment used in manufacturing, trafficking or cultivation of illegal drugs and drug paraphernalia. The type of property that may be forfeited has been expanded since 1970 to include assets derived from criminal activity such as cash, securities, negotiable instruments, and real property.

What are the differences between civil and criminal forfeiture procedures?

Civil procedures	Criminal procedures
• assets can be seized without arrest or conviction	• assets can be seized only after arrest and, in most States, conviction
• hearsay evidence can be used, eliminating the need to identify confidential informants and undercover agents	• government must prove that owner's assets are related to drug trafficking or other criminal activities
• the government's initial burden of proof is "probable cause;" the ultimate burden of proof is "preponderence of the evidence"	• hearsay evidence cannot be used
	• forfeiture requires a criminal conviction (a finding of guilt "beyond a reasonable doubt")

Based on a recent U.S. Supreme Court ruling, fees paid to attorneys for representation in criminal cases are subject to forfeiture if they were paid with illegal drug money. In a Supreme Court case, a law firm represented a defendant who was eventually convicted of running a multi-million dollar marijuana operation and sentenced to 17 years in prison. The government established at a civil trial that he paid his legal fees with illegal drug proceedings and secured their forfeiture. The Supreme Court has ruled that while a defendant has a right to counsel, she or he has no right to hire the attorney of his choice with illegal drug proceeds. Lawyers are exempt from prosecution under the new money laundering rules when they accept a fee of laundered drug money to represent a criminal defendant.

In 1990, the DEA seized assets valued at more that $1 billion. Not all property that is seized is eventually forfeited. Seized property may not be forfeited because the suspected drug criminal may not have owned the property that is seized, the relationship of the property to illegal drug proceeds cannot be proven, or innocent parties may have a partial interest in the property.

The disposition of the forfeited property is controlled by state and federal law. In many cases, the seizing agency may use the assets once they have been declared forfeited by a court.

According to a recent study, 17 states distribute the proceeds of drug forfeiture to drug law enforcement, and 10 states require that a certain portion of the forfeiture go into drug treatment and education programs. Many states distribute the proceeds to the general accounts.

Drug Arrests

Uniform Crime Reports estimate that state and local agencies made almost 1.1 million arrests of drug use violators in 1990. The DEA, which makes most of the federal drug arrests, made approximately 22,000 arrests in fiscal year 1990. Two-thirds of the drug abuse violations arrests by state and local agencies were for possession of drugs, 34 percent were for heroin or cocaine possession and 24 percent for marijuana possession. While possession is the most prevalent drug arrest offense, the share of arrests for the manufacture and sale of drugs has been increasing since 1980. Now, it appears that drug arrests make up 8% of all state and local arrests.

In Federal prisons, the rising proportion of offenders committed for drug offenses exceeded 50% in 1990

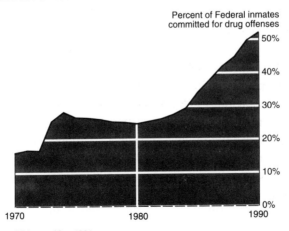

Percent of Federal inmates
committed for drug offenses

Source: Bureau of Prisons, May 1991.

In State prisons, the proportion of inmates admitted for drug offenses has increased

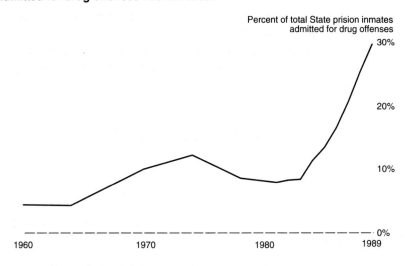

Percent of total State prision inmates admitted for drug offenses

30%

20%

10%

0%

1960   1970   1980   1989

Source: BJS, *Prisoners in 1991,* Bulletin, May 1992, table11.

Drug Treatment Programs

Drug treatment programs for offenders typically include individual counseling, group counseling, urine testing and referral to a support group. Other treatments or services may include therapeutic communities, drug education, behavior modification and even acupuncture. Services intended to enhance an offenders ability to remain drug free may also be provided. These services could include academic education, job training, job placement, employment interviewing, and job search skills training.

The actual content of treatment programs varies with the overall treatment philosophy and intensity. Intensity refers to the amount of time a person spends in a program activity. A program in which a person spends eight hours a week for six months, for example, will likely include a broader range of interventions and/or more detailed involvement in activities than one in which a person spends four hours a week for six months.

Many drug offenders are supervised in the community. Drug treatment is mandated for most drug using probationers and parolees.

Usually, offenders in the community who are in treatment programs are assigned to drug-free programs. Relatively few are sent to methadone maintenance programs or other programs that involve pharmacological treatment.[9]

It is difficult to conduct comprehensive treatment programs in local jails because most inmates are not incarcerated for more than three months.

DISCUSSION QUESTIONS

1. What programs should be used to control drug abuse?

2. What are the arguments in favor of legalizing drugs? Against legalizing drugs?

3. What new laws are needed to combat drug abuse?

ENDNOTES

[1] The majority of material from this chapter was taken from a December, 1992 report by the Bureau of Justice Statistics entitled, "Drugs, Crime and The Justice System."

[2] National Institute on Drug Abuse, *National Survey on Drug Abuse: Population Estimates*, "National Institute on Drug Abuse, (Washington D.C.: Government Printing Office, 1991).

[3] Bureau of International Narcotics Matters, U.S. Department of State, *International Narcotics Control Strategy Report*, (Washington D.C.: Government Printing Office, March, 1992).

[4] Barbara A. Manili, Edward F. Connors, and Darrel W. Stephens, "Police Drug Testing," *NIJ Research in Action*, NIJ-105191, (May, 1987).

[5] Randall Guynes and Osa Coffey, "Employee Drug-testing in Prison Systems," *NIJ Research in Action*, NCJ-112824, (August, 1988).

[6] Executive Order 12564, "Drug Free Federal Workplace," (September 17, 1986).

[7] J. Thomas McEwen, Barbara Manili, and Edward Connors (National Institute of Law Enforcement and Criminal Justice Research Project), "Employee Drug Testing Policies in Police Departments: A Summary Report," (Washington D.C.: Government Printing Office, October 1986).

[8] *National Treasury Employees' Union v. Von Raab*, 489 U.S. 656 (1989): *Skinner v. Railway Labor Executive's Association*, 489 U.S. 602 (1989).

[9] Marjorie Marlette, "Drug Treatment Programs," *Corrections Compendium*, (August, 1990): p.15.

OUR CRIMINAL JUSTICE SYSTEM — TODAY AND TOMORROW

I am not afraid of tomorrow, for I have seen yesterday and I love today.

—William Allen White

TODAY IN CRIMINAL JUSTICE

The previous chapters of this book have discussed the entire criminal justice system from the initial arrest to final disposition. In this section, the present state of our system is summarized — it is not a flattering report. This, however, does not mean that our criminal justice system is failing. By and large we tend to blame the criminal justice system for the broad failures of our society. However, the criminal justice system was not designed to be the *primary* peacekeeper of our society. The system is designed to a *assist* citizens as the primary crime fighters. Crime fighting, as a citizen involvement activity, is accomplished through reporting crime, witnessing, testifying, and upholding an intolerance of crime.

Present Status

Crime Rates — Although crime rates have stabilized in recent years, there is still an enormous amount of crime in our society. In addition, the degree of violence in our society is much too great.

Caseloads — Our caseloads in the courts have continued to climb. This results in more pressure being placed on prosecutors to plea bargain, thus limiting the number of cases being tried in court.

Crime-fighters — Adding more police is not the simple solution to reducing crime as was once thought. Unfortunately, it is impossible to measure the amount of criminal activity **not** taking place due solely to the presence of police. However, the effect of actually seeing a law enforcement officer makes the public feel safer by reaffirming that the "law" is close by. The police have been effective in assisting communities in establishing community based programs to reduce crime and as fear-reduction agents. The concept of police as crime fighters is largely a fictional role.

Increased Inmate Populations — The states are now being "tougher" on criminal sentences and, therefore, sending more people to prison and jail. The number of persons imprisoned in the United States has skyrocketed in recent years resulting in severe pressure on the corrections system. We must either spend an increasingly larger portion of our tax dollars on new facilities or increase alternative sentencing.

Conservative Supreme Court — Our U.S. Supreme Court has become more conservative in the past two decades, especially in the areas of search and seizures.

Limits on Discretion — Because of real or perceived injustices in the past which are attributed to the discretionary aspects of criminal justice, movement in the direction of limiting the discretion of law enforcement and judicial officers started in the 1990s and will probably continue in the future. The limitations include requiring police officers to justify decisions regarding the formal or informal handling of criminal code violations. For example, for many years police officers had discretion regarding the arresting of persons suspected of driving under the influence. Presently, many police departments require officers to arrest all individuals suspected of driving under the influence. In addition, judges are being restricted by the use of mandatory sentencing guidelines and minimum sentence requirements for certain crimes.

SUMMARY OF FUTURE TRENDS

The goal in this section is not to explain our present system, but rather to set the stage for *change*. To be successful in the future, we need to constantly ask ourselves the question: Why not? Instead of looking for reasons why new systems, methods, or procedures won't work, we should ask: How can we make it work? Too often governmental agencies exist for many years unimpeded by progress. In order to develop and maintain an effective criminal justice system, we need to look at not only how it was done in the past, but consider how we can do it *better* in the future. Our present system was developed for a rural America. Yet, we are no longer a rural nation and have not been for many years. As noted by the reading included in this chapter, the future will bring change for all of society.

Our use of technology in law enforcement has increased substantially since 1970 when then-Governor Ronald Reagan inaugurated the California Law Enforcement Telecommunications System (CLETS). CLETS now uses cellular communications, with automatic switching to state department of motor vehicles and FBI databases, with an inquiry response time of approximately 10 seconds. In 1970, CLETS handled about 100,000 messages daily. In 1993, there were over one million messages per day with over 22,000 hookups into the system. One can only imagine what the next few years will bring with the acceleration of our communications technology.

The 1990s will be remembered as the age of computers. Not only have computers completely changed our lives, but they have also had a significant impact on our criminal justice system. With the use of computerized equipment, we are now electronically monitoring persons under house arrest who would otherwise be adding to the overcrowding of our jails. In addition, there has been revolutions in the police records and communication systems, staff training, weaponry, and criminal investigation and tracking, etc.

911 System

The police receive a call on "911." A hysterical voice pleads for an ambulance. The caller states that her baby is having trouble breathing and then hangs up without giving her address. When the 911 system was first introduced to this country, this was a common problem. Today, the computer *enhanced 911* systems employ computer software to speed call tracing, contact emergency crews, dispatch vehicles, or view information such as the physical disabilities of the caller or the presence of hazardous material.

The newer generations of the *enhanced 911* system are working to improve emergency response. A problem like helping emergency crews physically locate people, especially in rural areas, is being solved by interfacing Geographic Information Systems (GIS).[1] GIS technology has the ability to relate database attributes such as chemicals stored on a site with mapped locations. When operators enter an address or use a "mouse" or "wand" to pick a location on a map automatically brought up on their computer screen, they can then view the area and any attributes attached to the area.

Today, when calls come in on 911, operators can use the computerized maps to instantly show the origin of the call. The map also displays other information regarding the location, such as hazards, location of fire hydrants, construction in progress, etc. When a call that requires police assistance is received, the computer can tag the nearest available patrol car and provide the best travel route for the car. Other uses of GIS mapping are currently being explored. For example, if there is a series of breaking-and-entering in a common area, the GIS can correlate times and methods of operations and be mapped.

The maps are updated daily. Along with this, local telephone companies submit daily changes in telephone installation. These changes, along with many others, are then used to constantly upgrade these maps. Similarly, when someone purchases or leases property, the record automatically becomes a part of the 911 system.

Policing

The future of policing will largely be controlled by three elements: funding, personnel and computer based technology.

Funding will be paramount. Without money, agencies will be unable to progress and keep pace with the community's needs. Upgrading equipment and facilities along with professionalizing staff will be secondary to maintaining skeleton operations with shrinking funds. Already we see the beginnings of this throughout our nation. As population centers expand and jurisdictional realignment takes place we choose not to allocate the funds needed to effectively police these newly developed areas. Yet, the general public and politicians alike decry the slow response of law enforcement, the mailing in of complaints versus having an officer come out and "take" a complaint, the constricting of targeted offenses on which agencies center their goals, etc. For the most part, law enforcement is shackled by constant or declining budgets while the requests for services increase.

As our population changes from a large Caucasian majority to a more ethnically diverse society, the work force in the criminal justice field should do the same. Perhaps this will help sensitize law enforcement to various cultural groups. The blending of more varied ethnicity into our police force will correspond with the increase of minimum educational requirements for officers. Therefore, not only will we develop into a police force with more compassion and understanding of cultures other than one's own but also a police force of more educated officers.

Computerization will lead to the most remarkable transformation of law enforcement. As agencies develop into highly sophisticated and technologically advanced crime fighting forces, much will change. For example, traffic infractions will be handled by computer. A speeding motorist "caught on laser" will be sent his/her ticket via mail with accompanying photographs of the vehicle and supporting data. The fine will be mailed-in and a computer will dispense with the case.

Communications will be impacted by computers through link-ups between databases containing both personal and criminal records. Access to records will be virtually instantaneous with patrol units becoming interactive through their on-board computer systems. "Hard" copies will be eliminated as the system develops into a paperless information net. Current documents will be "imaged" into the system. First officers on the scene will be able to provide computer assembled life-like suspect composites that will then be broadcast throughout the area to all agencies and patrol units, thus enhancing the ability to apprehend suspects quickly. Criminal tracking will become highly advanced with both the U.S and international law enforcement benefiting from the free flow of paperless information.

Call response can be greatly enhanced. For example, the Menlo Park Police Department now employs sophisticated earthquake technology to locate and verify gunshots reported through the local 911 system. Officers are then able to respond quickly to the specific location instead of having to canvas the area to determine the actual site of the shots.

Computerized satellite technology enhances law enforcement's ability to respond and reconnoiter events such as the L.A. riots and the Branch Davidian's standoff in Waco, Texas. Through information gleaned from such technology, agencies are capable of preparing engagement strategies and determining the overall scope of a situation.

In-service training will use the concept of distance learning as an alternative to sending people to distant locations to attend conferences and workshops. **Distance learning** refers to the delivery of educational programs by way of interactive television hook-ups. Interactive refers to the ability of viewers in distance locations to interact with presenters rather than being passive television viewers (i.e., much like a typical seminar held today, only the seminar leader will "present" via satellite link). The cost savings should be quite significant in saving worker hours and travel expenses. No longer will agencies lose an officer while they attend a conference and have to juggle personnel to fill-in; an entire shift will be able to attend a training seminar at their own facility.

Within the next 10 to 25 years, computer-based training will become the standard with a college education as a minimum entry level requirement. With newer technology will come an increase in constitutional challenges ranging from "invasion of privacy" issues to unlawful search and seizure. Traditional crime will escalate in relation to the increased disparity between the "haves" and the "have nots" of our society. Police administration will assume a more goal-oriented style of proactive leadership.

In the long term, law enforcement will achieve a professional status. This will be due, in part, to the higher educated entry level officer coupled with the mandatory continuing education required for advancement. High technology crime will become more complex. Our laws will need revising in order to address these new crimes. Law enforcement and apprehension will require more specialized training. Medical break-throughs will enable us to not only identify, but to also "treat" violence.

Adjudication

Public attitudes towards the efficiencies and fairness of our courts are also being measured. Citizen groups are becoming more aggressive in their watch over court processes — usually focusing on the trial courts with a general emphasis on more public access to what goes on in court (i.e., plea bargaining, fairness issues, witness and juror treatment, etc.) Judges have also come under great scrutiny. Debate over the amount of time a judge may spend on the bench and discretion in sentencing are prevalent. Currently, more and better research and evaluation into the courts is taking place. The effect of all this will be a streamlined process with the challenge of balancing efficiency with justice.

Court reform will ultimately lead to improvement of the court process. Unification of jurisdictions along with parallel administrative issues should provide economies of scale and the hope of a more efficient handling of cases and their respective flow through the courts. The formation of a centralized judicial authority should eliminate jurisdictional and procedural disputes.

Sentencing

Alternative forms of sentencing will continue to be an innovative way to impose punishment on offenders. Not only do the decreased costs of these types of sanctions merit further use, but the idea of warehousing non-violent offenders has proven to be uneconomical and inappropriate. Imposing fines similar to those used in the European systems, coupled with split sentencing, community service and shock incarcerations will be the mainstay in dealing with the first time offender, juveniles and non-violent criminals. However, once offenders either fail to respond to alternative sentencing or continue to commit crimes, prison sentences will be imposed much as they have been in the past.

Probation and Parole

Parole and probation reform will parallel the dynamic changes foreseen in alternative sentencing. Currently, both parole and probation are failing due to the enormous caseloads levied on very few professionals. Probation is decreasing as a result of demand from the public for criminals to be punished first and rehabilitated second. Probation has lost most of its "punishment" element and is now perceived by many as the criminal "getting off the hook."

Shock probation and parole will continue to grow in popularity. Again, reserved for the non-violent offender, this form of rehabilitation will prove effective, less costly and more corrective. As more research is undertaken and the results reviewed, the general conclusion today is that a "little taste of prison" can go a long way toward curtailing any future criminal activity.

The issue of caseloads will be the most difficult to correct. Here again, because of the scarcity of funding, adding personnel seems remote. The future seems to lie in technology. With advances and applications to house arrest and the like, probation and parole officers might eventually be capable of "tracking" their clients without physically making contact. Time and date stamped call-ins from clients and other similar forms of monitoring will become available. Those clients who actively seek to make their rehabilitation into society fruitful will be electronically screened and officers will be able to verify their pattern of achievement through computer readouts. Only cursory in-person follow-up will be necessary. By using a screening process such as this, officers will then be able to more fully concentrate on those clients who resist or are having difficulty integrating back into society. With the use of monitoring devices these same clients will also show certain patterns so that individualized corrective action can be applied.

Unfortunately, there is no quick fix for the current situation and a much more complicated process must be undertaken. Probation and parole philosophy must be re-evaluated and its mission restated to comply with current goals of our society. Community supervision, risk tolerance, accountability, process methodology clarification and public approval must be taken into consideration. New guidelines for the successful integration of clients back into society, coupled with adequate public safeguards, must be developed.

Jails and Prisons

With the implementations of alternative sentencing and modernization of parole and probation, our jail and prison systems will change. Overcrowding will be an issue for years to come, but a more fundamental change will be surfacing in the new way we employ these facilities.

As more non-violent criminals are moved out of long-term incarceration, jails and minimum security prisons will become centered around shock programs and pretrial/presentencing holding facilities. Medium and high security prisons will continue to be reserved for violent and long-term offenders. New facilities, such as the California prison at Pelican Bay, will become our maximum security prisons designed for those offenders who prove to be too violent for high security prisons and pose an increased risk to officers and other prisoners alike.

By further dividing and separating the classes of offenders so as not to mix non-like criminals, it is the hope of the system to make security more effective and efficient and allow offenders to rehabilitate more successfully. In essence, non-violent offenders will be located at different facilities than violent offenders.

Juveniles

The "coddling" of juvenile violent offenders will continue to be an area of great debate. As more and more juveniles under the age of majority and below that subjective "responsible for their actions" line (which currently rests at a about 15 years of age) commit more violent crimes, we'll continue to see 14, 12, and 10 year old children held accountable for heinous acts. Many dollars will continue to be spent on this issue, but the question remains if any concrete progress is really being made in dealing with these "hardened" juveniles.

The use of shock incarceration and "boot camp" type facilities will probably come to the forefront for juveniles. These alternatives provide the necessary elements of punishment, discipline, self-esteem improvement, education, safety for the public and ultimately rehabilitation back into a productive member of society. With juveniles, we seldom ever accept the punishment of "locking them up and throwing away the key." Unfortunately, some cases will continue to so offend society that public safety is the only issue sought and; therefore, life imprisonment will begin at a very early age.

Experts tend to agree that the way to prevent juvenile delinquency is through improved family life and education. Here again, these societal issues are not capable of being dealt with through the criminal justice system. Hence, until we, as a society, deal with gangs, drugs, lack of education, limited job potentials, minimal or nonexistent family environments, etc., the system can only deal with the symptoms of a greater disease. Currently juvenile delinquents, for the most part, are not thought of as being criminals only recalcitrant youth; that opinion is not likely to change.

Professionalization of Personnel

The term "profession" is an abstract ideal occupational model.[2] To be considered a profession is an ideal status for which occupational groups, including public safety officers, strive. The concept of striving toward "professionalism" refers to: (1) the extent to which the focus of specialization is occupational as opposed to individual or organizational, (2) the extent to which the occupation stresses the process by which the means (tactics) and the ends (goals) are achieved, and (3) the extent to which there is a body of codified knowledge which can be transmitted abstractly. [3]

The status of professionalism includes autonomy, professional authority, and the power to determine the character and curriculum of the educational process. For example, many consider a professional law enforcement or corrections agency as one in which management, efficiency and rationality are emphasized and politics is excluded.

So often, the problem with professionalism is that it has come to mean insulation from outsiders with excessive attention to personal prestige and the creation of a special language understood only by members of that profession.[4] If we are to professionalize public safety officers, we need to overcome these problems. In addition, we need to develop a clear criteria as to what will be considered performance indicators for the officers and eliminate the confusion over the nature of the functions of our public safety officers.

Accreditation

Four law enforcement associations: International Association of Chiefs of Police (IACP), National Organization of Black Law Enforcement Executives (NOBLE), National Sheriffs' Association (NSA), and Police Executive Research Forum (PERF) have combined to form the Commission on Accreditation for Law Enforcement Agencies (CALEA). The purpose of this commission is to establish and administer an accreditation process for law enforcement agencies. Accreditation is considered as one method to professionalize the police and improve police services.

Presently, CALEA has researched, developed and adopted over 900 standards. The standards are grouped into 48 categories. Standards are also classified as either mandatory or non-mandatory standards. The standards cover five major subject areas: (1) the role, responsibilities, and relationship with other departments; (2) organization, management, and administration; (3) law enforcement operations, operation support and traffic law enforcement; (4) prisoner and court-related services; and (5) auxiliary and technical services.[5]

Departments applying for accreditation must comply with the mandatory standards. Voluntary compliance with non-mandatory standards serves as evidence that a department is moving toward higher professionalism. The standards are designed to concentrate on desired results. The methods of obtaining the results are left to the individual departments. There is a four step accreditation process: application, application profile questionnaire, self-assessment, and final review by the commission.

Many police executives consider accreditation a costly, un-needed make-work scheme. One state police chiefs' association at an annual conference passed a strongly worded resolution against accreditation. Many executives contend that the accreditation program is a federally funded pie-in-the-sky project and that it is based on objectives born from naivete and is too ambitious.

The following three articles on the future of criminal justice are included for your review and discussion. They are presented as a means of sparking your imagination and enlightening you as to the present state of certain aspects of our society. They also afford insight into the social, political, and economic sledgehammers that will be pounding the system in the near-term.

EXHIBIT 18-1

THE FUTURE OF LAW ENFORCEMENT: DANGEROUS AND DIFFERENT

Alvin and Heidi Toffler

Before we begin, a question. Does anyone reading this think the years ahead are likely to be tranquil?

If so, quit reading, or prepare to disagree. For what follows contradicts the complacent views of straight-line trend spotters and polyanna politicians. It is based on the premise that we are moving into some of the most turbulent years in the history of this Nation.

If correct, we can expect this turbulence to put enormous new strains on our entire law enforcement and justice system. It will make law enforcement far more complex, dangerous, and different.

To understand why, it isn't necessary to replay familiar statistics on choked courts, overcrowded prisons, tight budgets, and all the other problems besetting the justice system today. Rather, the growing crisis in American law enforcement has to be seen in context. For it is only a small part of a much larger phenomenon.

America-A Nation of Change

The fact is that almost all the major systems on which our society depends-from the transportation system and the health system to the postal system and the education system-are in simultaneous crisis.

We are witnessing the massive breakdown of America as we knew it and the emergence of a strange, anew 21st-century America whose basic institutional structures have yet to be formed. The 1990s will either see a further deterioration of old systems and the social order that depends on them, or a serious effort to restructure America for the 21st century.

Either way, we are likely to put tremendous new pressures on people in their jobs, homes, and communities with results that will show up in tomorrow's crime statistics. Failure to prepare in advance for the turbulent 90's could produce a grave breakdown in public security.

America-As-We-Knew-It—the one we grew up in, the one we still remember from 1950s television or from those ads showing pert young bobby soxers sipping Coca Cola at the soda fountain—was an industrial America. It was the place that built the best cars, shipped the most steel, turned out the longest production runs of consumer products, and fitted everyone (more or less) into a nuclear family. It was basically a blue-collar America. It was "Smokestack America."

This "Smokestack America" has since been battered by the most accelerated technological revolution in history. Computers, satellites, space travel, fiber optics, fax machines, robots, bar coding, electronic data interchange, and expert systems are only the most obvious manifestations. All this has been combined with globalization of the economy, rising competition, and many social and cultural changes as well.

The "New America" emerging from these upheavals has an economy increasingly based on knowledge. When many of our grandfathers came to this country, speaking a foreign language and knowing nothing of American culture, their intelligence didn't count for much in the job market. What employers mostly wanted was muscle. Millions at the bottom of the pile were able to find work because they had muscle. They actually entered into the economy before they entered into the culture.

Today this is becoming impossible. More and more jobs presuppose skills, training, and education. As "muscle work" disappears, fewer openings remain for those on the bottom rung. A young person must now enter into the mainstream culture before he or she can enter into the legitimate economy. And millions don't. The results are clear in our inner cities.

It is simple-minded to blame crime on poverty. There are plenty of societies in which poverty does not produce crime. But it is equally witless to assume that millions of poor, jobless young people—not part of the work-world culture and bursting with energy and anger—are going to stay off the streets and join knitting clubs.

Fully 25 years ago, some futurists began forecasting massive dislocations, calling for radical changes in education, and trying to warn the country. Futurist analysis and forward thinking on the part of U.S. government agencies could have prevented at least some of today's problems. Unfortunately, these early warnings were ignored, and today's law enforcement agencies are desperately struggling to pick up the pieces.

Will the same thing happen in the '90s? Only worse? The systemic crisis facing America will not just affect ghetto kids. Then new complexity of everyday life (you need a manual to operate the simplest gadget) affects everyone, and the passing of "Smokestack America" has left millions of middle-class Americans stranded and disoriented. Expecting one kind of life, they find themselves plunged into another, frustrated and future-shocked.

Indeed, as early as 1970, we warned that the American nuclear family was about to be "fractured" — not because of permissiveness but because of radical changes in the work force, technology, communications, and economics. The subsequent collapse of the nuclear family and its replacement with a family system made up of many different models — two-career couples, childless couples, much married couples, etc. — has had a massive impact on law enforcement.

One of its consequences has been a frightening increase in the number of singles and loners in society and a loosening of all social bonds. Forced to be highly mobile, torn away from their root communities and families, and lacking support systems, more and more individuals are being freed from the social constraints that kept them on the straight and narrow. These individuals are multiplying, and that fact alone suggests further social turbulence in the years ahead.

We all know that law enforcement is society's second line of defense. Crime, drug abuse, and sociopathic behavior generally are first held in check by social disapproval—by family, neighbors, and co-workers. But in change-wracked America, people are less bonded to one another, so that social disapproval loses its power over them.

It is when social disapproval fails that law enforcement must take over. And until the "social glue" is restored to society, we can expect more, not less, violence in the streets, white-collar crime, rape and misery—and not just in the inner cities.

Impact of Technology

It is said that generals always try to fight their last war over again. This is what the French did in the 1930s when they built their immense and costly "Maginot Line."

French generals, steeped in trench-warfare thinking, paid little attention to the weapons of the future — air power, highly mobile land forces, blitzkrieg tactics. As a result, their guns were pointed in the wrong direction, and the Nazis swept across France in a few weeks.

The question facing law enforcement professionals is the same one that faced the French military: Is law enforcement in America still fighting today's wars with yesterday's weapons?

The high-speed technological revolution alone — a revolution that has barely begun — will introduce new weapons and methods for police and criminals alike. Already experimentation with electronic monitoring of parolees has begun, and the FBI is exploring expert systems to help solve crimes.

Science fiction writers and some futurists talk about a future in which drugs and electronic brain simulation can be used to control behavior 24 hours a day (an Orwellian prospect), or about undersea prisons and space prison colonies. In addition, breakthroughs in genetics, birth, technologies, bizarre new materials, software, and a thousand other fields will shake up our economy yet again, dislocate additional millions, and provide new opportunities for creative criminals.

Many of these will raise the deepest of legal, political, and moral issues. Is the theft of a frozen embryo kidnapping or mere burglary? What bio-monitoring technologies should be admitted as evidence? What new invasions of privacy will become technically possible? What are the consequences of such technologies for democracy and the unique American Bill of Rights? How must present criminal codes be changed to deal with previously unimaginable issues? Can the Constitution itself remain unchanged?

On the one hand, what makes America special is its profound commitment to individual freedom. On the other hand, when social disorder reaches intolerable levels, citizens begin to demand the most punitive, most intrusive, most anti-democratic measures.

Only by beginning now to analyze future technological and social changes systematically can law enforcement become anything more than a series of too-little, too-late crash programs. By thinking these matters through in advance—jointly with other agencies of government—law enforcement officials can begin to influence the social and political policies that would prevent, not merely suppress, crime.

Only by exploring long-range options can we begin to define the limits of governmental power and individual rights. Only by thinking ahead will our law enforcement system be able to protect both American society and its constitutional rights.

For law enforcement agencies and civil libertarians alike, dedicated to preserving not only order but also democracy, it is essential to step into the future now.

Social Change

Futurism, or long-range thinking, is not only a matter of technology. Even more important is a grasp of social changes bearing down the freeway toward us.

With the collapse or restructure of the major systems in society, we must also expect high levels of community conflict as power shifts dramatically away from old industries to new, from bureaucratic organizations to more flexible ones, from the uneducated to the educated, and potentially, from law-abiding citizens to those who would take advantage of widening cracks in the system. In short, law enforcement professionals starting out now face approximately 25 years of a society that is confused, rent with conflict, struggling to find a new place in the world, and bombarded by destabilizing technological changes and economic swings.

What Lies Ahead

No one knows the future. No crystal ball can provide firm answers. Forget straightline trend extrapolation and the people who peddle it. Trends are usually spotted when they are already half over. Trends top out or convert into something radically different if they continue long enough. They do not provide any explanation of why anything is happening. They typically do not reveal interrelations. More importantly, in periods of structural upheaval, trends are canceled, reversed, turned upside down, and twisted into totally new patterns. That is the definition of an upheaval.

But the fact that no one can be sure of the future, and that simplistic trend projection doesn't work, shouldn't leave us helpless. First, there are many other techniques to help us model change. Second, "prediction" isn't what futurism is all about, in any case.

Futurists cannot hit the bull's eye all the time. But far more important than trying to forecast, they can help us to imagine more possible scenarios and alternative tomorrows. This widening of our imagination is crucial to survival in a period of accelerated, destablizing change. It smartens our decision making in the here and now.

To illustrate the point, 25 years ago, in an article in which we coined the term "future shock," we called for more attention to be focused on the future, more long-range thinking. Ten years ago, we sat in the home of a former Japanese prime minister and were lectured by two top Japanese industrialists, who warned that American industry would suffer badly in the competitive battles ahead if its managers continued to bury their heads in the present. Today, this theme has become common among American mangers, and Uncle Sam, himself, is beginning to echo it.

Specifically, Richard Darman, the President's Budget Director, has urged a shift in the national attitude toward the future. Attacking what he calls "now-nowism," Darman defined that disease as "our collective short-sightedness, our obsession with the here and now, our reluctance to adequately address the future."

Therefore, we believe that it is necessary for every arm of law enforcement, federal, state, and local alike, to assign some of their best thinkers to the task of probing the future, and to plug their findings into decision making at every level—including at the very top.

When agencies begin to focus on the future, some questions naturally arise. What should a community's law enforcement budget be? How should law enforcement personnel be trained? What skills will be needed? What new technologies will they face and need? What new forms or organization will have to be created? How should forces be deployed? What provisions should be made for continually updating missions?

Practical questions such as these can't be answered intelligently if an agency's total attention is consumed by the present — no matter how hard it is pressed — if, in other words, it too is guilty of "now-nowism."

A Final Thought

It is the proud function of law enforcement to help guarantee the survival of the same democratic system that imposes limits on its actions. These very limits make our system of justice better than that of some banana republic characterized by death squads, terrorists, and narco-nabobs.

To guarantee democracy's future in the dangerous decades to come, all the agencies that form part of the American justice system need to rethink their assumptions about tomorrow and to pool their findings. They must not only know that they can never get it "right" but also realize that the very act of asking the right questions, or shaking people out of their mental lethargy, is essential to survival.

[Reprinted from the *FBI Law Enforcement Bulletin*, January 1990, pp.7-12.]

EXHIBIT 18-2

THE CHANGING FACE OF AMERICA

Robert C. Trojanowicz and David L. Carter

In the next century America's population will change considerably. According to demographers, in less than 100 years, we can expect white dominance of the United States to end, as the growing number of blacks, Hispanics, and Asians together become the new majority.

As we approach the 21st century, we already see white America growing grayer. In the past decade, there has been an estimated 23-percent increase in the number of Americans 65 and older. In fact, more people of retirement age live in the Unite States now than there were people alive in this country during the Civil War.

But while the average age of all Americans is now 32, the average age of blacks is 27; Hispanics 23. By 2010 more than one-third of all American children will be black, Hispanic, or Asian.

These dramatic changes in the overall make-up of American society have profound implications for law enforcement, particularly because many of the legal and illegal immigrants flooding into this country are of different races, ethnic groups, religions, and cultures. Many do not have even a rudimentary knowledge of the English language.

To understand fully what such immigration will mean for policing in the 21st century requires exploring some crucial questions. Who are these new immigrants? How many are there? Why do they come here? What new demands will they place on law enforcement in the future? How can the police prepare today to meet these changing needs?

The New Immigrants

For many of us, the word "immigrant" evokes two vivid images: 1) The wave after wave of Europeans flooding through Ellis Island, and 2) the metaphor of the "melting pot." These two memories often converge in a romanticized view of the past as a time when those "poor, hungry, huddled masses" from other countries required only a generation or two for their offspring to become full-fledged Americans. However, a closer look shows that many immigrant groups found the path to full assimilation difficult. For many this meant struggling to find ways to blend in without losing their unique cultural identities.

Our past experience should also forewarn us that race constitutes the biggest barrier to full participation in the American dream. In particular, the black experience has been unique from the beginning because most African Americans did not come here seeking freedom or greater opportunity, but were brought to this country as slaves. And the lingering problem of racism still plays an undeniable role in preventing blacks from achieving full participation in the economic and social life of this country.

De facto segregation persists in keeping many minorities trapped in decaying crime and drug-riddled, inner-city neighborhoods. Though blacks constitute only 12 percent of the total U.S. population, as a result of "white flight," many of this country's major cities have minority majorities, while the suburbs that surround them remain virtually white.

The role of race as an obstacle to full assimilation and participation is of obvious concern since almost one-half of all legal immigrants over the past decade have been Asians— Chinese, Filipino, Indian, Korean, Vietnamese, and Kampucheans (Cambodians)— and slightly more than one-third have been from Latin America. Though 9 of 10 Hispanics are counted as "white," there is no doubt that they face discrimination because of their Hispanic ethnicity. At the same time, only 12 percent of the immigrants since 1980 have been Europeans, whose experience would be likely to mirror more closely those of their counterparts in the past.

Because minorities are expected to continue to exhibit higher birth rates than whites, demographers expect minorities to constitute an even larger percentage of young people in this country in the near future. By 2020 a majority of children in New Mexico, California, Texas, New York, Florida, and Louisiana will be minorities— blacks, Asians, and Hispanics.

White males have traditionally dominated our society, in power and wealth as well as sheer numbers. Over the past few decades, both minorities and women have made significant gains, particularly in the business world. Yet, both groups still earn significantly less than their white male counterparts, and they have yet to attain leadership roles in the public and private sectors equal to their respective numbers in society.

Certain questions naturally arise. In the future, will the power and wealth of white males erode as their numbers decline? Will minorities band together as a new coalition or splinter apart into competing special interests? How will mainstream attitudes change along the way? Are we embarking on a new era of tolerance and cooperation or a new era of hostility, in which various groups will battle each other for status, dollars, and power?

The Numbers

When we look at the number of legal immigrants arriving each year, their overall numbers appear deceptively small compared to the more than 255 million people who already live here. In fiscal year 1988, a total of 643,000 newcomers arrived, but their potential impact becomes clearer if we remember that would mean roughly 6.5 million new residents in just the next decade, even if immigration rates did not rise. And the picture becomes clearer still when we consider that many immigrants often cluster in specific areas, which makes their combined impact on certain communities far greater than if they were dispersed evenly nationwide.

Shortly after the turn of the 21st century, Asians are expected to reach 10 million. Today's 18 million Hispanics may well double by then. Included in such totals, of course, are the illegal immigrants who find their way into America each year. While the actual numbers are unknown, the 1987 law that granted amnesty to those undocumented aliens and agricultural workers who qualified allowed roughly 3 million to stay.

Another indicator is that the Border Patrol now apprehends roughly 900,000 people who try to enter illegally each year, down 800,000 from 1986, the year before the employer sanctions of the new Federal immigration legislation went into effect. Again, we most often think first of undocumented aliens as being Mexican nationals and other Latin Americans who penetrate our southern borders; but these figures also include substantial numbers of people from the Pacific Rim and the Caribbean, as well as the Irish, Canadians, and Western Europeans who often come in as tourists and then decide to stay.

Why They Come

Current U.S. immigration policy gives highest priority to reuniting families. Among the 265,000 legal immigrants in 1988 subject to limitations (quotas based on country of birth), almost 200,000 were admitted on the basis of "relative preference," that is, they were related to a permanent resident or citizen of the United States. Immediate relatives (spouses, parents, and children) of U.S. citizens are exempt from restrictions, and in 1988, they constituted approximately 219,000 of the 379,000 in the exempt category.

The next largest category of legal immigrants admitted is refugees and those seeking asylum, roughly 111,000 in 1988. To qualify under these provisions, applicants must persuade the Immigration and Naturalization Service (INS) they are fleeing persecution at home, not that they are simply escaping poverty. An article in the Wall Street Journal alleged that the INS routinely rejects applicants from Haiti and El Salvador and that it is also difficult for Nicaraguans, Ethiopians, Afghans, and Czechs to qualify.

The fourth largest category of legal immigrants includes those given preference on the basis of their education and occupation, less than 54,000 in 1988— only 4 percent of that year's total. Morton Kondracke in an article in *The New Republic* notes, "…this tiny number provided 52 percent of the mathematicians and computer scientists who came in and 38 percent of the college teachers."

Chances are, however, that the immigration policy will not change dramatically in the near future, though efforts will be made to allow more people with preferred job skills to immigrate. The question is whether they should be admitted in addition to or instead of those scheduled to be reunited with their families. This also has racial implications, because shifting from family to occupational considerations would mean a shift from Asians and Latin Americans toward more Europeans.

The Law Enforcement Challenge

All of these issues have obvious implications for law enforcement, but perhaps the first challenge is to remember that generalities tend to be false. Each immigrant, whether legal or illegal, arrives not only as part of a larger group but also as an individual with unique gifts— and faults.

Particularly where newcomers cluster together in poor neighborhoods with high crime rates, the police, perhaps even more so than the population at large, must guard against stereotyping. Some newcomers may be too timid to interact widely in their new communities; yet, they may contact the police. The police, therefore, have a tremendous responsibility because those first impressions matter, not just in terms of how new arrivals will see the police but how they view the entire society.

Imagine how much Asians and Latin Americans have to learn, especially if they are not proficient in English. Who will assure them that the public police do not use torture or keep files on their activities? Will they understand the difference between the public police and private police? Will they really believe we have no secret police? Many of today's new arrivals come from places where the police are feared, not respected, and the last thing they would be likely to do is ask an officer for help or share any information. We have had our whole lives to understand the written and unwritten rules of this society, with all their nuances. It is unreasonable to expect immigrants to absorb these cultural characteristics in even a few years.

Police officers so often see people at their worst, not their best. And because police officers focus so much attention on crime, there is always the danger that they will have a distorted view of who the "bad guys" are and how many there are of them. This temptation to generalize from a few to the many is a particularly critical problem for the police in the case of immigrants.

A small fraction of the immigrants coming in will be career criminals, eager to ply their trades here. The police have had to battle Asian drug gangs and Jamaican posses, as well as the alleged hardened criminals that entered this country as part of the Mariel Boat Lift.

Moreover, there will always be the larger group that turns to crime when faced with economic hardship. Police departments must take steps to ensure that officers remain sensitive to the reality that the majority of the newcomers are law-abiding people, eager to build a new life.

Because police departments are a microcosm of a larger society, it would be naive to assume that everyone who wears the uniform is free of bias. In addition, the statistics verify that there is a link between race and crime, but the mistake lies in seeing this as cause and effect.

Studies show that blacks are arrested for violent crimes at rates four times higher than their overall numbers would justify; Hispanics at rates two and a half times what they should be, even though they are often poorer than blacks. But we have only to look at the rates of violent crimes in the black-run nations of Africa, which are nowhere near as high as they are here, to see that our problems are not caused by their genes but by our culture. Perhaps the increasing minority numbers will help make this society more color blind.

Unfortunately, many of these new immigrants will become victims, particularly of violent crimes that disproportionately afflict minorities. Ignorance of our laws and customs can make them easy targets for all kinds of predators. Fear of the police will also work against them. And if they cannot speak the language, at least not well, it may be difficult for them to share information.

Toward a Solution: Community Policing

As even this cursory analysis shows, immigrants face all the problems, and more, that everyone in this culture faces. The primary challenge for law enforcement will be to find ways to meet their needs with special concern for their racial, ethnic, cultural, and religious diversity— and their specific vulnerabilities.

A community policing approach offers law enforcement officers unique flexibility in tailoring their response to meet local needs in ways that promote sensitivity and respect for minority concerns. This new philosophy and organizational strategy proposes that only by decentralizing and personalizing police service will law enforcement be able to meet the needs of an increasingly diverse society.

Community policing rests on the belief that no technology can surpass what creative human beings can achieve together. It says that police departments must deploy their most innovative, self-disciplined, and self-motivated officers directly into the community as outreach specialists and community problem-solvers. Only by freeing these new community policing officers (CPOs) from the isolation of their patrol cars, so they can interact with people face-to-face in the same areas every day, can departments develop the rapport and trust necessary to encourage people to become active in the process of policing themselves.

In addition to serving as full-fledged law enforcement officers, CPOs would work to reduce fear of crime and the physical and social disorder and neighborhood decay that act as magnets for a host of social ills, including crime and drugs. They also can serve as community's ombudsmen to city hall, to ensure prompt delivery of vital government services, and as the community's link to the public and private agencies that can help.

Particularly in the case of immigrants, community policing allows the department an opportunity for mutual input and enrichment. CPOs can help educate immigrants about our laws and customs and how to cope with our culture. Equally important, this grass-roots, two-way information flow allows immigrants the opportunity to teach the department how to take their particular concerns into account, with dignity and respect for their cultural identities.

The Right People for the Job

One of the more difficult problems that police departments will continue to face is how to develop the capacity to speak to new immigrants in their native tongues. It is often easier in theory than in practice to recruit qualified bilingual candidates from immigrant populations, especially since many come from countries where police work may not be a respectable career.

This issue raises more questions than answers. How many officers should be bilingual? How proficient must they be? Should foreign language be a requirement for college degrees in criminal justice? What will it cost police departments to meet this need? Is this an opportunity to use civilian volunteers? Can a department develop the capacity to speak to all in their native tongues?

Such a changing society also will demand that the police remain sensitized to the issue of how to serve people who exhibit racial, ethnic, religious, and cultural diversity. This is a two-fold concern. First, it implies that departments must establish and enforce guidelines to ensure existing officers discharge their duties with care and concern. Second, it means that departments must recruit candidates who are the best capable to handle the increasing challenge posed by the future.

To recruit officers from minority populations is a logical response to this challenge. However, a study by the Center for Applied Urban Research on the Employment of Black and Hispanic Officers shows recent efforts aimed at minority recruiting have produced uneven results. Almost one-half of the big city police departments made significant progress in hiring black officers; yet, 17 percent reported a decline. Forty-two percent of the departments made gains in hiring Hispanics, but almost 11 percent reported a decline. Part of the reason related to whether the departments pursued affirmative action plans, but there are also concerns that some minorities leave because of better career opportunities elsewhere, often because policing is perceived as falling short in providing meaningful career development. Overall, however, a 1989 study by the Police Executive Research Forum (PERF) found that in cities with a population of 50,000 or more, the number of black and Hispanic police officers were generally proportionate to the population.

The PERF study also indicated that college-educated officers exhibit the greatest sensitivity to the diversity that will increasingly become the hallmark of this society. The study also verified that the officers with at least some college education are not only increasing in numbers in the rank and file but also in police management as well. But again, retaining these officers can be difficult. Therefore, research supporting the widespread perception that community policing not only makes officers feel safer but also that it provides job enlargement and job enrichment, indicating that community policing may be a potent new way to keep the best people for the challenges that lie ahead.

Police Policy Toward Illegal Immigrants

The obvious obstacle in building trust between the police department and immigrants who are here illegally stems from their fears that the police will inform INS officials about their status. One chief of police in a border city wrestled with this issue and decided that the police must serve the needs of all members of the community. The department's policy is that it will not inform INS about undocumented residents except, of course, in cases where the police arrest someone for a crime.

The chief based his decision on the argument that it is the job of the INS, not the police, to track down and deport illegals. He also believes that this policy has helped his department gain the trust of the entire community, so that people in the community are now far more willing to share the information that the police need to do their best job. This is a decision that more chiefs will face in the future, and they must weigh the best interests of the department and the community within the dictates of their individual consciences.

Serving the Entire Community

The successful assimilation of new immigrant groups, particularly those of different races, will depend on changing attitudes in mainstream society. This is of particular concern, because current trends portend a society in which the youngest members will increasingly consist of minority youths, while the ranks of the elderly will remain far whiter.

These trends also show that younger workers, many of whom will be minorities in low-paying service jobs, increasingly will be asked to pay for the needs of primarily white retirees, whose health care costs alone may prove staggering.

Adding to these generational tensions is the incendiary issue of crime, with its overlay of age and race considerations. The bulk of the crimes committed in this society are perpetrated by the young, at rates far beyond what other industrialized Western nations endure. Though the elderly exhibit lower-than-average rates of actual victimization, they rank among the groups with the greatest fear of crime. In some neighborhoods, we see the elderly becoming virtual prisoners of fear. Indeed, this self-imposed imprisonment which reduces their exposure to the threat explains in part why they are not victimized more often.

Because crime and youth are so strongly linked, perhaps our aging society foretells a steep decline in our overall rates of crime. Crime rates have already begun to fall as the bulge of the "baby boomers" continue to grow out of their most crime prone years, but not as much as had been anticipated.

Various factors raise concern that we may not soon see a dramatic drop in crime— the growing gap between rich and poor, drugs, teenage pregnancy, illiteracy, high unemployment among minority youths, the continued proliferation of guns, and alarming rates of child abuse and neglect. Even if we are fortunate enough to see a substantially safer future during our lifetime, we can also expect that people will begin to demand more. For example, the police will be asked to pay more attention to other wants and needs that are now often ignored or given short shrift because of the current crisis posed by serious crime.

Conclusion

Community policing offers an important new tool to help heal the wounds caused by crime, fear of crime, and disorder. In one community that might mean a community police officer recruiting elderly volunteers from a senior center to help immigrant youths become more fluent in English. This offers the hope that those retirees will overcome their fears, while at the same time enhancing a young person's opportunity to perform well in school and on the job.

In a different neighborhood, the challenge could be for the CPO to encourage blacks, Hispanics, and Asians to cooperate together in persuading area businesses to help provide recreational activities for juveniles. The possibilities are bound only by the imagination and enthusiasm of the officers and the people they are sworn to serve, if the police are given the resources, time, and opportunity to work with people where they live and work.

It would be naive to suggest that community policing is a panacea that can heal all the wounds in any community. But it has demonstrated its ability to make people feel safer and improve the overall quality of community life. Today's challenge is to find new ways for law enforcement to contribute to make the United States a place where all people have an equal chance to secure a piece of the American dream for themselves and their children. Therefore, the urgent message is that we must begin preparing now, so that we can do even more toward this worthy goal in the ever-changing future.

[Reprinted from *FBI Law Enforcement Bulletin*, January 1990.]

EXHIBIT 18-3

RESEARCH AND DEVELOPMENT IN CORRECTIONS: THE FUTURE IS ALMOST HERE

John P. Conrad

The Future Is Almost Here

> *Lo, children and the fruit of the womb are a heritage and gift that cometh of the Lord. Like as the arrows in the hand of the giant: even so are the young children.*
>
> *—Psalms CXXVII*

For reasons irrelevant to criminal justice this life-long Californian is spending a winter month in Philadelphia. One of the benefits of this experience is exposure to the *Philadelphia Inquirer*, a surprisingly innovative newspaper. To restrain its readers from unbridled euphoria during an otherwise unusually joyous holiday season, the editors have

published a series of articles on the "no-parents children."
For a penologist with an eye to the future of our occupation,
the series has been sobering to read. For child welfare
workers the story of children without parents in Philadelphia
must be appalling. We are faced with unprecedented
problems, and the response to them from the social workers
who have to cope is candid and alarming. They have never
before seen children like these. They don't know what to do.

There are 5,400 children in the city's foster-care
system, a third of them under 5 years old. The number is
increasing every day. The problem is the mothers who need
crack so desperately that they cannot and do not care for
their kids.

A juvenile police officer told the Inquirer, "We are
getting this more and more. It is unbelievable. These kids
are being left alone for hours and days at a time because
Mom is out doing her drug thing."

It is nothing new for police and child welfare workers
to cope with abandoned children. For years newspapers
have run heart-wrenching stories about engaging foundlings
left on somebody's doorstep or perhaps in a garbage can.
If they're cute enough an adoptive home can be found for
them; if not, the authorities will have to pay for their foster
care. What's new is the crack baby. This child is so new,
so bizarre, and so different that nobody has thought of a
constructive program for his nurture and hopeful growth.
Mom is so preoccupied with her drug thing that it's hopeless
to capture her attention, let alone to expect her to do
something for her kids. Even if she could be distracted from
her pipe, what on earth could this poor and unskilled woman
do for them?

Consider the physiology of the crack baby. At the
University of Pennsylvania Hospital about 20 percent of the
women giving birth have used cocaine just before going into
labor. The same is true at the Temple University Hospital.
According to the gynecologists, cocaine constructs the
blood vessels, cutting off oxygen and nutrients to growing
fetuses. When born, they're underweight babies, often with
damaged central nervous systems. They are irritable, easily

frightened, and do not eat or sleep well. As they grow, they can't concentrate and have trouble getting along with other kids.

The Inquirer's staff reported numerous examples of bizarre behavior by these small children. They're all small— after all, crack hasn't been around very long. There's one account:

Mrs. Theresa Jemison is an experienced and successful foster-mother. She's been one of the mainstays of the city's foster-home services for 18 years, and has successfully made homes for 23 children over that time. She agreed to take in two little brothers, 4 and 5 years old, in August 1988. In March 1989 she decided that she couldn't manage them and returned them to the Department of Human Services. When she first got them, she picked them up, filthy and smelly, in her car. By the time she reached home they'd torn apart the car's interior. "Everything they could tear off they had torn off." The older boy was well aware of his mother's problem. They'd been taken away because she'd been smoking crack. "We can't go home to Mommy until she gets off the pipe."

These were angry children. They would try to scratch out each other's eyes, they tore holes in the upholstery, they gouged holes in the bedroom walls and dug out fistfuls of plaster. In kindergarten they beat up other children, kicked the teacher, sassed the principal, and were so destructive that they had to be sent to separate sessions.

Finally, Mrs. Jemison gave up. She had to tell the boys that they were leaving. "It was very hard. I told them they were leaving. I was trying not to say to them they were leaving because they were bad." She was pretty sure what was ahead for them. They would fail in one foster home, move along to another, and on and on. "Most of the time they don't know if they are coming or going. They are unable to learn because there hasn't been anything stable in their lives...Every time these kids are uprooted it's like a little bit of life is going out. It's draining out of them."

Once she met the boys' mother. "She was dirty. Her hair was uncombed. She smelled terrible." She told Mrs.

Jemison that her children had been taken for no reason. Her kids were clean and her house was neat. "They should have taken the five kids from down the street. They're in a whole lot worse shape."

What's Ahead for Corrections?

We live in an age when alarm about the future is a staple of speculation for pessimists. There is always something new to worry about, and there are plenty who seize on the newest downward trend. I have always tried to avoid this tendency, but stories about crack babies appear so often and so luridly in big city newspapers that it seems to be time for us to give some thought to what we penologists are going to be up against. Philadelphia is certainly not alone. Wherever there is an inner city underclass, crack is to be found, and in abundance. In this city of more than a million and a half, 5,400 homeless crack kids does not seem numerically significant. But the number is growing all the time, and there are precious few Mrs. Jemisons who will take some of them into their homes for even a few months, let alone the long years of affectionate care that any child should have.

Perhaps it's too early to tell, but it sounds to me as though we have hundreds of little boys and girls who are programmed for serious trouble when they get old enough for initiatives in delinquency. As Mrs. Jemison plausibly predicts, they will be shuffled from foster home to foster home. At best they will find a foster parent like Mrs. Jemison who can take it for a few months and is then exhausted by their demands on her time, strength, and patience. A lot of them will be placed in homes where they'll be beaten and abused, sometimes in response to their own violence and destructiveness, sometimes because there are adults who take out their frustrations on any available child.

Anyone who has taken life histories for presentence investigations will recognize a sad and familiar tale that repeats itself time and again. Here is a young man who was shifted from home to home until adolescence and then couldn't take it anymore. He ran away, was picked up by the police, and returned to the agency responsible for him. Finally he runs away again, and nobody picks him up until he is in deep trouble— a mugging, a burglary, an assault. His schooling ended in junior high, but his score is about third or fourth grade, and often less. He doesn't have any skills, not even criminal skills. The prospect ahead is dismal. He will be hard to convince that going to the prison school is worth the modest effort required. There are always exceptions but this young man is a prospect for life-long recidivism. His social history is not confined to the male sex; there are plenty of female counterparts, ill-fitted for work and what is even more ominous, ill-fitted for motherhood. A lot of them are crack mothers, producing kids that even Mrs. Jemison can't handle.

These are bad enough stories, and most of my readers will have heard them too often. What depresses me is the prospect of crack babies growing up. Here we have children, most of whom will inevitably wear out the ingenuity and patience of men and women of goodwill who take them into their homes. Keep in mind that many, perhaps most, foster home placements work out very well. After all, Mrs. Jemison has a record of 23 successes. Crack children are different. Their violence, their inability to relate to others, and their poor concentration are danger signs, the signs that distinguish the people that we call sociopaths— for want of a better term.

What to Do?

Perhaps crack babies will grow up to become perfectly nice young people, but we shouldn't count on it. The chances are that they'll be bad news wherever they are— in a juvenile hall, on a probation caseload, in a "youth training school," or, finally, in a mental hospital or a prison. It isn't too early to think about them seriously and to find out what can be done to help them live normal law-abiding lives.

It's unlikely that foster-home care is an answer. Will it be possible to design small residential placements with professionals in charge who can take on a contingent of these kids— six, seven, or eight at the most— and see them through their school years? Are there psychiatrists, psychologists, and social workers who are willing to devote some of their lives to this kind of experiment? I think of Dr. Bruno Bettelheim and his persevering work with autistic children. Could crack children attract another such psychiatrist?

Another experiment might mix some crack kids with others whose troubles don't include a prenatal exposure to cocaine. Maybe peer influences might be positive. Maybe behavior modification methods might affect some of them. Why not try?

Perhaps the answer may be pharmacological. Something may be developed which will settle them down without converting them into zombies. Any program like that would have to depend on more content than daily doses of medications, but we know how often tranquility is mistaken for success in therapy.

Another strategy that is much more urgent than improvising care of these tragic children will be aggressive outreach to pregnant crack addicts. It should not be impossible to find them, get them into a prenatal clinic, and see to it that they are seen weekly throughout their pregnancies. We are told that for most of these women, the first time they see an obstetrician is in the delivery room of an overcrowded hospital. We can do better than that, and we must.

All of the above calls for a lot of research and development. We ought to know better than to let these ominous matters slide until an outraged public demands that something must be done about dangerous young thugs who have in common a history of crack from the time when they were in their mothers' wombs. With hundreds of these people growing up, there will be crises. Let's avert as many of them as we can.

The record of criminal justice in the solution of problems is anything but positive. The best we can do with most is to pick up the failures of others and administer procedures mandated by the law as fairly as we can. We hope that the crack epidemic will subside and that physicians and social workers will help the children of addicts make good lives possible for them. The prospects for such successes are hardly bright. We will certainly have to accept a lot of them in our caseloads and in our cell-blocks. We have some time to get ready for them. Our clinicians, our custodial staffs, and our researchers should be watching the successes and failures of the agencies struggling with these wretched kids. We should keep abreast of the research on crack and its effects. Surely something will work, something we can use.

As the nineties begin, our pundits are bubbling over with optimism about practically everything, from foreign affairs to the future of the computer. The horizon for corrections seems uniquely bleak. More prisons will be needed to cope with the swelling stream of incoming convicts. Our success in changing them for the better is far from reassuring. And in a few years, well before the nineties come to an end, we seem likely to have a new breed of convicts on our hands, men and women who as children were bad news for everyone who had to deal with them. To adapt the metaphor of the psalmist, they were arrows in the hands of the malevolent giant of our national indifference to their parents and the conditions of our slums.

[Reprinted from *Federal Probation*, March 1989, pp.62-64]

FAITH AND TRUST IN OUR SYSTEM

"Faith and trust in the system" is a catch-all phrase encompassing all components of the criminal justice system. If public faith and trust in any one component of the system is lost, the system itself will fail. Today, naysayers point towards the recent Rodney King incident as a focal point for their calls of alarm that the system is, in fact, crashing. More within reason is the simple explanation that as any system emerges, matures and continues the necessary element of perpetual change vital to meet the needs of a dynamic constantly changing environment, there will be stumbles along the way. Perhaps a more important focus would be on how the system deals with and, if found necessary, corrects or at least takes steps to ensure the precipitating event does not happen again.

We are fortunate that we live in a society where naysayers have a platform from which they can address the public and call for change. Whether these issues are prisoner rights, racial inequities, police abuse, political corruption, etc., they are brought to the forefront for debate via television, print media or local forum. Very seldom do citizens hear about the good things that make our system the envy of the world. The public becomes conditioned to hearing only about what is wrong with our system and, therefore, accepts the media accounts as the norm instead of realizing that pain, suffering, corruption and abuse sell better than the normal flow of everyday criminal justice news. The result is a distorted public view of reality imposed on the public by the media. It is no surprise that criminal justice finds it difficult to live up to public expectations. The public expects Perry Masons, Bill Fridays, Sherlock Holmes, and all-knowing benevolent jurists. Perhaps with the new breed of television shows that depict "true life" patrol operations, fallible prosecutors, and competent, yet human jurists, a more mainstream public expectation of our criminal justice personnel will evolve.

Problems do exist, but we tend to identify and correct those problems which are truly individualized within a component of the system and not rather a symptom of a greater problem of society. The Rodney King incident is an excellent example of this. All the corrective action centered on the Los Angeles Police Department (i.e., training, firings, prosecuting of individual officers) improved the department but had minimal effect on the crucial underlying social issues faced in South Los Angeles. Consequently, police brutality was simply a triggering event. The symptom was cured but not the disease. In other words, to "correct" the police doesn't solve the underlying problem; it simply will move the triggering event for, in this case, rioting. The true issues concern lack of jobs, poor education, gang violence, etc. Unfortunately, because law enforcement is responsible for "order maintenance" they tend to be involved whenever flair-ups of this nature arise and, as too often is the case, law enforcement is focused upon for the quick cure.

All in all, the future holds great challenges for our system of criminal justice. Faith and trust will continue to see its peaks and valleys. For the most part, trust is alive and well, and faith is the fabric that bonds our society to its high ideals which, in turn, spill over into our criminal justice system. One thing that can alter our faith and trust in the system is ignorance. If our society intellectually stagnates or allows the majority of the population to become uneducated as to the "American way of life," then we are in peril.

Without thinking minds and individuals yearning for more knowledge and striving to better themselves and society, the criminal justice system will become impotent. The cornerstones of our society are based around intellectual freedom and American compassion. This too is the foundation of our criminal justice system and is why we can tolerate the question and debate the issue of "have we lost faith and trust in our system?" A thinking, compassionate America will never allow our system to fail because of the constant bolstering brought about by the intellectual challenges encouraged by the system and, in turn, fed upon by the system so that it may continue to evolve.

DISCUSSION QUESTIONS

1. Explain the rationale for accreditation of police departments.

2. What determines whether or not a department is a professional department?

3. What changes can we expect within the next 10 years in our local police and other criminal justice agencies?

4. How can we prepare for the future?

ENDNOTES

[1] Laura Lang, "Mapping Improves 911 Service," *Government Technology*, vol. 6, no. 8, (August, 1983): pp. 16-20.

[2] *Juris and Feuille*, (1973), p. 7.

[3] Hervey A. Juris and Peter Feuille, "The Impact of Police Unions: Summary Report," (Washington D.C.: Government Printing Office 1973).

[4] John J. Broderick, *Police in a Time of Change*, (Morristown, NJ: General Learning Press, 1977), p. 200.

[5] Raymond E. Arthurs, Jr., "Accreditation: A Small Department's Experience," *FBI Law Enforcement Bulletin*, (August 1990): pp. 1-5.

GLOSSARY

ABDUCTION The crime of kidnapping by force, fraud or by criminal persuasion.

ABET To aid, encourage, or incite another to commit a criminal offense.

ABSCOND To leave one's usual residence; to conceal oneself in order to avoid legal proceedings; to disappear, sometimes with the property of others.

ACCESSORY One who, though not the actual perpetrator of a felony, is in some way concerned with the commission of it.

ACCOMPLICE One involved with others in the commission of a crime.

ACCUSATION The legal charge that a person is guilty of a criminal offense, subject to later adjudication.

ACQUITTAL The dismissal by a jury or a judge of criminal charges brought against an accused person, absolving him from further prosecution for the same offense.

ACT Something done or established; laws passed by legislatures.

ACTION A lawsuit; a proceeding taken in a court of law. May be civil or criminal.

ADJUDICATION A judgement or decision, usually by a court.

ADMISSIBLE EVIDENCE Evidence which may legally be received by a trial court.

ADMISSION A self-incriminatory statement by a subject falling short of an acknowledgment of guilt.

ADULT A person of majority age. In common law, a person who has attained the age of 21. By law in some states, one who has attained the age of 17 or 18.

ADVOCATE An attorney who speaks or writes on behalf of his client.

AFFIDAVIT A written statement of fact, signed and sworn to before a person having authority to administer an oath.

AFORETHOUGHT Planned beforehand; premeditated; deliberate.

AGENT One authorized by a party to act in that party's behalf.

AGGRAVATED ASSAULT Assault with a deadly weapon or with force likely to produce great bodily harm.

AID AND ABET To knowingly assist, encourage or urge someone to commit a crime.

ALLEGATION A statement of fact made in a legal proceeding, which the person stating it intends to prove.

ALLOCUTION To speak to; warning or advising with authority.

APPEAL A petition to a higher court seeking to modify the judgement of a lower court.

APPELLANT A person who initiates an appeal from one court to a higher court.

APPELLATE COURT A federal or state judicial tribunal which reviews cases originally tried or decided by inferior tribunals. The appellate court acts without a jury and is primarily interested in correcting errors in procedure or in the interpretation of law by the lower courts.

ARBITRATOR An impartial person chosen by the parties to solve a dispute between them.

ARGUMENT A statement to a judge or jury, of counsel's reasons why the client should prevail in a lawsuit.

ARRAIGNMENT The initial court hearing for a defendant where he is advised of the charges and his rights.

ARREST The apprehension of a person in order that he may be held to answer an alleged crime before a magistrate.

ARSON (UCR) In Uniform Crime Reports terminology, the burning or attempted burning of property with or without intent to defraud.

ASSAULT A threatening gesture, an attempted battery.

ATTEMPT An effort to commit a crime amounting to more than mere preparation or planning for it, which, if not prevented, would have resulted in the completion of the act attempted.

ATTORNEY GENERAL The chief legal officer of the United States or of a state.

AUBURN SYSTEM A correctional system established in the nineteenth century at the Auburn, New York prison, imposing silence, individual confinement at night, congregate work during the day, harsh discipline and strong security measures. (Cf., The Pennsylvania System.)

AUTOPSY Examination of a dead person to determine, among other things, the cause and manner of death.

AUXILIARY SERVICES All services which assist the police line officer in the performance of his duty. They include records, identification, communications, detention, property and evidence, and crime laboratory.

BAIL To effect the release of an accused person from custody, in return for a promise that he or she will appear at a place and time specific and submit to the jurisdiction and judgment of the court, guaranteed by a pledge to pay to the court a specified sum of money or property if the person does not appear. **II.** The money or property pledged to the court or actually deposited with the court to effect the release of a person from legal custody.

BAILIFF An officer assigned to court duty for the purpose of peace keeping, prisoner custody, and whatever the judge may require.

BATTERY An unlawful touching, striking, beating, or wounding of another's person without consent.

BENCH WARRANT A judicial order issued for the arrest of an individual, usually for appearance failure.

BEYOND A REASONABLE DOUBT In evidence, proof satisfied to a moral certainty. Degree of proof required in criminal cases for conviction.

BILL OF RIGHTS The first ten amendments to the United States Constitution.

BIND To hold by legal judgement; e.g., to bind over a party accused of a crime to appear before a higher trial court.

BOND In court, a promise by a defendant, usually with surety, normally pertaining to future appearance.

BOOKING The administrative record of arrest; normally involves photographing and fingerprinting of the arrestee.

BRIBERY Giving or receiving anything of value to influence exercise of a judicial or public duty.

BRIEF A printed summary of a legal case.

BURDEN OF PROOF The duty of providing disputed facts of a case at trial.

BURGLARY Entry into a building with intent to commit a felony or theft.

CALENDAR A list of cases arranged for trial in court.

CAPITAL CRIME A crime punishable by death.

CASE LAW Judicial precedent generated by resolving unique legal disputes.

CASELOAD (COURT) The number of cases requiring judicial action at a certain time or the number of cases acted upon in a given court during a given time period.

CERTIORARI See Writ of *Certiorari*

CHALLENGE An objection; challenges to potential jurors may be "peremptory" (no reason need be given) or "for cause", which under law disqualifies the jury or juror from sitting. The number of peremptory challenges allowed to each party is usually prescribed by statute.

CHANGE OF VENUE Removal of a suit from one county or district to another for trial; also applied to removal of a suit from one court to another within the same jurisdiction.

CHARGE Instructions given by the court to a jury as to the principles of law which should guide it in arriving at a decision; an accusation; a formal complaint, information or indictment.

CHIEF JUSTICE The highest judicial officer of the United States or of a state.

CIRCUIT COURT Court with jurisdiction extending over several counties or districts.

CIRCUMSTANTIAL EVIDENCE Evidence of an indirect nature; existence of principal facts is inferred from surrounding circumstances.

CITATION Reference to a constitutional, statutory, precedential case or other persuasive material used in legal writing; a written summons to appear in court.

CIVIL LAW Law governing property disputes between persons or groups.

CIVIL LIBERTIES Rights recognized as properly belonging to all individuals subject to specified limits.

CLEMENCY In criminal justice usage the name for the type of executive or legislative action where the severity of punishment of a single person or a group of persons is reduced or the punishment stopped, or a person is exempted from prosecution for certain actions.

CODE A collection, compendium of laws; e.g., state penal code.

COMMISSION A body of persons appointed to do certain things; the act of perpetrating an offense.

COMMON LAW That body of law originated, developed, formulated and administered in England, and adopted by most of the states; that part of law, and custom having universal application.

COMPETENT Legally qualified or capable.

COMPLAINANT One who makes a complaint; the plaintiff.

COMPLAINT The charge made before a proper officer that an offense has been committed by a person named or described; under rules of civil procedure, a pleading which must be filed in court to commence an action.

COMPUTER CRIME A popular name for crimes committed by use of a computer or crimes involving misuse or destruction of computer equipment or computerized information, sometimes specifically theft committed by means of manipulation of a computerized financial transaction system, or the use of computer services with intent to avoid payment.

CONFESSION A direct acknowledgment of the truth of the guilty fact as charged.

CONSTITUTIONAL LAW Law derived from, related to, or interpretive of a constitution.

CONTEMPT An offense against the dignity and good order of the court, the Congress of the United States, state legislatures, and in some instances, against administrative agencies.

CONTRABAND Goods exported or imported in violation of law; goods, the possession of which constitutes a violation of law.

CORONER An official possessing authority to hold inquests into deaths; a medical examiner who is a licensed physician.

CORROBORATIVE EVIDENCE Additional testimony to reinforce a point previously the subject of proof.

COUNT In criminal law, each part of an indictment which charges a distinct offense.

COURT An agency or unit of the judicial branch of government authorized or established by statute or constitution, and consisting of one or more judicial officers, which has the authority to decide upon cases, controversies in law, and dispute matters of fact brought before it.

COURT CLERK An elected or appointed court officer responsible for maintaining the written records of the court and for supervising or performing the clerical tasks necessary for conducting judicial business; also, any employee of a court whose principal duties are to assist the court clerk in performing the clerical tasks necessary for conducting judicial business.

COURT OF RECORD A court in which a complete and permanent record of all proceedings or specified types of proceedings is kept.

COURT REPORTER A person present during judicial proceedings, who records all testimony and other oral statements made during the proceedings.

CREDIBILITY Veracity of a witness; the degree of credit assigned to testimony.

CRIME Commission or omission of any act, in violation of law, without justification, for which a penalty has been imposed as a sanction against such commission or omission.

CRIME INDEX In Uniform Crime Reports terminology, a set of numbers indicating the volume, fluctuation, and distribution of crimes reported to local law enforcement agencies, for the United States as a whole and for its geographical subdivisions, based on counts of reported occurrences of UCR Index Crimes.

CRIME, STATUTORY Crime created by written statute, as distinguished from the common law.

CRIME, WHITE-COLLAR Nonviolent crime for financial gain committed by means of deception by persons whose occupational status is entrepreneurial, professional, or semiprofessional and utilizing their special occupational skills and opportunities; also, nonviolent crime for financial gain utilizing deception and committed by anyone having special technical and professional knowledge of business and government, irrespective of the person's occupation.

CRIMINAL HOMICIDE The causing of the death of another person without legal justification or excuse.

CRIMINAL INTENT Malice evidenced by a criminal act.

CRIMINAL JUSTICE SYSTEM An organizational system consisting of police, courts, and corrections designed to enforce standards of conduct in defense of individuals and the community.

CRIMINAL LAW An act prohibited or required by law, to which a penalty is attached for committing the act or omission.

CRIMINAL MOTIVE Mental self-inducement, specifically a reason, causing one to intend, and afterward commit crime.

CRIMINOLOGY The study of criminal behavior, legal norms, and social attitudes toward various types of crimes and criminals.

CROSS-EXAMINATION The questioning of a witness by opposing counsel after direct examination.

CULPABILITY I. Blameworthiness; responsibility in some sense for an event or situation deserving of moral blame. **II.** In Model Penal Code (MPC) usage, a state of mind on the part of one who is committing an act, which makes him or her potentially subject to prosecution for that act.

DEADLY FORCE Employment of force designed or likely to produce death or great bodily harm.

DEFAMATION The uttering of spoken or written words tending to injure the reputation of another for which action for damages may be brought.

DEFENDANT The party against whom a criminal or civil action is brought, warrant issued or indictment found.

DELINQUENCY In the broadest usage, juvenile actions or conduct in violation of criminal law, juvenile status offenses, and other juvenile misbehavior.

DELINQUENT A juvenile who has been adjudged by a judicial officer of a juvenile court to have committed a delinquent act.

DEPOSITION Testimony reduced to writing under oath or affirmation.

DETERMINATE SENTENCE A term of imprisonment for an exact period of time.

DIRECT EVIDENCE That means of proof tending to show existence of a fact in question, without intervention of proof of any other fact; distinguished from circumstantial evidence.

DIRECT EXAMINATION Initial questioning of a witness by the party calling him.

DISCOVERY A method by which opposing parties to a lawsuit may obtain all factual information in possession of opposing party.

DISPOSITION In criminal justice usage, the action by a criminal or juvenile justice agency which signifies that a portion of the justice process is complete and jurisdiction is terminated or transferred to another agency, or which signifies that a decision has been reached on one aspect of a case and a different aspect comes under consideration, requiring a different kind of decision.

DISTRICT ATTORNEY County prosecutor; D.A.

DISTRICT COURT Trial court established in United States judicial districts; state court established for hearing and deciding causes within their jurisdiction.

DOCTRINE A principle of law, often developed through court decisions; a precept or rule.

DOUBLE JEOPARDY Common-law and constitutional prohibition against second prosecution after a first trial for the same criminal offense; "jeopardy" attaches at certain stages in trial but an acquittal is always a bar to retrial.

DUE PROCESS OF LAW Compliance with the fundamental rules for fair and orderly legal proceedings; the observance of rules designed for the protection of individual rights and liberties.

DURESS Unlawful constraint exercised upon one forced to do some act that otherwise would not have been done.

ENTRAPMENT The act of officers or agents of the government of inducing a person to commit a crime not contemplated by him, for the purpose of instituting criminal prosecution against him. Entrapment is a legal defense.

ENTRY Insertion of any part of the body into land or buildings. Insertion of a pole or hook may also constitute entry.

EVIDENCE Proof, either written or unwritten, of allegations at issue between parties. It may be direct or indirect, the latter including circumstantial evidence.

EXCLUSIONARY RULE Legal prohibitions against prosecution's use of evidence illegally obtained.

EX POST FACTO LAW A law passed after the occurrence of a fact or commission of an act.

EXTRADITION The surrendering by one state or country to another of one accused or convicted of an offense committed within the jurisdiction of the requesting state or country.

FELONY A crime punishable by death or imprisonment in state prison.

FINE The penalty imposed upon a convicted person by a court, requiring that he or she pay a specified sum of money to the court.

FORCIBLE RAPE (UCR) Sexual intercourse or attempted sexual intercourse with a female against her will, by force or threat of force.

FORENSIC Belonging to, or applied in, courts of justice.

FRAUD Acts which have as their objective the gain of an advantage by deceitful or unfair means; deliberate misrepresentation or concealment.

GOOD TIME In correctional usage, the amount of time deducted from time to be served in prison on a given sentence(s), and/or under correctional agency jurisdiction, at some point after a prisoner's admission to prison, contingent upon good behavior and/or awarded automatically by application of a statute or regulation.

GRAND JURY A body of persons, not less than twelve, nor more than twenty- four, whose duty it is, on hearing evidence for the prosecution in each proposed bill of indictment, to decide whether sufficiency of a case is made on which to hold the accused for trial.

GRAND LARCENY More serious than petit larceny; classified according to the value or type of the object.

GROSS NEGLIGENCE Acts of commission or omission of a wanton or willful nature, showing reckless disregard of the rights of others, under circumstances reasonably calculated to produce injury.

GUILTY PLEA A defendant's formal answer in court to the charge(s) contained in a complaint, information, or indictment, claiming that he or she did commit the offense(s) listed.

HABEAS CORPUS See Writ of Habeas Corpus.

HABITUAL OFFENDER A person sentenced under the provisions of a statute declaring that persons convicted of a given offense, and shown to have previously been convicted of another specified offense(s), shall receive a more severe penalty than that for the current offense alone.

HAMMURABI CODE The earliest written code relating to ancient penal practices; the Code of the Babylonian King Hammurabi written circa 2,000 B.C.

HEARING A proceeding in which arguments, witness, or evidence are heard by a judicial officer or administrative body.

HEARSAY EVIDENCE Statements offered by a witness, based upon what someone else has told him and not upon personal knowledge or observation. Usually, inadmissible, but exceptions are provided by rules of evidence.

HOMICIDE The killing of a human being by another. It may be excusable, as when committed by accident, and without any intent to injure; justifiable, if committed with full intent, but under such circumstances as to render it proper and necessary; felonious, when committed willfully and without sufficient justification.

HUNG JURY A trial jury whose members are unable to agree upon a verdict.

ILLEGAL SEARCH AND SEIZURE An act in violation of the Fourth Amendment of the U.S Constitution: "The right of people to be secure in their persons, houses, papers and effects, against unreasonable searches and seizures, shall not be violated, and no warrants shall issue but upon probable cause, supported by oath or affirmation and particularly describing the place to be searched and the persons or things to be seized."

IMMATERIAL Not material, essential, or necessary; not important or pertinent; not decisive; of no substantial consequence.

IMPEACH To charge a public official with a crime or with misconduct in office; to prove that a witness has a bad reputation for truth and veracity, and is therefore unworthy of belief.

INADMISSIBLE That evidence which cannot be admitted or received.

INCITE To encourage, stimulate, or induce a person to commit a crime.

INCOMPETENT Disqualified, unable or unfit. A judge or juror is incompetent, when from interest in the subject matter, he is an unfit person to decide a controversy; testimony is incompetent when it is not such as by law ought to be admitted; a witness is incompetent, when by law he may not testify.

INCRIMINATING STATEMENT A statement which tends to establish guilt of the accused or from which, with other facts, his guilt may be inferred.

INDETERMINATE SENTENCE A term of imprisonment leaving the exact period of punishment to be decided by correctional authorities.

INDEX CRIMES Eight major offenses designated as "Part I" crimes used in the Uniform Crime Reports of the Federal Bureau of Investigation: murder, forcible rape, robbery, aggravated assault, burglary, larceny, motor vehicle theft, arson. (crime index.)

INDICTMENT An accusation in writing by a grand jury charging a person with a crime.

INDIGENT One who is needy and poor. Qualifies a defendant for court appointed counsel.

INDIRECT EVIDENCE Proof of collateral circumstances, from which a fact in controversy, not directly attested by witnesses or documents, may be inferred or presumed.

INFORMATION A written accusation before a magistrate, made upon oath by a prosecutor, charging one or more persons with having committed a crime; a criminal complaint filed in superior or circuit court.

INHABITED DWELLING A structure used exclusively or in part specifically for residential purposes.

INDEX CRIMES See Crime Index.

INJUNCTION A court order commanding a person to do, or to refrain from doing, an act which would injure another by violating his personal or property rights.

IN LOCO PARENTIS In the place of a parent.

IN RE In the matter of. Often used in juvenile, nonadversary cases.

INTENT Design; resolve to do some act; determination of the mind.

JUDGMENT The statement of the decision of a court, that the defendant is acquitted or convicted of the offense(s) charged.

JURISDICTION The territory, subject matter, or persons over which lawful authority may be exercised by a court or other justice agency, as determined by statute or constitution.

JURY INSTRUCTIONS A statement given by the judge, setting forth the law applicable to a particular lawsuit heard by a jury and about to be decided by it.

JUVENILE In the context of the administration of justice, a person subject to juvenile court proceedings because a statutorily defined event or condition caused by or affecting that person was alleged to have occurred while his or her age was below the statutorily specified age limit of original jurisdiction of a juvenile court.

JUVENILE COURT The name for the class of courts which have, as all or part of their authority, original jurisdiction over matters concerning persons statutorily defined as juveniles.

KIDNAPING Transportation or confinement of a person without authority of law and without his or her consent, or without the consent of his or her guardian, if a minor.

LARCENY Unlawful taking or attempted taking of property other than a motor vehicle from the possession of another, by stealth, without force and without deceit, with intent to deprive the owner of the property permanently.

LATENT Hidden; not readily visible.

LAW ENFORCEMENT The generic name for the activities responsible for maintaining public order and enforcing the law, particularly the activities of prevention, detection, and investigation of crime and apprehension of criminals.

LAW ENFORCEMENT AGENCY A federal, state, or local criminal justice agency or identifiable subunit of which the principal functions are the prevention, detection, and investigation of crime, and the apprehension of alleged offenders.

LAW ENFORCEMENT OFFICER An employee of a law enforcement agency who is an officer sworn to carry out law enforcement duties.

MANDATORY SENTENCE A statutory requirement that a certain penalty shall be set and carried out in all cases upon conviction for a specified offense or series of offenses.

MAGISTRATE A judicial official; a judge.

MALA IN SE Criminal acts wrong in themselves, whether prohibited by human laws or not, as distinguished from mala prohibita.

MALA PROHIBITA Criminal acts, not evil in and of themselves, but criminal only by statute.

MARSHAL A federal officer whose duty is to execute the process of the United States court; in some jurisdictions.

MIRANDA RIGHTS The set of rights which a person accused or suspected of having committed a specific offense has during interrogation, and of which he or she must be informed prior to questioning, as stated by the U.S. Supreme Court in deciding *Miranda v. Arizona* and related cases.

MISDEMEANOR An offense punishable by incarceration, usually in a local confinement facility, for a period of which the upper limit is prescribed by statute in a given jurisdiction, typically limited to one year.

MISTRIAL An erroneous trial lacking some fundamental requisite, or a jury's inability to reach a verdict.

MITIGATING CIRCUMSTANCES The opposite of aggravated circumstances; Circumstances surrounding the commission of a crime which do not in law justify or excuse the act, by which in fairness may be considered as reducing the blameworthiness of the defendant.

MODUS OPERANDI The method of operation; common criminal procedure.

MORAL TURPITUDE An act of baseness, vileness or depravity.

MOTOR VEHICLE THEFT (UCR) Unlawful taking or attempted taking, of a self-propelled road vehicle owned by another, with the intent to deprive him or her of it permanently or temporarily.

MOTIVE A specific reason for commission of a crime.

MURDER AND NONNEGLIGENT MANSLAUGHTER (UCR) In Uniform Crime Reports terminology, intentionally causing the death of another without legal justification or excuse, or causing the death of another while committing or attempting to commit another crime.

NEGLIGENCE, CRIMINAL An act or omission which a reasonable person would refrain from, by reason of which another person is endangered.

NEGLIGENCE, GROSS The intentional failure to perform a manifest duty in reckless disregard of the consequences as affecting the life or property of another.

NEGLIGENCE, WILLFUL A willful determination not to perform a known duty, or a reckless disregard of the safety or the rights of others.

NO BILL A refusal by a Grand Jury to issue an indictment.

NOLO CONTENDERE No contest; a plea in a criminal action, having the same legal effect as a plea of guilty.

OBSTRUCTION OF JUSTICE The intentional hindering of or obstructing an arrest, proceedings, conviction or punishment of accused persons.

OMISSION The neglect to perform what the law requires.

ORDINANCE A law, statute, or legislative enactment; particularly of cities and counties.

ORGANIZED CRIME A complex pattern of activity which includes the commission of statutorily defined offenses, in particular the provision of illegal goods and services but also carefully planned and coordinated instances of fraud, theft, and extortion, and which is uniquely characterized by the planned use of both legitimate and criminal professional expertise, and the use for criminal purposes of organizational features of legitimate business, including availability of large capital resources, disciplined management, division of labor, and focus upon maximum profit; also, the persons engaged in such a pattern of activity.

PARENS PATRIAE A doctrine by which the government supervises children and other persons who are under a legal disability.

PAROLE The status of an offender conditionally released from a prison by discretion of a paroling authority prior to expiration of sentence, required to observe conditions of parole, and placed under the supervision of a parole agency.

PAROLEE A person who has been conditionally released by a paroling authority from a prison prior to the expiration of his or her sentence, and placed under the supervision of a parole agency, and who is required to observe conditions of parole.

PAROLE VIOLATION An act or a failure to act by a parolee which does not conform to the conditions of parole.

PENOLOGY The branch of criminology concerned with government policies and practices in dealing with persons convicted of crimes.

PEREMPTORY CHALLENGE The right to challenge a juror without assigning a reason for the challenge. In most jurisdictions each party of an action, both civil and criminal, has a specified number of such challenges and after using all his peremptory challenges he is required to furnish a reason for subsequent challenges.

PERJURY A false statement under oath or affirmation, willfully made in regard to a material matter of fact.

PLAIN VIEW Legally observable. An exception to the general requirement of a valid search warrant to legitimize a search or seizure.

PLAINTIFF One who initiates a lawsuit.

PLEA A defendant's formal response to the charge in an indictment or to a civil lawsuit.

POSSE COMITATUS The power of a county to call on all able-bodied adults to assist the sheriff in preserving the peace.

PRECEDENT An adjudged case or court decision furnishing an example or authority for an identical or similar case afterwards arising from a similar question of law.

PRECINCT A police district; a minor political subdivision of a county or city.

PRELIMINARY HEARING A hearing held in a lower court in felony cases to determine if there are reasonable grounds to hold ("bind over") a defendant for trial in the felony trial court.

PREMEDITATION A design or intention, formed to commit a crime or do an act before it is done.

PREPONDERANCE OF EVIDENCE The greater weight of evidence, in merit and worth. Standard of proof in civil cases.

PRESUMPTION A conclusion or inference, drawn from the proven existence of some fact or group of facts.

PRINCIPAL In criminal law, any person who aids, abets, or counsels in the commission of a crime. All principals are equally guilty.

PRISON A state or federal confinement facility having custodial authority over adults sentenced to confinement.

PRISONER A person in physical custody in a confinement facility, or in the personal physical custody of a criminal justice official while being transported to or between confinement facilities. A person in physical custody in a state or federal confinement facility.

PROBABLE CAUSE A reasonable ground of suspicion supported by circumstances sufficiently strong in themselves to warrant a reasonable person to believe the accused guilty; in police operations, authority to arrest.

PROBATION A judicial function placing a convicted offender or juvenile delinquent under court supervision, often under the supervision of a probation officer.

PROCEDURAL LAW A branch of law prescribing methods to be used to determine and enforce substantive law.

PROSECUTOR An attorney who is the elected or appointed chief of a prosecution agency, and whose official duty is to conduct criminal proceedings on behalf of the people against persons accused of committing criminal offenses. Also called "district attorney," "DA," "state's attorney," "county attorney," and "U.S. attorney" and any attorney deputized to assist the chief prosecutor.

PUBLIC DEFENDER An attorney employed by a government agency or sub-agency, or by private organization under contract to a unit of government, for the purpose of providing defense services to indigents; also, occasionally, an attorney who has volunteered such service. The head of a government agency or subunit whose function is the representation in court of persons accused or convicted of a crime who are unable to hire private counsel, and any attorney employed by such an agency or subunit whose official duty is the performance of the indigent defense function.

RECIDIVISM Repeated return to criminal behavior, especially following imprisonment.

REHABILITATION The process whereby an individual loses the desire and intent to commit criminal acts and accepts the behavior standards of society.

ROBBERY (UCR) The unlawful taking or attempted taking of property that is in the immediate possession of another by force or threat of force.

SANCTION The power of enforcing a statute or inflicting a penalty for its violation; a penalty or reward directed at a person or group to discourage or encourage specified behavior.

SEARCH WARRANT A document issued by a judicial officer which directs a law enforcement officer to conduct a search at a specific location, for specified property or persons relating to a crime(s), to seize the property or persons if found, and to account for the results of the search to issuing judicial officer.

SEIZURE The act of taking possession of property, e.g., for a violation of law or by authority of a warrant.

SELECTIVE ENFORCEMENT The application of enforcement effort against specific types of crimes or violations prevalent in particular areas and at certain times.

SENTENCE The penalty imposed by a court upon a person convicted of a crime. The court judgment specifying the penalty imposed upon a person convicted of a crime. Any disposition of a defendant resulting from a conviction, including the court decision to suspend execution of a sentence.

SHERIFF The elected chief officer of a county law enforcement agency, usually responsible for law enforcement in unincorporated areas and for the operation of the county jail.

SIMPLE ASSAULT (UCR) Unlawful threatening, attempted inflicting, or inflicting of less than serious bodily injury, in the absence of a deadly weapon.

SPEEDY TRIAL The right of the defendant to have a prompt trial, as guaranteed by the Sixth Amendment of the U.S. Constitution. "In all criminal prosecutions, the accused shall enjoy the right to a speedy and public trial. . ."

STARE DECISIS Literally, "to stand on the decision"; legal precedent; to follow past decisions.

STATUTE A law enacted by the legislature of a state of nation.

STATUTE OF LIMITATIONS A statute limiting the period during which crimes may be prosecuted and which, after lapse of the prescribed period, serves as a legal bar to prosecution.

STATUTORY RAPE Sexual intercourse with a minor female, not involving force or violence. In California called unlawful sexual intercourse.

SUBPOENA A court order or writ commanding attendance in court under penalty for failure to do so. May command appearance as well as production of documents.

SUBSTANTIVE LAW That part of law defining crimes and regulating rights.

SUPERIOR COURT A court of record or general trial jurisdiction, superior to the lowest court. In some states known as circuit court.

SUPREME COURT In the federal court system, the highest national appellate court. In most state court systems, the highest state court of appeals. (In New York state, a trial court.)

SUSPECT An adult or juvenile considered by a criminal justice agency to be one who may have committed a specific criminal offense, but who has not been arrested or charged.

TERRORISM A violent act or an act dangerous to human life in violation of the criminal laws of the United States or of any state to intimidate or coerce a government, the civilian population, or any segment thereof, in furtherance of political or social objectives.

THEFT Generally, any taking of the property of another with intent to deprive the rightful owner of possession permanently.

TRIAL BY COURT A trial in which the judge decides the law and the facts (i.e., guilt or innocence in a criminal case).

TRIAL BY JURY A trial in which the jury decides the law and a jury decides the facts (i.e., guilt or innocence in a criminal case).

TRUE BILL An indictment or bill of indictment issued by a grand jury.

UCR An abbreviation for the Federal Bureau of Investigation's "Uniform Crime Reporting" program.

VENUE The county in which a lawsuit should be tried; the county from which the jury is selected for the trial of a lawsuit. See Change of Venue

VERDICT In criminal proceedings, the decision of the jury in a jury trial or of a judicial officer in a nonjury trial.

VICTIM A person who has suffered death, physical or mental anguish, or loss of property as the result of an actual or attempted criminal offense committed by another person.

VOIR DIRE The preliminary examination of a prospective juror to determine qualifications to serve as a juror; preliminary examination of a witness to determine his competency to speak the truth.

WARRANT A written order issued by a magistrate directing an officer to make an arrest or conduct searches or seizures.

WHITE-COLLAR CRIME See Crime, White-Collar.

WILLFUL Intentional; deliberate.

WITNESS In criminal justice usage, generally, a person who has knowledge of the circumstances of a case; in court usage, one who testifies as to what he or she has seen, heard, otherwise observed, or has expert knowledge of.

WRIT A formal written order issued by a court commanding an individual identified in the order to do, or abstain from doing, some specified act.

WRIT OF *HABEAS CORPUS* An order issued by a court to an official holding a person in custody, ordering the person's release or appearance before the court for a ruling on the legality of the custody.

WRIT OF PROHIBITION An order, issued by a superior court to a lower court, demanding that the latter refrain from exercising jurisdiction over some specific suit then before it.

WRIT OF *CERTIORARI* An original writ or action whereby a cause is removed from an inferior to a superior court for review. A dominant avenue to the United States Supreme Court.

INDEX